THE WESTERN SAN JUAN MOUNTAINS

THE WESTERN SAN JUAN MOUNTAINS

THEIR GEOLOGY, ECOLOGY, AND HUMAN HISTORY

MANAGING EDITOR: ROB BLAIR

TECHNICAL EDITORS:
TOM ANN CASEY
WILLIAM H. ROMME
RICHARD N. ELLIS

UNIVERSITY PRESS OF COLORADO
FORT LEWIS COLLEGE FOUNDATION

© 1996 by the University Press of Colorado

Published by the University Press of Colorado
P.O. Box 849
Niwot, Colorado 80544
Tel. (303) 530-5337

The University Press of Colorado is a cooperative publishing enterprise supported, in part, by Adams State College, Colorado State University, Fort Lewis College, Mesa State College, Metropolitan State College of Denver, University of Colorado, University of Northern Colorado, University of Southern Colorado, and Western State College of Colorado.

Library of Congress Cataloging-in-Publication Data

The western San Juan Mountains : their geology, ecology, and human
  history / managing editor, Rob Blair.
      p. cm.
    Includes bibliographical references and index.
    1. San Juan Skyway (Colo.)—Guidebooks. 2. San Juan Mountains
  (Colo. and N.M.)—Description and travel. 3. Geology—San Juan
  Mountains (Colo. and N.M.) 4. San Juan Mountains (Colo. and N.M.)—
  History. 5. Ecology—San Juan Mountains (Colo. and N.M.)
  I. Blair, Rob, 1943– .
  F782.S18W47 1996
  917.88'30433—dc20   95-41819
                                                                  CIP

This book was set in Galliard and Gill Sans.

Front cover photo: Twilight Peaks looking north (Photo by Rob Blair).
Back cover: Landsat image courtesy of the USGS EROS Data Center.

The paper used in this publication meets the minimum requirements of the American National Standard for Information Sciences— Permanence of Paper for Printed Library Materials. ANSI Z39.48-1948
∞

10 9 8 7 6 5 4 3 2

CONTENTS

PART I
PHYSICAL ENVIRONMENT ALONG THE SAN JUAN SKYWAY

PART II
BIOLOGICAL COMMUNITIES ALONG THE SAN JUAN SKYWAY

PART III
HUMAN HISTORY ALONG THE SAN JUAN SKYWAY

PART IV
POINTS OF INTEREST AROUND THE WESTERN
SAN JUAN MOUNTAINS

MAPS

FOREWORD

BY GOVERNOR ROY ROMER

Our sense of place comes from knowing where we are, where we have been, and where we are going. Knowing a place means exploring all aspects — geography, history, biology — that make it unique and special. The 235-mile highway loop known as the San Juan Skyway passes through the towns of Durango, Silverton, Ouray, Ridgway, Telluride, Dolores, Cortez, and Mancos, allowing travelers to study the many facets of southwestern Colorado. Throughout history this has been a dynamic region — the landscape has been shaped not only by time but also by those who have lived here.

The authors explore four aspects of this rich region: the physical environment, the biological communities, human history, and important points of interest around the Western San Juan Mountains. To understand the human history of this area, one must understand the physical and biological environment — both have changed those who have inhabited this part of Colorado. We also begin to understand how the people who have lived here have adapted to and shaped the physical and biological communities. From the Anasazi to the miners to today's skiers, each has left an indelible mark.

I encourage you to read this book and use it as a guide to the area. It can help you understand how the physical environment was created, appreciate the plant and animal life, and learn the history of the diverse human populations who have lived here. The Skyway is a common thread linking our past, present, and future.

I have spent a great deal of time in this part of Colorado. As a young boy I worked at my family's grain elevator in Dove Creek.

Working in southwestern Colorado allowed me to do my own exploring of this special place, with its unique spirit and sense of history. I always learn something new when I visit. As a student of history, I appreciate and commend the efforts of all of the authors who contributed to this project. Whether you are a resident or a visitor, I am sure you will find this book an excellent guide as you travel along the San Juan Skyway.

PREFACE

Everything simple is wrong. Everything complex is useless.
— *Paul Valeri*

The preceding quotation summarizes the dilemma we faced in producing this text. If we wrote about the complex topics in simple terms, much of what we said would be incorrect. But if we wrote them as if communicating with experts, few readers would be able to understand us. Thus, this book is aimed toward a mid-range group, the amateur naturalist and historian. The glossary at the end of the book defines many of the technical terms used.

This book was assembled because there is no single reference that covers the western San Juan Mountains in the detail it deserves and that treats this region as a system. These ancient mountains control the weather and climate, which in turn determine the animal and plant communities present. All of these factors have guided human activities.

The San Juan Skyway, one of fifty-four designated National Scenic Byways across the United States (as identified by the U.S. Forest Service in 1988), forms a loop through the heart of the western San Juans. In addition, this highway was designated by the State of Colorado Scenic Byway Commission as a State Scenic and Historic Byway. Most of the places and scenery discussed in the text can be seen from this byway or from tributary roads.

This book has four parts. The first part (Chapters 1–9) concerns the physical environment and includes a description of landform evolution, geologic history, economic geology, and weather. The second section (Chapters 10–13) describes the various ecosystems encountered, primarily with reference to vegetation zones because they remain relatively fixed and are easy to identify. The third part (Chapters 14–18) focuses on the human history of the area, beginning with the earliest known inhabitants, followed by the incursion of the Spanish and, later, miners searching for the "mother lode." The fourth section (Chapters 19–21) is a "points of interest" guide around the Skyway, the Alpine Loop, and the railroad between Durango and Silverton.

This book should be treated as a first approximation of our present knowledge of the western San Juan Mountains. Some of the ideas presented here are still being developed. We invite readers with additional information to help us develop an even better second approximation.

All royalties from this book go to the Skyway Undergraduate Research Fund handled by the Fort Lewis College Foundation. The intent here is to expand our knowledge of this unique region by promoting research by students at the undergraduate level. Donations can be made to this fund by contacting the Fort Lewis College Foundation at Fort Lewis College, Durango, Colorado.

ROB BLAIR, MANAGING EDITOR

ACKNOWLEDGMENTS

All authors and editors of this book volunteered their own time and effort and paid their own expenses. All chapters were reviewed either by fellow authors and editors or by outside experts. Only the outside reviewers will be acknowledged here. Audrey DeLella Benedict read the entire manuscript and made many insightful suggestions. Fred Vanden Bergh drafted many of the maps and figures, such as the Stratigraphic Chart and those found in Chapters 2 and 6, and helped prepare the maps in Chapter 19. Carolee Kohn helped compile the bibliography and produced some of the tables. Pat Blair read the manuscript and helped prepare the maps in Chapter 19. Indirectly, the U.S. Forest Service has contributed to this book through its development of the San Juan Skyway and its funding of research that led to some of the findings discussed in Chapter 14. Chapter acknowledgments include — Chapter 1: Mary Gillam, Sandi Williams; Chapter 7: Tom Westervelt, Fred Johnson; Chapter 9: Dick Armstrong, Tim Brown, Nolan Doesken, Michael Gillespie, George Kiladis; Chapters 10–13: John F. Reed, J. Page Lindsey, Jeff Redders; Chapter 14: Kevin Black, Alan Reed; Chapter 15: David Breternitz, Alan Kane, Ann Bond; and Chapter 18: Gay Smith. We also wish to thank all those students and others not listed individually who not only contributed to our knowledge base but also inspired us to further our research.

THE WESTERN SAN JUAN MOUNTAINS

PART I

PHYSICAL ENVIRONMENT ALONG THE SAN JUAN SKYWAY

Chronostratigraphic units (age estimates in million years)			STRATIGRAPHIC CHART FOR THE WESTERN SAN JUAN MOUNTAINS, COLORADO*	
CENOZOIC	QUATERNARY	(.01) HOLOCENE	STREAM DEPOSITS	
		(1.5) PLEISTOCENE	GLACIAL DEPOSITS	
	TERTIARY	(5) PLIOCENE	LATE ANDESITES AND RHYOLITES: Hinsdale Formation / Sunshine Peak Tuff (22)	
		(24) MIOCENE	ASH-FLOW TUFFS : Carpenter Ridge, Fish Canyon Tuffs, Sapinero Mesa, (~28, concurrent) Dillon Mesa, Blue Mesa, Ute Ridge Tuffs	
		(37) OLIGOCENE	EARLY ANDESITES (30-35): San Juan Formation (informal name)	
		(58) EOCENE	NACIMIENTO, SAN JOSE FORMATIONS, TELLURIDE CONGLOMERATE	
		(66) PALEOCENE	ANIMAS FORMATION	
MESOZOIC	CRETACEOUS		KIRTLAND SHALE	
			FRUITLAND FORMATION	
			PICTURED CLIFFS SANDSTONE	
			LEWIS SHALE	
			MESA VERDE GROUP	CLIFF HOUSE SANDSTONE
				MENEFEE FORMATION
				POINT LOOKOUT SANDSTONE
			MANCOS SHALE	
			DAKOTA SANDSTONE	
			BURRO CANYON FORMATION	
	JURASSIC	(144)	MORRISON FORMATION	BRUSHY BASIN MEMBER
				SALT WASH MEMBER
			JUNCTION CREEK SANDSTONE	
			WANAKAH FORMATION	
			ENTRADA SANDSTONE	
	TRIASSIC	(208)	DOLORES FORMATION	
		(245)	WINGATE SANDSTONE ?	
PALEOZOIC	PERMIAN		CUTLER FORMATION	
	PENNSYLVANIAN	(286)	HERMOSA FORMATION	HONAKER TRAIL MEMBER
				PARADOX MEMBER
				PINKERTON TRAIL MEMBER
		(320)	MOLAS FORMATION	
	MISSISSIPPIAN	(360)	LEADVILLE LIMESTONE	
	DEVONIAN		ELBERT FORMATION	
		(408)	OURAY LIMESTONE	
	SILURIAN	(438)		
	ORDOVICIAN		Stippled areas indicate the geologic record is missing	
		(505)		
	CAMBRIAN	(570)	IGNACIO QUARTZITE	
PRE-CAMBRIAN	PROTEROZOIC		TRIMBLE Gr, ELECTRA LAKE Gb (1460), EOLUS Gr (1460) AND RELATED ROCKS	
			UNCOMPAHGRE FORMATION (1500 - 1700)	
			TENMILE Gr (1720), BAKERS BRIDGE Gr (1720), TWILIGHT Gr (1800), IRVING FORMATION AND VALLECITO CONGLOMERATE	
	ARCHEAN	(2500)		

Modified after MacLachlan 1981.

CHAPTER I

ORIGIN OF LANDSCAPES

ROB BLAIR

The San Juan Skyway, a 235-mile highway loop in southwestern Colorado, winds its way up, over, and through canyons, mesas, plateaus, mountains, plains, and valleys. The sheer variety of landforms makes the Skyway a veritable classroom for the student of geomorphology. One explanation for the large diversity of landscapes on this route is that the Skyway straddles two major physiographic provinces, the Southern Rocky Mountains and the Colorado Plateau (Fig. 1.1). Each of these regions contains a unique suite of landforms and structures.

The Southern Rocky Mountains province dominates the Skyway loop and is represented specifically by the San Juan mountain range. Regionally, the province is associated with anticlinal arches, intervening basins, and glaciated mountains, all at alpine and subalpine altitudes (Pirkle and Yoho 1985). The Front Range is an example of an eroded anticlinal arch; South Park and the San Luis Valley are intervening basins; and the San Juan Mountains constitute one of many glaciated ranges.

The Colorado Plateau province lies within the four states of Utah, Colorado, Arizona, and New Mexico. The southwestern portion of the Skyway falls mostly within the Navajo section of the Colorado Plateau and partly within the Canyonlands section. Geologically, the plateau can be described as a large elevated block consisting of several thousand feet of Paleozoic and Mesozoic sedimentary rock (Thornbury 1965). The horizontal to gently dipping strata are disrupted in places by laccolithic mountains

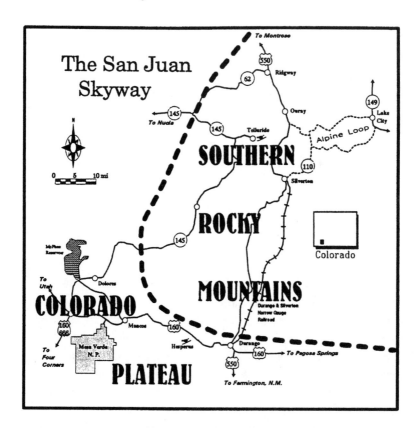

Fig. 1.1   Generalized boundary of Colorado Plateau and Southern Rocky Mountain provinces across the San Juan Skyway.

(Sleeping Ute Mountains, Cortez), monoclines (Hogback Monocline, Durango), upwarps (Monument Upwarp, Utah-Arizona border), basins (San Juan Basin, northwestern New Mexico), collapsed salt anticlines (Paradox Valley, Colorado), and faults (House Creek Fault, Dolores). Centers of volcanic activity mark much of the plateau perimeter. The region, however, is most noted for its colorful canyons and mesas.

The boundary between the Colorado Plateau and the Southern Rocky Mountains is broadly defined as the zone in which sedimentary formations rise onto the uplift of the San Juan Mountains (Hunt 1956).

LANDSCAPE ORIGIN

Geologic processes can be classified as either endogenic or exogenic. Endogenic processes are those that are generated underground and include mountain building and volcanic activity. Exogenic processes are those that occur upon the earth's surface and are represented principally by weathering and erosion. The endogenic and exogenic processes act simultaneously to reshape the surface.

At this boundary between the earth's crust and atmosphere, there is an exchange of energy and movement of materials that creates "interference" patterns. We call these patterns *landforms*, which collectively produce *landscapes*. A simple interference pattern results when wind blows across water to form wave trains or over sandy regions to form sand dunes. In these instances the wind is the energy driver, and the surface medium is homogeneous. However, when a system consists of multiple energy drivers such as running water, glaciers, and tectonic uplift and a variety of rocks (some soft, some hard, some shattered), then the landscapes become incredibly complex. Moreover, the landforms change and evolve through time. Such is the situation around the San Juan Skyway.

LANDSCAPE FACTORS

Several key factors often have great influence in shaping a region's geomorphology. In my view, seven main factors have helped create the Skyway landscape. These seven are not of equal importance, nor do they represent all influences on the evolving landscape. The factors are:

1. the presence of hard, resistant igneous and metamorphic rocks

2. the presence of alternating soft and hard sedimentary strata

3. episodic uplift and deformation

4. late Cretaceous plutonic activity

5. late Tertiary volcanic activity

6. multiple glaciations

7. postglacial processes

HARD "BASEMENT" ROCKS

To anyone who has flown over the San Juan Mountains, their most striking features are the jagged, sharp-pointed peaks jutting into the air. With few exceptions, the most spectacular of these peaks consist of resistant rock. For example, seven 14,000-foot-high (4,267 m) peaks in the immediate vicinity of the Skyway are composed of hard igneous plutonic rock. Mount Eolus, Mount Windom, and Sunlight Peak in the Needle Mountains are composed of Eolus Granite (Cross, Howe et al. 1905). El Diente, Mount Wilson, and Wilson Peak in the San Miguel Mountains are carved from granodiorite associated with the Wilson Peak stock (Bromfield and Conroy 1963), and Mount Sneffels, west of Ouray, is made up of granodiorite-related rocks (Tweto et al. 1976). North of the Needle Mountains stands the spectacular Grenadier Range, composed of hard quartzites of the Uncompahgre Formation. Vestal, Arrow, and Garfield Peaks were hewn from these quartzites, perhaps the hardest of all naturally occurring rocks.

VARIABLE HARDNESS OF SEDIMENTARY STRATA

The distinct layered look of sedimentary rock comes about because of successive episodes of deposition. The layers show up as differences in color, texture, and hardness. Topography reflects variable hardness in particular, because the resistant layers form cliffs, whereas the softer layers break down to form slopes or hollows beneath cliffs. For example, the prominent cliff-forming layers in the upper Animas Valley include the Leadville-Ouray Limestone and the Hermosa Formation (see Stratigraphic Chart, p. 2). The Junction Creek Sandstone forms a popular rock-climbing cliff just north of Durango, and the Dakota Sandstone caps Animas City Mountain at Durango and the valley walls around the town of Dolores. Mesa Verde would not exist as a plateau if it were not for the Point Lookout and Cliff House Sandstones.

Two common slope-forming layers are the Morrison Formation and the Mancos Shale. Slopes below the Dakota Sandstone just north of Durango and around Dolores comprise the Morrison Formation. The prominent gray slopes below the cliffs around Mesa Verde National Park are composed of Mancos Shale. These slope-forming units are made up of mudstones and shales, which weather rapidly because their binding cement is not strong.

EPISODIC UPLIFT

Uplift and deformation have occurred episodically throughout the geologic history of the San Juans and are responsible for the tilting of sedimentary strata, faulting, erosion surfaces, and the uplift of mountains. The approximately 15,000 feet (4,550 m) of Phanerozoic strata found in the vicinity of Durango (Lee et al. 1976, Fig. 3, p. 144; Baars and Ellingson 1984, Fig. 7, p. 12) record at least eleven erosion events. These episodes are preserved as unconformities (note the wavy lines in the Stratigraphic Chart, p. 2), four of which are known to record local uplift in the early Cambrian, Permian, late Cretaceous, and late Tertiary. The last two events together produced the tilting of sedimentary strata that form a cuesta at Mesa Verde and hogbacks at Durango.

Deformation has buckled and broken the earth's upper crust to create fracture zones and fault blocks. The uplifted Grenadier and Mount Sneffels horst blocks of hard Precambrian quartzites, for example, form the backbone of the western San Juan Mountains. These blocks are bounded by faults that have shifted several times since the Precambrian (Baars and Ellingson 1984). Erosion frequently occurs along fracture zones to create stream valleys or prominent escarpments. Examples include Mineral Creek, which closely follows the ring fractures west of Silverton associated with the Silverton Caldera. The steep slopes immediately south of Ouray are partly the result of the east-west-trending Ouray Fault.

LATE CRETACEOUS PLUTONIC ACTIVITY

Along the western perimeter of the San Juan Mountains stand four structural domes created by the intrusion of mushroom-shaped plutons called laccoliths. These domes include the La Plata, Rico, San Miguel, and Sleeping Ute Mountains. The La Plata Mountains, for instance, formed from multiple intrusions of magma from a point source some 65 million to 67 million years ago (Cunningham et al. 1977). The magma invaded the near-surface sedimentary layers to produce a complex of dikes, sills, and laccoliths. These laccolithic mountains differ from the central San Juans principally because they eroded from a complex of interfingering plutons and sedimentary layers, whereas the San Juans eroded from a thick volcanic pile resting upon an eroded Precambrian crystalline basement.

LATE TERTIARY VOLCANIC ACTIVITY

The rocks in the San Juans record an unusual period of tectonic stability in early Tertiary time, about 40 million years ago. This crustal quiescence is revealed by a buried erosion surface found throughout much of the western San Juan Mountains and forms an angular unconformity beneath the Telluride Conglomerate, a cliff-forming unit exposed from Molas Pass to Telluride. The overlying rocks mark the beginning of vigorous uplift in the central and eastern San Juans that culminated in some of the most violent volcanic activity ever recorded on the planet.

Between 30 and 35 million years ago, large stratovolcanoes were built upon remnants of the erosion surface and created a broad volcanic plateau (Steven 1975). These stratovolcanoes probably looked much like today's Mount Rainier. This early stage of volcanism is recorded by the presence of the San Juan Formation, a mixture of andesitic flows, breccias, and intermediate volcaniclastic deposits. However, beginning around 29 million years ago the style of volcanic activity changed. Some of the stratovolcanoes were destroyed by sticky, high-pressure felsic magma that burst through ring fractures and vents to blast hundreds to thousands of cubic kilometers of volcanic ash into the atmosphere (Steven and Lipman 1976). The ejected magma emptied the holding chamber beneath the surface, causing the overlying crust to collapse into the void, creating a caldera. The expelled ash was then deposited as a thick blanket over the existing landscape. This sequence of events happened not once but at least fifteen times over various parts of the San Juan Mountains during a 7-million-year period. The northern Skyway area preserves a known record of four of these eruptions (see Chapter 6).

The mountains carved from these ash-flow tuffs, flows, and volcanic breccias have a number of general characteristics that set them apart from the plutonic mountains discussed earlier. The volcanic rock is brittle and fractures easily into angular fist- and head-sized chunks from hydration and freeze-thaw weathering processes.

Thus, summits appear as piles of rubble. Examples include the Red Mountains north of Red Mountain Pass. These summits are usually not as high as the plutonic rock summits seen in the Needle Mountains and elsewhere around the Skyway.

Some volcanic flow units and shallow intrusive rocks display vertical cooling cracks or columnar joints. Such features appear in the rocks exposed in Hendrick Gulch in north Ironton Park and in the summit rocks of Engineer Mountain, west of Coal Bank Hill. Because the volcanic rock breaks down so readily, there is an abundant supply of rock fragments to cascade down cliffs and slopes to form large talus cones, debris fans, and rock glaciers.

MULTIPLE GLACIATIONS

Perhaps no other erosional agent has left its mark on this landscape more than glaciation. It is principally responsible for the deep, U-shaped canyons and steep-walled mountain peaks seen around the Skyway (Fig. 1.2). This glacial signature was etched on a scattered late Pliocene erosion surface that truncated the

Fig. 1.2   Looking south from Dallas Divide. View shows glacial cirques, horns, and arêtes in the Sneffels Range. Photo by R. Blair.

Precambrian crystalline rocks and the late Tertiary volcanic rocks (Atwood and Mather 1932; Steven 1968).

The San Juan Mountains may have experienced fifteen or more glacial advances in the last 2 million years, but only six of these are recorded by glacial deposits. The evidence of the earlier glaciations has been destroyed by the more recent ones and by erosion between glacial advances. Therefore, we cannot say when the region first became a refuge for glacial ice. However, we do know approximately when the glaciers disappeared. According to carbon-14 dating of organic sediments found in alpine bogs and lake sediments (Maher 1972, Carrara et al. 1984), the high glacial cirques in the San Juans were ice-free at least 15,000 years ago. Tree-ring data and Antarctic ice cores indicate that the planet experienced a glacial maximum some 18,000 years ago (Skinner and Porter 1987). The San Juans record this event with glacial deposits at the north edge of Durango and north of Ridgway. Thus, deglaciation must have taken place between 18,000 and 15,000 years ago.

For glaciers to grow, ice accumulation rates must be greater than ice ablation, or wastage, rates. The boundary between the ablation zone and the overlying accumulation zone is called the Equilibrium Line Altitude, or ELA, and corresponds roughly with the permanent snowline found in the highest mountain ranges. The ELA today lies between 12,200 and 12,300 feet (3,725–3,750 m) in the Grenadier Range (Leonard 1984). Only the highest peaks pierce this imaginary surface. The ELA varies from place to place because of local differences in topography, precipitation, and temperature. During the last global cooling, 18,000 years ago, the ELA dropped between 1,000 and 2,000 feet (300–600 m) and, in so doing, turned the huge upland surface of the San Juans into a dumping ground for snow and ice. The ice grew rapidly in thickness and finally into full-fledged glaciers.

The San Juan Mountains, during each maximum glacial episode, were covered with an ice-field complex covering about 1,900 square miles (5,000 sq km) (Atwood and Mather 1932). The ice field consisted of a thin layer of ice over the high divides and uplands, with streams of ice radiating out into river valleys like the arms of an octopus (Fig. 1.3). Some of the high peaks, such as Engineer, Sultan, Pigeon, and Turret, rose above the ice field, forming

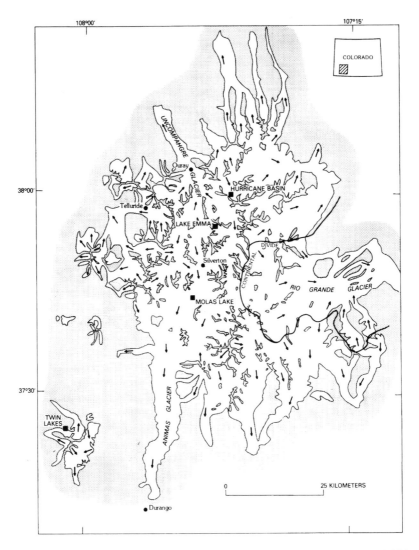

Fig. 1.3   The distribution and flow directions of glacial ice approximately 18,000 years ago in the San Juan Mountains, as inferred by Atwood and Mather (1932). Black squares indicate radiocarbon sites (from Carrara et al. 1984).

rock islands called nunataks by glaciologists. The tree line is esti-mated to have dropped by 2,100 feet (650 m) during these times (Maher 1961), and, of course, the valleys filled with ice were de-void of vegetation. The Animas glacier was one of the longest valley glaciers in the Southern Rocky Mountains. It extended for more than 40 miles (65 km) from Silverton to Durango. Once deglaciation commenced, the ELA rose above the San Juan "plateau," and the glaciers disappeared rapidly, leaving only a few small glaciers in north-facing cirques (Carrara et al. 1984). Glacial erosion, however, left its mark throughout the San Juan Mountains in the form of horns, cirques, hanging valleys, arêtes, and numerous U-shaped valleys.

In addition to causing erosion, the glaciers left deposits of lateral and end moraines. Lateral moraines line parts of both sides of the Animas Valley, and the best-developed end moraines are found at Durango and Ridgway. When the ice left the Animas and Uncompahgre Valleys, it left deep, U-shaped troughs that initially filled with water to form large proglacial lakes. The lakes quickly accumulated sediment and glacial outwash to form the flat-floored valleys seen today.

POSTGLACIAL PROCESSES

After each glaciation, the ongoing processes of stream erosion, mass wasting, and freeze-thaw modified the glaciated landscape. In particular, rivers cut deep canyons and built flights of terraces. River terraces reflect a complex response to major changes in the hydraulic flow of the river (Schumm 1977). Such changes may come about because of floods, sudden changes in gradient due to uplift or subsidence, channel blockage, or changes in climate. The majority of the well-developed river terraces in the Four Corners region represent the effects of multiple glaciations, where rivers were subjected over thousands of years to changes in discharge and sediment load. When the glaciers began their retreat, the valley floors were choked with sediment, which was being continuously reworked by braided streams across a broad floodplain. When discharges dropped, single channels formed and slowly carved into bedrock, leaving portions of the abandoned floodplain high and dry. The best terraces can be seen south of Durango (Fig. 1.4), but nearly every river has a few (Gillam et al. 1984).

The most common mass-wasting processes encountered around the Skyway drive are landslides, mudflows, debris flows, and creep. Landslides, for example, have continually modified the

Fig. 1.4 Looking northwest at Animas River terraces 4 miles south of Durango. Photo by R. Blair.

steep shale slopes and even the highway between Mancos and Hes-perus. A mudflow threatened the Telluride airport in the spring of 1987. Debris flows tend to be rare events, but their deposits can be seen at the north end of Ironton Park and at the base of nearly every avalanche chute. Soil creep can be recognized by the contin-uous curve of trees from trunk to tip. The basal curve noted in many trees, however, especially aspen, is caused by snow creep in winter during the first few years of tree growth.

Snow avalanches are also considered a mass-wasting phe-nomenon. Snow avalanches have accounted for 264 deaths in the San Juan Mountains between 1874 and 1991 (Dale Atkins 1991, personal communication), and thus they live up to their nickname, "white death." Most of these accidents occurred during the early boom days of mining, but even today hardly a year goes by that some unwary skier does not lose his or her life. The steep, treeless alleyways down gullies and slopes are avalanche paths. Whether an avalanche runs or not depends on the topography, nature of the snow, and local climatic conditions (Perla and Martinelli 1976).

Some avalanche zones run several times a year, some only once a year, and others perhaps only once in several decades.

Two general types of avalanches are recognized, point release and slab release. Point-release avalanches are loose-snow slides that begin from a point and spread out quickly into a fan-shaped flow. They are most common in the early winter and usually occur within forty-eight hours after a major snowstorm. The East Riverside slide in the upper Uncompahgre Canyon runs after virtually every major snowstorm. Slab-release avalanches have the potential to do the most damage because their release time is less predictable and because they can involve huge volumes of snow. They are more common in late winter and early spring. On March 3, 1963, the Reverend R. F. Miller and his two daughters were swept to their deaths by a large slab avalanche that bolted across U.S. 550 at the East Riverside slide, 5 miles south of Ouray (Gallagher 1967).

Freeze-thaw processes have left their signature, mostly above timberline, in the form of shattered rock, stone stripes and rings, flowing lobes of soil, and rock glaciers. Rock glaciers are lobate or tongue-shaped masses of angular rocks that can flow downslope at rates of several inches per year. Talus from rockfall is the most common source of debris, so most rock glaciers are found adjacent to cirque headwalls or cliffs. Rock glaciers have commonly been classified as either being ice-cored or ice-cemented (White 1976). The former are thought to have a solid core of ice perhaps tens of feet thick. In some instances this may be relict ice left over from a previous glacier. These rock glaciers are tongue-shaped and can exhibit meandering longitudinal furrows on their surface. Compression ridges commonly appear near their snouts. Ice-cemented rock glaciers are composed of angular rocks bound together by interstitial ice, and they can also exhibit a flowage signature.

More than 650 rock glaciers have been recognized in the San Juan Mountains (White 1979). This region has perhaps the largest concentration of this kind of feature in the conterminous United States. Of these rock glaciers, approximately 61 percent are actively moving, 28 percent are tongue-shaped, but only 6 percent are thought to be ice-cored (White 1979). Rock glaciers and other

Fig. 1.5 Looking northwest at the Imogene Basin rock glacier. U.S. Geological Survey photo by A. C. Spencer and E. Howe 1899.

freeze-thaw phenomena can be seen at the base of Mount Snowdon southeast of Molas Pass and above timberline along the Ophir Pass and Imogene Pass four-wheel-drive roads (Fig. 1.5).

REFERENCES

Atwood, W. W., 1915. Eocene glacial deposits in southwestern Colorado. U.S. Geological Survey, Professional Paper 95, pp. 13–26.

Atwood, W. W., and K. F. Mather, 1932. Physiography and Quaternary geology of the San Juan Mountains, Colorado: U.S. Geological Survey, Professional Paper 166, 176 pp.

Baars, D. L., and J. A. Ellingson, 1984. Geology of the western San Juan Mountains, in D. C. Brew, ed., *Field Trip Guidebook*, Geological Society of America, Rocky Mountain Section, 37th Annual Meeting, pp. 1–45.

Bromfield, C. S., and A. R. Conroy, 1963. *Preliminary geologic map of the Mount Wilson Quadrangle San Miguel County, Colorado.* U.S. Geological Survey Map MF-273.

Carrara, P. E., W. N. Mode, M. Rubin, and S. W. Robinson, 1984. Deglaciation and postglacial timberline in the San Juan Mountains, Colorado: *Quaternary Research*, v. 21, no. 1, pp. 42–55.

Carrara, P. E., D. A. Trimble, and M. Rubin, 1991. Holocene treeline fluctuations in the northern San Juan Mountains, Colorado, U.S.A., as indicated by radiocarbon-dated conifer wood. *Arctic and Alpine Research*, v. 23, pp. 233–246.

Cross, W., E. Howe, J. D. Irving, and W. H. Emmons, 1905. *Geologic atlas of the United States, Needle Mountain Quadrangle, Colorado.* U.S. Geological Survey, Folio 131, 14 pp.

Cunningham, C. G., C. W. Naeser, and R. F. Marvin, 1977. *New ages for intrusive rocks in the Colorado mineral belt.* U.S. Geological Survey, Open File Report 77-573, 7 pp.

Gallagher, D., 1967. *The snowy torrents: Avalanche accidents in the United States 1910–1966.* U.S. Department of Agriculture, 144 pp.

Gillam, M. L., D. Moore, and G. R. Scott, 1984. Quaternary deposits and soils in the Durango area, Southwestern Colorado, in D. C. Brew, ed., *Field Trip Guidebook,* Geological Society of America, Rocky Mountain Section, 37th Annual Meeting, 209 pp.

Hunt, C. B., 1956. Cenozoic geology of the Colorado Plateau. U.S. Geological Survey, Professional Paper 279, 99 pp.

Lee, K., R. C. Epis, D. L. Baars, D. H. Knepper, and R. M. Summer, 1976. Road log: Paleozoic tectonics and sedimentation and Tertiary volcanism of the western San Juan Mountains, Colorado, in R. C. Epis and R. J. Weimer, eds., *Studies in Colorado field geology,* Colorado School of Mines, Professional Contributions 8, pp. 139–158.

Leonard, E. M., 1984. Late Pleistocene equilibrium-line altitudes and modern snow accumulation patterns, San Juan Mountains, Colorado, U.S.A. *Arctic and Alpine Research*, v. 16, no. 1, pp. 65–76.

MacLachlan, M. E., 1981. Stratigraphic correlation chart for western Colorado and northwestern New Mexico, in R. C. Epis and J. F. Callender, eds., *Western Slope Colorado,* New Mexico Geological Society Thirty-second Field Conference, pp. 75–79.

Maher, L. J., 1972. Nomograms for computing 0.95 confidence limits of pollen data. *Review of Paleobotany and Palynology*, v. 13, pp. 85–93.

Maher, L. J., 1961. Pollen analysis and post-glacial vegetation history in the Animas Valley. Ph.D. thesis, University of Minnesota, Minneapolis, MN.

Perla, R., I., and M. Martinelli, Jr., 1976. *Avalanche handbook.* U.S. Department of Agriculture, Agriculture Handbook 489, 238 pp.

Pirkle, E. C., and W. H. Yoho, 1985. *Natural landscapes.* Dubuque, IA: Kendal/Hunt, 416 pp.

Schumm, Stanley A., 1977. *The fluvial system.* New York: John Wiley & Sons, 338 pp.

Skinner, B.J., and S. C. Porter, 1987. *Physical geology.* New York: John Wiley & Sons, 750 pp.

Steven, T. A., 1968. *Critical review of the San Juan peneplain, southwestern Colorado.* U.S. Geological Survey, Professional Paper 594-I, pp. I1–I19.

Steven, T. A., 1975. Middle Tertiary volcanic field in the southern Rocky Mountains, in B. F. Curtis, ed., *Cenozoic history of the southern Rocky Mountains,* Geological Society of America, Memoir 114, pp. 75–94.

Steven, T. A., and P. W. Lipman, 1976. *Calderas of the San Juan volcanic field, southwestern Colorado.* U.S. Geological Survey, Professional Paper 958, pp. 1–4 and 10–16.

Thornbury, W. D., 1965. *Regional geomorphology of the United States.* New York: John Wiley & Sons, 609 pp.

Tweto, O., T. A. Steven, W. J. Hail, Jr., and R. H. Moench, 1976. *Preliminary geologic map of Montrose 1° × 2° Quadrangle, southwestern Colorado, 1:250,000.* U.S. Geological Survey, Miscellaneous Field Investigations Map MF-761.

White, G. P., 1979. *Rock glacier morphometry, San Juan Mountains, Colorado.* Geological Society of America Bulletin, Part II, v. 90, p. 924–952.

White, S. E., 1976. Rock glaciers and block fields, review and new data. *Quaternary Research,* v. 6, p. 77–97.

CHAPTER 2

PALEOTECTONIC HISTORY

Douglas C. Brew

To unravel the geologic story of southwestern Colorado, one must understand its paleotectonic history. The field of tectonics looks at the processes that deform the earth's crustal rocks on the global scale; paleotectonics examines such processes over the span of geologic time. The geological evolution of a region such as the San Juan Mountains might not seem to require a mechanism of global dimensions to explain it, yet the fundamental forces that have shaped this region are of that scale.

For about 1.8 billion years southwestern Colorado has been in a position on the North American continent where its crustal rocks have been affected by tectonic activity. The mountainous terrain of the region is an obvious reflection of such activity; less obvious evidence is found in the igneous, sedimentary, and metamorphic rocks of the region. Subtle details of rock composition, variations in the thickness of sedimentary rock units, and the regional distribution patterns of specific units have recorded the influence of tectonism through geologic time. The record is not perfect; nevertheless, it reveals a fascinating, complex story.

To understand what drives local or regional tectonism, one must understand plate tectonics. This theory holds that the outer portion of the earth consists of several rigid plates; some underlie oceanic basins, and others encompass both oceanic and continental regions. These plates are in motion relative to each other and to the interior of the earth.

Plate motion is clearly the major process shaping present-day geological activity, and the same process appears to have characterized past geological history. To better understand how plate tectonics has shaped the San Juan region, we must first examine the basic tenets of plate tectonic theory.

PLATE TECTONICS

The theory of plate tectonics gives rise immediately to several questions: What is the nature of the plates? What allows and controls their motion, the directions and rates? What drives this process? Before proceeding, we must first examine these questions.

PLATES: WHAT ARE THEY?

The plates are pieces of the outer, essentially rigid layer of the earth known as the *lithosphere*. Fitting together a bit like pieces of a moving and ever-changing jigsaw puzzle, they are roughly 65 miles (100 km) thick under continents and slightly thinner in oceanic regions. A quick glance at the map of the modern configuration of plates (Fig. 2.1) reveals that some plates include both continental and oceanic regions (e.g., the North American plate), whereas others are largely oceanic (e.g., the Pacific plate).

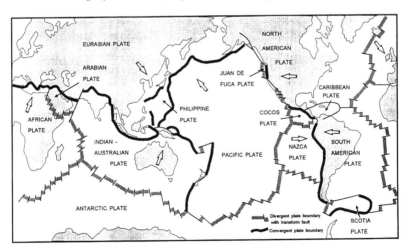

Fig. 2.1   The modern configuration of plates. Subduction zones indicated by heavy lines, spreading centers by stippled lines, transform boundaries by single lines. Arrows show relative directions of plate motion.

It's quite clear that the present-day plate arrangement differs from those of earlier geologic times. Indeed, the origin and subsequent transformation of any continent or ocean basin can be explained in terms of plate tectonic evolution. Through geologic time, continents (or even "supercontinents") have formed, have been added to, and perhaps have later fragmented; ocean basins have opened, closed, and reopened. Throughout this rearranging of the earth's geography, continental rocks have been preserved, and the total area of continents has increased, even though the form and distribution of continents have been continuously changing. It follows, then, that continental rocks should be relatively ancient. Radiometric dating confirms this; the oldest continental rocks are approximately 4 billion years old. The oldest rocks found along the San Juan Skyway are not quite this ancient, having been dated at about 1.8 billion years old (see Chapter 3).

By contrast, rocks that constitute the oceanic lithosphere have been dated at only 150 to 200 million years old. The oceans clearly have been transitory features. They have opened, widened, and then closed as the plates went on their inexorable journeys.

HOW DO PLATES MOVE?

Answering the question of how plates are able to move is relatively easy. Underlying the lithosphere is a zone extending from about 45 to 65 miles (70–100 km) beneath the surface to a depth of approximately 160 miles (250 km). Long known to seismologists as the "low velocity layer," this zone, called the *asthenosphere*, possesses pressure-temperature conditions that render the rocks of the interior soft and capable of slow flow. The lithospheric plates are thus in a sense floating on this underlying "plastic" layer; it allows them both to move horizontally over the earth's surface and to rise or fall as the plate is loaded (by the accumulation of sediment) or unloaded (by the erosional removal of rock).

HOW FAST DO PLATES MOVE?

The speed at which a plate moves is not impressive when compared to an automobile's velocity over the San Juan Skyway. Slow motion in plate tectonic terms may be about 2 inches (5 cm) per year, whereas rapid motion will be anywhere from 4 to 6 inches

(10–15 cm) per year. Speed is not everything, however, and this slow-moving geological process, given immense amounts of time and comparable amounts of momentum associated with a moving plate, has been relentlessly rearranging the face of the globe for most of its history.

WHAT GOES ON AT PLATE BOUNDARIES?

Although no portion of the earth's surface is truly devoid of geological activity, the most concentrated and significant activity takes place at the boundaries between plates. Plate boundaries are of three types: divergent boundaries, or spreading centers; convergent boundaries, or subduction zones; and transform boundaries. What is the nature of each type of boundary, and what activity characterizes them?

Where two plates are moving away from each other, the earth's crust is splitting apart, and the boundary is known as a *divergent boundary* or *spreading center* (see Fig. 2.2). At such boundaries, new lithosphere is being created. Earthquakes and volcanic activity accompany the process, and voluminous amounts of basaltic magmas and lavas rise into the fracture zone to provide the raw material for new crust. When such a process is initiated within a continent, the crust becomes fractured, faulted, and distended, and the dominant extensional (as opposed to compressional) activity literally pulls the crust apart. The East Africa Rift Valleys and the Rio Grande Rift of the western United States are good examples of such activity. When this process is not arrested, continents may break apart, and the pieces ultimately may separate. Divergence along the submarine spreading center that follows such a breakup not only produces some of the world's most extensive, albeit submerged, mountain ranges (e.g., the Mid-Atlantic Ridge) but also serves as the locus of growth of the ocean basins.

Where two plates move toward each other, one plate (always oceanic lithosphere) slides beneath the other and sinks into the interior of the earth, where it is ultimately consumed (see Fig. 2.2). Such boundaries are known as *convergent boundaries* or *subduction zones*. Most, but not all, involve the oceanic plate being subducted either directly beneath the edge of a continent (e.g., the subduction along the western coast of South America) or beneath major

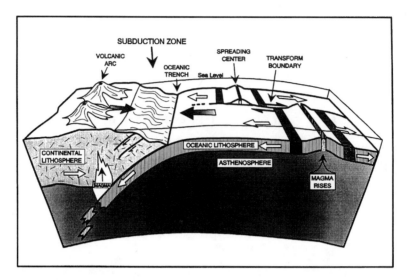

Fig. 2.2   The three types of plate boundaries; arrows show relative motions of plates. At spreading centers, note the successive addition of strips of oceanic lithosphere as rising magma fills the fracture and is subsequently split. A transform boundary, with side-by-side motion, connects offset segments of the spreading center. In the subduction zone, note the oceanic trench where the subducting plate sinks. Magmas generated at the contact between the subducting plate and the upper plate either cool beneath the surface to form intrusive igneous bodies or are erupted to form a volcanic arc. The subducted plate is consumed.

offshore island complexes adjacent to a continent (e.g., the sub-duction beneath the Japanese island arc). Modern subduction zones, such as those surrounding the Pacific Ocean, have as their hallmark belts of volcanic mountains (or "volcanic arcs") situated adjacent to oceanic trenches, which mark the zone where the sub-ducting plate sinks into the earth's interior. These associations are commonly known as "arc-trench systems."

Subduction zones are the sites of some of the most intense geological activity known. Folding, faulting, and widespread meta-morphism associated with igneous activity of all sorts take place and commonly produce extremely complex geology in the arc-trench systems. The igneous, sedimentary, and metamorphic rocks gener-ated in and around subduction zones are similarly complex.

This type of plate boundary, the only one in which litho-spheric plates (oceanic lithosphere, hence oceans) are consumed, has produced the major mountain belts of the world. Where continent-size blocks raft in on the incoming subducting plate, the continental material is too buoyant to take the plunge, and the ensuing collision and suturing together of the continental materials creates larger continents and some of the world's most impressive mountain ranges. The Himalayas were born of such a collision, as were the Alps. On a different scale, if smaller blocks of continental materials (sometimes called "microcontinents") are swept into a subduction zone, they, too, will be added to the edge of a continent but as a collage of accreted "terranes."

Plate boundaries in which two plates slide by each other side by side are known as *transform boundaries* (Fig. 2.2). These are sometimes termed "conservative" boundaries, as plate materials are neither created nor consumed but rather are "conserved." Although such boundaries are not typically accompanied by significant igneous activity, deformation of rocks in the zone surrounding the contact between the plates is commonly intense, and the earthquake activity may be both severe and frequent.

The San Andreas Fault system of Mexico and California is a transform boundary between the Pacific plate and the North American plate. Baja California and southern California are slowly and spasmodically but inexorably moving northwest relative to the remainder of North America, with consequences well known to the inhabitants of those regions.

WHAT CAUSES PLATE MOTION?

No universally accepted explanation for the drive behind plate motion exists. Most hypotheses invoke slow circulation within the asthenosphere, typically described as "convectional circulation," but whether or not this constitutes an *active* mechanism that actually propels plates along is open to question.

Others suggest that plates may be driven by *slab pull* as lithosphere slabs sink in subduction zones, and/or by *slab push*, which occurs as newly created oceanic lithosphere slides off the sides of an elevated mid-oceanic ridge or rise of a spreading center. Such a mechanism is gravity driven and has the appeal of being conceptually a simple system. Whether or not it actually works, however, is not clearly established. For the moment, then, geology and geologists are in the curious but familiar position of employing and cataloging the outcomes of a global system that clearly operates today and has operated in the past.

THE TECTONIC EVOLUTION OF THE SAN JUAN MOUNTAINS

With an understanding of plate tectonics as a guide, we can now explore how the theory relates to the geologic history of the San Juan Mountain region. This history can be divided into seven distinct segments, some of them times of relative quiescence, others characterized by intense tectonic activity.

THE PRECAMBRIAN

The San Juans' Precambrian rocks, a complex of igneous, metamorphic, and sedimentary rocks, are found mainly in the core of the mountain range (see Chapter 3). The oldest of these rocks, almost 1.8 billion years old, appear to represent the materials of ancient volcanic arcs. For example, the complex association of metamorphosed volcanic and sedimentary rocks found within the Irving Formation is comparable to what one might find in modern arc-trench systems in the western Pacific Ocean. The Irving Formation is exposed in the Animas Valley southeast of Electra Lake and at the U.S. Forest Service campground east of Haviland Lake (see Points of Interest 26).

The similarity of these ancient rocks to those of modern-day subduction zones suggests that the Precambrian rocks of Colorado were formed within a subduction zone. The orientation and location of this zone are not clear, however, because the limited exposure of these rocks makes it difficult to reconstruct such details. The broad patterns and ages of Precambrian rocks within the western United States suggest that the main mass of ancestral North America lay to the north, its southern edge lying along the southern border of present-day Wyoming (Condie 1986, Hoffman 1989). The subduction zone (or succession of zones) in which the Precambrian rocks of the San Juans were formed presumably was oriented more or less east-west and lay

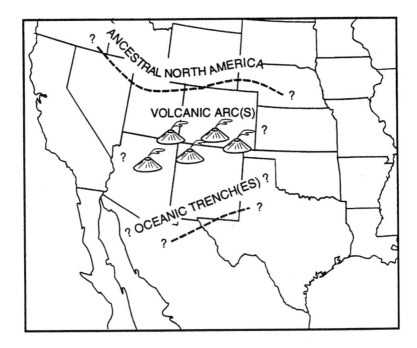

Fig. 2.3   Very generalized picture of the Precambrian paleotectonic setting. The southern edge of "Ancestral North America" in this figure coincides closely with the southern border of Wyoming (Condie 1986, Hoffman 1989). The Precambrian rocks in the broad belt that includes Colorado, New Mexico, Arizona, and Utah appear likely to have formed in a succession of volcanic arc–oceanic trench systems (subduction zones) that migrated south through time. The exact locations of these arcs and trenches are not clearly established.

off the southern coast of the continent. A generalized map of the presumed relationships appears in Figure 2.3.

Perhaps the most significant events of this period, in terms of their impact on later geologic development, occurred late in the Precambrian. Whereas earlier Precambrian tectonism was dominantly compressional in nature as the ancestral continent grew along its southern edge (see Chapter 3), the late Precambrian saw the continent broken apart by a rifting episode that commenced in certain parts of ancestral western North America about 1.4 billion years ago and was completed approximately 850 million years ago (Dickinson 1977, Stewart and Suczek 1977).

The best direct evidence of the breakup of the continent appears in Precambrian rocks to the west and southwest of the Four Corners region. The younger Precambrian rocks of the Grand Canyon region, an association of sediments and basic igneous rocks preserved in downdropped, or tilted, fault blocks, serve as a classic example of the *rift valley stage* (Dickinson 1974) of a developing spreading center. The evidence suggests that the western edge of North America was redefined at this time. This new edge of the continent (known to geologists as the Wasatch Line) faced west toward a widening ancestral Pacific Ocean and became a profound geologic boundary that strongly influenced both sediment deposition and the subsequent tectonic evolution of western North America (Fig. 2.4).

More important to our story, however, is what happened to the fundamental structure of the "basement" rocks underlying the western edge of North America. Studies of both modern rift valley regions and their ancient counterparts show that the fragmentation associated with rifting and subsequent spreading affects a linear belt that may extend as much as 325 miles (500 km) to either side of the initial rift zone (Dickinson 1974). The subsequent behavior of the San Juan region indicates that the basement rocks were indeed broken up into an assortment of large blocks bounded by fractures created in the late Precambrian rifting. These fractures were to play an important role in the geologic evolution to come.

THE EARLY AND MIDDLE PALEOZOIC

From the end of the Precambrian through the early Pennsylvanian Period, the region was part of the relatively stable edge of the North American continent (Fig. 2.4; also, see Chapter 4). Although subduction and volcanism resumed farther to the west in what is now western Nevada and California, the Four Corners region was largely unaffected by this activity and alternately lay either slightly below or slightly above sea level. The region was submerged in late Cambrian time and perhaps also during the Ordovician and Silurian. However, rocks of the latter two periods are not preserved here; they may have been removed by erosion during a time of emergence in the early and middle Devonian (see Chapter

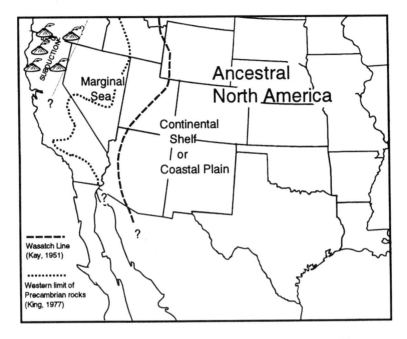

Fig. 2.4   Paleotectonic setting in early and mid-Paleozoic time. The western limit of Precambrian rocks marks the ragged edge of Ancestral North America, produced by late Precambrian rifting. The "Wasatch Line" marks the approximate edge of the continental shelf/coastal plain early in this time interval; the region east of this line was an emergent coastal plain at times, a shallowly submerged continental shelf at other times.

4). The late Devonian and Mississippian saw the return of a shallow sea that persisted up to the close of the Mississippian.

    Although there was no large-scale tectonic activity from late Precambrian through Mississippian, local evidence suggests that the basement blocks underlying the shelf were not altogether quiet. Subtle differences in sedimentary facies or rock types, differences in the thickness of rocks of a given time interval, and an occasional missing rock unit imply that the shelf was not a seamless, flat depositional surface. At the close of the Mississippian Period, the entire region, along with adjacent parts of Utah, Arizona, and New Mexico — virtually the entire continental shelf region of southwestern North America — was uplifted and exposed to erosion (see Chapter 4).

THE ANCESTRAL ROCKIES

In the Pennsylvanian Period, the relative quiet of the preceding 320 million years was broken, literally, as large blocks of the earth's crust began to shift. In Colorado two large raised blocks, the Uncompahgre Uplift and the Ancestral Front Range Uplift, became major sources of sediment. Two downdropped blocks adjacent to these mountainous regions, the Paradox Basin (southwest of the Uncompahgre) and the Central Colorado Trough (between the two uplifts), became the primary centers of deposition (Fig. 2.5; also see Chapter 4).

According to Kluth and Coney (1981), several factors combined to initiate and shape this episode of tectonism. First and

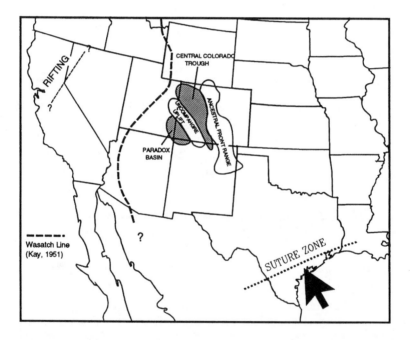

Fig. 2.5 Paleotectonic setting and major tectonic elements in Colorado in Middle Pennsylvanian time (after Kluth and Coney 1981). Note that only the Colorado tectonic elements are shown; numerous uplifts and basins also developed at this time in adjacent areas. The suture zone on the Gulf Coast region marks the approximate boundary between two continental blocks. The arrow shows the relative movement of the southern block; this motion was also imparted to the southwestern corner of Ancestral North America.

foremost was a collision between two continental blocks along a subduction zone located in the Gulf Coast region (Fig. 2.5). The impact is recorded in the folded and faulted rocks of the Marathon region in western Texas and the Ouachita Mountains of Oklahoma and Arkansas. Second, the southwestern part of North America was peninsula-like; the bulk of North America lay toward the northeast, so the southwestern extremity was somewhat fragile. If, as Dickinson (1977) suggests, rifting was occurring at this time west of the Wasatch Line, the lack of support was even more pronounced. When we remember that this region was thoroughly broken up into large basement blocks at the close of the Precambrian, it's not difficult to understand why the "peninsula" failed when hit from the south. A combination of inherited Precambrian fragility and strong plate motions revived the old fractures and produced the uplifts and basins of the Ancestral Rockies.

POST-ANCESTRAL ROCKIES, PRE-LARAMIDE TIME

Following the formation of the Ancestral Rockies, quiet prevailed once again. The mountain blocks were lowered by erosion, and the adjacent basins filled up with sediment (see Chapter 5). By the Triassic Period, the mountains had been beveled off, and the region returned to the continental shelf–coastal plain state of previous times (Fig. 2.6). The "tectonic quiet" prevailed until the end of the Cretaceous, when the Laramide Orogeny broke the spell.

THE LARAMIDE OROGENY

In the late Cretaceous the Four Corners region was once again inundated. This time, however, it was covered by a huge, shallow sea that extended east as far as present-day Minnesota and from the Gulf of Mexico to the Arctic Ocean. Subduction-driven deformation and uplift to the west generated highlands that prevented the sea from extending much farther west than the Four Corners region; these uplifts shed sediments eastward to the sandy shores of the vast inland sea (Fig. 2.7).

Rates of plate motion increased dramatically in late Cretaceous time, moreover, with two significant outcomes. First, the rapid convergence deformed rocks of the earth's crust farther and farther inland from the actual subduction zone itself. Once again

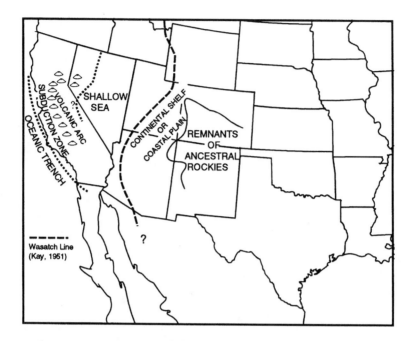

Fig. 2.6 Paleotectonic setting in early Triassic time. Only low-lying remnants of the Ancestral Rocky Mountains remained and merged westward into the continental shelf–coastal plain. A subduction zone with a volcanic arc was established along the western edge of the continent (after Kay 1951, MacLachland 1972, Collinson and Hasenmuller 1978).

the Precambrian weaknesses in the crust were exploited, and once again blocks began to rise or fall. The San Juan Dome, San Juan Basin, and other major structural features in and around the Four Corners region and the Southern Rocky Mountains began to acquire their present-day form (Fig. 2.8).

The second major consequence of rapid convergence was a wave of subduction-related volcanic activity that swept inland. Volcanic activity in the La Plata Mountains at the close of the Cretaceous Period is revealed by the intrusive igneous rocks now exposed there and by the distinctive McDermott Formation, an apron of volcanic debris to the south (see Chapter 5). No trace of the volcanic superstructure that must have existed at that time remains, but its former presence is unquestionable (see Chapter 6).

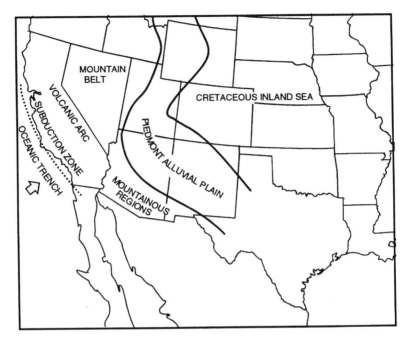

Fig. 2.7 Paleotectonic setting and paleogeography in late Cretaceous time. At this time the Point Lookout Sandstone was being deposited in southwestern Colorado. The mountainous region east of the volcanic arc was undergoing deformation, folding and faulting as the rates of convergence in the subduction zone increased. Arrow shows relative motion of the Pacific plate (after McGookey et al. 1972).

With the volcanism and structural deformation of the Laramide Orogeny, the sea retreated from the region for the last time, and the stage was set for the most recent events.

THE EARLY CENOZOIC

It seems clear that during times of rapid plate convergence in subduction zones, the subducted plate descends at a very shallow angle into the earth's interior. In the extreme case, the plate may even extend in a subhorizontal position just beneath the overlying plate. The late Cretaceous–early Tertiary rocks and events appear to have developed in such a setting; the strong deformation of the crust and the volcanism that occurred during the Laramide Orogeny are exactly what would be predicted (Fig. 2.9A).

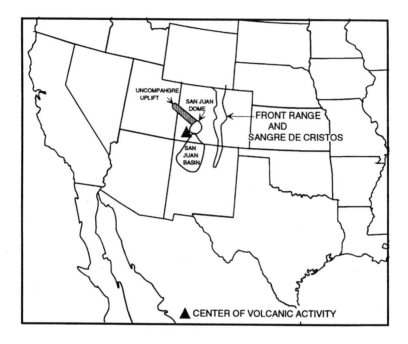

Fig. 2.8 Major features formed by the Laramide Orogeny in the region in and around the San Juan Skyway; note that not all Laramide features are shown (after Tweto 1980 and Kelly 1955).

As plate motion slowed down in the early Tertiary, the subducting plate sank at a steeper and steeper angle into the interior of the earth. Furthermore, the nature of plate motion along the far western edge of North America changed dramatically as a relatively hot zone of spreading was pulled into the subduction zone. This spreading center, the southern remnant of which is now called the East Pacific Rise, halted subduction along a gradually lengthening portion of the west coast (Fig. 2.10). Now the Pacific plate, rather than subducting beneath the North American plate, was sliding horizontally to the northwest along what had become a transform boundary, the San Andreas Fault system.

Of what consequence are these developments to southwest Colorado? As subduction slowed and the subducting plate sank at a steeper and steeper angle into the earth's interior, hot material from the mantle below rose into the space formerly occupied by the descending plate, and an episode of violently explosive volcanism

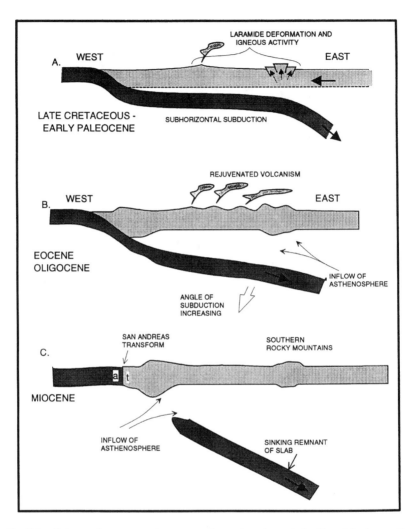

Fig. 2.9 Schematic east-west cross-sections showing subducting slabs beneath the southwestern United States at different times. Arrows show relative direction of motion in all diagrams except C, where the Pacific plate (west of the San Andreas transform) is moving away (a) from the reader in a northerly direction and the North American plate is moving toward (t) the reader (also see Fig. 2.10) (diagrams modified from Dickinson 1977).

ensued in many localities in the Southwest, including the San Juan Mountains (Fig. 2.9B). Furthermore, the cessation of subduction and the gradual sinking and disappearance of the last piece of the

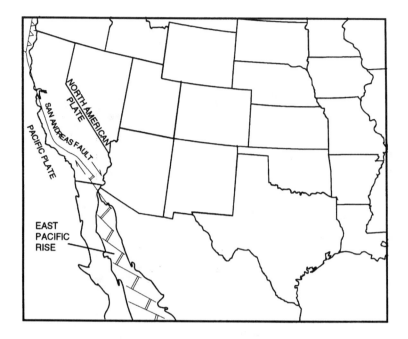

Fig. 2.10   Plate motion along the edge of the southwestern part of the North American continent today. The San Andreas transform connects to the East Pacific Rise, which consists of a series of offset spreading centers connected by short transform faults in the Gulf of California (after Dickinson 1977).

subducting slab sustained the volcanism. Volcanic activity began about 30 million years ago; the present-day San Andreas transform system had its beginnings about 30 million years ago. The two events are apparently not unrelated.

THE LATE CENOZOIC

Many significant events during the past few tens of millions of years have helped shape the San Juan Mountains into their present form, including widespread glaciation (see Chapter 1). Plate tectonics has played a diminishing role in the evolution of the region. We may be tempted to think that violent tectonic activity in the San Juans is a thing of the past, but we should remember that the Rio Grande Rift, an incipient but failed (?) spreading center, lies

EARTHQUAKE DISTRIBUTION 1882–1991

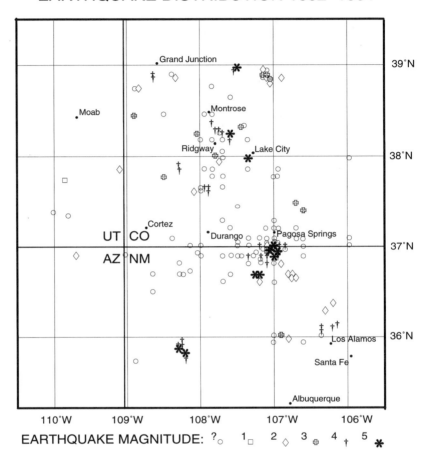

EARTHQUAKE MAGNITUDE: ?○ 1□ 2◇ 3⊞ 4† 5✳

Data from U.S. Geological Survey, National Earthquake Information Center (May 10, 1991)

Fig. 2.11   Map showing the distribution of earthquake epicenters in the Four Corners area. Each symbol represents the location of a recorded earthquake. Data from U.S. Geological Survey, National Earthquake Information Center.

to the east in the San Luis Valley. And although we tend to think this region is exempt from major earthquakes, a glance at an epi-center plot of recent earthquakes (Fig 2.11) reveals that the crust in the Four Corners region continues to adjust to regional stresses. The final chapter is not yet written.

REFERENCES

Collinson, J. W., and W. A. Hasenmuller, 1978. Early Triassic paleogeography and biostratigraphy of the Cordilleran migogeosyncline, in D. G. Howell and K. A. McDougall, eds., *Mesozoic paleogeography of the western United States,* Pacific Section, Society of Economic Paleontologists and Mineralogists, Pacific coast paleogeography symposium 2, pp. 175–187.

Condie, K. C., 1986. Geochemistry and tectonic setting of early Proterozoic supracrustal rocks in the southwestern United States. *Journal of Geology,* v. 94, pp. 845–864.

Dickinson, W. R., 1977. Paleozoic plate tectonics and the evolution of the Cordilleran continental margin, in J. H. Stewart, C. H. Stevens, and A. E. Fritsche, eds., *Paleozoic paleogeography of the western United States,* Pacific Section, Society of Economic Paleontologists and Mineralogists, Pacific coast paleogeography symposium 1, pp. 1–17.

Dickinson, W. R., 1974. Plate tectonics and sedimentation, in W. R. Dickinson, ed., *Tectonics and sedimentation,* Society of Economic Paleontologists and Mineralogists, Special Publication 22, pp. 1–27.

Hoffman, P. F., 1989. Precambrian geology and tectonic history of North America, in A. W. Bally, ed., *The geology of North America: An overview,* Geological Society of America, Decade of North American Geology, v. A, pp. 447–512.

Kay, M., 1951. *North American geosynclines.* Geological Society of America, Memoir 48, 143 pp.

Kelly, V. C., 1955. *Tectonics of the Four Corners region.* Durango, CO: Four Corners Geological Society, Guidebook, first field conference, pp. 108–117.

King, P. B., 1977. *The evolution of North America.* Princeton, NJ: Princeton University Press, 197 pp.

Kluth, C. F., and P. J. Coney, 1981. Plate tectonics of the Ancestral Rocky Mountains, *Geology,* v. 9, pp. 10–15.

MacLachlan, M. E., 1972. Triassic system, in W. W. Mallory, ed., *Geologic atlas of the Rocky Mountain region,* Denver: Rocky Mountain Association of Geologists, pp. 166–176.

McGookey, D. P., et al., 1972. Cretaceous system, in W. W. Mallory, ed., *Geologic atlas of the Rocky Mountain region,* Denver: Rocky Mountain Association of Geologists, pp. 190–228.

Stewart, J. H., and C. A. Suczek, 1977. Cambrian and latest Precambrian paleogeography and tectonics in the western United States, in J. H. Stewart, C. H. Stevens, and A. E. Fritsche, eds., *Paleozoic paleogeography of the western United States,* Pacific Section, Society of Economic Paleontologists and Mineralogists, Pacific coast paleogeography symposium 1, pp. 1–17.

Tweto, O., 1980. Tectonic history of Colorado, in H. C. Kent and K. W. Porter, eds., *Colorado Geology,* Denver: Rocky Mountain Association of Geologists, pp. 5–9.

CHAPTER 3

PRECAMBRIAN ROCKS

JACK A. ELLINGSON

The highest peaks of the San Juan Mountains make for some impressive scenery east of U.S. Highway 550 between the Needles store and Molas Lake. The rocks of these peaks were formed during the Precambrian Era between 1.8 and 1.3 billion years ago. Precambrian rocks are also exposed in the steep walls of the spectacular Uncompahgre Canyon south of Ouray and in a small outcrop just north of Rico. Several episodes of uplift and erosion that occurred since the formation of these rocks, especially the glacial erosion during the Pleistocene, have given us this grand landscape. Mountain goats have nothing on geologists who work in the high San Juan Mountains. The exposures of rock are rugged and steep, access is limited, supplies must be carried, and the field season is short.

THE PRECAMBRIAN

The length of time represented by the Precambrian is about 87 percent of all geologic time from the formation of the earth, about 4.6 billion years ago, to the start of the Paleozoic Era, about 570 million years ago. The Precambrian is divided into two major parts, the older Archean and younger Proterozoic (see geologic time scale on the Stratigraphic Chart, p. 2). The Precambrian rocks of the San Juan Mountains were formed near the middle of the Proterozoic Era.

The terms used in this chapter for the various Proterozoic rock units are the ones used in the current literature. However, not all those who labor in the area agree with this usage. Much geologic work remains to be done before we will understand the Proterozoic rocks of the San Juans.

The Proterozoic rocks in the Animas Valley have been changed from igneous or sedimentary "parent" rocks to metamorphic rocks by heat, pressure, and chemically active fluids. These three agents of metamorphism modify rocks deep in the earth beneath regions of active mountain building.

At least two periods of Proterozoic metamorphism are recorded in the Precambrian rocks of central and southern Colorado (including the San Juan Mountains). During the first, about 1.75 billion years ago, the rocks heated to about 600 degrees Celsius. This episode of metamorphism was part of a mountain-building event called the Boulder Creek Orogeny (Barker 1969, Hutchinson 1976). The second and more mild metamorphic episode occurred about 1.5 billion years ago with rocks heated to about 450 degrees Celsius. This episode was part of a mountain-building event called the Silver Plume Orogeny (Bickford et al. 1969, Hutchinson 1976).

OLDER PROTEROZOIC ROCKS

About 1.8 billion years ago, basaltic lavas were extruded in the Skyway region along the southern margin of what is now the continent of North America (see Chapter 2). The basaltic rocks were intruded by magma that formed light-colored granitic rock and darker rocks of variable composition. About 1.75 billion years ago (Barker 1969) the basalt, the granitic rocks, and the rocks of variable composition were metamorphosed during the Boulder Creek Orogeny. The heat, fluids, and deforming pressures caused all of these rocks to flow in the solid state and recrystallize, forming the gneissic and schistose rocks now exposed in the Animas Valley from Rockwood to Coal Bank Pass and in the Animas Canyon south of Silverton. The basaltic rocks were metamorphosed to a dark schist called the Irving Formation (Barker 1969). During this process the dark iron- and magnesium-rich minerals in the basalts were converted to a black, prismatic mineral called hornblende. Because hornblende is a member of a group of minerals called amphiboles, the dark schist containing hornblende is called amphibolite. The light-colored granitic rock and rocks of variable composition were metamorphosed to form a unit called the Twilight Gneiss (Cross et al. 1905). A gneiss contains small lenses of quartz and feldspar and thin, crenulated layers of dark minerals, often biotite and hornblende. David Gonzales (personal communication 1994) used zircons to establish an age of 1,780 ± 3 million years for the granite, one of the parent rocks of the Twilight Gneiss.

Following the Boulder Creek Orogeny, during the interval 1.72 to 1.667 billion years (Barker 1969), magma intruded the Irving Formation and the Twilight Gneiss, forming the plutons called the Bakers Bridge Granite and the Tenmile Granite (Fig. 3.1). Both granites contain quartz, feldspar, biotite, and minor amounts of other mica and clay minerals. The Tenmile Granite, unlike the Bakers Bridge Granite, is moderately foliated. Many granitic dikes cut the Tenmile Granite, and they are very similar to the small plutons and dikes in Whitehead Gulch just south of Silverton. On the basis of age and composition, Barker (1969) tied these Whitehead Gulch intrusives to the nearby Ten Mile Granite.

YOUNGER PROTEROZOIC ROCKS

The mountains formed by the Boulder Creek Orogeny had eroded to a surface of low relief by about 1.5 billion years ago. The rocks of the Uncompahgre Formation were deposited on this surface as sand, gravel, and clay in a shallow marine environment dominated by waves, tides, and storms (Harris 1990). Water depth varied with time from subtidal to deltaic, forming thick layers of mudstone and sandstone with interlayered pebble conglomerate (Harris 1990).

Rocks of the Uncompahgre Formation experienced low-grade metamorphism during the Silver Plume Orogeny and several more recent episodes of deformation (Tewksbury 1985). In the exposures between Coal Bank and Molas Passes, the Uncompahgre is a bedded sequence, at least 8,000 feet (2,450 m) thick, of white to purple sandy and pebbly quartzite interlayered with massive beds of gray slate, phyllite, and minor schist. The layers stand

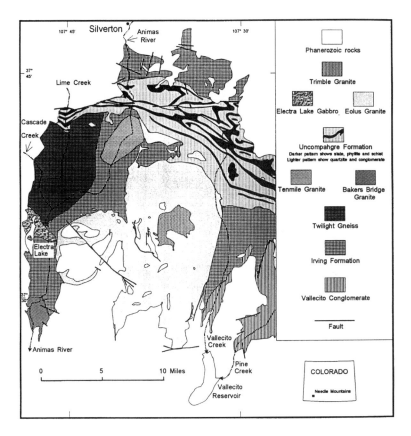

Fig. 3.1 Sketch map of Precambrian rocks of the Needle Mountains, southwestern Colorado (modified from Barker 1969).

on edge, a testimony to their deformation, with the slate layers forming valleys between the more resistant ridges of quartzite.

The Uncompahgre Formation also crops out south of Ouray where the Uncompahgre River and Red Mountain Creek have cut a spectacular canyon into the quartzite. A small exposure of quartzite, probably the Uncompahgre, crops out just north of Rico.

East of the Animas River from the Purgatory area, the Uncompahgre Formation is cut by the Eolus Granite, a batholith that crystallized about 1.435 billion years ago (David Gonzales, personal communication 1994). The Eolus Granite is not deformed, suggesting that the Uncompahgre Formation and the Silver

Plume Orogeny are older than 1.46 billion years old (Silver and Barker 1968, Bickford et al. 1969, Harris 1990, David Gonzales, personal communication 1994). The Electra Lake Gabbro, a small pluton located between U.S. 550 and the Animas River near the Needles store, is also about 1.435 billion years old (David Gonzales, personal communication 1994). The Electra Lake Gabbro intrudes the Irving Formation and the Twilight Gneiss and, like the Eolus Granite, is not deformed.

SUMMARY

Geologic history, like any history, becomes more difficult to decipher as the events being studied get older. The Proterozoic rocks exposed in the western San Juan Mountains constitute an island surrounded by the igneous rocks of the San Juan volcanic field on the north and east and the Paleozoic and Mesozoic sedimentary rocks on the south and west. At least twice during the Proterozoic, rocks of the San Juan Mountains were folded, faulted, metamorphosed, uplifted, and eroded. These rocks suffered some of these indignities again as younger events unfolded in the Paleozoic, Mesozoic, and Cenozoic. We can at best gain an incomplete profile of these rocks; their full histories, no doubt, will never be known.

REFERENCES

Barker, F., 1969. *Precambrian geology of the Needle Mountains, southwestern Colorado*. U.S. Geological Survey, Professional Paper 644-A, 35 pp.

Bickford, M., G. Wetherill, F. Barker, and Lee-Hu Chin-Nan, 1969. Precambrian Rb-Sr chronology in the Needle Mountains, southwestern Colorado. *Journal of Geophysical Research*, v. 74, pp. 1660–1676.

Cross, W., E. Howe, J. D. Irving, and W. H. Emmons, 1905. *Geologic atlas of the United States, Needle Mountain Quadrangle, Colorado*. U.S. Geological Survey, Folio 131, 14 pp.

Harris, C. W., 1990. Polyphase suprastructure deformation in metasedimentary rocks of the Uncompahgre Group: Remnant of an early Proterozoic fold belt in southwest Colorado. *Geological Society of America Bulletin*, v. 102, pp. 664–678.

Hutchinson, R. M., 1976. Precambrian chronology of western and central Colorado and southern Wyoming, in R. C. Epis and R. J. Weimer, eds., *Studies in Colorado Field Geology,* Golden, CO: Colorado School of Mines, no. 8, pp. 73–77.

Silver, L. T., and F. Barker, 1968. Geochronology of Precambrian rocks of the Needle Mountains, southwestern Colorado: Part 1, U-Pb zircon results. *Geological Society of America,* Special Paper 115, pp. 204–205.

Tewksbury, B. J., 1985. Revised interpretation of the age of allochthonous rocks of the Uncompahgre Formation, Needle Mountains, Colorado: *Geological Society of America Bulletin,* v. 96, pp. 224–232.

CHAPTER 4

PALEOZOIC HISTORY

John A. Campbell

Probably the most confusing aspect of studying the geology of any area is trying to fathom the lengths of time involved. Human references to time — days, months, years, even an average life span — are simply too short. As a result, geologists have evolved a system that uses strange-sounding words for intervals of time. These words come from the geographic area where these rocks were first studied. For example, the time span known as Cambrian was first studied in Wales, the Latin name for which was Cambria. The other names on the geologic time scale have similar origins. (Please refer to the Stratigraphic Chart, p. 2, which is modified from MacLachlan 1981.) The era from about 570 to about 245 million years ago is called the Paleozoic. This vast time span is subdivided into shorter units called periods; they are, from oldest to youngest, the Cambrian, Ordovician, Silurian, Devonian, Mississippian, Pennsylvanian, and Permian. Because of erosion or nondeposition, rocks of a particular age may not be present everywhere. Such breaks in the geologic record, called unconformities, are an important part of the geologic history of an area. In southwestern Colorado, including the area traversed by the San Juan Skyway, rocks of Cambrian, Devonian, Mississippian, Pennsylvanian, and Permian age are present (Steven et al. 1974), whereas the Ordovician and Silurian are absent (Fig. 4.1).

Individual layers, or strata, of rock that were deposited in an area during a period of time are given local names by geologists.

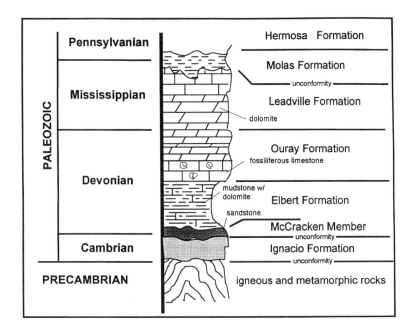

Fig. 4.1   Lower Paleozoic formations: not to scale, thickness approximate. These formations range from about 50 to 180 feet (15–55 m) in thickness, with all combined about 500 feet (150 m) thick (Steven et al. 1974).

These layers are called formations. Thus, the Cambrian-aged rock layer in the San Juan Skyway area is called the Ignacio Quartzite or Ignacio Formation (Fig. 4.1). The name *Ignacio* comes from a small lake located northeast of Electra Lake where there are good outcrops of the Ignacio. The Paleozoic rock layers that were deposited in this area, along with their ages and formation names, are shown in Figure 4.1, as are the unconformities.

By careful study of the rock's composition, physical features (such as the size of the particles or grains that make up a deposit), and any fossils that might occur, geologists can figure out the environments in which the deposit formed. These factors suggest that the upper part of the Ignacio Formation was deposited in shallow marine water very close to shore. By fitting together all the depositional environments of the various layers in the order they formed, the geologist can build the geologic history of an area.

This chapter will outline the Paleozoic geologic history for the portion of Colorado covered by the San Juan Skyway.

EARLY PALEOZOIC HISTORY

Notable differences between early and late Paleozoic geologic history exist in the area of the San Juan Skyway. Thus, it will be useful to discuss these time segments separately. During the early Paleozoic (Cambrian through Mississippian), this area was either exposed to weathering and erosion or was covered by a shallow, warm, widespread ocean. During the late Paleozoic (Pennsylvanian and Permian), a major mountain chain formed just north of the Skyway area, and sediment-laden streams flowed across it into a sea located just west of the area.

At the start of the Paleozoic, about 570 million years ago, the area of the San Juan Skyway was above the sea and was exposed to extensive weathering and erosion. The landscape was barren and almost flat, with low, rounded hills and perhaps a few cliff-scarps in the areas along northwest-southeast-trending faults. Sediment-choked streams flowed off the higher land to the sea. No land plants or animals had yet evolved into existence. The rocks exposed were Precambrian (see Chapter 2). Weathering must have produced a deep soil zone on these rocks, but erosion and the very slowly advancing sea eventually removed most of this material. Erosion was so complete that it removed most of the early Paleozoic deposits and younger Precambrian deposits that might have formed except for some of the stream deposits. This period of early Cambrian weathering and erosion probably lasted more than 50 million years.

The first formation of sedimentary rock, the upper Cambrian Ignacio Quartzite (Fig. 4.1, see Points of Interest 27), consists of sandstones and shales having lenses of very coarse quartzite conglomerate along the boundary with the underlying Precambrian rocks. The sandstones and shales were deposited in a shallow sea that slowly advanced from the west across the long-exposed continent (Lockman-Balk 1972). The evidence for this marine invasion comes partly from scattered primitive brachiopod fossils. As this sea advanced, breaking waves and coastal currents reworked the existing soil, washing away some of the very fine mud and leaving behind the sand and shales. Over time this material was cemented to form sandstone and shale. The scattered fossils in these rocks authenticate the age and depositional environment.

The topography beneath this upper Cambrian sea was low and hilly. As a consequence, the thickness of the Cambrian deposits is greater in areas where valleys once existed and thinner or nonexistent across the tops of ancient hills. Boulders and cobbles may have collected either in talus piles at the foot of the cliffs in the area of faults (Baars and See 1968) or in sediment-clogged stream channels (Campbell 1994). At the time of maximum flooding by the sea, some of the peaks in the San Juan Skyway area stood above water as islands. Toward the end of Cambrian time this sea slowly withdrew, leaving the area again in the grip of weathering and erosion (Foster 1972, Gibbs 1972).

The next Paleozoic rocks that formed in this area are of upper Devonian age (Fig. 4.1). These contain fossils that help determine the rocks' age and the depositional environment in which they formed (Cross and Larsen 1935). The Stratigraphic Chart (p. 2) indicates that the time span between the Cambrian-aged Ignacio Formation and the overlying upper Devonian formations is about 140 million years. What went on during this interval? Weathering and erosion may be the best answer, but it is interesting to note that rocks of upper Cambrian, Ordovician, and Silurian age found elsewhere in the Colorado are not present here. Were they deposited here, then later eroded away? Or were they never deposited? This is a typical puzzle facing geologists when trying to understand unconformities, one for which there may not be a clear solution.

The Upper Devonian formations that are present are the sandstones and shales (plus a little conglomerate) of the Elbert Formation (Fig. 4.1) and the limestone and dolomite of the overlying Ouray Formation. The Elbert Formation formed in about the same way as the Cambrian Ignacio Formation: A slowly advancing sea moved across the area from west to east, reworking older, weathered rocks (Campbell 1970, Baars 1972, Campbell 1994). The resulting rocks are sandstones and shales that formed in shallow, near-shore marine environments. At the base of the Elbert lies a prominent, sometimes conglomeratic sandstone called the McCracken Member of the Elbert Formation (Fig. 4.1, see Points of Interest 23). The McCracken Member probably represents the "beach," or the deposit closest to the shore of this advancing sea. This body of water pushed much farther east than the earlier Cambrian sea and was probably deeper; even the hills were eventually covered. The Elbert rests directly on Precambrian rocks in some places, without any Ignacio in between.

Offshore in this advancing Devonian sea, in quieter and deeper water, calcium and calcium/magnesium carbonate formed a "lime" mud. This material later was compacted and cemented to form limestone and dolomite (Campbell 1970, Baars 1972, Campbell 1994). These carbonate rocks, known as the Ouray Formation (Fig. 4.1), contain many fossils of creatures that lived in this shallow, warm sea.

This watery expanse probably lingered through the end of Devonian time and into the beginning of Mississippian time. Some geologists think the sea might have briefly retreated, then readvanced between the Devonian and Mississippian time, but if this happened, not much evidence of such an event is left. The early Mississippian Leadville Formation (Fig. 4.1) comprises limestone and dolomite very similar to the Ouray, but it contains fossils that are Mississippian in age. These rocks also formed in shallow, warm, clear marine waters (Craig 1972). The best present-day example of such an environment would be near the Bahama Islands.

This Devonian-Mississippian sea finally began to retreat from the San Juan Skyway area in late Mississippian time. The limestone and dolomite of the Leadville Formation were exposed to weathering and erosion. The climate must have been much like that of Florida today, hot and wet. The deep weathering caused the formation of many solution features, such as sinkholes and caves, and a red tropical soil developed on top of the limestone (Craig 1972, Mallory 1972). Evolution of this soil zone, called the Molas Formation (Fig. 4.1), took all of the late Mississippian and perhaps part of the early Pennsylvanian as well. A slowly advancing Pennsylvanian sea reworked the Molas soil, which now contains Pennsylvanian marine fossils in some places (Mallory 1972).

Outcrops of these lower Paleozoic formations can best be seen along the Skyway from about Hermosa northward to Coal

Bank Hill and from Molas Lake northward to the south edge of Silverton along U.S. Highway 550. The best outcrops stand along the south side of Coal Bank Hill.

LATE PALEOZOIC HISTORY

The major geologic event that distinguishes the late Paleozoic from the lower Paleozoic was the formation of a significant mountain chain just north of the San Juan Skyway area. This mountain system consisted of a series of ranges extending diagonally from southwestern Oklahoma across the Texas panhandle into Colorado and northeastern Utah (Mallory 1972). The southern edge of these mountains was only as close as Montrose, Colorado, but that was close enough to influence Skyway geologic history. This chain probably started forming in late Mississippian time and continued developing throughout Pennsylvanian and early Permian time, a span of about 70 to 80 million years. Geologists call this Paleozoic range the Ancestral Rocky Mountains. The range that influenced the Skyway area is called the Uncompahgre Uplift (Mallory 1972). As mountains are lifted up, weathering and erosion go to work, producing a great deal of sediment and depositing it as a thick wedge at the foot of the uplift. The Hermosa Formation (Fig. 4.2) was created as streams deposited great volumes of sediment carried from the Ancestral Rocky Mountains.

Simultaneously, a sea advanced into this area from the west. It did so at various times across the area, modifying the sediment at the foot of the mountains and leaving behind remains of marine animals and some limestone and gypsum deposits, which are interbedded with the stream deposits.

The Hermosa Formation is thus the result of several different depositional environments (Mallory 1972) and has been divided into members (Fig. 4.2). The lower part of the formation, stream-deposited sandstones interbedded with marine sandstones and shales, is called the Pinkerton Trail Member. The middle unit, which consists mostly of gypsum in the Skyway area and contains limestones to the west, is called the Paradox Member. The upper unit, which also contains stream sandstones and marine sandstones, shales, and limestones, is called the Honaker

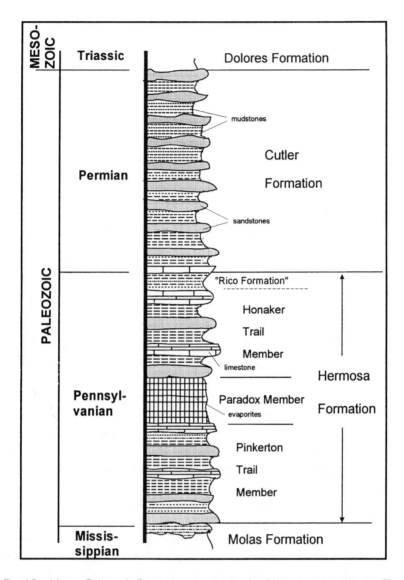

Fig. 4.2   Upper Paleozoic formations: not to scale, thickness approximate. The Hermosa is about 2,500 feet (760 m) thick, the Cutler about 2,000 feet (610 m) thick (Steven et al. 1974).

Trail Member (Fig. 4.2). These members are often difficult to distinguish from each other in the Skyway area except where all three are exposed just north of Durango at the village of Hermosa (see

Points of Interest 19, 43, 126). Some geologists identify a fourth unit, called the Rico Formation (Fig. 4.2), for the upper part of the Hermosa in some parts of the Skyway area. Recognition of these members is important, because the major oil fields of western Colorado and southeastern Utah occur in the limestones of the Paradox Member.

Mountains with sediment accumulation at their base persisted into lower Permian time, but the sea retreated farther west and no longer influenced sedimentation in the Skyway area (Rascoe, Jr., and Baars 1972). The result was the Cutler Formation (Fig. 4.2), which consists of sandstones and shales that were deposited by streams flowing from the north and west (Campbell 1980). These sediments rest on the gray-colored Hermosa Formation and have been oxidized ("rusted") to a bright red color; they are thus easily identified throughout the Skyway area (see Points of Interest 14, 54, 79, 95, 127).

Weathering and erosion continued, slowly wearing down the mountains during late Permian time and partly removing previously deposited sediments. The result was the development of yet another unconformity, this one spanning late Permian time (Rascoe, Jr., and Baars 1972). With this period of weathering and erosion, late Paleozoic geologic history for the San Juan Skyway area comes to a close. At the end of Paleozoic time this area consisted of low, rounded mountains with sluggish streams struggling to carry off the products of weathering and erosion, a setting that continued into Mesozoic time.

Outcrops of the upper Paleozoic formations are present in a number of places around the Skyway. The best places to observe them are along U.S. Highway 550 just north of Durango in the Animas Valley and northward along the Hermosa Cliffs to the Purgatory ski area.

The modern San Juan Skyway area reveals very little evidence of what the land looked like at various times during the Paleozoic. Most of the information comes from the geologic study of other places, principally the Appalachian Mountains in the eastern United States. We do know that from Cambrian to Silurian time there were no land plants or animals, but by Devonian time primitive plants had developed and a forest existed, and by late

Devonian time primitive land-dwelling vertebrates, amphibians, were present. Reptiles soon appeared, and an ancient forest flourished during Pennsylvanian time. Large reptiles evolved during Permian time, and prehistoric forest persisted. We will use our imaginations to place these creatures in the Paleozoic Skyway area, as there are few fossil clues.

REFERENCES

Baars, D. L., 1972. Devonian system, in W. W. Mallory, ed., *Geologic atlas of the Rocky Mountain region,* Denver: Rocky Mountain Association of Geologists, pp. 90–99.

Baars, D. L., and P. S. See, 1968. Pre-Pennsylvanian stratigraphy and paleotectonics of the San Juan Mountains, Southwestern Colorado. *Geological Society of America Bulletin,* v. 79, no. 3, pp. 333–350.

Campbell, J. A., 1994. Revision of the lower Paleozoic stratigraphic nomenclature and depositional systems, San Juan Mountains, Colorado (abstract), in *Abstracts with Programs,* Rocky Mountain Section, Geological Society of America, p. 7.

Campbell, J. A., 1980. Lower Permian depositional systems, and Wolfcampaign paleogeography, Uncompaghre Basin, eastern Utah and southwestern Colorado, in T. D. Fourch and E. R. Magathan, eds., *Paleozoic paleogeography of the west-central United States,* Denver: Rocky Mountain Section, Society of Economic Paleontologists and Mineralogists, pp. 327–340.

Campbell, J. A., 1970. Stratigraphy of the Chaffee Group (Upper Devonian), west central Colorado. *American Association of Petroleum Geologists Bulletin,* v. 54, no. 2, pp. 313–325.

Craig, L. C., 1972. Mississippian system, in W. W. Mallory, ed., *Geologic atlas of the Rocky Mountain region,* Denver: Rocky Mountain Association of Geologists, pp. 100–110.

Cross, W., and E. S. Larsen, 1935. *A brief review of the geology of the San Juan region of southwestern Colorado.* U. S. Geological Survey, Bulletin 843, 138 pp.

Foster, N. H., 1972. Ordovician system, in W. W. Mallory, ed., *Geologic atlas of the Rocky Mountain region,* Denver: Rocky Mountain Association of Geologists, pp. 76–85.

Gibbs, F. K., 1972. Silurian system, in W. W. Mallory, ed., *Geologic atlas of the Rocky Mountain region,* Denver: Rocky Mountain Association of Geologists, pp. 86–89.

Lockman-Balk, C., 1972. Cambrian system, in W. W. Mallory, ed., *Geologic atlas of the Rocky Mountain region,* Denver: Rocky Mountain Association of Geologists, pp. 60–75.

MacLachlan, M. E., 1981. Stratigraphic correlation chart for western Colorado and northwestern New Mexico, in R. C. Epis and J. F. Callender, eds., *Western Slope Colorado,* New Mexico Geological Society Thirty-second Field Conference, pp. 75–79.

Mallory, W. W., 1972. Regional synthesis of the Pennsylvanian system, in W. W. Mallory, ed., *Geologic atlas of the Rocky Mountain region,* Denver: Rocky Mountain Association of Geologists, pp. 111–137.

Rascoe, Jr., B., and D. L. Baars, 1972. Permian system, in W. W. Mallory, ed., *Geologic atlas of the Rocky Mountain region,* Denver: Rocky Mountain Association of Geologists, pp. 143–165.

Steven, T. A., and P. W. Lipman, 1974. *Map of the Durango Quadrangle, southwestern Colorado.* U.S. Geological Survey, Miscellaneous Investigations Series Map I-764.

CHAPTER 5

MESOZOIC AND CENOZOIC HISTORY

JOHN A. CAMPBELL AND DOUGLAS C. BREW

The Mesozoic Era lasted from about 245 million to 66 million years ago. It, like the Paleozoic, is divided into shorter intervals called periods. The periods of the Mesozoic are the Triassic, Jurassic, and Cretaceous (see Stratigraphic Chart, p. 2). These periods are not of equal length: the Cretaceous is the longest, about 78 million years, and the Triassic the shortest, about 37 million years. By looking again at the Stratigraphic Chart, one can see that Mesozoic formations, like those of the Paleozoic, include unconformities, with much of the Triassic and some of parts of the Jurassic missing. These breaks in the geologic record are due to erosion, nondeposition, or a combination of the two.

The geologic history of the San Juan Skyway area during the Mesozoic provides an interesting contrast to that of the Paleozoic. Whereas in the early Paleozoic deposition of sediments took place in shallow, warm seas, during the first part of the Mesozoic this area was subjected to periods of weathering and erosion and deposition by streams, lakes, or wind. In the latter part of the Mesozoic, sediments were deposited in a sea that covered much of central North America, whereas in the later Paleozoic the sediments were deposited by streams at the foot of an ancient mountain chain. We have divided the following discussion into two sections to reflect the two depositional styles evident in the Mesozoic geology of the San Juans region.

EARLY MESOZOIC GEOLOGIC HISTORY

Weathering and erosion of the landscape, particularly of the Ancestral Rocky Mountain chain that formed in late Paleozoic time, continued into the early part of the Mesozoic. No deposits of early Triassic time are known in the Skyway area (MacLachlan 1972). The oldest preserved deposits are those of the late Triassic Dolores Formation (Fig. 5.1, Points of Interest 14). This formation was deposited by streams, lakes, and wind (Blodgett 1984). The resulting sandstones, shales, and siltstones are typically oxidized ("rusted") to a bright red and thus are difficult to distinguish on the outcrop from the underlying Permian Cutler Formation. However, an angular unconformity exists between the Cutler and the Dolores in many places; it can best be seen in the Ouray area (Weimer 1980). This unconformity indicates movement along faults in the northern side of the Skyway area during late Permian or early Triassic time.

Weathering and erosion again dominated following the creation of the Dolores Formation. This interval continued through the early Jurassic, by which time all vestiges of the Ancestral Rocky Mountains were gone. The Skyway area was now low, flat, and probably not very heavily vegetated. A desert was starting to form (Peterson 1972), and the wind blowing across the area deposited sand in large dunes. Cross-bedding in these sandstone beds is highly variable but indicates a wind that blew from the northwest toward the southeast. This desert was very large, covering a vast area of the western United States (Peterson 1972). Later the sand was cemented together in a sandstone called the Entrada Formation (Fig. 5.1). North and perhaps west of the Skyway area there was a sea, the beaches of which may have been the source for the sand in the dunes.

The Wanakah Formation, which overlies the Entrada (Fig. 5.1, see Points of Interest 10, 80, 93, 131), comprises shales, siltstones, and a few sandstones and limestones, all of which were deposited in or near a large, shallow body of water. Some geologists think this body of water was a lake or playa that eventually covered the dunes in the Skyway area. Others think this may have been a shallow sea. No fossils or other clear indicators have been found to

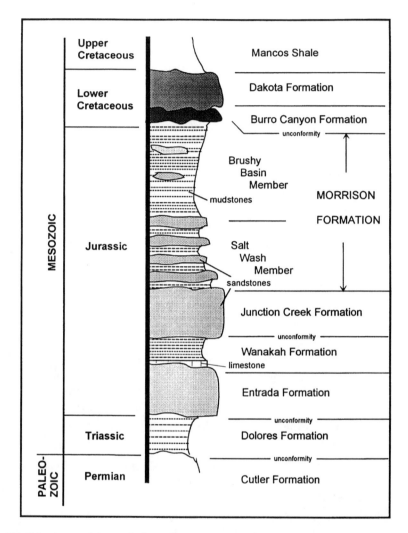

Fig. 5.1 Lower Mesozoic formations: not to scale, thickness approximate. The Dolores is about 600 feet (180 m) thick, the Entrada about 250 feet (76 m), the Wanakah and Junction Creek about 300 feet (90 m), the Morrison about 800 feet (245 m), and the Dakota–Burro Canyon about 300 feet (90 m) thick (Steven et al. 1974).

settle the issue, but the marine notion is the most popular (Peterson 1972). Following the deposition of the Wanakah Formation, the water dried up, and desert conditions returned. Again the wind deposited large sand dunes, which were later cemented to form the Junction Creek Formation (Fig. 5.1). This second Jurassic desert was not as widespread as the earlier, Entrada desert (Peterson 1972).

In late Jurassic time major geologic changes in the western part of the continent began greatly to affect the San Juan Skyway area. A major new mountain system began to form far to the west in what is now Nevada, along with many volcanoes. As soon as mountain systems form, they begin to shed sediment, and erosion accelerates. Sediments from the Jurassic Nevada mountains were carried by streams toward lower elevations to the east of the Skyway area. These stream deposits were later cemented into sandstones and shales that now are called the Morrison Formation (Fig. 5.1, see Points of Interest 11, 102, 134, 135). Many streams flowed eastward off these newly formed western mountains; as a consequence the Morrison Formation is very widespread in the western United States (Peterson 1972). The lower portion of the Morrison is known as the Salt Wash Member, and the upper part is called the Brushy Basin Member (Fig. 5.1). The Brushy Basin sandstones were probably deposited by streams that flowed into a large lake, and the shales formed from mud deposited in the lake. Both members contain some volcanic ash that blew in from the western volcanoes.

The Morrison Formation is of special interest, as it yields more dinosaur fossils than any other geologic layer. Many of the major dinosaur quarries of the West, including Dinosaur National Monument (Peterson 1972), are in the Morrison. Dinosaur remains have been found in the Skyway area, but no large concentrations are known. However, plant remains indicate that the vegetation lining the Morrison streams was transitional in development between the ancient plants of the Paleozoic and the modern plants of the Cenozoic. Evidently the swampy areas around these Morrison streams and the forested areas between streams were an ideal environment for the development of the giant reptiles of the Mesozoic.

Stream deposition continued into early Cretaceous time with the formation of the Burro Canyon Formation (Fig. 5.1). The mountains were still present to the west; thus, the streams still flowed to the east. About this time the lowland area to the east, in present-day eastern Colorado, was flooded by an interior seaway (McGookey et al. 1972). This sea gradually spread westward to cover the Skyway area in late Cretaceous time.

LATE MESOZOIC HISTORY

As noted in the introduction to this chapter, the difference between early Mesozoic and late Mesozoic history is the presence of a seaway. This persistent body of water started invading eastern Colorado in early Cretaceous time but did not reach the San Juan Skyway area until late Cretaceous time (McGookey et al. 1972). Streams flowing from the mountains in the west continued to dominate the area in early Cretaceous time. Sands deposited by the streams solidified to become part of the Dakota Formation (Fig. 5.1, see Points of Interest 11, 102). As the sea advanced from the east it reworked these stream sands, forming near-shore marine deposits. The Dakota is a mixture of these two depositional environments, with more marine deposition east of the Skyway area and more stream deposits to the west. The western volcanoes were still present, and the Dakota contains some volcanic ash beds. The Dakota is also of interest because it contains oil and gas south and west of the Skyway area.

This late Cretaceous sea continued to flood west into what is now Utah. Sediment from the mountains continued to be dumped into the sea, but only the fine-grained sediment was deposited in the deeper water of the Skyway area (McGookey et al. 1972). As a result, thick offshore marine mud accumulated, compacted, and cemented with time into the Mancos Shale (Fig. 5.2, see Points of Interest 1, 84, 140, 144, 149). This shale contains the fossilized remains of a variety of marine animals that attest to the depositional environment and age. Volcanoes still existed to the west, so there are ash beds in the Mancos Shale.

After a time this sea began to retreat to the east. Sediment continued to flow from the mountain uplift to the west such that the sediment-laden streams pushed in after the retreating sea (McGookey et al. 1972), depositing beach and near-shore sands that eventually cemented to form the Point Lookout Sandstone (Fig. 5.2, see Points of Interest 143, 153). The overlying stream

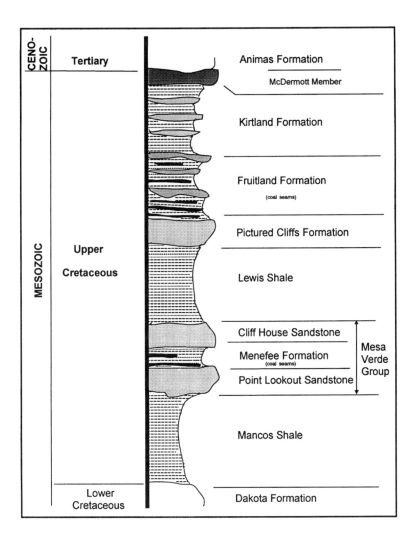

Fig. 5.2   Upper Mesozoic formations: not to scale, thickness approximate. The Mancos is about 2,400 feet (730 m) thick, the Lewis about 2,700 feet (820 m). The Point Lookout, Menefee, Cliff House, and Pictured Cliffs Formations are about 350 feet (107 m) thick apiece. The Fruitland is about 400 feet (120 m) thick, the Kirtland about 1,200 feet (366 m) thick, and the McDermott about 300 feet (90 m) thick (Steven et al. 1974).

deposits, which include sands, muds, and abundant plant material, became sandstones, shales, and coals of the Menefee Formation (Fig. 5.2, see Points of Interest 143, 153). (The coal from
this formation is mined locally to heat homes and to run the famous local train; it once fired the furnace of the smelter that used
to be the hub of Durango's existence.) The sea retreated, and the
streams from the west flowed past the Skyway area, but the marine environment and the shoreline would return with the next
advance of the water.

   The sea did return, moving from east to west, reworking the
stream deposits and depositing more beach and near-shore sands.
These became the Cliff House Sandstone (Fig. 5.2, see Points of
Interest 143). (It should be noted that the Point Lookout Sandstone, Menefee Formation, and Cliff House Sandstone together
constitute what is locally defined as the Mesa Verde Group.) The
sea continued to push west beyond the Skyway area, placing the
region deeper underwater. Mud accumulated in a thick deposit
that became the Lewis Shale (Fig. 5.2, see Points of Interest 2).
Like the Mancos Shale, the Lewis contains marine fossils to support the interpretation of environment and age of deposition (Mc-
Gookey et al. 1972). As before, volcanoes were active to the west,
and ash beds are present in the Lewis Shale.

   A final retreat of the sea took place, with the streams close
behind (McGookey et al. 1972). This time the solidified beach and
near-shore sands became the Pictured Cliffs Sandstone (Fig. 5.2,
see Points of Interest 2). The overlying stream deposits of channel
sands, over-bank shales, and abundant plant debris formed the
sandstones, shales, and coals of the Fruitland Formation (Fig. 5.2,
see Points of Interest 2, 3). These coals, presently mined south of
the Skyway area, fire the Four Corners and San Juan power plants.
They have also been extensively drilled south and southeast of Durango for "coal-bed methane," a new source for natural gas. The
beach and near-shore sandstones that formed with the advance and
retreat of the sea are the chief reservoirs for oil and gas in the San
Juan Basin, which lies south of the Skyway area.

   Stream deposition continued, but now without much accumulation of plant material, and the sea continued to retreat into
eastern Colorado (McGookey et al. 1972). The resulting deposits

are the sandstones, shales, and coals of the Kirtland Formation (Fig. 5.2). With the formation of the Kirtland deposits, the geologic episodes controlled by the western mountains and their eastward-flowing streams came to a close. Another major change in the geologic setting was about to occur.

At the end of the Cretaceous Period, about 66 million years ago, molten rock, or magma, began working toward the surface from deep within the earth (McGookey et al. 1972, Steven et al. 1972). It forced its way into all the sedimentary layers previously formed, up through the Dakota Formation and into the base of the Mancos Shale. These intrusions folded the rock layers into a large, dome-shaped highland complex now called the La Plata Mountains. As always occurs in mountain building, the overlying rocks were stripped off as they started to uplift. The stream and mudflow deposits at the foot of the La Plata Mountains became the sandstones, shales, and conglomerates of the McDermott Formation (Fig. 5.2), which makes up the south-dipping purple cliffs seen west of the Animas River and 2.5 miles south of Durango. Some geologists think volcanic activity might have been associated with the formation of the La Plata Mountains, but that has been difficult to prove. Thus, from the flat plain of the stream-deposited Kirtland Formation, mountains of considerable relief rose. The creation of the La Plata Mountains was just the first of several major geologic changes affecting the San Juan Skyway area.

Following the emergence of the La Plata Mountains and the deposition of the McDermott Formation, new forces caused the regional uplift, folding, and faulting that formed the geologic structure of the present-day Rocky Mountains (see Chapter 2). This mountain building took place all across the western United States, including the Skyway area. Once again, as the mountains were uplifted, sediments were stripped off and deposited around their base (Robinson 1972), this time by streams flowing southward from the Needle Mountain area of the San Juan Mountains. These became the sandstones, shales, and conglomerates of the Animas Formation (Fig. 5.2). These events occurred at the very end of Mesozoic time and continued into Cenozoic time, thus bringing to a close this chapter of San Juan Skyway geologic history.

The widely publicized Cretaceous-Tertiary boundary associated with the extinction of dinosaurs probably occurred during the deposition of the McDermott Formation, but no local outcrop reveals this boundary.

CENOZOIC GEOLOGIC HISTORY

The Cenozoic history of the San Juan Mountain region falls naturally into three different pieces; the volcanic history (the subject of Chapter 6), the glacial history (Chapter 1), and the history revealed by the sediments and sedimentary rocks of Cenozoic age that are found mostly at the foot of the mountains, primarily along the northern edge of the San Juan Basin (south of U.S. 160) and to the south within the basin. It is to these deposits and this history that we now turn.

The composition and characteristics of the rocks and unconsolidated sediments shed from the San Juans offer numerous clues about how the region evolved during the Cenozoic. For example, the composition and size of the particles in gravels or conglomerates provide information about the nature and proximity of source areas. Thick accumulations of sediment suggest elevated source lands and similarly high rates of erosion, and the distributions of the deposits often point to a particular area as a source. Although the specific landscape features — volcanic centers, major drainages, alluvial plains, and such — may have long since vanished, the sedimentary deposits produced by them testify to their former existence.

Cenozoic sedimentary deposits fall into three major groups: 1) the older units, Paleocene through Eocene in age, including the Animas, Nacimiento, and San Jose Formations and Telluride Conglomerate (see Stratigraphic Chart); 2) the older, high-level pediment and terrace gravels of Pliocene(?) and Pleistocene age, including the Bridgetimber Gravel and gravels of the Mesa Mountains; and 3) the younger, lower-level alluvial terrace gravels and other depositional features of Pleistocene and Holocene age associated with the major drainages, and in particular with glacial end moraines in the Animas, La Plata, and Uncompahgre River drainages.

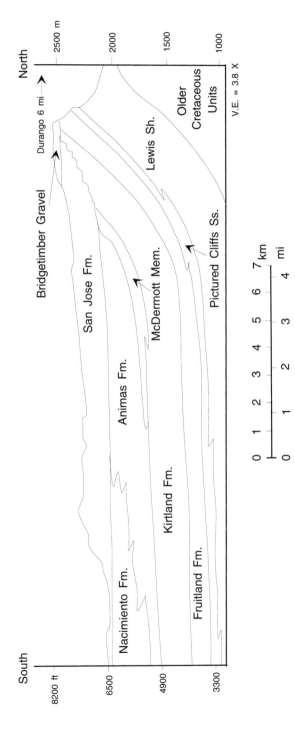

Fig. 5.3 Diagrammatic cross-section showing stratigraphic relationships of late Cretaceous and Tertiary units. View from U.S. 50 south of Durango (modified after Condon, 1990).

OLDER UNITS

The oldest of the Cenozoic bedrock units, the Animas Formation (or upper Animas) of Paleocene age (Fig. 5.3), consists of stream deposits. Coarser conglomerates and sandstones of the Animas were deposited on alluvial fans originating in the Needle Mountains, and finer shales and sandstones were deposited south of the fans in low-gradient, meandering streams with extensive floodplains (Sikkink 1987). Still farther south the Animas Formation grades laterally into the Nacimiento Formation, a complex of stream and lake sandstones, shales, and mudstones. A mixture of sandstones, sandy shales, and tuff beds called the San Jose Formation (Fig. 5.3) conformably overlies the Animas and Nacimiento Formations but locally steps to the north beyond them. The San Jose, of Eocene age, is also interpreted to be of stream and lake origin. The general stratigraphic relationships among these bedrock units of Cenozoic age (Condon 1990) and their relationships to underlying and overlying units are shown in Figure 5.3.

At this point there is a significant gap in the record, expressed by the unconformity between the San Jose Formation and the overlying, high-level pediment and terrace gravels, the oldest of which are apparently late Pliocene in age. The Oligocene, Miocene, and most of the Pliocene epochs are unrepresented by the sediments on the southern flank of the San Juan Mountains.

To the north, the Telluride Conglomerate of late Eocene and early Oligocene age rests upon a widespread late Eocene erosion surface (unconformity) and is exposed in outcrops in the vicinity of Silverton, Ouray, and Telluride (see Points of Interest 43, 68, 85, 106, 113). Near Telluride the formation attains thicknesses in excess of 1,000 feet (305 m) (Cross and Larsen 1935). Initially, these coarse sediments may have been associated with pediments but were later associated with alluvial fans developed in response to mountain uplifts in the north and central San Juans. The upper layers of the Telluride Conglomerate contain volcanic clasts that mark the onset of andesitic volcanism in the San Juan Mountains (see Chapter 6).

OLDER HIGH-LEVEL PEDIMENT AND TERRACE GRAVELS

Older, high-level gravel deposits of restricted distribution unconformably overlie the Cenozoic units described above. The oldest of these and the only formally named unit, the Bridgetimber Gravel, is known from a single locality, Bridgetimber Mountain, located on the divide between the La Plata and Animas River drainages. The composition of the clasts in these gravels suggests a source area in the La Plata Mountains and deposition by an ancestral La Plata River, but the exact age and depositional environment of the gravels are uncertain. Originally considered remnants of a formerly more extensive peneplain, or pediment, the gravels were later interpreted to be as old as late Pliocene in age. Others, however, have interpreted the gravels to be glacial outwash deposits of early Pleistocene age.

Gravels of the Mesa Mountains (Gillam, Moore, and Scott 1984) located east of the confluence of the Animas and Florida Rivers resemble the Bridgetimber Gravels in terms of their elevation above the adjacent drainages, but they clearly were deposited by an ancestral Animas River. Although most workers interpret them as early Pleistocene deposits, they could be as old as late Pliocene and thus equivalent in age to the Bridgetimber Gravels.

YOUNGER TERRACES, GRAVELS, AND ASSOCIATED FEATURES

The youngest Cenozoic sediments and geomorphic features in the region consist chiefly of an array of terraces and associated gravels along the Animas River, Uncompahgre River, and other major drainages. In addition, there are some local, relatively small alluvial fans, deposits of windblown silt or loess, and lenses of volcanic ash, the product of a violent eruption of the Yellowstone Caldera in northwestern Wyoming some 600,000-plus years ago (Gillam, Moore, and Scott 1984).

The terraces and associated gravels form a nested array of "steps" flanking the major rivers, and those associated with the Animas River can be traced southward to the junction with the San Juan River near Farmington, New Mexico, and beyond. This sequence of terraces records, in the words of Gillam, Moore, and Scott (1984), "climatic perturbations . . . superimposed on a long-term trend of valley incision in response to late Tertiary or Quaternary uplift." The older terraces, higher in elevation and with greater degrees of weathering and dissection and thicker loess blankets, are graded to specific glacial end moraines and clearly represent outwash terraces formed by glacial meltwaters. They are primarily climatic in origin, whereas the youngest of the terraces, not coupled to any glacial features, have formed by continued riverine downcutting in response to regional uplift. These processes continue to the present day.

REFERENCES

Blodgett, R. H., 1984. Nonmarine depositional environments and paleosol development in the upper Triassic Dolores Formation, southwestern Colorado, in D. C. Brew, ed., *1984 Field Trip Guidebook,* 37th Annual Meeting, Rocky Mountain Section, Geological Society of America, pp. 46–61.

Condon, S. M., 1990. *Geologic and structure contour map of the Southern Ute Indian Reservation and adjacent areas, southwest Colorado and northwest New Mexico.* U.S. Geological Survey, Miscellaneous Investigations Series, Map I-1958.

Cross, W., and E. S. Larsen, 1935. *A brief review of the geology of the San Juan region of southwestern Colorado.* U. S. Geological Survey, Bulletin 843, 138 pp.

Gillam, M. L., D. Moore, and G. R. Scott, 1984. Quaternary deposits and soils in the Durango area, southwestern Colorado, in D. C. Brew, ed., *1984 Field Trip Guidebook,* 37th Annual Meeting, Rocky Mountain Section, Geological Society of America, pp. 149–182.

MacLachlan, M. E., 1972. Triassic system, in W. W. Mallory, ed., *Geologic atlas of the Rocky Mountain region,* Denver: Rocky Mountain Association of Geologists, pp. 166–176.

McGookey, D. P., et al., 1972. Cretaceous system, in W. W. Mallory, ed., *Geologic atlas of the Rocky Mountain region,* Denver: Rocky Mountain Association of Geologists, pp. 190–228.

Peterson, J. A., 1972. Jurassic system, in W. W. Mallory, ed., *Geologic atlas of the Rocky Mountain region,* Denver: Rocky Mountain Association of Geologists, pp. 177–189.

Robinson, P., 1972. Tertiary history, in W. W. Mallory, ed., *Geologic atlas of the Rocky Mountain Region,* Denver: Rocky Mountain Association of Geologists, pp. 233–242.
Sikkink, P.G.L., 1987. Lithofacies relationships and depositional environments of the Tertiary Ajo Alamo Sandstone and related strata, San Juan Basin, New Mexico and Colorado, in J. F. Fassett and J. K. Rigby, Jr., eds., *The Cretaceous-Tertiary boundary in the San Juan and Raton Basin, New Mexico and Colorado,* Geological Society of America, Special Paper 209, pp. 81–104.
Steven, T. A., H. W. Smedes, H. J. Prastka, P. W. Lipman, and R. L. Christiansen, 1972. Upper Cretaceous and Cenozoic Igneous rocks, in W. W. Mallory, ed., *Geologic Atlas of the Rocky Mountain region,* Denver: Rocky Mountain Association of Geologists, pp. 229–232.
Weimer, R. J., 1980. Recurrent movement on basement faults: A tectonic style for Colorado and adjacent areas, in H. C. Kent and K. W. Porter, eds., *Colorado Geology,* Denver: Rocky Mountain Association of Geologists, pp. 23–35.

CHAPTER 6

VOLCANIC ROCKS

JACK A. ELLINGSON

The San Juan volcanic field is part of a much larger volcanic region that was active throughout the Southern Rocky Mountains from about 40 million to 18 million years ago (Fig. 6.1). Most eruptive centers lie within the region bounded by the Rocky Mountains on the east, the Colorado lineament on the north, and the Uncompahgre–San Luis Uplift on the south. The volcanic activity within this triangular area produced lavas and pyroclastic debris that covered all of south-central Colorado and the north-central part of New Mexico.

The eruptions that formed this middle Tertiary volcanic field began with the formation of stratovolcanoes made of alternating layers of lava and ash of andesitic composition. Geophysical evidence suggests that at this time one or more batholiths intruded to shallow levels in the crust. Early in the history of this intrusive activity, lava and ash were generated at deeper levels from magmas of the intrusion. The rocks formed from these first eruptions blanketed a late Eocene erosion surface of low relief (Epis and Chapin 1975). As eruptions continued, the volcanic aprons enlarged, forming a continuous cover of volcanic rocks. Because of extensive erosion, the exact size of this volcanic cover cannot be determined. However, the lavas and ash of these early eruptions still account for about two-thirds of the volcanic rocks in the San Juan Mountains (Steven 1975).

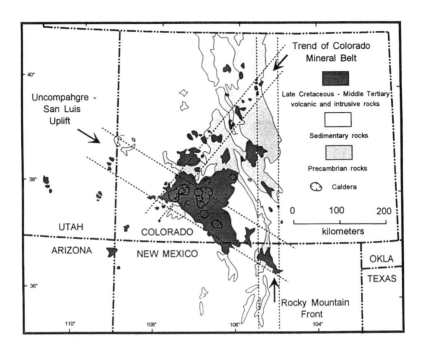

Fig. 6.1   Distribution of volcanic rocks in the Southern Rocky Mountains.

As the magma chamber enlarged and continued its relentless push toward the surface, the volcanic eruptions in the San Juans area became more violent. The near-surface magma supported the overlying roof and volcano. Once the magma breached the surface, the roof rapidly collapsed, forming a cylindrical pit, or caldera, 5 to 15 kilometers in diameter. The vented magma produced ash-flow sheets; fifteen have been identified in the San Juans, according to Steven and Lipman (1976). Each eruption was many times more powerful than the May 18, 1980, eruption of Mount St. Helens, and each caldera produced characteristic ash flows. Fifteen calderas have been identified, and two others are postulated by U.S. Geological Survey geologists.

Figure 6.2 shows the San Juan volcanic field, the largest remaining portion of the original volcanic field in the Southern Rocky Mountains. In this chapter I will discuss only the volcanic rocks of the western San Juan Mountains.

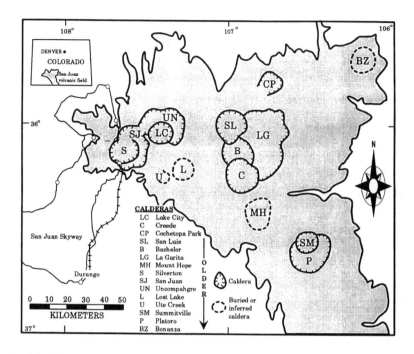

Fig. 6.2 Sketch map of the western San Juan Caldera complex after subsidence. Darker lines indicate better control (modified from Steven and Lipman 1976).

GENERAL GEOLOGY

The volcanic rocks of the western San Juan Mountains rest on deformed and eroded igneous, sedimentary, and metamorphic rocks ranging in age from lower Tertiary to Precambrian. Erosion by running water and glacial ice have greatly reduced the volcanic blanket covering the older rocks.

The prevolcanic rocks of the Needle Mountains south of Silverton include Precambrian gneiss, schist, quartzite, and slate overlain on the south and west by Paleozoic and Mesozoic sandstone, shale, and limestone. Precambrian quartzite is exposed in Uncompahgre Canyon south of Ouray and is overlain to the west and north by Paleozoic and Mesozoic sedimentary rocks. Late Cretaceous and early Tertiary intrusions resemble in composition the mid-Tertiary volcanic rocks of the San Juans. These intrusive rocks are resistant to erosion and form the rimrocks in several locations, especially in the Ophir, Lizard Head, Wilson Peak, and La Plata Mountain areas. Graysill Mountain and Engineer Mountain north of the Purgatory ski area are also capped with the erosional remnants of these older, small plutons.

One or more of these late Cretaceous or early Tertiary intrusive bodies broke the surface and became volcanic. The evidence for this can be seen in the layers of purple conglomerate, sandstone, and shale called the McDermott Member of the Animas Formation, located west of the Animas River about 3 miles south of downtown Durango. In the conglomerates, clasts of all sizes are randomly mixed, indicating rapid deposition, possibly as mudflows. Boulders, cobbles, and pebbles are 99.9 percent fine-grained, porphyritic andesite. The volcanic source for the McDermott is unknown, but intrusive rocks of similar age and composition are found in the La Plata Mountains.

VOLCANIC ROCKS OF THE STRATOVOLCANOES

The oldest mid-Tertiary rocks of the western San Juan Mountains were erupted from stratovolcanoes between 35 and 30 million years ago (Lipman et al. 1973). The volcanoes were subsequently destroyed by erosion and buried by layers of volcanic ash during the eruptions of the calderas. The rocks from these stratovolcanoes formed the San Juan Formation and comprise lava flows, flow breccias, mudflows, and conglomerate of intermediate composition, mostly of andesite.

The remnants of these stratovolcanoes in the western San Juans are recognized near Larson Creek, at the head of the Cimarron River, at Matterhorn Peak, and near Camp Carson (Lipman et al. 1973). In general, lava flows and layers of flow breccias thin as they move away from a volcanic vent. This thinning is visible in the San Juan Formation in the vicinity of the San Juan and Uncompahgre Calderas (Fig. 6.3). Thus, it is postulated that one or more stratovolcanoes existed in the area of the calderas and were destroyed by caldera eruptions (Lipman et al. 1973).

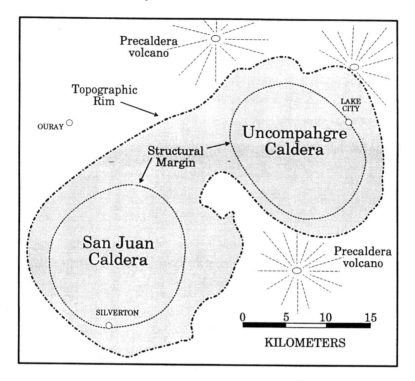

Fig. 6.3   Sketch map of the San Juan and Uncompahgre Calderas (modified from Steven and Lipman 1976).

FORMATION OF CALDERAS

A batholith, suspected of being the source of the volcanic activity for the stratovolcanoes, is postulated to have lain beneath the calderas of the central and western San Juan Mountains (Fig. 6.2). This assumption is based on a negative gravity anomaly, which suggests the presence of rock of lower density. Closely spaced gravity contours indicate that the intrusion occurred relatively close to the surface. Steven and Lipman (1976) suggest that the change in eruption style in the region about 29 million years ago was caused by the intrusion's nearing the surface, then producing violent eruptions. Lower confining pressures on the magma caused gas to separate, then violently erupt. The volcanic structures collapsed into the evacuated portions of the magma chamber and formed the calderas, as seen in the western San Juan Mountains, for example, in the Uncompahgre, San Juan, Silverton, and Lake City Calderas.

UNCOMPAHGRE AND
SAN JUAN CALDERAS

Three of the four calderas considered here formed within a period of about 1 million years, between 28 and 27 million years ago. The caldera-forming eruptions appear to have begun with the formation of the Dillon Mesa Tuff (Table 6.1). There are other ash deposits in the area from calderas in the eastern and southern San Juans, but the Dillon Mesa Tuff appears to be radially distributed around and to thicken toward the Uncompahgre Caldera (Lipman et al. 1973) and so must be tied to it.

Following the deposition of the Dillon Mesa Tuff, the San Juan and Uncompahgre Calderas collapsed simultaneously with the deposition of the Sapinaro Mesa Tuff. This massive eruption spread a "blanket" deposit of rhyolitic ash generally less than 330 feet (100 m) thick over a wide area to the north and east (Table 6.1). Continued eruptive activity within the caldera produced a rock unit known as the Eureka Member of the Sapinaro Mesa Tuff. This tuffaceous stratum of rhyolitic ash contains many rock fragments of granite and quartzite derived from the basement rocks beneath the caldera, as well as masses of landslide and avalanche debris from the collapse of the caldera walls. The Eureka Member is up to 2,300 feet (700 m) thick in some places (Lipman et al. 1973). The failure of the steep caldera walls caused the San Juan and Uncompahgre Calderas to expand and form a single topographic rim encompassing both craters (Fig. 6.3).

Smaller and milder eruptions continued in the calderas following the major caldera-forming events. Domes and thick flows of silicic and intermediate composition interfinger with reworked volcaniclastic sediments. These deposits are especially well exposed within the San Juan Caldera and are called the Burns Formation.

As these intracaldera eruptions continued, the lavas changed to dark-colored andesite. This material was more fluid and covered the floor of the calderas more evenly. Gradually the extrusive activity stopped, and volcaniclastic sedimentation covered the caldera floors. These rocks of andesite and volcaniclastic sediment are called the Henson Formation (Steven and Lipman 1976).

One of the interesting things about caldera formation is the bulging or doming of the central block following the initial collapse,

Table 6.1 Volcanic rocks of the western San Juan Mountains. Data from Lipman et al. 1973; Steven and Lipman 1976.

Volcanic Rocks of the Western San Juan Mountains*

Rock Unit	AGE (M.Y.)	Est. Volume Cubic Mi	Thickness Feet	Composition	Source for Unit
Hinsdale Formation	18.0	Plugs & Flows	?	Porphyritic rhyolite Porphyritic andesite Alkalic olivine basalt	Lake City Caldera
Sunshine Peak Tuff	22.5	125–200	3300	Silicic rhyolite	Lake City Caldera
—EROSION— Crystal Lake Tuff	26.7 - 27.8	15–60	160 - 660	Rhyolite	Silverton Caldera
Henson Formation	?	?	?	Andesite and associated sediments	San Juan Caldera
Burns Formation	?	?	?	Porphyritic rhyodacite quartz latite and sediments	San Juan Caldera
Eureka Mem.	27.8 - 28.4	?	2300	Rhyolite	Uncompahgre and San Juan Calderas
Sapinero Mesa Tuff	27.8 - 28.4	>625	160 - 330	Rhyolite	
Dillon Mesa Tuff	27.8 - 28.4	15–60	20 - 200	Rhyolite	Uncompahgre(?) Caldera
—EROSION— San Juan Formation	34.7- 31.1	>15,500	?	Andesite, rhyodacite, and mafic quartz latite	Numerous stratovolcanoes
UPLIFT & EROSION McDermott Member	65- 80(?)	?	0 - 330	Mudflows of andesitic boulders, gravel, sand, and silt	La Plata Mountains(?)

SAPINERO

*Data from: Lipman, Steven, Luedke and Burbank, 1973; Steven and Lipman, 1976

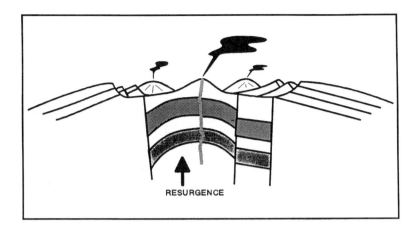

Fig. 6.4   Cross-section of a resurgent caldera. Note the doming of the caldera block.

a process known as resurgence. Pressure drops in the evacuated magma chamber during the eruption, causing magma to rise. As it does so, the magma competes for space with the downdropped block in the center of the caldera (Smith and Bailey 1968). This renewed movement of magma toward the surface deforms the caldera block, uplifts it, usually in the form of a dome, and breaks it radially, concentrically, or both, with differential movement of the major segments (Fig. 6.4).

These features are nicely exposed in the Creede Caldera in the central San Juan Mountains. This caldera block, called Snowshoe Mountain, is nearly 10 miles (16 km) in diameter and rises about 3,300 feet (1,000 m) above the moat at the edge of the caldera. The layers of volcanic ash in this dome have outward dips of 25 to 40 degrees. The dome is broken by faults displacing rocks downward as much as 4,000 feet (1,200 m) (Smith and Bailey 1968).

SILVERTON CALDERA

Rocks from ring-fracture volcanism, sedimentation, and landslide debris nearly filled the Uncompahgre and San Juan Calderas, creating the Eureka Member and Burns and Henson Formations (Table 6.1). The resurgent doming in both calderas

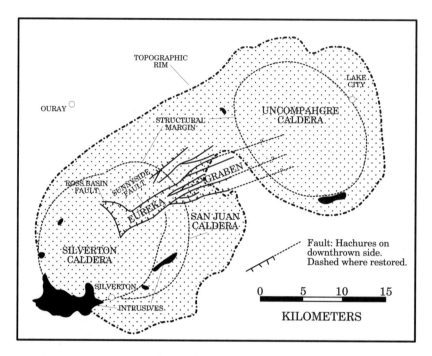

Fig. 6.5   Sketch map of the Silverton Caldera, Eureka Graben, and associated volcanic complex (modified from Steven and Lipman 1976).

started shortly after collapse and continued during the accumulation of the intracaldera formations, as shown by the fact that the older, Eureka rocks have steeper dips than the Henson rocks. The resurgence fractured the San Juan and Uncompahgre Domes in a northeast-southwest direction, forming a fault system called the Eureka Graben (Fig. 6.5). In the center of the San Juan Caldera, the trend of these faults abruptly changes to northwest-southeast, possibly in response to breaking along a deeply buried Precambrian zone of weakness.

During the resurgence of the San Juan Caldera, an eruption formed the Crystal Lake Tuff and evacuated the region under the southern part of the caldera. Collapse of this area produced the Silverton Caldera (Fig. 6.5 and 6.6). The ring fractures on the western and southern parts of the San Juan Caldera appear to have been reactivated during the collapse of the Silverton Caldera. Faulting and folding at the Eureka Graben accommodated the

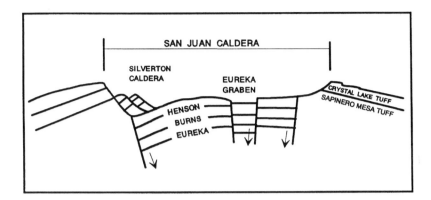

Fig. 6.6   Cross-section of the Silverton Caldera.

caldera formation on the north. Maximum displacement on the south is more than 3,800 feet (600 m) (Steven and Lipman 1976).

The Crystal Lake Tuff is relatively small in volume compared to the Sapinaro Mesa Tuff of the San Juan–Uncompahgre Caldera complex. Steven and Lipman (1976) say there is no evidence of resurgent doming of the Silverton Caldera.

LAKE CITY CALDERA

A period of about 4 million years of limited volcanic activity in the western San Juan Mountains followed the formation of the Silverton Caldera. About 22.5 million years ago, eruptions began again in the central and southwestern parts of the Uncompahgre Caldera, producing the Sunshine Peak Tuff (Table 6.1). Simultaneously, an elliptical block 7.5 to 9 miles (12–15 km) in diameter collapsed, forming the Lake City Caldera (Fig. 6.7) (Lipman et al. 1973). Again, landslide debris mixed with the erupting ash. The Sunshine Peak Tuff is about 3,300 feet (1,000 m) thick within the Lake City Caldera. Around the margin of the caldera floor, lava flows and domes of viscous lava cover some of the Sunshine Peak Tuff.

Unlike the Silverton Caldera, the Lake City Caldera underwent resurgence, which caused the central dome to dip 20 to 25 degrees (Lipman et al. 1973). Faults paralleling the northeastward extension of the Eureka Graben cross the caldera floor, with displacements of 33 to 50 feet (10–15 meters). Steven and Lipman

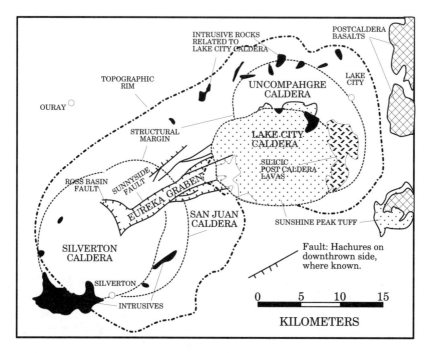

Fig. 6.7 Sketch map of the Lake City Caldera and associated volcanic complex (modified from Steven and Lipman 1976).

(1976) state that the resurgence resulted from upward movement of magma, now exposed as granitic bodies in the bottoms of several valleys cutting into the caldera floor.

HINSDALE FORMATION

The Lake City Caldera was the last of the fifteen or so calderas to form in the San Juan volcanic field. However, volcanism did not stop with deposition of the Sunshine Peak Tuff and associated rocks. To the east, starting about 26 million years ago, the Rio Grande Rift began to develop (Noblett and Loeffler 1987). Associated with the rifting was basaltic volcanism of the Hinsdale Formation (Table 6.1). Erosional remnants of these basalts rest on the Sunshine Peak Tuff just 6 to 9 miles (10–15 km) east of the Lake City Caldera. This change from silicic ash to mafic lava may represent the major change from volcanism of the San Juan volcanic field of the mid-Tertiary to volcanism of the Rio Grande Rift of the late Tertiary and Quaternary.

SUMMARY

Of fifteen calderas recognized in the San Juan Mountains, only the Lake City Caldera retains topographically recognizable segments of the original caldera wall (Steven and Lipman 1976). Stream and glacial erosion have destroyed the bowl-shaped topographic expression of the calderas. However, the disruption of the older drainage patterns by the many ash-flow sheets and the influence of caldera rims can still be seen in the current drainage patterns, especially near the Lake City and Silverton Calderas.

Mineral Creek on the west and the Animas River on the east and south flow in valleys that outline the Silverton Caldera just inside its structural rim. Henson Creek and the upper part of the Lake Fork of the Gunnison River flow in valleys that nearly encircle the Lake City Caldera, suggesting that the topography of the caldera controlled the original drainage across the post-eruption landscape.

REFERENCES

Epis, R. C., and C. E. Chapin, 1975. Geomorphic and tectonic implications of the post-Laramide, late Eocene erosion surface in the Southern Rocky Mountains, in B. F. Curtis, ed., *Cenozoic history of the Southern Rocky Mountains,* Geological Society of America, Memoir 144, pp. 45–74.

Lipman, P. W., T. Steven, R. Luedke, and W. Burbank, 1973. Revised volcanic history of the San Juan, Uncompahgre, Silverton, and Lake City calderas in the western San Juan Mountains, Colorado. U.S. Geological Survey, *Journal of Research,* v. 1, no. 6, pp. 627–642.

Noblett, J. B., and B. M. Loeffler, 1987. The geology of the Summer Coon volcano near Del Norte, Colorado, in S. S. Bues, ed., *Geological Society of America Centennial Field Guide,* Rocky Mountain Section, Geological Society of America, pp. 349–352.

Smith, R. L., and R. A. Bailey, 1968. Resurgent cauldrons, in R. Coats, L. Hay, and C. A. Anderson, eds., *Studies in volcanology,* Geological Society of America, Memoir 116, pp. 613–662.

Steven, T. A., 1975. Middle Tertiary volcanic field in the southern Rocky Mountains, in B. F. Curtis, ed., *Cenozoic history of the southern Rocky Mountains,* Geological Society of America, Memoir 114, pp. 75–94.

Steven, T. A., and P. W. Lipman, 1976. *Calderas of the San Juan volcanic field, southwestern Colorado.* U.S. Geological Survey, Professional Paper 958, pp. 1–4 and 10–16.

CHAPTER 7

ORE DEPOSITS AND MINERALS

Scott Fetchenhier

Gold! Silver! The fabulous riches of the San Juans were discovered in the last quarter of the nineteenth century, and hordes of prospectors poured into the area. Every miner had romantic visions of wealth and dreamed of enjoying the success of Leadville's Horace Tabor or Silverton's Stoiber brothers (of Silver Lake Mine fame). El Dorado lay over the next ridge, just waiting to be found. Mining towns and civilization sprang up with each new discovery. Some disappeared almost as quickly, products of the boom-and-bust economics of the mining and metal industries. Gold and silver were the driving forces that caused men to throw caution to the wind and to migrate westward from their homes and families in the East.

Some of the greatest mines in Colorado, such as the Sunnyside, Camp Bird, and Idarado, have produced millions of tons of ores containing gold, silver, lead, zinc, and copper over the last 100 to 120 years. But the settling of southwestern Colorado and the great mining discoveries of the past would not have occurred had it not been for geologic events that happened millions of years ago (see Chapter 6).

GEOLOGY

STRUCTURAL CONTROLS

The Silverton and Lake City Calderas, along with a downdropped block of ground between them called the Eureka Graben, were the

"Hey, I got news for you, sweetheart! ...
I *am* the lowest form of life on earth!"

most important structural features for localization of later ore bodies in this area (see Chapter 6, Fig. 6.7).

Doming and collapse of the Silverton Caldera was accompanied by radial and concentric faulting. These faults, when open, acted as a plumbing system for later upward migration of hot, acidic, mineral-laden waters. These hydrothermal solutions, charged with metals such as gold, silver, lead, zinc, and copper, leached from the surrounding rocks and percolated upward over long periods of time. As these ore fluids encountered lower temperatures and pressures near the surface, they precipitated minerals along the sides of the faults as veins and altered and leached the surrounding host rock. These veins were often shattered by recurrent fault movement and then cemented by subsequent episodes of ore deposition.

The most productive ore deposits in the San Juans were open, space-filled vein deposits. Vein ores were most often confined within fault walls or within a zone of multiple fractures within a faulted area. Veins are tabular, greater in length (strike) and depth below ground than in thickness. They often pinch and swell both vertically and horizontally and change direction depending on the brittleness and composition of the surrounding host rocks.

LITHOLOGIC CONTROLS

The San Juan Tuff, Eureka Rhyolite, Burns Latite, Telluride Conglomerate, and varied limestone and sandstone layers in the older sedimentary series were the most favorable host rocks for vein ore bodies. Smaller amounts of production came from replacement ore bodies in sedimentary rocks. Hydrothermal solutions, migrating upward along veins, would, upon encountering a favorable host rock such as limestone, eat away and replace the original rock with ore minerals. Many of the deposits in Rico, Ouray, and the lower levels of the Camp Bird and Idarado Mines were of this type and are called *replacement bodies.* Intrusions of molten laccoliths, stocks, dikes, and sills also exerted local control on ore deposition, especially in the La Plata Mountains, Rico, Ouray, the Red Mountain breccia pipes, western Ophir, and the Yankee Boy Basin southwest of Ouray.

MINERALOGY

The San Juan ore deposits contain a wide variety of minerals and
native elements. Gold and silver occur in their native forms and in
complex combinations of tellurides. Silver also occurs in tetrahe-
drite/tennantite, pyrargyrite, proustite, argentite, and argentiferous (silver-bearing) galena. Base metals are found in galena (lead),
sphalerite (zinc), chalcopyrite (copper), pyrite (iron), and hubnerite (tungsten), as are subsidiary amounts of less economic minerals.
White, milky "bull" quartz is the most common gangue, or waste
mineral, accompanied by rhodonite, rhodocrosite, calcite, barite,
and fluorite. Ransome identified more than seventy-seven mineral
species in his study of the San Juan mining districts in 1901.

SILVERTON AREA

Silverton is synonymous with the famous Sunnyside Mine, one of
Colorado's largest gold mines, which contained more than 60
miles of underground workings. The original Sunnyside vein was
discovered by R. J. McNutt and George Howard in August 1873
on the northern shores of Lake Emma. The Sunnyside Mine lies
within the downdropped block, or graben, between the Silverton
and Lake City Calderas. The numerous veins within the mine are
large and continuous. Some, such as the Washington, are more
than 100 feet (30 m) wide in places. The mine primarily has produced lead, zinc, and copper, along with gold and silver. The veins
consist of a complex intermixing of galena, sphalerite, pyrite, chalcopyrite, tetrahedrite, quartz, and rhodonite deposited over different intervals of time. Mineralization took place approximately 17
million years ago (Casadevall 1976) at the Sunnyside, well known
for its native gold and rhodochrosite specimens.

The Sunnyside produced more than 800 tons of ore a day
in the 1990s, when it was last active. The ore was trucked 7 miles
from the portal of the 2-mile-long American Tunnel in Gladstone
to the Mayflower Mill, about a mile and a half northeast of Silverton. The large tailings piles below the mill are the final waste
products of ore milling. The Gold King Mine on the western border of the Sunnyside Mine and Eureka Graben was one of the
area's biggest producers in the early 1900s. Some of the Sunnyside's

last production came from veins that were followed onto Gold King property.

Silverton sits on the southern edge of the Silverton Caldera, a block of ground that subsided over 2,000 feet (610 m) along its southern edge (Steven and Lipman 1976). The present river valleys generally follow the concentric fractures, or ring faults, that border the caldera and run northeast along the upper Animas River and west along Mineral Creek. These faults continue up and over Red Mountain Pass and into Ironton Park. Many of Silverton's primary mines, such as the Shenandoah Dives and the Pride of the West, are located on faults that radiated out and to the south from this caldera.

A small stock of quartz monzonite was intruded along the ring-fault zone and lies beneath and south of the town of Silverton. The sediments bordering the stock to the southwest show evidence of contact metamorphism and mineral deposition related to the intrusion. The mines of Sultan Mountain lie southwest of town on two veins, the Little Dora and the Hercules/North Star, both of which parallel Mineral Creek. Two other veins, the Champion/Empire and the Alletha, parallel the Animas River valley. The veins pinch and swell, are narrow, and are not continuously mineralized with ore but contain ore shoots interspersed with stretches of barren quartz. The ores consist of pyrite, galena, and chalcopyrite, with some sphalerite and tetrahedrite. Quartz, barite, and calcite make up most of the remaining vein material.

Between Red Mountain Pass and Silverton there are several mines of smaller magnitude. The Brooklyn Mine, northeast of the Ophir Pass turnoff and east of U.S. 550, produced some gold, zinc, and copper from claylike seams that contain interspersed heavy pyrite, sphalerite, chalcopyrite, and quartz, along with small amounts of rhodocrosite. Farther up the valley, at the foot of Red Mountain Pass, stand the remains of the town of Chattanooga, which supported the Silver Ledge Mine to the north. The Silver Ledge ore deposit consisted of a small irregular chimney of galena and silver that was mined by a shaft sunk to a depth of 400 feet (122 m). The old shaft house can still be seen towering above the water-filled shaft partway below Red Mountain Pass.

RED MOUNTAIN PASS AREA

The Red Mountains are part of and adjacent to the ring-fault zone of the Silverton Caldera. The area was subjected to intense hydrothermal activity that leached and altered the volcanic rock to clay or hardened and silicified the rock to make it almost unrecognizable. Pyrite was disseminated throughout the rocks and later oxidized to the reds, yellow oranges, and browns evident on the mountains today.

The Red Mountain ore bodies were most often shallow, elliptical, vertical chimneys containing rich pods and lenses of galena and silver. The chimneys, or pipes, which are often associated with small intrusions of quartz latite, consisted of highly brecciated rock, often altered to clays in the middle and capped by erosion-resistant silica. The brecciated, or broken, rock within the pipes could have been formed by the explosive release of hot gases or by hot acidic waters that ate away at the volcanic rock as it migrated along faults or fractures. The intrusion of the quartz latites also could have led to the fracturing of the surrounding rock (Burbank 1941). Later, metal-laden waters migrating upward precipitated minerals in the open spaces between the broken rock fragments.

Some of these pipes, such as the Guston, Robinson, and National Belle, have silicic caps that dominate the adjacent countryside. The National Belle pipe, called "the knob," rises almost 200 feet (61 m) above the surface. The upper silicic cap of the National Belle was laced with caves formed by the action of acidic solutions. Later solutions cemented together the broken rock of the chimneys and lined the caves with heavy sulfides of galena, sphalerite, pyrite, chalcopyrite, enargite, covellite, chalcocite, and rich silver minerals such as tetrahedrite, proustite, and pyrargerite. The caves contained oxidized ores, whereas sulfide ores extended several hundred feet beneath the surface. The pipe eventually bottomed out in uneconomical pyrite. Sorted ores from some of the mines ran as high as 20,000 ounces of silver to the ton, but the general grade of the ore bodies was substantially lower.

The mineralized zones were small but extremely rich in silver. Unfortunately, they were often mined out quickly, and large amounts of money were spent trying to find similar ore bodies in the same vicinity. The playing out of the ore bodies, an inability to pump out the large amounts of water that seeped into the shafts, the high acidity of the water (which destroyed machinery), and the silver collapse of 1893 all led to the closure of the mines. The Joker Tunnel was started below the mines in 1904 and completed in 1906 as an ambitious project to dewater the mines and extract the ore at lower depths, but the target minerals played out within a few years (Sloan and Skowronski 1975).

A large, low-grade, disseminated gold deposit was discovered on Red Mountain No. 3 in the early 1980s but will not be mined by strip-mining methods unless the value of gold increases substantially. Molybdenum has also been found at depth but is presently uneconomical to mine.

IDARADO MINE

The buildings and tailings ponds just below Red Mountain Pass are part of Colorado's famous Idarado Mine, whose 80 miles of workings extend west as far as Telluride. The mine was continuously worked from the mid-1940s to its closure in 1978. The Idarado connects some of the area's earliest and most famous mines, such as the Ajax, Smuggler-Union, Tomboy, Liberty Bell, Alamo, Virginius-Revenue, Pandora, Flat, Japan, Flora, Cross, Ansborough, Handicap, Montana-Argentine, Black Bear, and Barstow. The Treasury Tunnel below Red Mountain Pass ran 8,670 feet (2,644 m) to the Black Bear vein, and the Mill Level Tunnel stretched 7,150 feet (2,180 m) from the Pandora mill at Telluride to the Argentine vein (Hillebrand 1957). The distance from Red Mountain Pass to Telluride through tunnels and raises is 6 miles.

Most of the vein systems mined at the Idarado are in faults radial to the Silverton Caldera. The larger veins trend generally northwest. One of the most famous veins, the Montana-Argentine, is more than 16,000 feet (4,875 m) long and 5 to 7 feet (1.5–2 m) wide and has been mined to a depth of more than 3,500 feet (1,067 m). The vein coexists with an andesite dike that intruded and followed a fault radial to the caldera. The Montana-Argentine vein consists of 60 to 70 percent quartz, with heavy sphalerite, galena, pyrite, chalcopyrite, gold, and some silver along with calcite, rhodocrosite, and fluorite. The vein in some areas splits into multiple parallel fractures filled with minerals. Much of the ore has been shattered by subsequent fault movement and cemented together by later mineralization (Hillebrand 1957). Between 1947 and 1972 more than 4.8 million tons of ore worth $88 million were mined from the Montana-Argentine, predominantly from the favorable host rocks of the San Juan Tuff (Mayor and Fisher 1972).

In localities where the veins passed through the lower Telluride Conglomerate, large replacement ore bodies of lead, zinc, and copper were mined. Such veins existed both at the Idarado and at the Camp Bird Mine, to the north. The cementing matrix of calcite and limestone clasts within the conglomerate was easily altered and replaced by acidic ore solutions containing galena, sphalerite, chalcopyrite, and pyrite. The ore bodies were confined to the more permeable middle and basal parts of the formation as solutions spread out from the veins. Vein intersections localized the ore solutions and created concentrated replacement. The large replacement ore body in the middle Telluride Conglomerate along the Argentine vein was 3,500 feet long, 30 feet thick, and 25 feet wide (1,067 m × 9 m × 7.6 m) (Mayor and Fisher 1972).

IRONTON PARK–UNCOMPAHGRE CANYON

Some of the park's deposits are similar to the Red Mountain pipe deposits. These veins are associated with an area of replacement ore within the Ouray-Leadville Limestone at the Saratoga Mine on the eastern side of Ironton Park. Most of the vein deposits in the Uncompahgre River valley between Ouray and Ironton Park narrow as they pass through the Precambrian slates and phyllites and widen upon entering the San Juan Tuff. Though often located in strong structures, the ore deposits are small and uneconomical.

OURAY AREA

There were two periods of mineralization in Ouray, both related to igneous activity. The first episode involved emplacement of a quartz monzonite stock that fed a laccolithic intrusion into upper Cretaceous sediments northeast of Ouray in the late Cretaceous–early Tertiary. The second resulted from the collapse of the Silverton Caldera during the Tertiary.

The brownish-stained area above and northeast of Ouray is a quartz monzonite intrusion locally known as the "Blowout." It was emplaced along a zone of weakness that formed at the intersection of two major structural elements: an old Paleozoic anticlinal flexure, the axis of which is the northwest-trending Uncompahgre Valley, and a group of northeast-trending, late Cretaceous–Eocene dikes that cross the valley (Burbank 1940). Igneous dikes were emplaced along faults or zones of weakness. A second type of dike formed from the violent escape of hot gases, water, and vapors along faults and fractures. The gases tumbled the rocks within the fault and left a crack filled with rubble, or breccia. This type of structure is called a clastic dike. Later, mineral-rich solutions recemented or replaced these clastic dikes with lead and silver ores (Burbank 1940).

Several episodes of mineralization that produced contact metamorphic, vein, and replacement deposits appear to have occurred simultaneously with or later than the intrusion of the quartz monzonite. The earliest deposits were low-grade contact metamorphic deposits adjacent to the intrusion. Pyritic and gold replacement ore bodies formed in the Pony Express Limestone and Dakota Sandstone, whereas galena and silver were deposited in veins farther north (Fig. 7.1).

Hot solutions migrating along faults, fractures, dikes, and bedding planes boiled or vaporized upon nearing the earth's surface as pressure was released. The solutions leached silica from sandstones and redeposited it along channelways and porous spaces in the Dakota Sandstone. The resulting quartzite was brittle, fractured easily, and offered an easy pathway for future ore solutions to follow. Small caves and pockets were leached out of favorable beds, leaving open space for future ore deposition. Later, metal-rich solutions migrated slowly up faults, bedding planes, and flexures in the quartzite. They replaced more permeable limestones and porous sandstones adjacent to channelways and faults and filled the earlier dissolution pockets with pyrite, chalcopyrite, galena, and, later, native gold.

Gold producers such as the American Nettie, Jonathan, and Wanakah Mines stand high up on the cliffs above Ouray. The honeycombed tunnels and shafts form a complex maze, following

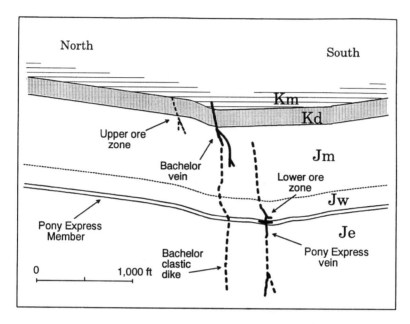

Fig. 7.1   Generalized cross-section through the Pony Express and Bachelor veins, Mancos Shale (Km), Dakota Sandstone (Kd), Morrison Formation (Jm), Wanakah Formation (Jw), and Entrada Sandstone (Je). The Pony Express is the basal member of the Wanakah Formation (modified after Burbank 1940).

myriad dikes, faults, and replacement channels within favorable beds. Tunnels chase in every direction from one pocket of ore to another. Exploration geologists in the early 1980s were rumored to have unwound balls of string to mark their way back to the mine entrances, so complex and confusing are the mine workings. In some areas large tabular ore bodies 10 feet (3 m) thick were mined, leaving rooms the size of football fields.

Some of the more productive deposits of the area were narrow gold-bearing veins close to the Blowout and silver-bearing veins to the north (such as the Bachelor-Syracuse) emplaced along a clastic dike. These veins were widest where they passed through the permeable Pony Express Limestone or the brittle Dakota Quartzite. Much of the Pony Express Limestone within 1,000 feet (305 m) of the monzonite stock is a brittle magnetite-garnet-pyroxene skarn.

A second, later stage of mineralization was related to the Silverton volcanic centers. Collapse of the caldera formed northwest-trending faults that extend almost as far as Ouray. The northernmost of these faults, the Grizzly Bear vein, contains Silverton-type ores of galena, sphalerite, chalcopyrite, argentiferous tetrahedrite, hubnerite, and beautiful rhodocrosite. With the exception of the Grizzly Bear, most of the deposits south of Ouray are narrow, sporadic, and generally uneconomical.

CAMP BIRD MINE

The Camp Bird Mine lies 6 miles southwest of Ouray, adjacent to and north of the Idarado workings. It was originally mined for silver, primarily on a sulfide streak on the footwall of the vein. Rich gold-bearing quartz on the hanging wall of the vein had been thrown away as waste, its riches unknown. Thomas Walsh initiated a sampling program in 1896, discovered the gold in this quartz, and bought the surrounding properties. The mine produced high-grade gold until the early 1920s, when the richest ore bodies were exhausted and production slowed. The mine has produced primarily base metals since the early 1940s. More than 2.5 million tons of ore, primarily from the Camp Bird vein and replacement bodies at depth, have yielded more than 1.4 million ounces of gold and 4.5 million ounces of silver (Hutchinson 1988). Most of the faults that host veins at the Camp Bird mine radiate northwestward from the Silverton Caldera and are parallel to the structures found at the Idarado Mine. Many of them were first intruded by andesitic dikes and later filled with vein material. The Camp Bird vein, though related to the collapse of the Silverton Caldera, trends east to west at an angle across the radiating faults.

The Camp Bird vein structure consists of distinct parallel veins of varying age and mineralization within one fault zone. Quartz, galena, sphalerite, pyrite, and chalcopyrite occur in ore shoots of varying length and from 3 to 10 feet (1–3 m) wide. A quartz hematite stage was deposited in veins 6 to 18 inches (15–46 cm) wide at approximately the same time as the sulfide stage. Later movement shattered both volcanics and ore, fragments of which were later recemented by quartz containing high concentrations of gold in the upper levels of the mine. This part of the vein structure varies from 1 to 5 feet (0.3–1.5 m) wide and is some-times parallel to or cuts across the earlier vein deposits. The latest stage of mineralization consisted of barren quartz deposition (Hutchinson 1988). At the Camp Bird Mine, replacement ores of galena, sphalerite, pyrite, and chalcopyrite occur in the basal mem-ber of the Telluride Conglomerate where it is crossed by the northwest-trending Orphan, Gordon, and Walsh veins. More than 560,000 tons of ore were mined from these ore bodies 700 feet (213 m) below level 14 of the Camp Bird (Hutchinson 1988).

Other veins to the northeast of the Camp Bird are related both to the Silverton Caldera and to emplacement of the Stony Mountain stock. This stock is exposed on Stony Mountain be-tween Yankee Boy and Governor Basins and consists of gabbro-granodiorite, which was emplaced during middle to late Tertiary time. A swarm of andesitic dikes, faults, and veins radiate out from the stock center. Limited mining occurred on related veins, such as the Ruby Trust, but ore bodies were sporadic and small.

TELLURIDE AREA

The famous mines of Savage and Marshall Basins, northeast of Tel-luride — the Smuggler-Union, Tomboy, and Argentine — are lo-cated on parallel veins and dikes trending northwestward, away from the Silverton Caldera. All of these mines have been consoli-dated into the extensive workings of the Idarado Mine. The Pan-dora mill, at the east end of town, had a capacity of 1,800 tons a day. The resulting tailings were stockpiled in the valley below or pumped back through the Idarado workings to Ironton Flats.

OPHIR AREA

The swarms of faults, dikes, and related vein deposits between Tel-luride (to the north) and the Ophir Pass road (to the south) are related to two different geologic events: formation of the Silverton Caldera and intrusive activity near Ophir. The collapse of the Sil-verton Caldera produced radiating faults that trend northwest to-ward Telluride and west from the western edge of the crater. Concentric faults in this area trend north and northeast, following the circular pattern of the caldera to the east.

A linear zone of weakness that runs from the Ophir Needles east toward Lookout Peak and Ophir Pass, parallel to Howard Fork, apparently acted to localize a variety of intrusions. Two large stocks of diorite were intruded into the Ophir area. One of these makes up the Ophir Needles northeast of the Ophir Loop, and the other, a stock east of the Needles, is exposed on the northern valley walls of the Howard Fork of the San Miguel River. The emplacement pressures exerted by these stocks produced radial faults, many of which were then intruded by andesitic dikes and later filled with veins. In addition to the two larger stocks, several smaller quartz porphyry intrusions crop out northwest of Ophir Pass. A zone of horsts and grabens (alternating blocks of uplifted and downdropped ground) trends eastward just to the north of Ophir Pass and appears to be related to the zone of weakness. Hydrothermal solutions migrating up along this zone deposited minerals in fracture openings and formed fissure veins that, as elsewhere in the San Juans, are often brecciated and cemented with additional mineralization. The formations most favorable for fracturing and deposition were the San Juan Formation and the Telluride Conglomerate.

Gold was produced from west-trending quartz veins in the area south and southeast of Telluride. The veins consisted predominantly of quartz, some pyrite, and minor sulfides. Mines on these veins included the Mayflower, Contention, Weller, Fairview, and Savage.

Farther south, the veins at the head of Bridal Veil Basin and the northern valley walls of the Howard Fork predominantly bear silver and base metals. These consist of chalcopyrite, tetrahedrite, pyrite, sphalerite, galena, silver, and gold, along with quartz, ankerite, barite, and rhodocrosite. The larger producers at the head of Bridal Veil Basin were the Lewis and Little Dorritt Mines. The Carbonero Mine was one of the larger producers in the Howard Fork Valley, yielding more than 100,000 tons of ore containing silver, gold, lead, zinc, and copper (Vhay 1962).

The consolidated properties of Alta Mines Inc., one of the larger mining operations in the area, lie in Palmyra and Gold King Basins. Most of the past production came from the Palmyra and Alta veins, which contained gold, silver, galena, sphalerite, chalcopyrite, and pyrite, along with quartz, calcite, barite, and rhodocrosite. Several long tunnels, including the St. Louis Tunnel in Palmyra Basin and the 6,000-foot Blackhawk Tunnel, underlie the properties. A tramline connected the Alta site with a mill in Ophir in 1910. Later, other mills were built near the portal of the Blackhawk Tunnel, but they burned down in 1929 and again in 1948. Together, the St. Louis and Alta properties produced 75,000 ounces of gold and 2.75 million ounces of silver, along with millions of pounds of lead and copper (Vhay 1962).

Northwest of the town of Ophir are the Gold King and Suffolk Mines. The area between the mines is crisscrossed with numerous quartz veins containing pyrite and gold. Mineralization by acidic hydrothermal solutions was so intense that large amounts of the surrounding country rock were replaced or pervaded with pyrite and gold. The veins and host rock on the sides of the veins were stoped, some completely to the surface. Several mines — the Globe, Gold Crown, and Suffolk — were combined into one property and worked through the Suffolk Tunnel in the late 1800s. Ore was shipped by aerial tram to a stamp mill in Ophir (Vhay 1962). The nearby Crown Point Mine produced from replacement ores containing silver-rich tetrahedrite, galena, and chalcopyrite, which were found in the metamorphosed limestones of the Pony Express Member of the Wanakah Formation.

RICO AREA

The Rico mining district was a small but extremely rich area that produced more than 83,000 ounces of gold and 14.5 million ounces of silver between 1879 and 1968 (McKnight 1974). Rico differs from many of the surrounding mining districts in that most of its ores typically occur as replacement bodies in limestone layers of the Hermosa Formation.

During Tertiary times magma swelling beneath the Rico area domed the surrounding sediments and uplifted a horst of ground now exposed as Precambrian rock. A large intrusion of quartz monzonite crops out east of town. Other igneous rock intruded as horizontal sills between sedimentary layers or as vertical dikes radiating out from the monzonite intrusion. Many of the area's faults trend east-west parallel to the elongation of the monzonite intrusion. These faults — the long, northwest-trending Blackhawk Fault and the northeast-trending Princeton Fault — were the main feeder channels for a majority of the ore bodies.

There are several types of deposits in the Rico district. These are contact metasomatic ore bodies adjacent to the monzonite intrusion, vein-type ores, and replacement ores found in favorable host rocks of limestone and gypsum. The contact metasomatic deposits of sphalerite, galena, and chalcopyrite in marbleized limestones of the Ouray-Leadville Limestone and basal Hermosa Formation could not be economically mined, and the silver ores of the vein deposits of Newman Hill were exhausted by 1900. Another small but valuable ore deposit mined chiefly at the famous Enterprise Mine, a silver-rich replacement of a dissolution bed of gypsum in the lower Hermosa Formation, averaged 221.5 ounces silver and .87 ounces gold to the ton. This ore body, found in 1887, was exhausted by 1900 (McKnight 1974).

The most common and heavily mined ore bodies of this century were massive sulfide replacement deposits of pyrite, galena, sphalerite, and chalcopyrite in the limestones of the Hermosa Formation. The ore bodies were localized by faults and minor breaks in favorable limestone beds. Heavy pyrite was concentrated closest to the faults with an outer halo of galena and sphalerite. Ore solutions migrated up faults, fractures, and bedding planes and spread out upon encountering the limestone. The ore deposits are located northeast of Rico on CHC Hill, to the east at Silver Creek, and to the southeast on Newman Hill. In later years the properties were consolidated under the ownership of the Rico-Argentine Mining Company and mined through the St. Louis Tunnel and Argentine shaft.

In addition to mining the massive replacement bodies for lead and zinc, the Rico-Argentine Mining Company extracted pyrite for the production of sulfuric acid. The sulfuric acid was used in the milling of uranium ores, but the end of the uranium boom forced the acid operation to close in 1964. The Rico-Argentine operation had shut down by the early 1970s.

Several years ago molybdenum was discovered east of Rico in a deeply buried molybdenum porphyry ore body (Tom Westervelt, written communication 1992), but interest waned with a fall in metal prices and a surplus of molybdenum. Rico, a once-proud boomtown, waits quietly for the next economic upswing.

What took millions of years to form has taken less than 120 years to discover and mine. Although most of the obvious ore deposits in the San Juans have been discovered, some probably still remain to be found, waiting for the prospector's pick or the roar of the drill to reveal the mountain's hidden riches.

REFERENCES

Burbank, W. S., 1941. Structural control of ore deposition in the Red Mountain, Sneffels, and Telluride districts of the San Juan Mountains, Colorado, in *Colorado Scientific Society Proceedings*, no. 5, pp. 396–408.

Burbank, W. S., 1940. *Structural control of ore deposition in the Uncompahgre district, Ouray County, Colorado, with suggestions for prospecting.* U.S. Geological Survey, Bulletin 906-E, pp. 189–265.

Casadevall, T. J., 1976. Gold mineralization in the Sunnyside Mine, Eureka Mining District, San Juan County, Colorado: Geochemistry of gold and base metal formation in the volcanic environment. Ph.D. thesis, Pennsylvania State University, University Park, PA.

Eckel, E. B., J. Williams, and F. Galbraith, 1949. *Geology and ore deposits of the La Plata district, Colorado.* U.S. Geological Survey, Professional Paper 219, 179 pp.

Hillebrand, J. R., 1957. The Idarado Mine, Colorado, in F. E. Kottlowski and B. Baldwin, eds., *Guidebook of southwestern San Juan Mountains, Colorado, eighth field conference*, Albuquerque: New Mexico Geological Society, pp. 287–486.

Hutchinson, R. M., 1988. Structure and ore deposits of the Camp Bird Mine, Colorado, in R. M. Hutchinson, ed., *Epithermal base-metal and precious-metal systems, San Juan Mountains, Colorado*, Society of Economic Geologists, Guidebook series volume 3, pp. 4–44.

Mayor, J. N., and F. S. Fisher, 1972. Middle Tertiary replacement ore bodies and associated veins in northwest San Juan Mountains, Colorado. *Economic Geology*, v. 67, no. 2, pp. 214–230.

McKnight, E. T., 1974. *Geology and ore deposits of the Rico district, Colorado.* U.S. Geological Survey, Professional Paper 723, 100 pp.

Ransome, F., 1901. *A report on the economic geology of the Silverton quadrangle.* U.S. Geological Survey, Bulletin 182, 265 pp.

Sloan, R. E., and C. A. Skowronski, 1975. *The rainbow route.* Denver: Sundance Limited, 415 pp.

Steven, T. A., and P. W. Lipman, 1976. *Calderas of the San Juan volcanic field, southwestern Colorado.* U.S. Geological Survey, Professional Paper 958, pp. 1–4 and 10–16.

Vhay, J. S., 1962. *Geology and mineral deposits of the area south of Telluride, Colorado.* U.S. Geological Survey, Bulletin 1112-G, pp. 209–310.

CHAPTER 8

ENERGY RESOURCES

T. L. BRITT AND J. M. HORNBECK

The scenic San Juan Skyway route lies in a relatively energy-poor corridor between two major oil- and gas-producing basins, the Paradox Basin to the west and the San Juan Basin to the south. Prolific oil fields associated with Pennsylvanian-age (300 million years) algal and oolitic carbonate reservoirs of the Paradox Basin are located 25 miles west of Cortez. The eastern edge of these productive Pennsylvanian trends is defined by drilling east and north of the town of Dolores, where both Ismay and Desert Creek test wells have been completed as producers. A few miles south of Durango is the northern margin of the San Juan Basin gas field, a huge natural-gas deposit second in size, within the lower forty-eight states, only to the Hugoton Field of Oklahoma, Kansas, and Texas. This basin is, among other distinctions, the world's largest area of coal-seam gas production, and development of this resource is expected to continue for several more years. East from Cortez approximately 20 miles, a series of small, shallow Cretaceous Dakota Sandstone oil and gas pools have been developed within the Mancos River valley.

Coal deposits underlie a large part of Montezuma and La Plata Counties, but thickness, mining costs, and transportation have restricted their economic development to small local markets. Recently, however, coal from the Durango area has been sold as far away as central Arizona, and production is increasing.

The Skyway route also skirts the southeastern end of the Uravan mineral belt, a large uranium/vanadium district with myriad individual mines and mills (now abandoned or inactive). Minor uranium/vanadium deposits lie in the Placerville district, which is bisected by the Skyway route, and these also are inactive.

Geothermal resources in the form of warm springs are present along U.S. Highway 550 between Durango and Ouray and in the Rico area. Cooling Tertiary intrusive rocks in the San Juan Mountains heat the water. A few of these sites have been turned into commercial spas, delighting tourists and locals alike.

URANIUM RESOURCES

The Skyway route traverses a section of the Colorado Plateau that played a pivotal role in the development of nuclear power. This area provided some of the earliest enriched radium for experimental purposes and, later, uranium for the early U.S. atomic bomb effort. In fact, one of the most common uranium oxide minerals, carnotite, was discovered in 1895 and described from a site in Sinbad Valley, Utah, about 60 miles northwest of Placerville, Colorado.

Recognition of carnotite, a powdery, yellow potassium uranyl vanadate (approximately $K_2O, 2UO_3, V_2O_5, 3H_2O$), as a possible source of radium sparked the first of three mining booms in this portion of the Colorado Plateau. The initial boom, called the Radium Era, lasted from 1900 to 1924 and produced about 200 grams of radium, which sold for about $100,000 per gram. This metallic radium was used for medical and scientific research as well as some industrial applications. Though local legend ascribes the radium originally identified by the Curies in 1898 to ores from this area, it seems more probable that they used Czechoslovakian materials in their initial work and finally isolated the element in 1910 using American ores (Smith 1960).

During the Radium Era, carnotite ore averaging less than 2 percent U_3O_8 (extremely high grade by current standards) was not considered worth milling, and most of it was discarded on the mine dumps. Early exploration focused primarily on shallow, oxidized ores containing minerals of the carnotite group. These enriched high-grade uranium ores were handpicked at the mines and

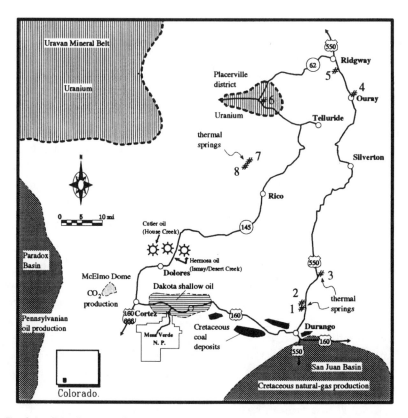

Fig. 8.1   Distribution of energy resources in and around the San Juan Skyway.

hauled by burro, freight wagon, and truck to Placerville, where they were shipped by narrow-gauge rail to Salida, Colorado, and then on to New Jersey by standard rail. Nearly all of the significant uranium mines from this era lay within the Uravan mineral belt (Fig. 8.1), located approximately 40 miles northwest of Placerville, but some production came from smaller deposits in the Placerville district just north and east of the townsite. The Radium Era suffered a fatal blow when higher-grade deposits were discovered in the Belgian Congo in 1915.

The second mining boom, the Vanadium Era, occurred from 1909 to about 1945. Whereas the Radium Era began slowly and reached a peak in 1920, only to be suddenly cut short by the Belgian Congo production, the Vanadium Era had two peak cycles.

The first coincided with the industrial development of the late 1920s, culminating in 1929. During the ensuing Depression years, all production essentially ceased. The rearmament boom of the World War II years caused a second peak from 1940 to 1945. The Vanadium Era cannot be viewed entirely independently from the Radium and Uranium Eras because of the intimate mineralogical association of vanadium with uranium in widespread uranyl vanadate minerals such as carnotite. Both vanadium and uranium enjoyed overlapping boom cycles attributable to their wartime applications — vanadium for high-quality steel, uranium for nuclear weapons. Because earlier mining for radium content had produced tailings containing substantial amounts of concentrated vanadium, the earliest sources of vanadium were the tailing piles of mines within the Uravan belt and at Rifle, Colorado. Additional deposits were discovered in the Placerville district (Fig. 8.2), and development yielded approximately 3 million pounds of metallic vanadium between 1909 and 1923. The associated uranium content of these ores averaged approximately .05 percent U_3O_8 and contributed 15,000 pounds to the nation's uranium resource base during that period.

Union Carbide Corporation organized the U.S. Vanadium Corporation in 1925 to take over assets and properties of the U.S. Vanadium Company, which had gone bankrupt trying to develop the Rifle, Colorado mine. One of the small firms that operated in the Placerville area of Colorado was the Primos Chemical Company of Pittsburgh, Pennsylvania. Another player in this crowded field, the Vanadium Corporation of America, was organized in 1919 largely to take over Primos's plateau holdings. The deposits around Placerville were in the Entrada Sandstone and contained little or no carnotite and thus very minor amounts of radium. Accordingly, they became of interest only after World War I, when the market for vanadium expanded. The Primos deposits had several advantages. They were located around the end of the narrow-gauge railroad, eliminating the expensive freight haul; there was an abundance of water available from the nearby San Juan Mountains; and the sandstone was firm but friable, so the mine workings stood well but the ore was not difficult to mine. Thus, Primos had the distinction of being the first year-round operator on the Colorado Plateau.

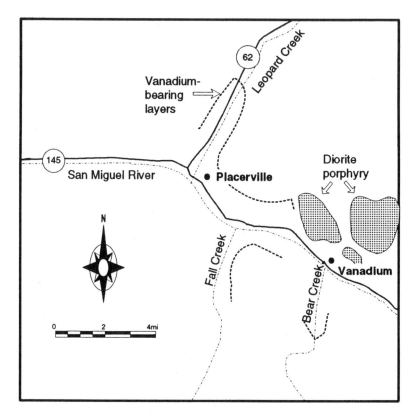

Fig. 8.2   The Placerville mining district, with outcrops of vanadium-bearing strata.

Shortly after its formation, the Vanadium Corporation of America acquired control of the much higher-grade vanadium deposits at Minasragra, Peru, and operations on the plateau were somewhat curtailed. This company finally expanded its plateau work in 1938 in response to competition from the U.S. Vanadium Corporation, as well as the armament demands preparatory to World War II.

The Uranium Era can best be described as the period from 1949 to 1978, during which time major finds occurred throughout the Colorado Plateau. The impetus for this boom was the Cold War nuclear weapons race and the development of nuclear power plants. The Colorado portion of this mineral belt produced 12.7 million tons of ore averaging 0.25 percent U_3O_8. The ore yielded 63.3 million pounds of U_3O_8 "yellow-cake" and 332 million pounds of vanadium oxide (V_2O_5) and represented the largest single source of uranium ore for U.S. consumption during this era.

The Placerville district, as previously mentioned, contributed a minor amount of U_3O_8 during the earlier eras but was not a significant contributor to the later uranium boom cycle because of its low grades and relatively small, high-cost deposits. Total modern production from the district is approximately 30,000 pounds of U_3O_8 and 970,000 pounds V_2O_5.

GEOLOGY OF WESTERN COLORADO URANIUM/VANADIUM DEPOSITS

Western Colorado harbors the oldest uranium mining area in the United States. This region, known as the Uravan mineral belt, is an arcuate belt extending from western Montrose and San Miguel Counties through southwestern Mesa County and into eastern Utah (Fig. 8.1). Production came from vanadium-uranium ores contained in sandstones, predominantly the Salt Wash Member of the Morrison Formation. Most of the uranium ores in Colorado, represented by the deposits in the Uravan mineral belt, occur in sandstones and conglomerates. Carnotite and uraninite (pitchblende), the most important uranium ore minerals, occur within carbonaceous materials in these deposits. The ore bodies are in irregularly shaped tabular, lenticular, or roll-type deposits.

Ore bodies are contained in continental sandstones, with the mineralized rock forming elongated, podlike masses and irregular bodies called "rolls." Roll ore deposits generally lie near the base of thick sandstone units where thin but well-defined mudstones are interbedded with thin sandstones (Shawe 1956). Rolls commonly include carbon and sulfur and occur in a socket-shaped cross-section, but these may be complicated by splits, bulges, loops, flat spots, or transitions into tabular-shaped deposits. Minor elements exhibit a skewed distribution across an ore body. In the Salt Wash Member of the Morrison Formation, layers rich in hematite or limonite, calcite, and selenium commonly occur in concentric arrangements on the concave side of roll ore deposits. Where numerous well-developed deposits lie in clusters, they are generally elongated and oriented in a common direction nearly perpendicular to the trend of the belt. The amount of ore in these deposits may range in size from less than a ton to several hundred thousand tons, with grades ranging from a trace to several percent uranium oxide (U_3O_8), generally averaging about 0.25 percent U_3O_8.

Small uraniferous vanadium deposits occur in the Entrada Sandstone near Placerville in San Miguel County and north of Graysill Mountain in San Juan County. Smaller similar types of deposits occur in the Lightner Creek area in La Plata County a few miles west of Durango. These uraniferous vanadium deposits are referred to as the "roscoelite type" because of the vanadium mica roscoelite that is always associated with them. This belt appears to be continuous within the Entrada Sandstone from the La Plata Mountains to the area near Placerville.

Table 8.1 shows production summaries and geologic occurrence for most of the known mines in the Placerville district. This output comes in addition to the 3 million pounds of vanadium and 15,000 pounds of uranium produced between 1909 and 1923.

GEOTHERMAL RESOURCES

Geothermal resources are present in the form of moderately hot waters that have passed near or through cooling Tertiary volcanic rocks of the San Juan Dome and related igneous bodies. These warm springs lie along U.S. Highway 550 between Durango and Ouray and along State Highway 145 in the Rico area (Table 8.2, Fig. 8.1). Although not of sufficient size and temperature to warrant development for electric power generation, some have been utilized as commercial spas and are popular tourist attractions. Table 8.2 is a summary based on the Colorado Geological Survey Report on geothermal resources of Colorado (Pearl 1972).

COAL RESOURCES

Deposits of high-quality coal underlie a large portion of La Plata and Montezuma Counties (Fig. 8.1), but several economic and geologic factors have limited development. The first written geologic report about coal in the Durango area was authored by geologists of the U.S. Geological Survey between 1905 and 1909 (Zapp 1949). However, Cross, Spencer, and Purington

Table 8.1   Uranium and vanadium production statistics for most of the known mines in the Placerville district from 1948 to 1978. In addition, 3 million pounds of vanadium and 15,000 pounds of uranium were produced between 1909 and 1923.

Mine	Location	Tonnage	Grade % U_3O_8 V_2O_5	lbs U_3O_8 lbs V_2O_5	Geologic occurrence and host rock ore mineral
Dolores County					
Blue Eagle	38N-19W	62	0.18 2.36	226 2,929	Strataform (bedded) deposit in SS of the Salt Wash member of Morrison Fm. Mineralization is of the carnotite-tyuymunite type.
South Barlow	40N-10W	115	0.11 2.79	254 6,419	Strataform roscoelite mineralization in Entrada SS.
Miscellaneous		170	0.18 2.19	533 7,851	Strataform roscoelite mineralization in Entrada SS.
COUNTY TOTALS		347		1,013 17,119	
La Plata County					
Good Hope Nevada Group	36N-10W (Lightner Ck)	650	0.07 1.66	956 21,578	Strataform roscoelite mineralization in Entrada SS.
San Miguel County (Placerville only)					
Alchemist	43N-10W	136	0.13 3.15	341 8,570	Strataform deposit of roscoelite in Entrada SS.
Bear Creek	42N-10W	14,919	0.05 2.01	15,302 600,070	Strataform deposit of roscoelite in Entrada SS.
Black King	44N-11W	3	1.35 0.05	81 3	Fault breccia in Permo-Triassic red-beds with uraninite & coffinite mineralization.
Crucible	43N-10W	13	0.07 1.58	17 410	No information.
Donegan	43N-10W	78	0.04 2.51	66 3,923	Strataform deposit of roscoelite in Entrada SS.
Fall Creek Group	43N-10W	8,232	0.07 1.91	11,804 314,084	Strataform deposit in Morrison Fm. roscoelite mineralization.
Joe Dandy Group	43N-10W	686	0.06 1.68	867 23,063	Strataform deposit of roscoelite in Entrada SS.
Leopard	44N-11W	150	0.14 2.54	430 7,610	Strataform deposit of roscoelite in Entrada SS.
Lizzie Group	43N-10W	398	0.05 1.47	374 11,699	No information.
Omega	44N-11W	8	0.09 1.68	14 269	Strataform deposit of roscoelite in Entrada SS.
COUNTY TOTALS		24,623		29,296 969,701	
DISTRICT TOTALS		25,620		31,265 1,008,398	

Table 8.2   Data from hot springs found along the San Juan Skyway (Pearl 1972).

HOT SPRINGS AROUND THE SKYWAY

SPRING see Figure 8.1	LOCATION Points of Interest (milepost)	DISCHARGE gallons per minute	TEMP ˚F(˚C)	SOURCE
#1. Trimble	POI 17 (mp 28) U.S. Hyw 550	200	100-110˚ (38-43˚) max 124˚ (51˚)	From faults in Cutler Formation
#2. Tripp	same as above	60	90˚ (32˚)	same as above
#3. Pinkerton	POI 22 (mp 35.5) U.S. 550	75	86˚ (30˚)	From faults in Elbert-Ouray Formation
#4. Ouray	POI 74	800 all springs	140-180˚ (60-82˚)	From faults in lower Paleozoic rocks
#5. Orvis	POI 82 (mp 102) U.S. 550	15-20	129˚ (34˚)	From fractures (?) beneath alluvium
#6. Lemon	POI 96 (mp 84) Co. 145	8	93˚ (34˚)	From faults in Dolores Formation
#7. Dunton	west of Co. 145	20	108˚ (42˚)	From faults in Morrison Formation
#8. Geyser	west of Co. 145	20	86˚ (30˚)	From faults in Dolores Formation

(1899) earlier made a brief discussion of some coal beds in the Hesperus area, 15 miles west of Durango.

Coal production was sufficient by 1882 to provide coke for the new San Juan smelter and heat for homes in Durango. In fact, the prosperity of Durango as an early settlement was anchored by the presence of ample coal and water to smelt the fabulous ores of the nearby Silverton district and to fuel the Denver & Rio Grande's narrow-gauge rail system, which hauled the ore.

According to Smith (1980), Durango entrepreneur John Porter used to tell of coming into the Animas Valley in 1875 with two saddlebags full of coal to use in assay work, only to notice large seams of coal cropping out in the area just east of the site where

Durango would eventually be established. Although disgusted that he'd hauled what proved to be excess baggage, Porter later turned his observation to commercial advantage, founding the Porter Fuel Company in 1890, which supplied 80 percent of the district's coal needs during the early years of settlement. At the turn of the century, miners were paid 50 cents per ton produced, so all "dead work," such as timbering, mucking, and maintenance, was essentially unpaid. Wages were probably close to 30 cents per hour.

GEOLOGIC DISCUSSION

Coal beds are present in the Dakota, Menefee, and Fruitland Formations of late Cretaceous age. Although each formation's coal is of a different age (Table 8.3), the environment favorable for coal development was similar in all three cases. Coal is a sedimentary rock formed by natural thermal and chemical changes acting on layers of abundant plant debris from a swamplike environment over millions of years. Increased depth of burial and associated higher temperatures continually improve coal quality, and the relatively

Table 8.3   Coal-bearing formations along the San Juan Skyway.

COAL-BEARING FORMATIONS ALONG THE SKYWAY		
AGE (millions of years)	FORMATION	THICKNESS AND QUALITY
Upper Cretaceous — 70	Fruitland	30 to 90 feet thick; medium volatile bituminous; low sulfur; seams 20 to 30 feet thick; tilted steeply to south.
Upper Cretaceous — 80	Menefee	10 to 20 feet thick; high volatile bituminous; low to moderate sulfur; only coals of commercial importance along the Skyway.
Upper Cretaceous — 110	Dakota Sandstone	0 to 5 feet thick; high volatile bituminous; thin discontinuous seams.

high rank of the Menefee and Fruitland coals suggests that they were several thousand feet underground at one time.

Dakota coals are thin and discontinuous and are not considered a significant source of energy. Fruitland coals, present at the surface just south of Durango, are thick and of good quality but are tilted southward at a very high angle, making them virtually impossible to mine. Southward into the San Juan Basin, however, these same Fruitland coals are a major new source of natural gas currently being developed by several oil and gas companies.

The only active mine along the Skyway route is the King Coal Mine (portal located in Hay Gulch, about 4 miles southwest of Hesperus), owned and operated by National King Coal, a subsidiary of W. C. Kirkwood Company. This mine was started in 1935 by Violet and Irvin Smith, who operated it as a small "mom and pop" mine that produced limited tonnages for local consumption. Violet Smith, who passed away in 1993, was a hardy individual who had little patience for regulators, especially U.S. Bureau of Mines inspectors, who often tried but seldom succeeded in visiting the King Coal Mine. Figure 8.3 is a photograph of the sign the Smiths posted to discourage federal mine inspectors. Violet backed up the warning with a loaded shotgun. In the early years at King Coal Mine, Violet and Irvin farmed during the daytime and

Fig. 8.3   Photograph of sign at entrance to King Coal Mine.

worked the coal vein at night. According to Duane Smith (oral communication 1991), Violet would prepare her young children for bed, put them in an empty coal car, and roll the car into the mine and onto a side drift while she and her husband dug coal by hand for several hours. Violet enjoyed playing the quintessential liberated woman competing successfully in a male-dominated society, but she also was a devoted mother, businesswoman, farmer, and civic leader. The Smiths sold the mine to Henrietta Mines of Vancouver in 1976. Henrietta then turned the property over to W. C. Kirkwood of Casper, Wyoming, in 1977. Kirkwood installed continuous mining machines and has steadily increased production since taking ownership.

The main minable seam lies in the upper part of the Menefee Formation and ranges from 4 to 7 feet (1.2–2.1 m) thick. A representative analysis of the coal is shown in Table 8.4. The coal seam dips (tilts) 1.5 to 3 degrees southward. Fault offsets of the seams are minimal. Excavation is by the room-and-pillar method using continuous mining machines. The coal does not require washing. Currently the mine operates on two eight-hour shifts and produces 180,000 tons per year. At that rate, there is enough coal under lease to last thirty more years. Coal from King Coal Mine is sold as far away as Clarkdale, Arizona (to Arizona Portland

Table 8.4   Typical analysis of Menefee coal (as received).

TYPICAL ANALYSIS OF MENEFEE COAL		
	Hay Gulch	Durango
Moisture %	3.5	2.4
Volatiles %	38	34.4
Fixed carbon %	53.7	55.8
Ash %	4.0	6.6
BTUs per lb	13,529	13,580
Sulfur wt %	0.8	0.8

Cement Company). This mine also supplies coal for the narrow-gauge locomotives that transport tourists daily between Durango and Silverton.

A second mine, the Peerless, has recently been active in removing a small amount of surface minable coal. The scar from this surface mine is visible 5 miles west of Durango on the north side of U.S. Highway 160. At this locality, there are two minable seams in the Menefee Formation, a lower seam 3 to 10 feet (1–3 m) thick and an upper seam 3 to 7 feet (1.5–2 m) thick. The owner of this property plans to develop an underground mine in the near future.

Coal reserve estimates for the Durango coal field vary with assumptions about the selling price of coal, mining costs, and transportation costs. In general, estimates are based on current costs and selling prices, as the word "reserves" implies they are recoverable at some economic benefit to the investor. The U.S. Geological Survey (Landis 1959) estimates that approximately 3.5 billion tons of coal, mostly Menefee, are present in the Durango coal field. Nearly all of this coal would require underground extraction methods. It's very likely that only a small fraction of this total resource estimate would be considered economically minable under current conditions.

OIL AND GAS RESOURCES

The southern and western legs of the San Juan Skyway route venture into a structural province known as the Four Corners Platform. This tableland, approximately 50 miles (83.3 km) wide, stretches between Durango and Cortez and separates two major Rocky Mountain oil- and gas-producing basins, the Paradox Basin to the west and the San Juan Basin to the south (Fig. 8.1). The steeply dipping strata of the Hogback Monocline define the eastern boundary between the Platform and the San Juan Basin. Along this sharp structural flexure, rocks exposed at the surface plunge southward into the basin. A short distance into the basin, hydrocarbons lie as much as 8,000 feet (2,438 m) below the surface. The western edge of the Four Corners Platform cannot be recognized nearly as easily on the surface. This edge, approximately 10 miles west of Cortez, is identified through subsurface well control.

Here an evaporite salt section in Pennsylvanian-age rocks begins to rapidly thicken to a width of more than 1,000 feet (305 m).

PARADOX BASIN

Almost all the oil and gas produced in the Paradox Basin comes from a series of stacked, porous carbonate reservoirs within the Pennsylvanian Paradox Formation. The most prolific production is related to algal mound buildups called the Ismay and Desert Creek intervals. During Pennsylvanian time large accumulations of the calcareous algae *Ivanovia* flourished on the sea floor, along with a rich fossil assemblage including brachiopods, fusilinids, foraminifera and an occasional *Chaetetes* coral. Sea-level fluctuations caused organic-rich shales to develop in close proximity to the algal mounds. This combination, once buried deeply enough to allow the generation of hydrocarbons, is an exploration geologist's dream come true. At depth the hydrocarbon-rich source shales charged the lithified porous algal mounds with oil and gas. These stratigraphic traps are still quite elusive and take tremendous technical effort (and a little luck) to locate at depths averaging 6,000 feet (1,828 meters).

Although oil was first discovered in the Paradox Basin in 1908, it wasn't until the mid-1950s that drilling revealed the true potential of the Paradox Formation carbonate reservoirs. In 1956 Aneth Field, a truly giant Desert Creek substage oil field, was discovered. Located approximately 30 miles (50 km) west of Cortez, Aneth has produced more than 280 million barrels of oil since its discovery. Although no other giant oil fields have been found, exploration continues on the Four Corners Platform. The eastern edge of the productive area is presently defined by successful completions of Ismay and Desert Creek wells just east of Dolores (Fig. 8.1). The only other hydrocarbons produced within the area came from a Permian-age Cutler sandstone in the House Creek area, just north of Dolores. This well produced a small volume of gas with limited extent and has been plugged.

SAN JUAN BASIN

Natural Gas. The southern leg of the scenic Skyway route skirts the San Juan Basin (Fig. 8.1), which holds the second-largest accumulation of natural gas in the continental United States in a series of relatively tight Cretaceous sandstone reservoirs. Since the discovery of natural gas in the basin in 1921, more than 25,000 wells have been drilled in the search for stratigraphically trapped gas in Pictured Cliffs, Mesa Verde, Gallup, and Dakota Sandstones (see Stratigraphic Chart, p. 2). These productive sandstones occur at depths ranging from 2,500 to 8,000 feet (762–2,438 m) and result from shoreline fluctuations during upper Cretaceous time. The shoreline sequences contain sandstone reservoirs that were deposited in coastal plain, deltaic, beach, and shallow offshore environments and have produced more than 15 trillion cubic feet (TCF) of natural gas. Additional reserves are still being found by continued exploration.

Coal-bed Methane. In the past few years, coal-bed methane, an entirely new and different source of clean natural gas, has been identified in the San Juan Basin. This unconventional source of natural gas is still being evaluated, with most of the interest focused on coals of the upper Cretaceous Fruitland Formation. The most prolific production begins just south of Durango and extends 30 miles (48 km) southward to Navajo Reservoir, thus making this the largest producing coal-bed methane area in the world. Unlike a conventional reservoir, which traps oil and gas only within its matrix porosity, coal beds additionally adsorb methane on a molecular scale. This adsorption provides for a much greater gas storage capability per unit volume of coal and greatly increases the recoverable reserves for each well. Global projections of recoverable gas from this newly identified resource are as high as the total amount of gas produced to date from all known conventional sandstone reservoirs combined. Obviously, it is too early to tell if these projections represent the true potential of coal-bed methane. It is certain, however, that coal-bed methane will be a significant addition to the hydrocarbon-rich resources of the San Juan Basin.

DAKOTA CHANNEL SANDS

Between Cortez and Durango, the Skyway travels through an area of numerous small, shallow Dakota Sandstone oil and gas fields. Scattered throughout the Mancos River valley, these fields produce oil from lower Dakota channel sandstone reservoirs occurring at a depth of approximately 1,200 feet (365 m). These sandstones average 30 feet (9.1 m) in thickness. After completion small volumes of oil, averaging five barrels per day, are lifted to the surface with the help of a pump jack.

MCELMO DOME

One other unique gas resource exists just west of Cortez in the area of McElmo Dome (Fig. 8.1). This large structure produces carbon dioxide from the Mississippian-age Leadville Limestone at depths averaging 8,500 feet (2,590 m). From here the gas is transported more than 500 miles (833 km) by pipeline to western Texas, where it is injected as a "flood" into older oil fields near the end of their productive life. Utilizing carbon dioxide in this way makes it possible to recover a higher percentage of the oil in place in the ground and extends the productive life of oil fields that otherwise would be plugged and abandoned.

REFERENCES

Cross, C. W., and C. W. Purington, 1899. *Geologic atlas of the United States, Telluride Quadrangle, Colorado.* U.S. Geological Survey, Folio 57, 18 pp.

Fassett, J., ed., 1988. *Geology and coal-bed methane resources of the northern San Juan Basin, Colorado and New Mexico.* Denver: Rocky Mountain Association of Geologists, 351 pp.

Fassett, J., ed., 1983. *Oil and gas fields of the Four Corners area,* volume III. Durango, CO: Four Corners Geological Society, pp. 728–1143.

George, R., H. Curtis, O. Lester, J. Crook, and J. Yeo, 1920. *Mineral waters of Colorado.* Colorado Geological Survey, Bulletin 11, p. 474.

Kuhn, E. H., 1989. *Directory and statistics of Colorado coal mines with distribution and electric generation map, 1989.* Colorado Geological Survey, Resource Series 29.

Landis, E., 1959. *Coal resources of Colorado.* U.S. Geological Survey, Bulletin 1072-C, pp. 131–232.

Lewis, E. L., 1966. The thermal springs of Colorado: A resource apprais-al. M.S. thesis, University of Colorado, Department of Geography, Boulder, CO, 91 pp.

Nelson-Moore, J. L., D. B. Collins, and A. L. Hornbaker, 1978. *Radio-active mineral occurrences of Colorado.* Colorado Geological Survey, Bulletin 40, 1054 pp.

Pearl, R. H., 1972. *Geothermal resources of Colorado.* Colorado Geologi-cal Survey, Special Publication 2, 54 pp.

Pratt, W. P., E. T. McKnight, and R. A. DeHon, 1969. *Geologic map of the Rico Quadrangle Dolores and Montezuma Counties, Colorado.* U.S. Geological Survey, Geologic Quadrangle Map GQ-797.

Shawe, D. R., 1956. Significance of roll ore bodies in genesis of uranium-vanadium deposits on the Colorado Plateau, in *Geology of uranium and thorium,* U.N. International Conference on Peaceful Uses of Atomic Energy, Geneva, v. 6, pp. 335–337.

Smith, C. T., 1960. From X-rays to fission, a metamorphosis in mining, in K. G. Smith, ed., *Geology of the Paradox Fold and Fault Belt, third field conference,* Durango, CO: Four Corners Geological Society, pp. 109–114.

Smith, D., 1980. *Rocky Mountain boom town: A history of Durango.* Al-buquerque: University of New Mexico Press, 215 pp.

Stevenson, G. M., and D. L. Baars, 1988. Overview: Carbonate reser-voirs of the Paradox Basin, in S. M. Goolsby and M. W. Longman, eds., *Occurrences and petrophysical properties of carbonate reservoirs in the Rocky Mountain region,* Denver: Rocky Mountain Association of Geologists Guidebook, pp. 149–161.

Zapp, A., 1949. *Geology and coal resources of the Durango area, La Plata and Montezuma Counties, Colorado.* U.S. Geological Survey, Oil and Gas Investigations Map OM-109.

CHAPTER 9

WEATHER AND CLIMATE

RICHARD A. KEEN

If you want to see some very fine weather, come to the San Juan country — in the summer.
— *Silverton Standard,* March 7, 1891

It only takes a day to drive the San Juan Skyway, but on the right day you can catch a whole year's worth of weather. It is not unusual — especially in the spring — to wake up with frost on the ground, drive through snow, hail, a thunderstorm, and 90-degree heat, and finish the day with a rainbow. The main reason for this variety is, of course, the mountains (Fig. 9.1). A loop around the Skyway takes you from the near-desert climate at Cortez, 6,000 feet (1,830 m) above sea level, to the high-country conditions on Red Mountain Pass, elevation 11,000 feet (3,350 m), and some hiking and climbing can take you 3,000 feet (910 m) higher onto the alpine tundra. On the average, temperatures drop about 4 degrees Fahrenheit for every 1,000 feet (305 m) of elevation gain, and the resulting 35-degree spread between Cortez and the summit of Mount Wilson can be the difference between summer and winter weather.

However, the mountains aren't the only factor that shape the climate of the western San Juans. Like most other places in the western United States, the San Juans are at the mercy of storms (called "cyclones" because of their circular wind patterns, or "lows" because of their low barometric pressure) sweeping off the Pacific Ocean. From November through April, one or two cyclones a week (on the average) strike the coast and head for the

Fig. 9.1   An afternoon storm brews up over the La Plata Mountains. Photo by Duane Smith.

Rockies. Most cyclones veer north of Colorado, but some slip south into Arizona and New Mexico.

Wispy cirrus clouds in the western sky are often the first sign of an approaching Pacific storm. Over the next twelve to twenty-four hours the clouds thicken and lower, and as the cloud deck envelops the highest peaks snow begins to fall along the ridges. Within a few hours the snow spreads to the valleys, though it may melt into rain before it reaches the surrounding low country.

From space a cyclone looks like a draining bathtub, with air streaming in toward the center. Water in a bathtub goes down the drain, but air in a storm rises as it nears the center. In the Northern Hemisphere the cyclone spins counterclockwise. The rising air expands and cools, and its load of moisture (humidity) condenses into clouds and snowflakes. The air gets an added upward shove where the wind blows up and over mountain ridges, complicating the pattern of snowfall. Though snow may fall over the entire San Juan area, the heaviest falls normally occur along the higher ridges and passes. Because of this "upslope" effect during storms, Red Mountain, Coal Bank, and Lizard Head Passes receive five to ten

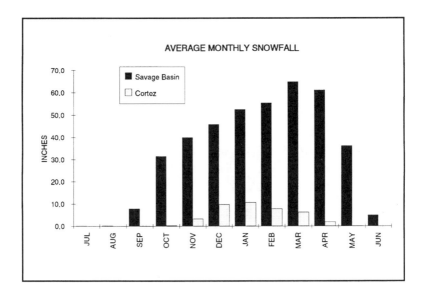

Fig. 9.2 Average monthly snowfall at Savage Basin (above Telluride) and Cortez. March storms bring the year's heaviest snows to the high country, but at lower elevations (such as Cortez's) many March storms bring rain instead, and January is the snowiest month of the year.

times as much snow each winter as do Cortez and Durango (Figs. 9.2, 9.3). Snow accumulations at lower elevations often melt before the next storm, but above 7,000 feet (2,130) the flakes continue piling up through the winter, reaching peak depths in early spring.

Frequent moderate snows from numerous storms tracking north of the area provide most of the winter's accumulation, but the heaviest individual falls come from storms that pass south of Colorado. It may seem strange that storms crossing the Arizona desert should be the heaviest snow producers for the mountains, but on this southerly track cyclones are better able to sweep moisture-laden air from the subtropical Pacific Ocean west of Mexico directly into the San Juans. Cyclones that have followed this path include the great storms of December 19–26, 1883; February 3–8, 1884, February 24–27, 1987; and February 15–26, 1993, each of which dumped 5 feet (or more) of snow in the mountains. Snowslides following the February 1884 storm blocked the rail line into Silverton, isolating the community until mid-April. By far

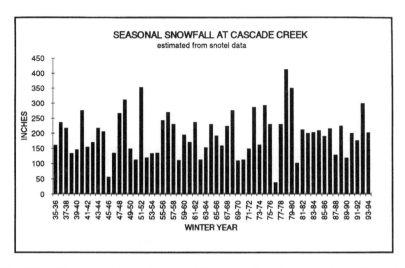

Fig. 9.3 Fifty-nine winters of seasonal (fall through spring) snowfall at Cascade Creek, near the Purgatory ski area, 1935–1936 through 1993–1994. Snowfall totals have ranged from 39 inches (1976–77) to 413 inches (1978–79), but overall there is no distinct trend to more or less snowy winters.

the worst winter for avalanches, though, was 1905–1906, with twenty-four avalanche fatalities in San Juan County. Numerous slides killed sixteen on Saturday evening, March 17, at the end of a week-long snowstorm, with twelve miners dying as they sat for dinner at their boardinghouse east of Silverton. Snow can plague the lowlands, too. The massive, slow-moving system of December 13–21, 1967, buried Cortez, Mesa Verde, and Durango under 3 to 4 feet of snow and forced emergency aerial hay drops to livestock stranded in the Four Corners area.

As the storm continues east onto the Plains, clearing skies move in from the west. Snow showers and flurries may linger in the mountains for part of a day after the clouds have parted over the lowlands. Northerly winds on the heels of the storm bring lower temperatures, and nighttime readings may dip to zero or lower. However, these cold air masses usually come off the Pacific Ocean. Bitter Arctic air from Siberia and Alaska usually stays east of the Continental Divide, and extremely low temperatures are actually quite rare in the San Juans. Whereas other mountain areas of Colorado have recorded temperatures in the range of 40 to 60 degrees below zero, the coldest ever seen in the San Juans is a comparatively mild 39 below, at Silverton. See Table 9.1 for a list of climatic extremes in San Juan Mountains.

With sunny skies and light winds, daytime temperatures may rise 30 to 40 degrees above the morning low. Pleasant winter weather may last less than a day or continue for a week or more before cirrus clouds announce the approach of the next storm.

Table 9.1   List of San Juan weather extremes.

* Hottest Day:	102 degrees at Durango, July 5, 1989; Fort Lewis, July 4, 1973; Mesa Verde, July 24, 1936.
* Coldest Day:	–39 degrees at Silverton, February 1, 1985.
* Most rain in one day:	8.05", Gladstone, October 5, 1911.
* Most precipitation in one month:	11.9", Red Mountain Pass, December 1983 (fell as snow).
* Most precipitation in one year:	58.1", Red Mountain Pass, October 1983–September 1984.
* Least precipitation in one year:	6.34", Cortez, 1950.
* Biggest snowstorm:	62" at Purgatory Ski Area, February 24–27, 1987.
* Most snow in one month:	144", Savage Basin, April 1917.
* Most snow in one winter:	(measured) 581", Savage Basin, 1928–1929; (measured) 490", Purgatory Ski Area, 1974–1975; (estimated) 749", Spud Mountain (near Coal Bank Pass), 1978–1979.
* Deepest snow on ground:	155", Purgatory Ski Area, April 13, 1975; 16 feet (184") at Animas Forks (drifts up to 70 feet), March 1884.
* Least snow in one year:	3.5", Cortez, 1934.
* Highest wind gust:	128 mph, Red Mountain Pass, January 1972.

Note: These are the most extreme weather events I could find record of. However, in such varied terrain as the San Juans, there's a good chance that even more extreme weather may have gone unrecorded.

By March, when most of the Northern Hemisphere is feeling the first touches of spring, winter still reigns in the San Juans (and all across the Rockies). March is, on average, the snowiest month of the year in the high country, and April is often not far behind. Silverton, Telluride, and Ouray rarely see bare ground before mid-April, and above 10,000 feet the snow doesn't clear out until June.

Spring arrives with a bang. One or two winterlike storms may cross the area in early May, bringing rain to the lowlands and wet snow in the mountains, but then the storm track shifts toward the northern United States and Canada. As a warm high-pressure system settles in over the Southwest, the winter's accumulation of mountain snow starts melting in earnest. During the most rapid melt, from mid- to late May, the volume of snow turned into water each day is equivalent to a widespread rainfall of nearly 1 inch, and by late May the Animas, Dolores, and Gunnison Rivers are running high. River flows typically peak during the first ten days of June, then decrease considerably by the end of the month as the mountains run out of snow.

June is the sunniest and driest month of the year. The sun shines on Durango an average of 12.4 hours per day, or 84 percent of the total daylight hours (Fig. 9.4), and rain falls on but four of June's thirty days. Pleasantly warm days follow cool, even frosty nights, and the day-to-night temperature swing often exceeds 40 degrees. Only occasionally do the cumulus clouds that dot the afternoon sky develop into showers or thunderstorms. All in all, June has the best weather of the year for outdoor activities.

July brings the southwest monsoon, a flow of moisture from the tropical Pacific into the southwestern United States. The air becomes more humid, and afternoon thunderstorms become common. Cortez averages about forty thunderstorms per year, and the higher mountains may see eighty or more (Fig. 9.5). More than half of these storms occur in July and August, when a hiker in the high country has a better than even chance of encountering thunder, lightning, and rain during the afternoon. Some of these storms (about three or four per year at any location) may drop small hail, but large, damaging hail is rare.

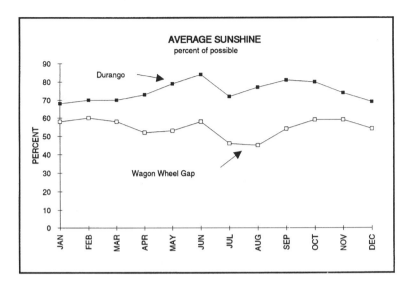

Fig. 9.4   Average monthly sunshine at Durango and Wagon Wheel Gap, expressed as a percent of total daylight hours for each month. Wagon Wheel Gap is at 9,600 feet elevation in the eastern San Juans.

As the monsoon weather tapers off in September and ceases in October, the air becomes cooler and drier. Rainy days become less frequent, cloudiness decreases, and the sun shines nearly as much as it did in June. Once in a while the flow of air from the southwest picks up a dying hurricane off the coast of Mexico and swings its soggy remnants into the San Juans. It doesn't happen often, but when it does the ensuing torrents of rain can lead to disastrous flooding — as in October 1911, October 1972, and July 1981. The remnants of Tropical Storm Norma spawned a tornado 12 miles west of Cortez on September 5, 1970. (Only two other tornadoes have ever been reported in the area. One appeared near Cortez, on April 25, 1985, in a developing snowstorm; the other touched down south of Durango on May 30, 1992. Neither caused injuries or serious damage.) For the most part, however, September and October are pleasant months, weatherwise.

Late October and early November bring the return of winterlike storms. The first few snowfalls may melt quickly, but by mid-November snow once again covers the ground at higher elevations. The chances of a white Christmas (1 inch or more of

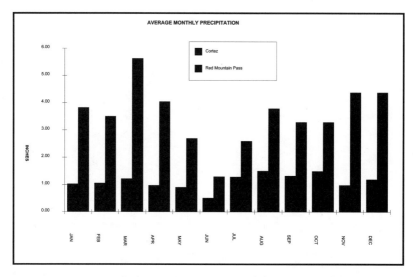

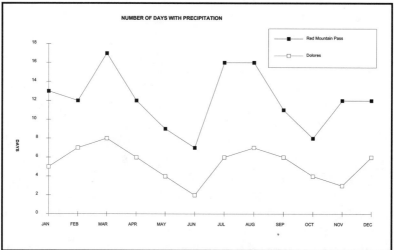

Fig. 9.5 *(Top)* Average monthly precipitation (rain and melted snow) at Red Mountain Pass and Cortez shows the distinct wet and dry seasons in the San Juans. *(Bottom)* More relevant, perhaps, for outdoor activities is the number of days per month with precipitation. Your picnic is most likely to be rained (or snowed) on in late winter and late summer, least likely in June or October.

snow on the ground) range from 40 percent at Cortez and 70 percent at Durango to more than 95 percent at Ouray, Silverton, and Telluride. December snows cover the lower elevations to close out a typical year of weather in the San Juans.

Not all years are typical, though. Average temperatures in some winters can be 20 degrees warmer than in others, and average temperatures for entire years may vary by 5 or 10 degrees — in effect, Durango may have Telluride's weather for a year or vice versa. During the past century the warmest year in the San Juans was 1934, followed by 1954 and 1981, and the coldest years were 1912, 1924, 1973, and 1979. The warmest decades were the 1930s and 1950s, whereas the 1910s, 1920s, and 1970s were generally cool across southwestern Colorado. There have been plenty of ups and downs on San Juan thermometers, but over the past century there has been no evidence that global warming (or cooling) has taken hold of the region. Temperatures for the most recent full decade, the 1980s, averaged about the same as those in the 1890s (Fig. 9.6).

For the most part, the San Juans lie in a semiarid area, and the amount of precipitation is more critical than the temperature to human endeavors (Fig. 9.7). Snow and rainfall can vary tremendously from one year to the next. Most mountain locations had only 3 to 6 feet of snow during the drought winter of 1976–1977, but ten times as much snow fell on the same places just two winters later. Early weather records show that the winters of the 1870s and 1880s were quite a bit snowier (perhaps twice as snowy, on the average) than they are now. The decades of the 1890s and 1950s were on the dry side, but over the past century there has been no long-term trend toward greater or lesser precipitation. There is, of course, no guarantee that the climate will remain so stable in the future. Tree-ring records indicate that the present century has been the wettest in 800 years. The sudden end of an earlier wet spell around A.D. 1170 may have driven the Anasazi from the San Juans — a historical lesson we should not ignore.

CLIMATE DATA

The range of climates found in the southwestern corner of Colorado is greater than that in many entire states. Table 9.2 summarizes climate data taken at weather stations along (and near) the

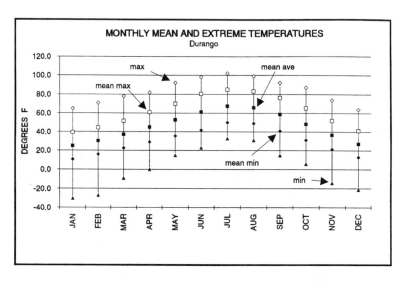

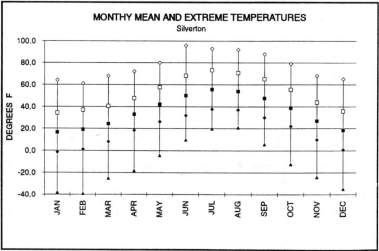

Fig. 9.6 The seasonal cycle of temperatures at Durango and Silverton. Shown for each month are the mean monthly temperature; the average daily high and low temperatures; and the highest and lowest temperatures ever recorded.

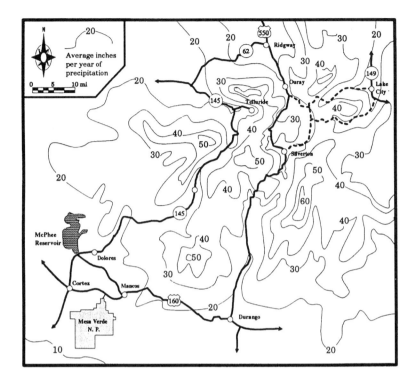

Fig. 9.7 Average annual precipitation around the San Juans. Precipitation includes rain and the water contained in snow and ranges from 12 inches per year near Cortez to 60 inches or more in the highest peaks. Data from Colorado Climate Center, Colorado State University, Fort Collins, CO.

San Juan Skyway, listed in order heading north from Durango. Among the places included are towns, mines, train stops, snow survey sites, ski areas, parks, and research stations — all places with an interest in reporting and recording the weather. A glance at these statistics reveals the incredible variety of climates: Cortez receives only 12 inches of precipitation per year, whereas Red Mountain Pass may expect an annual burial under 43 feet of snow. If you're planning a trip to the area, check the average temperatures and number of rainy (or snowy) days per year and dress accordingly. The data presented in Table 9.2 include:

Elevation (feet) — One of the most important factors in determining local climate.

Years of Record — The longer weather records have been taken, the more reliable the averages will be. It takes about ten or twenty years to come up with a truly representative average.

Average Temperature (Fahrenheit) — The average daily high and low temperatures for July and January give a good picture of the daily and seasonal ranges of temperature.

Temperature Extremes — The highest and lowest temperatures since records began. The longer the period of record, the more extreme these numbers are likely to be.

Average Annual Precipitation (inches) — Precipitation includes the water contained in snow, hail, sleet, etc., as well as rain. As a rule, 10 to 15 inches of snow melts down to 1 inch of precipitation.

Average Annual Snowfall (inches) — The total of all the individual storms in a year. For some locations this is estimated from U.S. Department of Agriculture/Soil Conservation Service snowpack data.

Deepest Snow on Ground (inches) — The greatest accumulated depth of snow ever measured.

Days with Precipitation — Average number of days per year with measurable rain (0.01 inch or more) or snow (0.1 inch or more).

REFERENCES

Armstrong, B. R., 1976. *Century of struggle against snow: A history of avalanche hazard in San Juan County, Colorado.* Boulder, CO: Institute of Arctic and Alpine Research, University of Colorado, Occasional Paper 18, 98 pp.

Armstrong, R. L., and J. D. Ives, 1976. *Avalanche release and snow characteristics.* Boulder, CO: Institute of Arctic and Alpine Research, University of Colorado, Occasional Paper 19, 256 pp.

Berry, J. W., 1968. Climates of the states — Colorado, in *Climatography of the United States 60–65,* U.S. Department of Commerce, Weather Bureau, 20 pp.

Bradley, R. S., 1976. *The precipitation of the Rocky Mountain states.* Boulder, CO: Westview Press, 334 pp.

Table 9.2 Climatic data around the San Juan Skyway.

Station	Elevation	Years Recorded	Average Temperature July Max.	July Min.	January Max.	January Min.	Temperature Extremes High	Low	Average Annual Precipitation	Snow	Deepest Snow on Ground	Days with Precipitation
Durango	6600	94	85	50	40	11	102	-30	19	71	82	84
Hermosa	6633	7	—	—	—	—	—	—	14	—	—	—
Tacoma	7300	38	—	—	—	—	—	—	22	139	54	87
Electra Lake	8300	24	—	—	—	—	—	—	26	145	—	86
Purgatory Ski Area	10200	17	—	—	—	—	—	—	—	232	155	—
Cascade Creek	8880	84	—	—	—	—	—	—	35	213	83	93
Spud Mountain (Coal Bank Pass)	10660	40	—	—	—	—	—	—	46	392*	121	—
Molas Lake	10500	40	—	—	—	—	—	—	29	208*	82	—
Silverton	9270	79	73	38	34	-1	96	-39	25	162	69	106
Red Mountain Pass	11200	40	64	39	26	7	77	-26	43	518*	125	145
Gladstone	10400	10	—	—	—	—	—	—	38	285	—	134
Ironton	9800	10	—	—	—	—	—	—	25	172	—	96
Ouray	7840	41	79	51	38	15	97	-22	23	150	49	98*
Ridgway	7000	6	80	43	38	1	88	-36	19	95	25	68*
Placerville	7320	40	—	42	37	6	—	—	18	87	45	93*
Telluride	8800	78	77	42	37	6	96	-36	23	184	64	106
Savage Basin (above Telluride)	11522	15	—	—	—	—	—	—	38	400	—	124
Ames	8700	9	75	44	36	11	88	-26	25	171	78	112
Trout Lake	9700	51	—	—	—	—	—	—	29	236	79	123
Lizard Head	10200	55	—	—	—	—	—	—	30	278*	83	—
Rico	8780	33	76	40	38	5	89	-36	27	173	89	96
Dolores	6970	41	84	51	41	12	99	-21	19	82	43	64
Cortez	6210	60	88	54	41	12	101	-31	12	41	21	59*
Mesa Verde National Park	7120	66	87	57	40	19	102	-20	18	86	39	68
Mancos	6940	20	83	50	40	11	96	-26	16	68	28	73
Fort Lewis	7600	57	80	48	37	9	102	-35	18	90	48	70

Note: *—estimated

Bradley, R. S., R. G. Barry, and G. Kiladis, 1982. *Climatic fluctuations of the western United States during the period of instrumental records.* Amherst, MA: Department of Geology and Geography, University of Massachusetts, Contribution 42, 169 pp.

Keen, R. A., 1987. *Skywatch: The western weather guide.* Golden, CO: Fulcrum Press, 158 pp.

Petersen, K. L., 1985. Climatic reconstruction for the Dolores project area (Chapter 20), in *Dolores archaeological program — studies in environmental archaeology,* Denver: U.S. Bureau of Reclamation.

Sherier, J. M., 1933. Climatic summary of the United States — Western Colorado, in *Climatography of the United States 10–22,* U.S. Department of Commerce, Weather Bureau, 33 pp.

PART II

BIOLOGICAL COMMUNITIES ALONG THE SAN JUAN SKYWAY

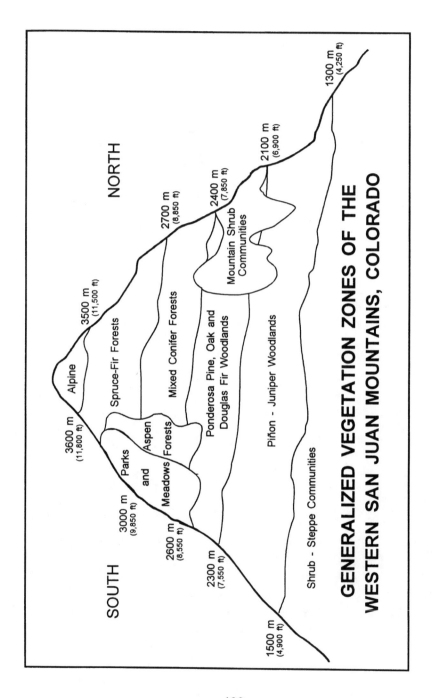

NORTH

SOUTH

3600 m
(11,800 ft)

3500 m
(11,500 ft)

Alpine

Spruce-Fir Forests

2700 m
(8,850 ft)

Mixed Conifer Forests

2400 m
(7,850 ft)

2100 m
(6,900 ft)

Mountain Shrub
Communities

1300 m
(4,250 ft)

Ponderosa Pine, Oak and
Douglas Fir Woodlands

Piñon - Juniper Woodlands

Aspen

Parks
and
Meadows Forests

3000 m
(9,850 ft)

2600 m
(8,550 ft)

2300 m
(7,550 ft)

Shrub - Steppe Communities

1500 m
(4,900 ft)

**GENERALIZED VEGETATION ZONES OF THE
WESTERN SAN JUAN MOUNTAINS, COLORADO**

Fig.   10.1 Major vegetation zones of the western San Juan Mountains.

CHAPTER 10

ECOLOGICAL PATTERNS

ALBERT W. SPENCER AND WILLIAM H. ROMME

A mantle of green vegetation covers the San Juan Mountains and softens the appearance of the rugged slopes and valleys. The plant life also provides homes for myriad creatures, large and small. The study of ecology centers on patterns in distribution of plant and animal species and the reasons for these patterns. In Part 2 we examine the ecology of the San Juan Mountains. In this chapter we give an overview of the broad patterns in climate, plant life, and animals found along the Skyway and cover some fundamental concepts of ecology. Chapter 11 presents a closer look at the often harsh conditions in the semiarid basins and foothills and considers some of the remarkable adaptations by which plants and animals cope with them. In Chapter 12 we move up to the high country, the dense mountain forests, and the treeless landscape above timberline and examine the different kinds of constraints and opportunities for organisms living in these environments. We conclude in Chapter 13 by discussing the wetlands and aquatic ecosystems found throughout the San Juans, from the foothills to the alpine basins.

In general, each species is found only in environments where the limiting factors are conducive to its survival. These limiting factors may be physical (for example, low temperatures or lack of water) or biological (for example, the presence of a competitor or predator). Most species do not occupy all the habitats that potentially could support them because they have never had the opportunity to spread into all suitable areas. In addition to understanding the distribution of individual species, the ecologist is concerned with assemblages of species, or biotic communities, and with the physical and biological factors controlling the distribution of these communities across the landscape.

One of the pleasures of walking or driving in the mountains lies in seeing everywhere evidence of the dynamic processes that shape the natural world. For example, driving north from Durango the road traverses stratum upon stratum of sandstones, shale, limestone, and volcanic deposits, each laid down under a different set of circumstances. This layer of sandstone represents a dune field tens of thousands of square miles in extent; those shales represent mudflats of a shallow inland sea; those red cliffs, a coastal plain in a tropical environment; the rimrock, the petrified sands of an ancient beach. The valley itself has been shaped by a river of ice that ran through hillsides clothed in spruce and fir and an alpine meadow where piñon and juniper now grow. To eyes that are open to the history of the planet, it is clear that life faces a ceaseless challenge to adapt to changing conditions. The living organisms found today along the San Juan Skyway are constantly responding to the endless sequence of changes. Life is still adjusting to the glacial retreat and to the arrival of humans, of European settlers and their livestock, and of modern technology. Travelers along the Skyway can observe the current state of the process and understand the factors that have helped create the biological communities visible from the roadway.

Fifteen thousand years ago, the climate of Durango was not greatly different from that seen today at the crest of Molas Pass (Pielou 1991). Musk oxen *(Ovibos moschatus)* grazed at times on the barren flats at the foot of the glacier, and alpine meadows bloomed on the hillsides above the great tongues of ice flowing out of the huge icefield at the headwaters of the Animas, Dolores, San Miguel, and Uncompahgre Rivers. Very likely there were no amphibians or reptiles in or around the Animas Valley then. As the glaciers melted back and temperatures warmed toward their present levels, species dispersed upstream from lower elevations. Many of the Arctic and northern Rocky Mountain animals that inhabited the area at the height of the glaciation became locally extinct; today only the pika *(Ochotona princeps)* and white-tailed ptarmigan remain to represent the glacial fauna. The changing of the guard is still continuing, in part because it may take thousands of years for species to expand their ranges and in part because the course of the climatic change fluctuates back and forth over periods of months, years, and centuries.

Many species living along the San Juan Skyway have very specific habitat requirements and are found only where these requirements are met. For example, cattails *(Typha latifolia)* and marsh wrens rarely live far from permanent water. Other species have such broad tolerances to physical factors that they could establish themselves at nearly any site if other species were not present. A mountain bluebird, for instance, seems equally at home on a sagebrush flat, in an area that has been clear-cut in the subalpine forest, or on a sunny alpine fellfield (a slope covered with large boulders). It can live and breed in any open place that has insects and other foods and a well-defended hole for a nesting site. A tansy aster (*Machaeranthera* spp.) thrives on heavy soils, sandy loams, and abandoned roadways consisting mainly of cobbles. It would probably cover any well-drained upland site, from sage desert to high pass, were no other species of plant present. Its actual distribution is limited to recently disturbed ground in sunny locations below timberline. An annual, it soon gives way to longer-lived species. Still other forms, such as lichens and the club moss (*Selaginella* spp.), can live on bare rock where no flowering plant could survive. And some organisms are completely dependent on the presence of another; the Abert's squirrel *(Sciurus aberti)*, for example, never persists for long away from the branches of the ponderosa pine *(Pinus ponderosa)*. Both physical and biotic factors can be important determinants of a species' range. Seldom does a single factor define an organism's distribution; more often the aggregate effect of many interacting factors sets the limits. We now should examine some of the major limiting factors in the San Juan Mountains.

PHYSICAL LIMITING FACTORS

The most powerful physical limiting factors are temperature and moisture. These vary greatly across the landscape, especially in relation to changes in elevation and topography. As moist air masses move inland from the Pacific Ocean and Gulf of Mexico, they strike the San Juan Mountains and are pushed upwards into the colder reaches of the atmosphere, where the air's water-holding capacity decreases and a large portion of the moisture falls as snow or rain. This augmented precipitation in the high country is the primary source of water for all human activities in the region, and it also supports extensive forests across the middle slopes of the mountains.

Average temperatures progressively decrease with increasing elevation. As a result of this gradient in precipitation and temperature, plant and animal species and biotic communities gradually change with altitude. A trip from the foothills to the top of one of the high peaks, representing a climb from 6,000 to 13,000 feet (1,800–4,000 m), is equivalent in many respects to a journey from southern Colorado to the edge of the Arctic Ocean in northern Canada. One experiences a similar pattern of climate changes and a comparable progression of vegetation zones by climbing either in latitude or in elevation. As a general rule of thumb, 1,000 feet (300 m) of elevational gain is comparable to 300 miles of northward travel.

At a certain point along this elevational gradient, the relative importance of the two limiting physical factors, temperature and moisture, changes. The threshold occurs roughly between 7,600 and 8,200 feet (2,300 and 2,500 m) in the San Juans. At lower elevations, scarce rainfall combined with hot summers makes water the principal limiting factor. Indeed, most terrestrial organisms in this semiarid zone have made remarkable adaptations to overcome or circumvent water stress. At higher elevations, water is still important, but acquiring enough heat energy to complete development and reproduction becomes ever more difficult. The depth and persistence of winter snowpack increase dramatically in this elevational zone; organisms must be able to cope with deep snow for several months each year.

Two additional factors — soil characteristics, traceable to the nature of the parent rocks, and topography — greatly accentuate the differences in water stress experienced at all elevations and often account for abrupt transitions from one type of biotic community to another. Several more or less distinctive zones of vegetation are apparent in the San Juan Mountains. Each zone lies within its own range of elevation, where conditions are suitable for growth of its component species. However, a given vegetation zone usually extends to lower elevations on north-facing slopes, where cooler and wetter conditions prevail, and on types of rock, such as sandstone, that form soils having high moisture-holding capacity. Similarly, each zone usually is found at higher elevations on south-facing slopes and on soils (such as those formed from shale) having low capacity to retain moisture. North-facing slopes are generally cooler and moister than south-facing slopes because the sun strikes the latter more directly most of the year. Valley bottoms at any elevation tend to be relatively cool and moist and support a distinctive assemblage of plants and animals that need more water than is available on the drier slopes and ridges.

A good spot to examine the effects of soil characteristics on the vegetation of an area is between Mancos and Dolores along Colorado 145, a few miles off the main highway. The land south of the road lies on Mancos Shale; the area north lies atop Dakota Sandstone. Ponderosa pine *(Pinus ponderosa)* dominates to the north, piñon *(Pinus edulis)* and juniper *(Juniperus* spp.) to the south. The biological differences in these communities are almost entirely due to the different soils of the two areas, which lie at the same altitude and share the same rainfall and temperature patterns.

Water moves through the sandy soils derived from the Dakota Sandstone much more rapidly than through the heavy clay soils arising from the Mancos Shale. A summer shower of a third of an inch (8 mm) will wet the sandy soil about 3 inches (75 mm) deep in twenty-four hours. Some of the moisture will move by gravity to even lower depths over time. The same amount of rain on Mancos soils will penetrate to less than half that depth, because the water will be tightly held by the clay particles. Much of the moisture in the surface soil will evaporate within days, and the deep layers will remain dry throughout much of the summer. The environments of the roots of plants in the two soil types thus differ radically even though the rainfall at the surface is nearly the same. Such effects contribute to the abrupt transitions from one community of organisms to another.

The steepness of a slope also is important for the vegetation. In many steep areas, especially at high elevations, snow avalanches occur frequently. Distorted aspens and stunted willows that can tolerate this kind of disturbance are commonly found growing in avalanche paths, although they are quite uncommon in the less disturbed areas nearby.

BIOLOGICAL LIMITING FACTORS

The presence and abundance of a species in a particular locality usually depends primarily on physical limiting factors. Most amphibians and reptiles, for instance, are only found within particular ranges in elevation, which suggests that temperature is the most important limiting factor for these animals. For many mammals and other groups of plants and animals, however, the presence or absence of other species may be more important limiting factors than temperature and moisture. For example, the valley pocket gopher *(Thomomys bottae)* occupies the low valleys and cuestas in the southern end of the Skyway area, leaving mounds and serpentine cylinders of soil at the surface as it mines for roots and living space. At some elevation in each major valley, however, possession of the soil passes to the northern pocket gopher *(Thomomys talpoides),* whose range extends even onto the thin soils of the alpine zone. There is almost no overlap in the ranges of these two species: it is almost as though a political border equivalent to the national boundaries of two countries had been established. No major change in climate or soil at the edge of their respective ranges can explain why one gopher species gives way to the other. The two gophers have nearly identical habits and requirements, but it would seem that there is room for just one of the two species at any one site.

Similarly, montane voles *(Microtus montanus)* occur almost exclusively in the tall tussocks of fescue grass (*Festuca* spp.) in mountain parks such as Big Bear Park, visible on Missionary Ridge from the pullout where U.S. Highway 550 crosses the railroad tracks at Shalona. Long-tailed voles *(Microtus longicaudus)* also inhabit the parks in the absence of the mountain vole, but they are restricted to clear-cuts, aspen groves, and shrubby grasslands when the montane vole is present.

Sometimes the competition is between native species and species introduced by humans. Domestic sheep carry lungworms that are frequently fatal when they infest young Rocky Mountain bighorn sheep *(Ovis canadensis)*. Therefore, the bighorns are largely absent from much of their former range now used as pastures for domestic sheep.

In contrast to the competitive interactions described above, cooperative, mutually dependent relationships exist between many pairs of species — neither can survive without the other. The yucca plant *(Yucca baccata)* and the yucca moth are good examples of this kind of symbiotic relationship. The female moth gathers pollen from yucca flowers, forms it into a ball, and carefully inserts it into another flower, thereby assuring pollination. Then she places just the right number of eggs into the ovary of the flower such that her offspring will be able to consume some but not all of the developing seeds. Yuccas rarely set seed without the moth to pollinate their flowers, and the moth can reproduce only in yucca flowers. Many kinds of flowering plants and insects have similar, mutually beneficial relationships.

ADAPTATIONS OF PLANTS AND ANIMALS TO LIMITING FACTORS

Plants and animals exhibit a variety of remarkable adaptations that enable them to cope with the kinds of limiting factors we have been discussing. Adaptations in animals may be illustrated via three contrasting species of amphibians.

Western spadefoot toads *(Scaphiopus multiplicatus)* inhabit many of the valleys below 7,000 feet (2,100 m), although they are seldom seen except following heavy summer thunderstorms. Their biggest problem in this semidesert environment is coping with the limited and unreliable supplies of water for breeding. They solve the problem by reproducing whenever water does become available and by having very rapid development so the young can mature before the temporary ponds dry up. After a heavy rainstorm, the 2- to 3-inch-long (6–8 cm), smooth-skinned, olive-drab animals make their way to temporary ponds, earthen tanks, and ditches. The females find mates by following the grating calls of the males. The eggs may hatch in fewer than three days, and the tadpoles grow quickly. The fastest-growing individuals assume predatory roles and consume their pondmates, thus growing even more rapidly on the easily assimilated diet of spadefoot flesh. Tadpoles can be ready for metamorphosis (the change into adult form) in as little as three weeks' time, having reached a length of 1 to 1.25 inches (2.5–3 cm). They move away from the pond as their parents already have done. Each one digs into the soil, coming to the surface to feed only when atmospheric humidity permits. When desiccation threatens, they dig even deeper and become dormant. Spadefoots are active less than 20 percent of the year and may remain dormant months or even years while they grow, develop eggs and sperm for future mating opportunities, and wait for favorable conditions to allow them to journey to the puddle where they were reared. They probably are limited to areas below 7,000 feet (2,100 m) because ponds at higher elevations do not provide the high temperatures required for their rapid development.

The life history of the tiger salamander *(Ambystoma tigrinum)* illustrates a more generalized adaptation to water limitations. The tiger salamander ranges from the basins and foothills to above timberline. It copes with the low temperatures at high elevations by extending its period of development. This adaptation restricts it to fairly permanent ponds and pools, in contrast to the spadefoot, which breeds in ephemeral ponds. Metamorphosis of the larval salamanders into the adult stage is triggered by oxygen stress, which elicits secretion of the iodine-containing hormone thyroxine. Some ponds are naturally deficient in iodine, and metamorphosis may be delayed indefinitely. Likewise, oxygen-rich water in deep ponds at high elevations may not stimulate the thyroid, allowing individuals to remain in the larval or juvenile state. These perpetually immature salamanders can grow larger than adults and may even reproduce while retaining their larval characteristics. However, they are unable to leave the water. The individuals that do metamorphose into adults can leave the pond and often wander great distances from the breeding site before descending into a burrow in soft earth.

A third type of adaptation in amphibians is seen in the boreal chorus frogs *(Pseudacris triseriata)*. These little terrestrial creatures attain lengths of around 1.5 inches (35 mm) and weights of less than 3 grams. They breed in temporary pools, seasonal marshy ponds, and cattail swamps and forage in nearby meadows and grasslands. Probably the most abundant amphibians in Colorado and among the most widely distributed, chorus frogs breed from above 11,900 feet (3,600 m) to below 5,000 feet (1,500 m) in the San Juan region. They solve the problem of low temperatures at high elevations by selecting heat-trapping ponds, foraging actively only during the warmest part of the day, and maturing while still at a small size. Breeding commences soon after the thaw, typically before the last snow and ice have disappeared from the marsh. The ponds favored by chorus frogs at high altitudes cool overnight to near freezing and often develop a thin covering of ice early each morning, but the water usually warms to between 77 and 86 degrees F (25–30°C) between noon and sundown. At low elevations chorus frogs are mainly active around dusk and dawn, and their breeding usually coincides with the season of high river water (or, nowadays, with irrigation flows).

Mammals also must cope with water and temperature limitations. Deer mice *(Peromyscus maniculatus)* are found almost everywhere along the San Juan Skyway. Indeed, campers must keep their stores of bread, grains, and snacks well protected or wake to find that the mice have transported amazing quantities of food into their own larders. This animal does not truly hibernate but depends on the food it has stockpiled to carry it through the winter. In years of heavy snow, populations may decline remarkably, presumably because long winters exhaust their food reserves. Probably some local populations are eliminated in exceptionally stormy years; the species' presence is soon restored by immigration from a population surviving nearby, usually at a lower elevation.

Lowland animals generally cope with water stress by avoiding the heat of the sun, by burrowing to find more humid conditions underground, by restricting their activities to evening or nighttime, or by making remarkable physiological adaptations for conserving water. The big ears of the black-tailed jackrabbit *(Lepus californicus)*, for example, permit it to transfer heat to the air by convection rather than evaporation; it also recovers much of the water evaporated from its air passages and lungs through condensation onto the cooled surfaces of its nasal cavities and subsequent resorption. Most remarkable, perhaps, is that its body temperature falls several degrees below optimum in the cool early morning, thus offsetting heat gain as it heats up later during the day and avoiding the evaporative water loss that would otherwise be required.

All the organisms in the lowlands have equally effective strategies for conserving water, an absolute necessity in an arid environment where ground temperatures routinely exceed 100 degrees F (40°C) for considerable periods each day during the warm season and where no rain may fall for weeks on end. Some of the larger animals and birds may be able to travel considerable distances to the few permanent streams or springs or to depressions in the rocky outcrops that hold water for extended periods after rains, but most lowland resident animals must rely on their food to make up any deficit in their water balance. Lizards, for example, obtain a small quantity of water with every insect ingested, and their kidneys excrete wastes in a form requiring almost no water. Pocket mice (*Perognathus* spp.) and kangaroo rats (*Dipodomys* spp.) consume carbohydrate-rich foods or select seeds rich in oils and fats, which yield metabolic water as they are broken down inside the cells of the body. Pocket mice also have a behavioral ploy for coping with drought: for example, in periods of both low food supply and drought, the pocket mouse spends a portion of its time in a state of torpor, conserving energy and breathing so slowly that almost no water is lost through its lungs. It also may spend less time searching for food on the exposed surface of the ground and thus stretches its resources until the hard times pass.

THE ROLE OF DISTURBANCE

The broad patterns in distribution of species and the zones of vegetation primarily reflect the underlying patterns of geology, topography, soil, and climate. Superimposed upon these broad patterns are others brought about by past disturbances (for example, fires, avalanches, or rock slides) and interactions among species (for example, the effects of browsing elk or of tree-killing bark beetles).

The boundaries between communities along a gradient of elevation are usually gradual; one type of vegetation blends into the next. Boundaries created by disturbances often are very sharp, however, as are boundaries between communities on two very different kinds of soil or between those on a steep north-facing slope and a steep south-facing slope.

Many kinds of disturbances are natural processes that have shaped the vegetation of the San Juan Mountains for thousands of years. Though they usually entail the death or injury of many individual plants, they may actually enhance the overall biological diversity of the area by creating new kinds of habitats and temporarily reducing the dominance of the most successful species, which otherwise might crowd out competitors. Consequently, most natural disturbances should be regarded not as disasters but as integral parts of the ecological system.

Humans also disturb the vegetation, of course, sometimes in ways that mimic the natural disturbances to which the system is well adapted. Thus, some level of grazing by livestock, cutting of timber, and hunting of game, if wisely planned and well regulated, may be no more deleterious to the integrity and stability of the San Juan Mountain ecosystems than the natural disturbances to which it has long been subjected. Unfortunately, many human activities in these mountains during the last century have been far greater in intensity and duration than natural disturbances, and the scars left by these activities are still evident. Nevertheless, in traveling the San Juan Skyway, one usually is struck less by the changes wrought by humans than by the remarkable diversity, resilience, and beauty of the natural landscape.

BIODIVERSITY IN THE SAN JUAN MOUNTAINS

The presence of the Rocky Mountain Cordillera, of which the San Juan Mountains are an impressive part, creates gradients in local temperature and annual precipitation. The range's high altitudes allow organisms adapted to conditions of the far north to extend their ranges to much lower latitudes than would otherwise be possible, bringing them into juxtaposition with organisms inhabiting arid regions of the southwest. The species of the two regions mix along the climatic gradients in the mountains.

In general, diversity decreases as elevation increases. A small deviation from the overall trend occurs in the forests at middle elevations, which support a variety of arboreal species, such as Abert's squirrel, chickaree, and pine marten *(Martes americana)*. A number of widespread species penetrate into the alpine zone while maintaining strong populations at low elevations. In fact, the majority of mammals encountered on the highest peaks belong to species equally at home on the arid plateaus and grasslands. However, very few of the northern species extend into lower elevations in the San Juans.

A dramatic example of the process of subtraction and diminished diversity is provided by the amphibians and reptiles. A semi-desert area just 25 miles southwest of Cortez harbors twelve species of lizards, at least ten species of snakes, and at least six species of amphibians, all native, an assemblage approaching the diversity of that great herpetofaunal center, the Sonoran Desert. By the time one has climbed to the top of Hesperus Hill or entered Rico, however, a determined search of the slopes and valleys turns up only two kinds of lizards, no more than two kinds of snakes, and perhaps four kinds of amphibians. All the reptiles would drop out of the list with another rise of 2,000 feet (600 m) in elevation, and only two amphibians reach to the treeline in a few locations. No reptiles or amphibians reach the summits of the fourteeners (i.e., 14,000-foot-high peaks).

Although the foothills and basins may appear barren and inhospitable compared to the green uplands, they harbor the majority of species of plants and animals to be found in this corner of Colorado. The diversity on any one acre tends to be low, but every rise and draw, ridge and canyon, outcrop and flat provides significantly varied conditions, permitting the region to support a great variety of species of both plants and animals. This pattern is evident in Table 10.1, which lists the vertebrate species found in each elevational zone in the San Juan Mountains. Apparently temperature is a more significant limiting factor for most vertebrate species than water, as the high elevations have ample water but low temperatures. Total land area also limits species diversity, with more species usually present in a larger area if all other factors are constant. The

Table 10.1   Numbers of vertebrate animal species at different elevations in the western San Juan Mountains and adjacent lowlands, Numbers in parentheses include extinct species and those whose ranges extend up to the margin of the San Juan region.

feet meters	4,600–5,899 1,400–1,799	5,900–7,199 1,800–2,199	7,200–8,499 2,200–2,599	8,500–9,799 2,600–2,999	9,800–11,100 3,000–3,400
AMPHIBIANS					
frogs, toads	7	6	4	3	1 (2)
salamanders	1	1	1	1	1
REPTILES					
lizards	13	8	4	3	1
snakes	13 (14)	9	2 (5)	4	0 (1)
MAMMALS					
INSECTIVORES					
shrews	2	3 (4)	3	3	3
CARNIVORES					
coyotes, foxes	4 (5)	3 (4)	3 (4)	3 (4)	3 (4)
bears	1	1 (2)	1 (2)	1 (2)	1 (2)
raccoon, ringtail	2	2	1	(1)	
weasels, badgers, skunks	7	7	6 (7)	6 (7)	6 (7)
cats	2	2	2	2 (3)	2 (3)
LAGOMORPHS					
rabbits	1	2	1	1	0
hares	1	1	3	2	2
pika	0	0	0	1	1
RODENTS					
porcupine	1	1	1	1	1
beaver	1	1	1	1	1
marmots	1	1	1	1	1
ground squirrels	5	4	4	3	3
prarire dogs	2	2	0	0	0
tree squirrels	0	1	2	2	1
pocket mice	2	2	0	0	0
kangaroo rats	1	1	2	1	1
gophers	1	2	2	1	1
harvest mice	1	1	0	0	0
deermice	4	4	3	1	1
grasshopper mice	1	1	0	0	0
packrats	3	2	1	1	1
voles	2	3	3	4	3
muskrats	1	1	1	1	1
jumping mice	0	1	1	1	1
UNGULATES					
pronghorn	1	1	(1)	0	0
deer	1 (2)	2 (3)	2	2	2
sheep	1	1	1	1	1

land area above 10,000 feet (3,000 m) is only one one-hundredth the area below that elevation, which further reduces the number of high-elevation species in the San Juans relative to low-elevation species.

MAJOR VEGETATION ZONES IN THE SAN JUAN MOUNTAINS

Moving from the semiarid basins and foothills to the frigid summits of the high peaks, one progresses through a sequence of vegetation zones (Fig. 10.1). The lowest elevations in the basins consist of greasewood-shadscale shrub-steppe and Great Basin sagebrush shrub-steppe (Kuchler 1964). Moving higher up into the foothills, one passes through piñon-juniper woodland, the mountain shrub community, and ponderosa pine–oak–Douglas fir forest. These communities are discussed in Chapter 11 (also see Points of Interest 1, 84, 138, 141, 143).

Above the foothills, one encounters mixed conifer forests, aspen groves, and mountain parks or meadows on the middle slopes of the mountains, above which stand the spruce-fir forests in the subalpine environment just below timberline. The highest peaks and ridges are capped with alpine meadows and fellfields lying above timberline. These high mountain communities are the subject of Chapter 12 (also see Points of Interest 29, 36, 43, 58, 88, 116).

Narrow strips of riparian vegetation slice through the vegetation zones of the foothills and mountains along streams and moist canyon bottoms. Riparian communities also thrive around lakes, ponds, and other wetlands. The unique environment and assemblage of species in riparian zones and the ecology of the major rivers are discussed in Chapter 13 (also see Points of Interest 15, 31, 56, 105, 128, 147).

REFERENCES

Kuchler, A. W., 1964. *Potential natural vegetation of the conterminous United States.* American Geographical Society Special Publication 36, 116 pp.

Pielou, E. C., 1991. *After the ice age: The return of life to glaciated North America.* Chicago: University of Chicago Press, 366 pp.

CHAPTER 11

BIOTIC COMMUNITIES OF THE SEMIARID FOOTHILLS AND VALLEYS

LISA FLOYD-HANNA, ALBERT W. SPENCER, AND WILLIAM H. ROMME

The semiarid foothills and valleys lying between 4,500 and 9,000 feet (1,400–2,750 m) occupy the largest area of the San Juan region. We will discuss the low-lying and broadest valleys, the mesas and cuestas, and the slopes and narrow valleys of the true foothills in turn, as though there were a uniform progression from one to the other. (In actuality, travelers continually pass from one to another as they drive the Skyway.) Five types of communities will be discussed: greasewood-shadscale shrub-steppe, Great Basin sagebrush shrub-steppe, piñon-juniper woodland, the mountain shrub community, and ponderosa pine–oak–Douglas fir forest. The communities, in the order listed, tend to occupy progressively higher elevations or better soil conditions.

Piñon-juniper woodland, Great Basin sagebrush-steppe, and greasewood-shadscale communities occur along less than 10 percent of the San Juan Skyway loop, but they are characteristic of the major area of the Colorado Plateau and the canyon country lying south, west, and north of the San Juan Mountains. Within this broad geographic region, the total area covered by arid vegetation types dwarfs that encompassed by the montane and alpine zones that dominate the Skyway scenery. The shrub-steppe habitats are also the ones most heavily exploited and altered by humans. From prehistoric times, people have lived, foraged, and farmed in the areas covered by these communities, which include the greatest expanses of arable land in the Four Corners region. The streams passing through them have been dammed and the waters spread out on irrigated fields so that cultivated grains and forage have displaced hundreds of thousands of acres of big sagebrush vegetation. Generations of cattle and sheep have stripped away many of the native grasses and forbs over much of this area. Indeed, many of the herbs found here are exotic weed species that have invaded the denuded ground. For instance, cheatgrass *(Bromus tectorum)*, a Eurasian weed, is a dominant grass in many parts of the Four Corners region.

SHRUB-STEPPE COMMUNITIES

Two kinds of semiarid shrub-steppe communities cover most of the area at the lowest elevations. *Steppe* is a Russian word for semiarid grassland. Low places in the major valleys, especially those carved out of marine shales such as the Mancos, have heavy, poorly drained, saline soils. These soils support greasewood *(Sarcobatus vermiculatus)*, shadscale *(Atriplex confertifolia)*, and other halophytic (salt-tolerant) plants such as sea blight (*Suaeda* spp.) and saltgrass *(Distichlis spicata)*. This greasewood-shadscale shrub-steppe community is widespread along the lower reaches of the San Juan Mountains but along the Skyway occurs only east of Cortez. To accommodate the additional water stress salts impose, halophytic plants secrete excess salt from their leaves and/or selectively exclude salt as their roots take up water. Both of these survival adaptations have a cost in metabolic energy, so the halophytes usually grow more slowly than plants that do not need to cope with excessive salt in the soil. Pluck and chew a leaf from the shadscale; you will taste the salt unless recent rains have washed away the deposits.

Annual species also constitute an important portion of the biota of both the greasewood and the sagebrush communities. The seeds of annuals very effectively meet the problem of avoiding water stress; they can lie dormant in the soil for months or even years until adequate rainfall stimulates their germination.

Great Basin sagebrush shrub-steppe communities develop in low-lying areas having deep, well-drained soils. The dominants are mainly grasses such as blue grama *(Bouteloua gracilis)* and galleta *(Hilaria jamesii),* a variety of other herbs, and big sagebrush *(Artemisia tridentata).* The sagebrush is easily recognized by its silvery foliage and pungent odor, whereas greasewood has pale green leaves and long, straw-colored spines.

Before the arrival of European agriculturalists, sagebrush shrub-steppe generally covered all of the low areas having deep, rich, well-drained soils in the San Juan region. Such soils often have been deposited over centuries by wind, most often on sandstone strata such as the Dakota Sandstone or on alluvial terraces along the major streams. The red soils exposed in the dryland wheat and bean fields north and west of Cortez and south of Durango are representative; they were once covered mainly by sagebrush. Sagebrush still dominates much of the Great Sage Plain around Cortez, whose underpinnings are Dakota Sandstone.

An important associate of big sagebrush is rabbitbrush *(Chrysothamnus nauseosus).* Though shorter-lived than big sage, this plant germinates more readily. It attains its greatest densities in recently disturbed sites. In winters, when vole numbers are high and herbaceous forage unavailable, the rodents eat the bark of rabbitbrush and may girdle nearly every stem. Sagebrush is scarcely touched and thus takes over.

The most obvious vertebrates in these communities are rabbits, prairie dogs, ground squirrels, birds, and lizards because they are active during the day. Most of the other mammals and snakes are nocturnal or so wary as to escape detection. A number of amphibians are also present but generally are active only during rainy seasons (for example, the spadefoot toad discussed in Chapter 10).

The best place to view the greasewood-shadscale shrub-steppe is east of Cortez along U.S. 160 in the valley of McElmo Creek. Great Basin big sagebrush shrub-steppe can be observed west of Mancos and north and west of Cortez, although much of this habitat has been converted to cultivated fields or pasturelands. An ecologically similar but floristically different sagebrush community lies west of Ridgway, north of the road, on Horsefly Mesa.

PIÑON-JUNIPER WOODLANDS

North America experienced 30 million years of drought from the late Paleocene into the Oligocene. Plants lacking drought tolerance became extinct, and the arid flora known as the Madro-Tertiary Geoflora survived. It is believed that the ancestral piñon-juniper association developed among this oak, locust, and chaparral shrub community. Piñon *(Pinus edulis)* gradually made a northward climb into the semiarid region now known as the Southwest. Piñon pines and their associated junipers bear witness to the gradual changes that allowed plants to survive in the arid southwestern climate. Piñon pine usually shares canopy dominance with one of two species of juniper, the Utah juniper *(Juniperus osteosperma)* or the Rocky Mountain juniper *(Juniperus scopulorum)*. This vegetation type was tremendously successful and now occupies approximately 42 million acres (17 million ha) of the Southwest at elevations of 5,000 to 7,750 feet (1515–2350 m). At elevations lower (and drier) than the piñon-juniper belt, few trees of any species survive except along streams.

Utah juniper is more abundant in the lower elevations of the piñon-juniper belt, whereas Rocky Mountain juniper most often occurs in the higher reaches. Junipers are often called "cedars" because of their aromatic wood, with an odor reminiscent of true cedar. They are slow-growing, often gnarled trees, and their berrylike cones are small and tight, housing from one to four tough seeds. These fruits may pass through the digestive tract of animals that feed on them, and the seed emerges in feces, ready to germinate into a new juniper tree. Seedlings are bluish in tint and typically succeed under mature piñons and other "nurse" plants.

Few trees exhibit such an array of drought-tolerating adaptations as do piñons. The leaves, shaped as needles, expose little evaporative surface, and that which is exposed is covered by thick wax with indentations protecting the stomata. (Stomata, openings in leaves that allow uptake of carbon dioxide from the air, are essential for photosynthesis but also allow water to escape from the leaf interior.) Indeed, pines are among the most drought-tolerant of all conifers in terms of their ability to photosynthesize under drought conditions. Their cells can withstand water loss, so they tolerate having their stomata open well into the dry summer months. Some evidence suggests that pines may photosynthesize at low rates even in winter months, when soil moisture freezes, creating a different type of drought.

Piñon pine produces large seeds, which, if placed in a suitable site, support growth of a large seedling until its roots reach soil water. Piñon pines and their associated junipers have been important to human populations throughout the Southwest, including the Anasazi, who from A.D. 400 to 700 settled as corn agriculturalists in this region. One major reason is that piñons provide large, edible seeds with thin coats. This rich resource becomes available in the early fall, and a large crop can be stored for winter.

The timing of piñon seed production is interesting. Instead of producing many seeds annually, all of the trees in a given geographic area wait until a certain point and then reproduce prolifically at the same time. This delay in the cycle is known as *masting* and, in piñon pines, occurs roughly every four to seven years. The physiological cause of masting is not easily explained. It may be that trees are "exhausted" internally by the reproductive effort and require years of growth to replenish internal supplies of energy and nutrients. Indeed, tree rings are significantly smaller during the reproductive year (Dickman and Kozlowski 1969), indicating a drain on internal resources and a trade-off between growth and reproduction. Nevertheless, it is mysterious how trees of all ages and developmental stages tend to mast simultaneously. Perhaps they respond to an environmental cue such as low temperature (Forcella 1981) or rainfall.

However, the survival value of masting for the piñon is understood: seed vectors — birds, such as piñon jays, and small mammals — eat their fill of seeds and cache the excess in the ground (Ligon 1978). Some of the cached seeds will not be retrieved and are essentially planted. The jays cache seeds in particularly good sites, increasing the success of seedlings in dry, difficult environments. Piñon seeds that fall to the ground and do not have cover or shade rarely survive. Thus, masting ensures that seeds are placed in "safe," germinable sites. Without the masting strategy, birds and mammals might simply eat all of the seeds produced each year (Vander Wall and Balda 1977).

Masting apparently is good for both the piñon tree and for the animals that function as seed vectors, for there is a remarkable co-evolutionary relationship between them. Piñon jays flock to piñon woodlands that are masting. Piñon trees display their seeds at an angle that enables piñon jays readily to retrieve the seed. The jays distinguish between those that are full of nutritive tissue and those that are not by weighing the seeds via a technique called "bill-clicking" (Ligon and Martin 1974). The seed coat also "advertises" seed quality, in that dark seeds are full whereas light ones may not contain nutritive tissue (Floyd and Hanna 1990). During the masting years, piñon jays breed in late winter and late summer (Ligon 1978).

What about human populations? Can they use such a variable food source? Data collected on the Dolores Archeological Project show that, as agriculture intensified, the use of piñon as food diminished, and the trees were used increasingly for construction and firewood (Floyd and Kohler 1990). Thus, whereas people of the Great Basin made consistent of single-leaf piñon *(Pinus monophylla),* which does not mast in the same way as the Colorado piñon, the Anasazi appear to have used Colorado piñon mainly as a supplemental food whenever masting made the seeds available.

Juniper woodlands have expanded into adjacent grasslands in historic times (West 1988). Although this tree had been confined to rocky habitats, it is now found also in fine-textured soils, where it is "invading" grasslands. There is some controversy about the exact causes of this recent spread of woodlands. It is likely that a cluster of conditions, including stress from overgrazing, periodic droughts, and fire suppression (fire kills trees but stimulates grasses), have assisted in the woodland invasion.

Representative stands of piñon-juniper woodland occur around Durango and Mancos, between Cortez and Dolores, along the San Miguel Canyon, and near Ridgway. The southern end of Mesa Verde National Park supports some of the best examples of this type.

THE MOUNTAIN SHRUB COMMUNITY

The mountain shrub community fills the vistas at many points along the Skyway. A shrub generally is a woody plant attaining a height less than 16 feet (5 m) and having many stems. Several of the species found in the mountain shrub community can attain tree size under optimum conditions, but they occur most often as shrubs.

An amazing variety of low-growing woody plant species make up the mountain shrub community. More than thirty-two species of true shrubs have been tabulated in the Durango area (Table 11.1). If native semishrubs (plants with a woody base and herbaceous top, or very low woody plants) and exotic introductions such as wild apple trees are included, the number of species approaches fifty. Without question, the mountain shrub community in southwestern Colorado is one of the most diverse forms of vegetation in the state.

The species are an admixture of forms important in adjacent communities — for example, Gambel oak *(Quercus gambelii)* from the ponderosa pine–oak–Douglas fir woodlands and antelope bitterbrush *(Purshia tridentata)* from the piñon-juniper community. A number of species, such as chokecherry *(Prunus virginianus),* hawthorn *(Crataegus* spp.), and box elder *(Acer negundo),* are shared with the riparian woodlands of the valleys; a few, such as squaw-apple *(Peraphyllum ramossissimum)* and fendlerbush *(Fendlera rupicola),* are characteristic of the mountain shrub community and abundant only there. The most important species, based on number of stems or area covered, include Gambel oak, mountain-mahogany *(Cercocarpus montanus),* fendlerbush, antelope bitterbrush, squaw apple, snowberry *(Symphoricarpos oreophilus),* serviceberry *(Amelanchier utahensis),* currants *(Ribes* spp.), barberry *(Berberis fendleri),* rose *(Rosa* spp.), skunkbush or squawbush *(Rhus trilobata),* banana yucca *(Yucca baccata),* narrowleaf yucca *(Y. angustissima),* and Davis's prickly pear *(Opuntia davisii;* an arborescent form), all of which occur at most sites.

Table 11.1 Percent cover of shrub species on slopes differing in aspect and substrate attributes. Samples were taken in the vicinity of Durango, Colorado.

Location	College Heights	Chapman Hill	College Heights	College Heights	Leyden Drive	Leyden Drive
Aspect	SS	NE	NW	NW	SSW	NNE
Substrate	Alluvium	Alluvium	Alluvium	Mancos	Mancos	Mancos
Species						
Gambel oak	0	13	17	56	77	70
Mountain-mahogany	0	26	32	17	12	18
Snowberry	0	0	3	0	0	6
Serviceberry	0	0.2	1	10	0	3
Barberry	0	0	0	0	0	1
Rose	0	0	0	0	0	1
Fendlerbush	29	16	15	14	0	0
Squaw-apple	9	24	18	0	11	0
Skunkbush	5	0	0	0	0	0
Bitterbrush	12	0	0	0	0	0
Big sagebrush	15	13	8	0	0	0
Horsebrush	2	0	0	0	0	0
Snakeweed	1	0	0	0	0	0
Prickly pear	1	0	0	0	0	0
Banana yucca	22	8	6	0	0	0
Narrowleaf yucca	0.2	0	0	0	0	0
Others	3	0	0	0	0	0
Bare	59	50	6.4	8	57	27

Most mountain shrub stands are found on steep or moderately steep slopes of 10 degrees or more. The local abundance of each species varies widely according to elevation, slope aspect, slope angle, soil type, water availability, adjacent plant communities, age of the stand, and past history of the site. On the slopes of the mesa where Fort Lewis College lies, fendlerbush, banana yucca, big sagebrush, bitterbrush, squaw-apple, and skunkbush are dominant components of a steep south-facing slope of alluvium; all except fendlerbush are absent from a nearby steep north-facing slope on a shale-derived substrate. The most important species on the latter site were oak, mountain-mahogany, fendlerbush, serviceberry, and snowberry. Even on the same substrate, the difference arising out of northern versus southern exposures is clear-cut (Table 11.1).

The variation in species composition between north-facing and south-facing slopes arises primarily because of the differences in soil water, snow loading in winter, and water availability during late spring and early summer. Steep south slopes are bare through much of the winter; the snow sublimates and melts away, and the surface becomes quite warm on sunny days. In contrast, snow accumulates throughout the winter on north slopes. Most of the water content of the snowpack soaks into the soil during the spring melt, and the plants on the north slope typically enjoy ample water supply during May and early June, a period frequently deficient in rain or altogether dry.

Characteristic animals of the mountain shrub community include the brush mouse *(Peromyscus boylei),* gray fox *(Urocyon cinereoargenteus),* rufous-sided towhee, blue-gray gnatcatcher, scrub jay, and sharp-shinned hawk. Many of the shrubs produce edible fruits attractive to various birds and mammals. The shrubs also support a rich assemblage of insects, which in turn support a diverse assortment of insect-eating mammals, birds, and reptiles.

One of the most interesting questions still puzzling biologists working in the San Juan Mountains is the unexpected predominance of the mountain shrub community over extensive areas at elevations of 6,000 to 9,500 feet (1,800–2,700 m), where piñon-juniper or ponderosa pine–oak–Douglas fir woodlands might be expected. Earlier workers attributed the situation to burning by native Americans (see Brown 1958) or concluded that the type represents a self-sustaining plant association (see Kuchler 1964). After studying the vegetation following fires in Mesa Verde National Park, Erdman (1970) concluded that mountain shrub stands represented a stage in a progression toward piñon-juniper woodland.

We also hypothesize that most mountain shrub vegetation constitutes a stage in the recovery of an area disturbed by fire or other agents and that the shrubland eventually will be replaced by woodland or forest if the process continues long enough. The reason shrub communities cover such a large proportion of the landscape is that fires and other disturbances usually recur at intervals shorter than the time required for establishment and maturation of fully stocked stands of trees. These disturbances are of a kind and intensity that precludes the emergence of forest or woodland but only briefly interrupts or retards the recovery and development of shrub communities. Recurring disturbances thus operate to maintain the shrub stage of succession and discourage the development of trees, even though the soils and climate are favorable for forests.

Fire is the most obvious agent of disturbance in mountain shrub communities (Brown 1958, Erdman 1970), but snow may be important also. Snow in the San Juans characteristically comes as feathery, wet, sticky flakes accompanied by little wind. On south-facing slopes, sunlight after a storm melts the snow or loosens it sufficiently to slide it off the shrubs and trees. The plants on north-facing slopes, however, may not receive the sun's direct rays for several weeks in early to mid-winter, and the snowpack builds up and weighs the branches down. By the time the sun is high enough to shine down the slope, most of the energy is reflected off the deep pack. All winter long the wet, heavy snow slowly creeps down the hill, crushing the plants beneath it. As it settles and re-crystallizes, it also acquires a firm hold on the branches. When the thaw comes, wet snow may roar downslope in avalanches, tearing plants out by the roots. Only the most limber and flexible plants can survive such a snowslide without being broken or uprooted. Trees such as piñons suffer much more than shrubs do. Evidence for the importance of this process comes from a field study carried out by Fort Lewis College students: the largest stems of most shrubs other than oaks on north-facing slopes were found to be less than ten years old, whereas stems of the same species on south-facing slopes could be as old as thirty-five years. Furthermore, the north-slope plants had skirts of numerous dead, depressed branches, whereas most of the branches of south-slope plants remained upright even after death.

Many problems remain in understanding fully the ecology of the mountain shrub community. For example, there are dense piñon-juniper groves at the lower end of Mesa Verde that have not burned for centuries, whereas the upper end of Mesa Verde has burned repeatedly during the last 150 years and is covered by mountain shrubs. Why has fire history been so different in these two adjacent areas that differ only slightly in climate and soils? One surely must invoke a multiplicity of factors to account for this observation, including possible differences in the probabilities of ignition and spread of fire.

The most important difference may be that piñon-juniper forests have a relatively small amount of fuel on the ground and a less continuous distribution over the surface. Compared to an open stand of shrubs, a mature piñon-juniper stand has scant herbaceous cover beneath and between the trees, and the mat of dead leaves and branches under piñons and junipers is commonly shallower and decomposes more rapidly than that under Gambel oak or ponderosa pine stands. This may be so because piñon and juniper usually grow on more alkaline substrates than oak or ponderosa pine; these substrates support more abundant and more active soil microorganisms. The fallen leaves of piñon and juniper also form a more compact layer on the ground than do the leaves of oak and ponderosa pine; the former may dry more slowly, decompose more rapidly, and burn less readily. The upshot is that mountain shrub stands may be inherently more flammable than piñon-juniper stands except under extreme weather conditions, when spectacular fires can occur in piñon-juniper forests (for example, the Long Mesa burn in Mesa Verde in 1989). Some piñon-juniper groves also may be "protected" from fire by adjacent cliffs or sparsely vegetated areas through which fire cannot spread. Ecologists remain unable to give an entirely satisfactory answer to the question of why mountain shrub communities occupy particular sites that could potentially support woodlands, but research is in progress.

The mountain shrub community is prominent west of Durango toward the crest of Hesperus Hill, east of Mancos descending Mancos Hill, north of Dolores in the river canyon, and in the northern portion of Mesa Verde National Park. Travelers will encounter less extensive stands along much of the Skyway route intermingled with other vegetation.

PONDEROSA PINE–OAK–DOUGLAS FIR WOODLANDS

The transition zone between the upper reaches of the semiarid foothills and the moist forests of the higher mountain slopes contains a variety of plant communities with species from both higher and lower elevations. Nearly pure stands of ponderosa pine *(Pinus ponderosa)* can be found on sandstone substrates at 6,500 to 8,000 feet (1,970–2,400 m). Shrubby Gambel oak *(Quercus gambelii)* commonly forms the major groundcover under ponderosa pine, but it grows to tree size in some favorable sites. Douglas fir *(Pseudotsuga menziesii)* grows best on cool, moist, north-facing slopes at these lower elevations, though it grows on a variety of sites in the mixed conifer forests higher on the mountain slopes. Depending on local soil and microclimatic conditions, a variety of grasses and wildflowers may be found in ponderosa pine–oak–Douglas fir woodlands. Look for the wild candytuft *(Thlaspi montana)* in early spring, the yellow mule's ears (*Wyethia* spp.) and balsamroot *(Balsamorrhiza sagittata)* in early summer, the showy red beardtongue *(Penstemon barbatus)* in midsummer, and a variety of white and purple asters (*Aster* spp.) in late summer.

Most of the ponderosa pine forests in southwestern Colorado were heavily logged around the turn of the twentieth century. Because they were readily accessible and the wood was of high quality for buildings, mine timbers, railroad ties, and the like, these were among the first forests to be cut by the European settlers in the region. If you look closely in a ponderosa pine forest today, you usually can see the old stumps of the nineteenth-century forest (Fig. 11.1). The majority of living ponderosas in these stands appear to have become established since the turn of the century. Many trees date from 1900 to 1930, a period when abundant seed crops coincided with favorable spring rains and when most of the large, old trees had recently been removed by loggers (White 1985) (Fig. 11.2).

Commonly the old stumps are less numerous but larger in diameter than the second-growth trees, suggesting that the pre-settlement forests were more open and contained larger trees than the ponderosa pine forests of today. Indeed, early accounts from this region frequently refer to ponderosa pine forests as "parklike," with abundant grass in the openings between trees. Today, with the dense tree canopy and the thick layer of pine needles on the ground, grasses and wildflowers probably are less abundant than they used to be (Covington and Moore 1994).

The major reason for the openness of the original ponderosa pine forests probably was fire (Cooper 1960). Tree-ring studies

Fig. 11.1   Young ponderosa pine forest near Dolores, Colorado, and stumps left by heavy logging in the early 1900s. Today's second-growth trees are denser and smaller than the trees that inhabited this forest prior to logging. Average diameter of stumps in this area is 27 inches (68 cm); average diameter of living trees today is around 8 inches (20 cm). Moreover, the pre-1900 trees were distinctly clumped, with grassy open areas between clumps. The open nature of this forest formerly was maintained by low-intensity fires that occurred every five to thirty-five years prior to 1900. Since 1900 there have been no fires in the area. The combination of fire suppression and heavy logging at the turn of the century has profoundly altered most of the low-elevation forests of the San Juan Mountains. Photo by W. H. Romme.

Fig. 11.2 Logging operation near Dolores, Colorado, in 1936. By the end of World War II, nearly all of the accessible, large trees had been removed from the ponderosa pine forests of the San Juan Mountains. In addition to trucks, narrow-gauge railroads were extensively used to haul logs out of the forest. Photo by J. W. Smith, Jr. Courtesy U.S. Forest Service.

have revealed that these forests burned every decade or so in the centuries before the onset of effective fire control in the twentieth century. Lightning evidently ignited most of the blazes, although native Americans may have set them in some times and places. Because the fires were relatively frequent, only small amounts of dead needles, branches, and other fuels accumulated between successive burns, and the fires were of relatively low intensity. Light blazes of this kind did not injure the thick-barked adult ponderosa pines, but they killed small trees and shrubs and prevented woody plants from filling the openings between the large adult trees. Here and there a site would be missed by fire for several decades, and in these places new ponderosa pines could grow to such a size that fires no longer injured them.

Clearly, the combination of logging and fire suppression has profoundly changed the structure of ponderosa pine forests in the San Juan Mountains. It is no longer feasible to allow uncontrolled fires to burn near towns and other settlements, but land managers are examining ways of restoring the natural ecological role of fire in ponderosa pine forests through a prescribed-fire program, in which fires are intentionally ignited during periods when cool, moist weather makes burns more controllable.

Ponderosa pine forests support a variety of wildlife species. Elk *(Cervus elaphus)* may be found here in the winter, and mule deer *(Odocoileus hemionus)* are year-round residents. Coyotes *(Canis latrans),* bobcats *(Lynx rufus),* and mountain lions *(Felis concolor)* are present but rarely seen. Most conspicuous are the noisy flocks of the small white-breasted nuthatches and mountain chickadees that glean insects from the foliage, the violet-green swallows catching insects on the wing, and the Abert's squirrels that thrive only in ponderosa pine forests and whose presence often can be detected from the sprigs of pine needles that they leave around the bases of the trees.

Ponderosa pine–oak–Douglas fir woodlands occur at several points between Telluride and Ouray and midway along the Animas Valley north of Durango.

REFERENCES

Brown, H. E., 1958. Gambel oak in west-central Colorado. *Ecology,* v. 39, pp. 317–327.

Cooper, C. F., 1960. Changes in vegetation, structure, and growth of southwestern pine forest since white settlement. *Ecological Monographs,* v. 30, pp. 129–164.

Covington, W. W., and M. M. Moore, 1994. Southwestern ponderosa forest structure: Changes since Euro-American settlement. *Journal of Forestry,* v. 92, no. 1, pp. 39–47.

Dickman, E. I., and T. T. Kozlowski, 1969. Seasonal variations in reserve and structural components of Pinus resinosa cones, *American Journal of Botany,* v. 56, no. 5, pp. 515–520.

Erdman, J. A., 1970. *Piñon-juniper succession after natural fires on residual soils of Mesa Verde, Colorado.* Provo, UT: Brigham Young University Science Bulletin, Biological Series, no. 2, 24 pp.

Floyd, M. L., and D. D. Hanna, 1990. Cone indehiscence in a peripheral population of piñon pines. *Southwestern Naturalist,* v. 35, no. 2, pp. 146–150.

Floyd, M. L., and T. Kohler, 1990. Prehistoric use and modern productivity of piñon pine in the Dolores archeological project area, southwestern Colorado. *Economic Botany,* v. 44, no. 2, pp. 141–156.

Forcella, F., 1981. Ovulate cone production in piñon: Negative exponential relationship with late summer temperature. *Ecology,* v. 62, no. 2, pp. 488–491.

Ligon, J. D., 1978. Reproductive interdependence of piñon jays and piñon pines. *Ecological Monographs,* v. 48, pp. 111–126.

Ligon, J. D., and D. J. Martin, 1974. Piñon seed assessment by the piñon jays, *Gymnohinus cyanocephalus. Animal Behavior,* v. 22, pp. 421–429.

Vander Wall, S. B., and R. P. Balda, 1977. Coadaptation of the Clark's Nutcracker and the piñon pine for efficient seed harvest and dispersal. *Ecological Monographs,* v. 47, no. 1, pp. 91–111.

West, N. E., 1988. Intermountain deserts, shrub steppes, and woodlands, in M. C. Barbour and W. D. Billings, eds., *North American terrestrial vegetation,* London: Cambridge University Press, 434 pp.

White, A. S., 1985. Presettlement regeneration patterns in a southwestern ponderosa pine stand. *Ecology,* v. 66, pp. 589–594.

CHAPTER 12

BIOTIC COMMUNITIES OF THE COOL MOUNTAINS

DAVID W. JAMIESON, WILLIAM H. ROMME, AND PRESTON SOMERS

Forest vegetation is restricted to areas of relatively high precipitation and moderate temperatures. Most of the forests in the San Juan Mountains are dominated by various species of evergreen coniferous trees. Evergreens are especially well adapted to environments with short growing seasons (because of long winters, summer droughts, or both) and scarce soil nutrients. Evergreen trees need not expend a large amount of energy and nutrients in growing a full set of new leaves every year. Evergreen forests are common in the harsh climates of the northeastern and Great Lake states, in Canada, Europe, and Asia, on the infertile soils of the coastal plain in the southeastern United States, and at middle to high elevations throughout the Rocky Mountain Cordillera.

Middle-altitude slopes of the San Juan Mountains are covered by mixed conifer forests, whereas higher elevations support spruce-fir forests (DeVelice et al. 1986, Romme et al. 1992). Alpine vegetation grows in areas above timberline. Interspersed within the coniferous forests are aspen groves and meadows, which provide a pleasant visual contrast to the dark green conifers and support a distinctive suite of plant and animal species. Mixed conifer and spruce-fir forests line many parts of the Skyway, especially in the vicinities of Silverton and Rico. The highway does not quite reach the true alpine zone, though it comes close at Red Mountain Pass and other high points.

MIXED CONIFER FORESTS

At middle elevations in the San Juan Mountains (7,500–9,500 ft; 2,270–2,880 m), forests are dominated by a variety of conifer species, including ponderosa pine *(Pinus ponderosa)*, southwestern white pine *(Pinus strobiformis)*, Douglas-fir *(Pseudotsuga menziesii)*, white fir *(Abies concolor)*, corkbark fir *(Abies lasiocarpa* var. *arizonica)*, blue spruce *(Picea pungens)*, and Engelmann spruce *(Picea engelmannii)*. A complex mix of environmental and historical factors interact to determine the presence and relative abundance of each of these species on any particular site. White fir appears to grow best on relatively fertile soils, blue spruce thrives in cold, wet valley bottoms, and ponderosa pine is restricted to locally drier, warmer conditions. Generally, however, a mixed conifer forest is indicative of relatively cool, moist conditions.

The southwestern white pine is particularly interesting because it reveals the floristic affinities between this area and the mountains farther south in New Mexico, Arizona, and Mexico. The San Juans mark the northern limit of distribution of southwestern white pine. In northern Colorado and on up the Rocky Mountain Cordillera, this species is replaced by the limber pine *(Pinus flexilis)*. Some authorities lump the southwestern white and limber pines into a single species, but even then the two forms are distinct, and the trees in the San Juans are clearly more similar to populations to the south than to populations elsewhere in Colorado.

Historically, mixed conifer forests appear to have been subjected to fires less frequently than ponderosa pine forests. Cooler, wetter conditions at the higher elevations where mixed conifer forests grow reduce fire hazards. However, when these forests did burn, the fires were sometimes very hot and killed all of the aboveground vegetation. The first trees to reestablish an extensive cover in the burned forests often were aspen. Today on the mountain slopes aspen groves often have fairly abrupt borders with the surrounding mixed conifer forest; some of these groves mark the sites of forest fires that raged during the late 1800s. Today young conifers, but very few young aspens, are becoming established in the shade of the adult aspens. Eventually these conifers will replace the aspens, and a mixed conifer forest similar to that which burned more than a century ago will once again be in place.

Numerous mammals and birds inhabit the mixed conifer forests. One that is specifically dependent on ponderosa pines is the Abert's squirrel *(Sciurus aberti)*. This large, gray tree squirrel is not often seen but is readily distinguished by the long tufts of hair that protrude upward from its ears. A smaller relative, the red squirrel *(Tamiasciurus hudsonicus),* lives wherever Douglas-firs or spruces occur and often announces its presence by its long, chattering alarm call. White-breasted nuthatches and pygmy nuthatches are common in conifer forests, where they feed on bark-dwelling insects.

SPRUCE-FIR FORESTS

As we approach timberline, reaching elevations of 9,500 to 11,000 feet (2,880–3,330 m), most of the tree species of the mixed conifer zone drop out, leaving forests of Engelmann spruce and corkbark fir. Growing conditions become increasingly severe at these high elevations, and few tree species are hardy enough to thrive in them. Frosts and even snow can occur at any time, and the growing season is extremely brief. Both spruce and fir grow in a spire shape, which is thought to be an adaptation to the heavy snows of the subalpine environment.

Engelmann spruce is a major timberline species throughout the Rocky Mountains, from southern Arizona into Canada. The distribution of corkbark fir resembles that of the southwestern white pine of the mixed conifer zone in that it reaches its northern limit of distribution in the San Juan Mountains. In northern Colorado and the northern Rockies it is replaced by subalpine fir *(Abies lasiocarpa* var. *lasiocarpa).* Thus we see one more piece of evidence of the San Juan's floristic affinity with New Mexico and Arizona.

Mixed conifer and spruce-fir forests are rich in animal life as well as plant life. Several species of warblers, nuthatches, and kinglets glean insects from the foliage; woodpeckers work over the trunks; and crossbills excavate seeds from cones. Black bears and smaller mammals forage for the various plant and animal foods available in the mixed conifer forest. Several species in the San Juans inhabit only mature forest stands that have not been disturbed by major fires or logging for decades or centuries (Romme et al. 1992); examples of such old-growth species include the goshawk owl and the pine marten *(Martes americana)*.

An inconspicuous but ecologically significant animal in spruce-fir forests is the spruce bark beetle *(Dendroctonus rufipennis)*. This tiny insect (less than an inch in length) bores into Engelmann spruce trees and lays its eggs in the inner bark. The eggs hatch, and the beetle larvae proceed to eat the inner bark, eventually girdling the tree if they are numerous. When the larvae mature, they bore their way out of the tree and fly to another tree to lay eggs for the next generation. Most of the time the beetle population is extremely low, and they kill only an occasional tree. Periodically, though, the population explodes, for reasons that biologists have not yet been able to understand, and the insects kill thousands of spruce trees over large areas. These outbreaks generally last a few years; then the beetle population crashes as suddenly and as mysteriously as it exploded.

The significance of spruce beetle outbreaks goes beyond the destruction of trees; the resulting "snags" provide important habitat for a great variety of other wildlife species. Woodpeckers excavate nesting holes, which are taken over in subsequent years by bluebirds, nuthatches, and other species. The dead branches provide perching sites for raptors and other birds. When a dead tree finally falls to the ground, it provides a substrate and food source for myriad small insects and fungi, which in turn form the base of the food chain for more conspicuous birds and mammals. Thus, except in commercial forests, whose wood we want for ourselves, a bark beetle outbreak really is not a disaster. On the contrary, it is one of several forms of natural disturbance that actually enhance the diversity and the ecological function of the forest ecosystem as a whole.

Thousands of Engelmann spruce trees were killed in the San Juans during beetle outbreaks in the 1960s. A recent study of tree rings and historic photographs has revealed that similar widespread outbreaks occurred over extensive portions of Colorado, including the San Juan Mountains, in the late 1800s (Baker and Veblen 1990). Trees and insects have coexisted for thousands of years in the Rockies, and we can be sure that outbreaks will occur again in the future, just as they have in the past. (When walking around in a beetle-killed forest, look for the three-toed woodpecker, a secretive bird that specializes in eating insects that attack coniferous trees.)

Forest fires have been infrequent in these cool, moist, subalpine forests. When they have occurred, however, the forest sometimes has grown back very slowly, as climatic conditions are marginal for tree growth even without disturbance. For example, the Lime Creek Burn between Durango and Silverton occurred in 1879, yet much of this area remains covered with subalpine meadows in which large dead trees still stand in mute testimony to the slow pace of ecological processes in the timberline environment. Many of the subalpine meadows we see near timberline may represent areas that burned decades or centuries ago and still have not reforested.

Presumably the forest will eventually reclaim its former area if no further disturbance occurs and if the climate remains suitable for tree growth throughout the decades or centuries required for this process to reach completion. Recent research suggests that the time frame of forest regrowth near treeline is comparable to the time frame of climate change in mountainous regions. For example, during the mid-1800s, a cool period throughout the Northern Hemisphere known as the "Little Ice Age," snowdrifts lasted longer into the summer in the La Plata Mountains, and the upper timberline appears to have been lower than it is today (Petersen 1985). At other times since the end of the last ice age, some 12,000 to 15,000 years ago, temperatures have been warmer and timberline has been higher than at present (Carrara et al. 1991, Pielou 1991).

The global climate is currently showing a strong warming trend, partly because of human activities but also partly through natural causes. The evidence of past climates in the San Juan Mountains indicates that this trend may be reversed at some time in the future, with dramatic effects on the vegetation near timberline. If we could stand back and watch the upper timberline within a time frame of hundreds or thousands of years, we would see a dynamic interplay of short-term climate change, fire, and a shifting mosaic of subalpine forests, meadows, and alpine zones.

ASPEN FORESTS

Aspen forests are conspicuous in the San Juan Mountains, especially in the fall, when entire mountainsides come alive with color.
This is the only major deciduous forest tree species in the region,
and it is interesting not only for its brilliant autumn hues but also
for some unusual ecological features (DeByle and Winokur 1985).
Aspen forests are made up of clusters of stems that all arise from a
common root system and are genetically identical. Thus, an individual aspen is not a single tree but rather part of a root system
comprising tens or hundreds of stems. These genetic groups can
be identified in the spring, as discrete groups of stems all put on
their new leaves simultaneously, or in the fall, when they all turn
the same color at the same time.

Aspen produces light, wind-dispersed seeds in early spring,
and the seeds are generally viable, but aspen seedlings are almost
never found in the wild in this region. It seems that they cannot
survive the dry spring conditions or the competition with other
plants on the moist sites that they require. Instead, nearly all aspen
reproduction occurs asexually, as the extensive root systems that are
already established sprout new stems. These root systems must
have developed from seedlings at some time in the past, as many of
today's aspen forests are growing in places that were covered with
glaciers 20,000 years ago, during the Pleistocene. However, we really do not know when today's aspen forests became established; it
may have been hundreds or even thousands of years ago, and the
trees have been persisting ever since by vegetative resprouting.

Despite its failure to reproduce sexually, aspen is clearly a very
successful species in the San Juan Mountains. One reason for this
great success is its ability to capitalize on natural disturbances such
as fire, avalanches, and soil creep. Even though a forest fire may
char all of the vegetation above the ground, the aspen's root system, insulated by the soil, survives the fire and sends up a prolifer-
ation of new stems in the next growing season. Fueled by abundant
energy reserves drawn from the entire root system, these young aspen trees may grow a meter or more a year, rapidly overshadowing
other species that have to start from seed. Aspen thus maintains
a prominent place for itself for decades or centuries following a

disturbance, though it may eventually be suppressed by conifers and other species more tolerant of shade and crowding. Old mixed conifer or spruce-fir forests often harbor gnarled or stunted aspen stems that appear to be barely persisting but whose root systems could respond vigorously if the forest were disturbed.

Though many groves of aspen sprouted after forest fires in the 1800s and early 1900s and are slowly being replaced by coniferous species, other aspen forests show no evidence of being overtaken by conifers. These persistent stands appear most often on moist, fertile sites at lower elevations, such as steep north-facing slopes and small draws or depressions. Natural disturbances, though they affect these sites, do not appear to be essential for the perpetuation of aspen in them. Aspen is a complex species with adaptations for a great variety of ecological conditions; characterizing it just as a "post-fire species," as some have done, is overly simplistic.

Aspen forests contribute more than just visual diversity to the forested landscape of the San Juan Mountains. They also contain a distinctive suite of herbs and shrubs and provide feeding and breeding habitat for a variety of animals. Old-growth aspen forests often support a greater abundance and diversity of breeding birds than nearby coniferous forests. Birds and mammals particularly take advantage of old aspen stems with rotten or hollow centers; these provide essential nesting cavities, which are a relatively rare commodity in many areas, especially where the forests are young. These cavities often start as fungal infections but are enlarged by birds such as the northern flicker and the hairy woodpecker. Typically the leftover cavities are appropriated by smaller birds, such as violet-green swallows and mountain bluebirds, which must nest in such sites but cannot excavate them. The Williamson's sapsucker is limited in the Skyway area to ponderosa pine forests containing aspens with nest cavities.

MEADOWS AND PARKS

The open meadows, or parks, that are interspersed throughout spruce-fir and mixed conifer forests are something of an enigma ecologically. It often is difficult to say just why a particular area is meadow rather than forest. Some meadows are found on old lake beds, where the fine-textured soils support grasses and herbs better than trees. Other meadows are on deep deposits of volcanic ash. Meadows near upper timberline may represent old burns where reforestation has not yet occurred. The bottom of a basin or valley at high elevation may become a meadow because cold air, which is heavier than warm air, flows down the slopes and pools in the bottom, effectively shortening the growing season for trees. Parks or grasslands near lower timberline often occur on shale substrates that are too dry to support forest. Frequently, however, the exact factors responsible for an area's being a meadow are not known.

Regardless of their origin, mountain meadows offer a pleasing visual contrast for the traveler, and they enhance the biological diversity of the region by providing an open habitat for nonforest plants and animals. Common meadow species include Thurber's fescue *(Festuca thurberi)*, other large bunchgrasses, and pocket gophers (*Thomomys* spp.); you will not find these species in dense forests. Elk, deer, and bear also feed in the meadows, although they make use of forest habitats as well.

ALPINE VEGETATION

Alpine landscapes have long been a source of fascination to people of many regions. The word *alpine* conjures up pleasant images of the Swiss Alps, with bright sunshine on flower-covered high mountain slopes, jagged peaks, and glacial ice. These images also find expression in a song from *The Sound of Music* that commemorates a little blue sunflower, the edelweiss. However, the beauty of the alpine terrain at midsummer belies the rigor of the environmental factors that create and maintain it. Low temperatures, a short growing season, and the topography at high elevations combine to create the treeless landscape. Quite simply, the alpine zone occurs where the seasonal input of solar energy is insufficient to support the growth of trees. These same factors are responsible for the low stature of alpine vegetation.

The word *tundra* is used regularly to refer to the treeless landscapes of both Arctic and alpine areas. Indeed, both types of land are treeless for largely the same reason: low temperatures during the growing season. However, the causes of low temperatures differ between the two regions. In the Arctic, low temperatures result mainly from the tilt of the earth's axis and the low angle at which the summer sun strikes the ground. Lower temperatures in alpine zones result most immediately from the thin atmosphere, which cannot absorb much solar heat, and from the natural cooling of rising air masses. Further, the nearly continuous light of the month-long Arctic summer is very different from the days and nights experienced by plants at lower latitudes. Light intensity in the Arctic is relatively low, because much solar radiation is absorbed as sunlight passes at a low angle through the atmosphere. In contrast, sunlight passes at a much higher angle and comes more directly through the thin atmosphere at high elevations farther south. Alpine areas at temperate latitudes receive greater intensities of damaging ultraviolet radiation than do Arctic regions or mid-latitude areas at lower elevations. Alpine areas in the Colorado Rockies also do not have the perennially frozen soil (permafrost) found in Arctic regions. Because of these differences, some ecologists restrict the use of the word *tundra* to Arctic treeless landscapes; treeless alpine landscapes would be termed *alpine meadows*.

Located on the upper slopes and summits of rugged mountains, alpine zones are characterized by great topographic diversity, which in turn exerts an enormous influence on the vegetation. For example, snow is deeper and melts more slowly on north-facing ridges than on south-facing ridges. Any irregularity of the ground's surface can affect habitat. Even small depressions accumulate slightly deeper snow cover, which melts to produce a wet depression, an oasis within otherwise drier surroundings. Moreover, boulders can create small-scale versions of slope effects; the soil on the south side of the boulder will be drier than soil on the shaded side. The effects of solifluction are probably better known than the word. As soil on a slope becomes saturated with meltwater, the force of gravity causes the wet soil to "slump," or creep downslope. The slumping tears the vegetation cover and exposes sections of bare soil. The exposed soil is unstable and can only support plants with shallow, flexible roots. Soil crevices of this kind are important habitats for mosses, which have no roots at all.

Wind also exerts an important influence on the alpine environment, both directly and indirectly. The direct effects are related mainly to the dryness of the wind, which has a terrible desiccating effect on exposed plants. Moreover, the wind carries ice crystals, which subject any unprotected plants or plant parts to severe mechanical damage. The effects of desiccation and mechanical damage are seen in the patches of gnarled, stunted trees, termed *krummholz*, at timberline. The tree commonly are "flagged" — that is, the windward side of each trees exhibits dead, ice-blasted limbs, whereas the leeward limbs have living foliage that maintains a tenuous vitality.

Wind affects alpine vegetation indirectly by modifying the influence of topography on soil moisture. Treeless alpine slopes offer little resistance to the passage of wind, and wind velocities at ground level are often very high. Consequently, most of the snow is blown away on many exposed sites in the alpine zone. These snow-free areas display severe drought conditions during the growing season, and the plants that can survive them are sparse and low in stature.

Snow blown clear of windward slopes accumulates on the leeward slope. Deep drifts accumulate just over a ridge, and in general the depth of the snowpack decreases with increasing distance from the ridge. This snow cover affects the plants in two ways. First, it provides a water source as it melts. The thinner snow cover toward the lower end of the snowdrift melts out quickly, resulting in dry conditions early in the growing season, whereas the deeper portion of the drift near the top of the slope melts more slowly and provides a more sustained moisture supply. This moisture gradient along the length of a snowdrift strongly influences the kind, abundance, and form of plants that can grow on the slope. Second, snow cover influences plants by affecting the length of the growing season. Deeper snow takes longer to melt, and therefore the plants under it have less of the already short alpine summer to grow. Late-lying snowdrifts are very interesting biologically, for they create habitats that are cold and moist and have very short growing seasons. These sites harbor unusual plant communities that often include Arctic plant species such as the whitlowwort *(Draba graminea)*.

One of the most intriguing aspects of an alpine landscape is the conspicuous absence of trees. Why can trees not grow in this environment? In most situations, it is advantageous for plants to be tall, as taller plants can acquire a greater share of the available light for photosynthesis. However, a tall tree requires a strong supporting stem. Growth and maintenance of a woody stem requires a substantial amount of energy and materials, yet the stem does not produce any food by photosynthesis, nor does it contain any reproductive structures. The alpine growing season is so short that plants barely have time to photosynthesize and store enough carbohydrates to sustain the most essential structures (roots, leaves, flowers) and to carry the plant through the long months during which photosynthesis is impossible. There simply is not energy to spare for wood production. Furthermore, a tall stem is exposed to desiccation and mechanical damage from the wind.

Given that large stature is a disadvantage, what kinds of attributes do enable plants to survive in the alpine environment? Some of the most interesting adaptations are related to growth form and reproduction. Most alpine plants are low herbaceous types, with prostrate woody shrubs second in abundance. The ground absorbs most of the sun's energy and re-radiates it to warm the air within a few inches above the soil surface. Low plants thus can absorb maximum warmth and energy for growth during the summer, and in the winter they are covered by an insulating layer of snow.

Alpine plants have other protective adaptations in addition to low stature. For example, most alpine grasses are bunchgrasses, which retain dead leaves from previous seasons. These old leaves provide mechanical protection and insulation for the plant's growing points, which are located at the base of the mass of old leaves. Other plants, such as the alpine dandelions (*Taraxacum* spp.), form rosettes, or dense clusters of basal leaves. Held flat against the ground, these rosette leaves offer little or no resistance to the wind and are less likely to be damaged. Moreover, the stem tip and growing point are recessed just below ground level and partially covered by the leaf bases. Some plants carry the rosette to an extreme and take a form rather like that of a pincushion. The very short leaves of these "cushion plants" are clustered tightly around one another and the stem so as to expose only the leaf tips to the elements. Examples are moss campion *(Silene acaulis)* and alpine phlox *(Phlox condensata)*. The cushion growth form is also seen in desert plants, and its common occurrence in the alpine provides further evidence of the rigorous growing conditions above timberline.

Most alpine plants are perennials. Indeed, the alpine environment is almost as inhospitable to herbaceous annuals as it is to trees. Consider the obstacles an annual plant must clear to complete its life cycle during the short alpine summer. The seed must have the right conditions for germination in early summer. A late frost could destroy the delicate seedling, or excessive cloudiness might retard photosynthesis and production of the sugars necessary for flower formation. On the very day that a flower is ready for pollination, cloudiness could make the temperature too cool for insects to visit. The summer might provide ideal growing conditions for up to five weeks, but an early frost could cause the young seeds to abort. Despite all these factors, there is one annual species, *Koenigia islandica* (it has no common name), that regularly completes its life cycle above timberline.

Though time and environmental vagaries work against annual plants, they favor alpine perennials. These are slow growers, but they are persistent. Early seedling growth usually focuses on establishment of a vigorous root system that can take up water and minerals. Only a small stem and a leaf or two might form by the end of the first season of life. The following year the existing leaves can get an immediate start at photosynthesis. The stem may grow a little and produce another leaf or two, but most of the sugars produced by photosynthesis are transformed into storage carbohydrates that are accumulated in the roots. Only after several seasons of such conservative growth will the plant become large and vigorous enough to support continued vegetative life and the added burden of flowering and seed production.

Despite the spectacular summer flower display, flowering and seed production are as fraught with hazards for alpine perennials as for the few alpine annuals. Consequently, nearly all alpine plants have evolved a common adaptation that enables them to attain the greatest possible reproductive success: they form precocious flower buds. Rather than initiating flower formation at the start of each growth season, perennials carry out this critical step at the end of the previous season. Most alpine plants are in full flower within two or three weeks after the snow melts. In the San Juans the snowmelt can be flooding local streams in the middle of June, but by July the season's floral display is in full bloom.

Only a handful of birds breed in the alpine zone: horned larks, rosy finches, water pipits, white-crowned sparrows, golden eagles, and white-tailed ptarmigans. With the exception of the white-tailed ptarmigan, all of these species leave alpine elevations for the winter to escape the deep snow, bitter cold, and harsh wind. The grouselike ptarmigan, a ground-dwelling bird, molts to a camouflage-white plumage and seeks shelter in the snow-covered willows and the krummholz near timberline, where it spends the winter huddled in relative safety feeding on young willow shoots.

Mammals that live in the alpine zone use one of three strategies to survive the winter: they may migrate to lower altitude (American elk, *Cervus canadensis*), hibernate (yellow-bellied marmot, *Marmota flaviventris*, and least chipmunk, *Eutamias minimus*), or they may remain active under the snow, using it as a protective cover. An example of this latter approach is seen in the northern pocket gopher *(Thomomys talpoides)*, which burrows year-round and is not much bothered by the extreme alpine environment as long as there is enough snow cover to prevent the soil from freezing. Deer mice *(Peromyscus maniculatus)* and montane voles *(Microtus montanus)* also remain active under the snow. One of the more interesting strategies is that of the pika *(Ochotona princeps)*, which lives in the protection of rock slides and gathers hay during the summer and early fall. This small relative of the rabbits and hares stores the hay among the rocks, then nests in it and feeds upon it during the long alpine winter.

There is a remarkable similarity between the list of plant species found on alpine peaks and those found in the Arctic. Indeed, some of the most common alpine plants also grow within sight of the Arctic Ocean. Plant geographers have proposed two possible explanations for these similarities. In the last century, Charles Darwin and others suggested that as the Pleistocene ice sheets formed some 2 million years ago, the ice dissected and destroyed much of the Arctic flora. However, many plants were able to escape extinction by slowly migrating southward along the flanks of the Rocky Mountains, ahead of the advancing ice sheets. When the climate began to warm and the glaciers retreated north-ward, remnants of the Arctic flora remained behind on high mountains, trapped at high elevations by the warming tempera-tures of the surrounding lowlands.

Others have suggested a second scenario. It has been argued that prior to the Pleistocene a well-developed Arctic-alpine flora was widely distributed across the Northern Hemisphere. The al-pine plants on today's mountain peaks are thought to be relics of that old flora. According to this theory, the Pleistocene ice sheet and its associated mountain glaciers dissected the flora's habitat, leaving behind the remnants we now see.

At present there is no consensus as to which hypothesis is correct. The data do not give us a clear picture. However, certain data provide interesting support for the second theory. The over-lap between the Arctic and alpine floras decreases sharply toward the south. In the southern Rockies, the number of species in com-mon with the Arctic stands at only about 25 percent. In addition, certain alpine natives have relatives not in the North American Arctic but in the mountains of central Asia. The most plausible ex-planation is that these Rocky Mountain and central Asiatic rela-tives descended from an old, dissected flora. Further, there is evidence that part of the Rocky Mountain flora originated nearby. Certain alpine species have their closest relatives not in the Arctic or on other continents but in the deserts west and south of the Rockies. The desert Southwest apparently supplied the stock from which certain alpine species evolved.

Alpine vegetation has several different forms. The most widespread and luxuriant type of alpine plant community is the al-pine meadow. Along the Skyway it is most easily observed in the vicinity of Molas Pass. Especially well-developed meadows lie on the mountain slopes across the Animas Canyon east of Molas Pass. Alpine meadow also can be seen in the upper Animas Can-yon north of Animas Forks. In such areas the meadow forms a lush carpet, often a blaze of yellow from the flowers of mountain avens (*Acomastylis rossii*) and cinquefoil (*Potentilla* spp.). Also abundant are the yellow, white, and rose-colored flowers of Indi-an paintbrushes (*Castilleja* spp.). The white-flowered stalks of the alpine bistort *(Bistorta bistortoides)* exist in patches. Among the most distinctive signposts of the alpine zone are the two- to three-flowered clumps of yellow *Hymenoxys grandiflora,* the "old man of the mountains."

Alpine meadow plants diminish in stature on the drier and more exposed upper mountain slopes and summits. The alpine avens and some cinquefoils persist but are very short. The brilliant magenta flowers of clover *(Trifolium brandegei)* are very conspicuous, and small cushions of the pink- or white-flowered moss campion *(Silene acaulis)* can be found.

Alpine marshes can be found around lakes and tarns. These areas are dominated by sedges (*Carex* spp.), although the patches of magenta-flowered elephant's heads *(Pedicularis groenlandica)* and occasional tufts of white cotton grass (*Eriophorum* spp.) add color. Near the lower limits of the alpine zone or in moist sites that enjoy some protection from wind, one can find dense thickets of shrubby willows (*Salix* spp.), which form mosaics with herbaceous alpine marsh species.

REFERENCES

Baker, W. L., and T. T. Veblen, 1990. Spruce beetles and fire in the nineteenth-century subalpine forests of western Colorado, U.S.A. *Arctic and Alpine Research,* v. 22, pp. 65–80.

Carrara, P. E., D. A. Trimble, and M. Rubin, 1991. Holocene treeline fluctuations in the northern San Juan Mountains, Colorado, U.S.A., as indicated by radiocarbon-dated conifer wood. *Arctic and Alpine Research,* v. 23, pp. 233–246.

DeByle, N. V., and R. P. Winokur, eds., 1985. *Aspen: Ecology and management in the western United States.* U.S. Department of Agriculture, Forest Service General Technical Report RM-119, 283 pp.

DeVelice, R. L., J. A. Ludwig, W. H. Moir, and F. Ronco Jr., 1986. *A classification of forest habitat types of northern New Mexico and southern Colorado.* U.S. Department of Agriculture, Forest Service General Technical Report RM-131, 59 pp.

Pielou, E. C., 1991. *After the ice age: The return of life to glaciated North America.* Chicago: University of Chicago Press, 366 pp.

Romme, W. H., D. W. Jamieson, J. S. Redders, G. Bigsby, J. P. Lindsey, D. Kendall, R. Cowen, T. Kreykes, A. W. Spencer, and J. C. Ortega, 1992. Old-growth forests of the San Juan National Forest in southwestern Colorado, in *Old-growth forests in the southwest and Rocky Mountain regions,* U.S. Department of Agriculture, Forest Service General Technical Report RM-213, pp. 154–165.

CHAPTER 13

WETLANDS, RIPARIAN HABITATS, AND RIVERS

PRESTON SOMERS AND LISA FLOYD-HANNA

Moisture is one of the premiere limiting factors for plants and animals, and where moisture is not limited one finds very distinctive communities of drought-intolerant species. Wetlands, defined as areas that remain moist through all or most of the growing season, include communities such as marshes and bogs. A special type of wetland is a riparian ecosystem (i.e., the area immediately adjacent to a flowing stream). In this chapter we discuss the characteristics and importance of the wetlands of the San Juans in general, then look more closely at the riparian vegetation that grows along the rivers and streams of the San Juan Skyway region. Finally, we discuss the aquatic ecology of a representative major river, the Animas.

WETLANDS

In a region characterized by low and seasonal precipitation, the presence of wetlands seems surprising. However, these isolated areas have a unique or persistent water source and are highly productive and diverse ecosystems, especially when set against an arid background. Often called the "thin green line," rich, wet ecosystems occur along waterways at both high and low elevations. Although wetlands make up only a fraction of the total land area in Colorado, it is estimated that 70 percent of the animals, including 80 percent of the vertebrate fauna, depend on wetlands for their permanent homes or for stops along their migration path.

Wetlands are disappearing all over the United States. In the last century, for example, Arizona and New Mexico have lost 90 percent of their original riparian and wetland ecosystems (Johnson 1989). A draft listing of the threatened native wildlife in Arizona compiled by the Arizona Game and Fish Department in 1988 named eighty-one vertebrate species associated with wetland habitats, of which 70 percent absolutely require wetlands and riparian sites to survive. Thus, the importance of wetlands extends beyond the ecological characteristics and processes we generally associate with them — for example, speedy nutrient cycling; rich, often oxygen-deficient soils; and reduction of river sediments.

Many of the western wetlands are seasonal, driven by snowmelt or other fluctuations typical of western hydrology. Sometimes, as in the wetland-rich San Luis Valley, a shallow water table provides for the characteristic wetland vegetation. In montane regions, wetland meadow vegetation is supported by a shallow water table fed by spring snowmelt. Other wetlands persist on the edges of rivers and streams.

Wetland plants have many adaptations that allow them to thrive in waterlogged soils. For example, their roots can tolerate low oxygen levels. They also have a low susceptibility to the toxins produced by microorganisms that occur in oxygen-deficient soils. Roots of wetland plants contain a spongy tissue full of large air spaces, which enhances oxygen uptake.

Distinctive wetland species in southwestern Colorado include cattails, many species of sedges, willows, cottonwoods, and horsetails (*Equisetum* spp.). In summer wetlands buzz with dragonflies and birds such as the rough-winged swallow and red-winged blackbird.

Wetlands are a threatened kind of ecosystem throughout the West and are protected by federal legislation. Many of the criteria used to define a wetland, however, are derived from the more common eastern types. Hydrological cycles, soil types, and plant species are used together to determine whether or not a site is a so-called "jurisdictional wetland" worthy of protection. There has been a strong lobbying effort to reduce the amount of land that falls into the wetland definition. Colorado wetlands, primarily because of their seasonal nature, may lose their protected status if legislation is weakened. At present, if a site is saturated for seven to ten days, it may qualify for wetland status. A proposed change in legislation would expand the minimum saturation time to twenty-one days. Such a change would eliminate up to 50 percent of protected sites.

Wetlands appear at many places along the Skyway and throughout the San Juans. A beautiful, low-elevation wetland ecosystem can be viewed from the highway just east of Mancos. Numerous examples of high-elevation wetlands lie near Molas Pass. These support different species than the wetlands in the foothills do, but they exhibit the same kinds of ecological conditions and processes.

RIPARIAN VEGETATION

Major streams in the foothills and basins of the San Juan region commonly are lined with riparian woodlands dominated by cottonwoods (*Populus* spp.). These woodlands and associated phreatophytic vegetation (composed of plants that require a perennial water source near the soil surface) have changed dramatically during the last century and a half in the western Great Plains and southwestern United States. Much of the change results from the fact that riparian areas were those first settled and developed for townsites, farmlands, and residential areas. Vast riparian lands have been cleared or modified beyond recognition. More recently, significant but subtle changes have taken place in the remaining "wild" or "natural" riparian communities. In the most common pattern, native cottonwoods have declined and been replaced by riparian scrub species such as sandbar willow *(Salix exigua)* or exotic phreatophytes such as tamarisk or salt cedar *(Tamarix ramosissima)* and Russian olive *(Elaeagnus angustifolia)* (Johnson 1979, Miller and Bowman 1985).

These changes are often attributed to the construction of dams, reservoirs, and irrigation diversion projects upstream of the affected areas. Such structures and their typical management regimes regulate stream flow at a relatively constant year-round level and drastically reduce spring and early summer snowmelt flows. Thus, the riparian areas downstream of these projects are no longer subjected to periodic scouring of the riverbanks and terraces. Ironically, by eliminating this natural form of disturbance and stabilizing the riparian environment, these human developments have severely impaired the reproduction of cottonwood and have allowed shrubby phreatophytes to invade on sites adjacent to the river channel that previously were bare or supported cottonwood seedlings.

Unregulated rivers typically meander in their floodplains; the Animas Valley upstream of Durango and the Dolores Valley upstream of Dolores offer good examples. These streams carry enough water in spring floods to cause their meanders to move sideways and downstream. The greatest erosion occurs on the outside and downstream portion of the bend of a meander, where the current is strongest. This scouring undermines and carries away alluvium deposited during a previous meander cycle. Often a mature cottonwood woodland has taken root on this older alluvium, and large trees are felled and swept away. By contrast, the current is weakest on the inside and downstream portion of the bend of the meander, and as a result a point bar of alluvium is deposited there (Leopold et al. 1964). Because erosion and deposition are greater in the downstream portion of each meander, the entire meander system moves down the valley over time. Thus, new point bars and beaches are deposited at successively lower levels each year, and older, higher deposits on the outsides of the meander bends are carried away.

The life cycle of the cottonwood is well adapted to this natural geomorphic process. Cottonwoods produce large quantities of small seeds, each surrounded by light fluff. These seeds are released and easily dispersed by wind or water in early summer — exactly the time that receding floodwaters are exposing newly created point bars and beaches. Seeds landing on these moist sites germinate promptly and begin to grow. Cottonwood seeds have a limited period (one to five weeks) of viability after their release, but once they germinate and are established as seedlings their roots may grow an average of 0.25 inches (6 mm) per day (Fenner et al. 1984). This rapid growth rate allows the roots to follow and maintain contact with the receding water table during the summer, reaching a depth of 29 to 65 inches (72–162 cm) by the end of the first growing season (Fenner et al. 1984).

Cottonwoods also can reproduce vegetatively in their early years. Once established, cottonwoods grow quickly, 6 to 13 feet (2–4 m) annually under ideal conditions, and stands thin themselves naturally. The trees achieve their maximum diameter and height in forty to fifty years (Hoover and Wills 1987). During this time the water table level under a typical cottonwood stand lowers as erosion degrades the river channel. Silt accumulation may lift the substrate above the water level. As the meander system moves down the floodplain, the distance between the cottonwood stand and the bend that laid down its substrate increases. At the same time, the distance between the stand and the approaching upstream bend decreases. Eventually the upstream bend encroaches on the stand, erodes away its substrate, and carries away the trees. By this time the trees typically have reached maturity or even have begun to decline in vigor.

The regulation imposed upon most rivers in the western United States halts or greatly retards this natural geomorphic process. Under the regime of constant flow and low-volume discharge, erosion of older deposits and deposition of new alluvium occur at a negligible rate. The current is not strong enough to scour the banks, and water coming from reservoirs lacks sufficient silt and sand for siltation to occur. Indeed, silt may be trapped in the reservoirs, and as a result the river channel may become "armored," or lined with cobbles and pebbles (Simons 1979).

Thus, a system once characterized by dynamic movements of alluvium has become stable. Cottonwoods are well adapted to take advantage of the dynamics of fluvial processes, but they are not favored by stability. Their roots need to be in contact with the water table, but this falls and stays low in the floodplains of many regulated streams. Cottonwoods have a short life span, they do not reproduce well vegetatively in their mature stages, and managed streams produce no new point bars and beaches on which seedlings can become established. Moreover, cottonwoods are intolerant of shading and competition by other plants (Hoover and Wills 1984). Shrubby phreatophytes invade stream banks in the absence of bank scouring, keeping cottonwoods from gaining a foothold on the areas closest to the water table. As a consequence, cottonwood woodlands of the high plains and much of the Colorado

River drainage are being replaced in many areas by non-native phreatophytes (for example, salt cedar) that support a lower diversity of native fauna and favor less desirable, introduced animal species such as the starling (Cohan et al. 1979).

We can see an example of this process in the Dolores River, whose headwaters rise in the Wilson Mountains of southwestern Colorado. In 1984 the McPhee Dam was completed 17 miles (27 km) downstream of Dolores, and McPhee Reservoir began to fill. This reservoir was designed and built as the primary water storage facility of the Dolores Project by the U.S. Bureau of Reclamation. It supplies irrigation water to a large region as well as municipal and industrial water for several local towns. Volume discharge from McPhee Reservoir is now regulated at three levels: 25, 50, and 75 cubic feet per second (ft^3/sec) (0.7, 1.4, and 2.1 m^3/sec). During the spring there are brief larger releases of up to 1,200 ft^3/sec (34 m^3/sec) for whitewater recreation. By contrast, the Dolores River in this reach formerly had peak flows of up to 5,540 ft^3/sec (156 m^3/sec), with a mean peak of 3,360 ft^3/sec (94 m^3/sec). The mean annual flow at the town of Dolores was 438 ft^3/sec (12.3 m^3/sec), with a historic minimum of 8 ft^3/sec (0.2 m^3/sec). However, the Montezuma Valley Irrigation System diversion, just below Dolores, often left the river dry downstream during the late summer.

The flow regime in the Dolores River downstream of McPhee Dam is now practically constant and quite low compared to levels during most months before construction of the dam. This area contains much riparian woodland that is heterogenous in age class and diverse in floral and faunal composition. Narrowleaf cottonwood *(Populus angustifolia)* is the dominant tree species, and stands of any age may be found. These stands, along with their associated trees and shrubs, have been developing and interacting with the fluvial processes of an unregulated stream. However, there is concern that as these stands of narrowleaf cottonwood decline naturally with age, there will be insufficient recruitment of new individuals into the population. The stable, low flows of the Dolores will likely eliminate the fluvial dynamics upon which cottonwoods are dependent and allow the invasion and establishment of scrubby phreatophytic communities along the river.

THE ANIMAS RIVER

The Animas River, one of the few unregulated waterways remaining in western Colorado, provides a good example of the ecology of major streams in this region. The Animas River originates at Animas Forks northeast of Silverton at an elevation of 11,120 feet (3,390 m) and flows southward to Farmington, New Mexico, where it joins the San Juan River. In its course, the Animas goes from high alpine to dry desert environments, undergoing many changes in its physical, chemical, and biological attributes.

The rate and volume of stream flow in the Animas vary greatly by season and year (Ugland et al. 1990). The typical seasonal minimum stream flow of 150 to 225 ft^3/sec (4.2–6.4 m^3/sec) at Durango occurs during the winter months of November through March, but there are wet years when the flow rarely falls below 300 ft^3/sec (8.4 m^3/sec). The lowest daily flow observed since recording started was 94 ft^3/sec (2.7 m^3/sec) on March 2, 1913. The seasonal maximum of 3,000 to 7,000 ft^3/sec (85–198 m^3/sec) occurs during the spring snowmelt period of late April through early June. There are years when the spring discharge exceeds the latter figure (U.S. Geological Survey data 1971–1990). Likewise, when there is a mild, dry winter and little snow accumulation in the mountains, there is little spring runoff. The most dramatic recent example of this occurred in the dry winter of 1976–1977; the following June the Animas peaked at only 1,220 ft^3/sec (34.6 m^3/sec) (U.S. Geological Survey data 1978). However, the greatest stream flows in the Animas have occurred not as a result of the spring snowmelt but during the occasional late summer and early fall floods, which result from the monsoon rains this area receives. The largest of these on record came on October 5, 1911, when the peak flow in Durango was 25,000 ft^3/sec (708 m^3/sec) (Ugland et al. 1990).

From the river's origin to Baker's Bridge, north of Durango, the gradient of the Animas varies from steep to moderate to steep again. Below Baker's Bridge the gradient becomes much more gentle, and in much of the valley between Baker's Bridge and Durango the river is slow and meandering in a wide, unconstrained reach of 17.4 miles (28 km) of river channel that traverses only

11.8 miles (19 km) of valley. At Durango the river gradient increases to a more moderate angle, and the channel meanders less; the Animas continues in that manner for the rest of its course within Colorado.

The upper Animas's high altitude, many tributaries, steep gradient, and narrow, shady canyons make the water temperature quite low even in summer. However, when the river reaches the valley below Baker's Bridge, it slows and meanders back and forth in the warmth of the sun, and the water temperature rises.

The water chemistry of the Animas River varies enormously along its course. The factor most relevant to aquatic life along most of the Animas is the presence and mining of highly mineralized deposits near its headwaters. In the upper Animas watershed, acidic runoff containing toxic levels of heavy metals comes from several sources. In the Silverton area and northward there are extensive exposed and underground ore deposits containing sulfides of iron, copper, antimony, arsenic, and zinc. These deposits also contain gold, silver, and manganese (Albrecht 1988). When iron pyrite (fool's gold) in these deposits is exposed to the atmosphere directly or indirectly, it undergoes a series of reactions with water and oxygen to produce ferric hydroxide and sulfuric acid. These reactions start in the ore deposits and continue within the streams that drain them. Ferric hydroxide is quite insoluble and precipitates out on the bed of the stream draining the deposits; thus, the rocks of the stream are coated with a light yellow to orange precipitate often called "yellow boy." The water in such streams typically is very acidic because the oxidation of pyrite produces sulfuric acid. The water draining such deposits also carries salts of the heavy metals mentioned above (Albrecht 1988, Western Aquatics 1985).

The ore deposits that pollute the upper Animas and some of its tributaries can be exposed to the atmosphere in several ways. First, naturally occurring steep mountainsides with surface ore deposits weather and erode away. Runoff from these exposed deposits is thought to contribute significantly to the heavy metal content and low pH of the streams in the Silverton area. Additionally, the valleys harbor iron bogs, such as those in the Cement Creek and Mineral Creek drainages, that act as reservoirs of acid and heavy metals. Spring snowmelt and summer thunderstorms can flush these materials into the main stream. Iron springs also rise within the drainages of these two creeks and may be additional natural contributors to the metal and acid load of these streams (Albrecht 1988, Western Aquatics 1985).

Mining has received more attention than any other source of pollution in the upper Animas watershed. Mining activities exposed large amounts of ore deposits in several ways. First, mineral-containing rock and earth were brought to the surface, and most was discarded near the mine mouth as a spoil heap or mine dump. (Such dumps appear today as yellow to orange-brown piles of rock on many of the mountainsides between Molas Pass and Ouray.) Here they were exposed to the atmosphere and weather, which flushed their toxins to the stream below. The high-grade ore was transported to a nearby mill, where it was ground to a fine texture and the desired materials were separated from it. The tailings, a fine gray mineral powder suspended in water, were traditionally discharged into the nearest stream. This practice once caused severe pollution of the Animas River throughout its length, but mining engineers began to curtail the problem around the middle of this century by impounding the tailings effluent in ponds (Albrecht 1988). The tailings ponds allowed the suspended materials to settle out, and the clarified water could be discharged to a stream. The perimeter of the pond was constantly raised through continual deposition of material, so that what was once a ground-level pond eventually became a huge, steep-sided tailings pile with a shallow pond on top. These light gray mounds are prominent features of the landscape in several places in the Silverton and Red Mountain areas. They erode by wind and water action and continue to contribute stream pollutants (Western Aquatics 1985).

In the mines themselves, pyrite and heavy metal deposits are exposed to water and oxygen. Groundwater enters mines throughout much of their extent, washes over the mineral deposits, and exits through the lowest opening. This mine drainage flows into streams, carrying with it sulfuric acid and salts of heavy metals (Albrecht 1988).

Of the various sources of low-pH water and heavy metals, the open mine portals and the exposed tailings piles are thought to be the most significant. It is technically possible to mitigate the pollution from these sources by sealing mines and removing tailings, but doing so would be exorbitantly expensive (Western Aquatics 1985).

The oxidation, weathering, and leaching of pollutants from these sources (naturally exposed deposits, iron bogs, mine dumps, tailings piles, and mines) occurs year-round. However, the greatest concentrations of heavy metals typically appear in the Animas and its affected tributaries in April and May. The heavy snowpack melts during this time of the year and percolates through the exposed mineral deposits. This leaching action, combined with the production of sulfuric acid (which mobilizes the heavy metals), results in a pulse of heavy metal contamination in the Animas during the spring runoff. Other pulses of pollutants occur after heavy rainstorms in the summer and fall (Western Aquatics 1985).

Upstream of Silverton, the Animas River is noticeably affected by the extensive mining that has occurred in this portion of the watershed over the past 120 years or more. However, the quality of the water here is actually better than it is downstream of Silverton: the pH is consistently higher, the heavy metal concentrations lower (Albrecht 1988). Aquatic macroinvertebrates such as mayflies and stoneflies are more abundant and diverse upstream of Silverton (Four Corners Environmental Research Institute 1975), and rainbow and brook trout can occasionally be caught there. These fish reproduce in the less polluted tributaries such as Cunningham Gulch, and some of the adults may migrate down to the Animas River and spend most of their time in the plume of a cleaner tributary (Japhet, personal communication 1991, Western Aquatics 1985).

The main reason water quality deteriorates so markedly below Silverton is that two tributaries, Mineral Creek and Cement Creek, enter the river in this area. Both of these creeks contain very high levels of sulfuric acid. Yellow to orange-brown deposits of sulfates, oxides, and hydroxides of iron cover the cobbles of these streams, and essentially no aquatic organisms live in them. These tributaries have dissolved iron and heavy metal volumes many times greater than what the Animas has absorbed above the two creeks' mouths. Their pH values are usually well below 7 (neutral) and are often below 4 (the acidity of vinegar). The low pH makes heavy metal concentrations more toxic than those same concentrations would be at pH values above 7 (Four Corners Environmental Research Institute 1975).

Fortunately, the volume of water discharged into the Animas River by Cement and Mineral Creeks is low compared to the amount in the main stream. Furthermore, their polluted waters are greatly diluted by the many tributaries between Silverton and Rockwood. Nevertheless, the Animas has very poor water quality for many miles downstream of Cement and Mineral Creeks. This fact can be verified simply by observing the stream from the narrow-gauge Durango-Silverton train; as one approaches Silverton in the upper portion of the canyon, the stream bed changes from the usual dark olive drab to light tan to brown and orange. This color difference indicates the absence of algae and other living organisms and the presence of precipitated iron compounds and accompanying sulfuric acid. The typical levels of cadmium, copper, iron, lead, and zinc in the Animas here greatly exceed the levels determined by the EPA to be toxic to freshwater organisms when they occur on a chronic basis (Albrecht 1988).

By the time the Animas River reaches Durango its chemistry has changed considerably. Many tributaries between Silverton and Durango dilute the more toxic water from the upper Animas. Several of these streams drain watersheds composed of sedimentary rocks and tend to have pH values above 7 and greater hardness and alkalinity values than the Animas has. Waters of this nature do more than merely dilute the toxic upper Animas water: they neutralize acids and precipitate heavy metals. Sediments at the confluences of major tributaries in the Animas Canyon and along the lower Animas typically have higher metal concentrations than sediments elsewhere in these stretches of the river. Although the river's heavy metal content decreases significantly from one end of the canyon to the other, the levels of copper, lead, and zinc at Baker's Bridge still typically exceed the EPA standards for chronic exposure by aquatic organisms, and cadmium and iron levels come close to exceeding these standards (Albrecht 1988).

The Animas River within and immediately below Durango is well known as a trout fishery. Both rainbow trout and brown trout are present in this stretch of river, and a Colorado-record trout — 23 pounds (10.4 kg) — was caught just upstream of the Main Street bridge. This record stood for several years during the 1960s until another, bigger brown trout was caught at nearby Vallecito Reservoir. This segment of river has even been considered for designation as a Gold Medal Fishery by the Colorado Division of Wildlife (Japhet, personal communication 1991). However, the existence of fish in a stream does not necessarily mean that it has excellent or even good water quality. The Animas trout fishery in Durango is wholly artificial. About 12,000 rainbow trout of catchable size are released into the Animas each year within Durango by the Colorado Division of Wildlife. Additionally, the agency stocks 20,000 rainbow trout fingerlings and 20,000 brown trout fingerlings annually (Japhet, personal communication 1991). There is a high mortality rate among these released fish, but those that survive do well and grow rapidly. The brown trout, which are wily and not caught by the average fisherman, occasionally grow to impressive sizes. These stocked fish are the sole basis of the Animas River sport fishery in Durango. The natural reproductive rates of trout in this area are extremely low (Japhet, personal communication 1991) for a variety of reasons.

The Animas supports greater trout survival and growth within Durango because this stretch of river has relatively low pollution levels, alkaline water with moderate carbonate and bicarbonate contents, moderately good habitat (rocky bottom, alternating pools and riffles), and reasonably abundant aquatic life. Because of the carbonates and other favorable aspects of the water chemistry, diatoms, green algae, and cyanobacteria (formerly called "blue-green algae") thrive on the cobbles and boulders of the riffles and on the rubble of the bottoms of the pools. These riffles also contribute oxygen to the water by causing turbulence and entrapping air from the surface. The combination of abundant oxygen and food in the form of various algae and cyanobacteria, as well as organic material washed into the river from the productive riparian areas and meadows upstream, supports good populations but a limited diversity of aquatic insects and other invertebrates. Of these aquatic macroinvertebrates, caddisflies are the most common. Species indicative of high water quality, such as stoneflies and mayflies, are less abundant in the Animas than in nearby rivers (Japhet, personal communication 1991). Nonetheless, these aquatic invertebrates provide the principal foods for the trout that lurk in the pools of the Animas.

Fish dispersed from the stocking program in Durango produce the sparse population of brown and rainbow trout for several miles both upstream and downstream of town. Brown trout may be found as far upstream as Baker's Bridge. Above Durango, in the valley where the river meanders, there is little suitable habitat for algae, aquatic invertebrates, and trout. The bottom and banks are generally sandy, and there are no cobbles or boulders to which aquatic organisms can attach themselves. This reach of the river is poor habitat for trout, but other fishes may be found here. Carp *(Cyprinus carpio)* are present in the Animas Valley above Durango, and they become increasingly more common as the river proceeds southward toward the state line. The same holds true for bluehead sucker *(Catastomus discobolus)*, flannelmouth sucker *(C. latipinnis)*, and white sucker *(C. commersoni)*. Occasionally black bullhead catfish *(Ictalurus melas)* may be present in the Animas Valley above Durango, but they are thought to be escapees from farm ponds in the valley. Speckled dace *(Rhinichthys osculus)* and fathead minnow *(Pimephales promelas)* also inhabit the river, primarily south of Durango (Japhet, personal communication 1991). An inconspicuous but interesting native fish in the Animas River and its tributaries, a small bottom-dweller called the mottled sculpin *(Cottus bairdi)*, thrives only in clean, cobble-bedded mountain streams.

Despite poor water quality in its upper reaches produced by both natural phenomena and human-caused pollution, the Animas River throughout much of its length is a beautiful and reasonably productive stream. It supports extensive plant and animal communities in its riparian zone. Water from the Animas irrigates many farms and furnishes towns with municipal water supplies. It has the potential to become an outstanding sport fishery. Whitewater sports and recreation opportunities created by spring and summer flows have developed. Thus, the Animas River is a precious resource worthy of protection and improvement through conservation and pollution abatement and control.

REFERENCES

Albrecht, C., 1988. Heavy metal concentrations in the Animas River, southwest Colorado. Senior thesis, Fort Lewis College, Department of Geology, Durango, CO, 27 pp.

Cohan, D. R., B. W. Anderson, and R. D. Ohmart, 1979. Avian population responses to salt cedar along the lower Colorado River, in R. R. Johnson and J. F. McCormick, technical coordinators, *Strategies for protection and management of floodplain wetlands and other riparian ecosystems* (proceedings of the symposium). Callaway Gardens, GA: U.S. Department of Agriculture, Forest Service GTR-WO-12, pp. 371–382.

Fenner, P., W. W. Brady, and D. R. Patton, 1984. Observations on seeds and seedlings of Fremont Cottonwood. *Desert Plants,* v. 6, pp. 55–58.

Four Corners Environmental Research Institute, 1975. Biological and chemical studies of selected reaches and tributaries of the Colorado River in the State of Colorado (unpublished report). Durango, Colorado, Four Corners Environmental Research Institute for the Colorado Department of Health, 95 pp.

Hoover, R. L., and D. L. Wills, eds., 1987. *Managing forested lands for wildlife.* Denver: Colorado Division of Wildlife and U.S. Department of Agriculture, Forest Service, Rocky Mountain Region, 459 pp.

Johnson, A. F., 1989. The thin-green line: Riparian corridors and endangered species in Arizona and New Mexico, in G. Mackintosh, ed., *In defense of wildlife, preserving communities and corridors.* Washington, DC: Defenders of Wildlife, pp. 35–46.

Johnson, R. R., 1979. The lower Colorado River, a western system, in R. R. Johnson and J. F. McCormick, technical coordinators, *Strategies for protection and management of floodplain wetlands and other riparian ecosystems* (proceeding of the symposium). Callaway Gardens, GA: U.S. Department of Agriculture, Forest Service GTR-WO-12, pp. 41–55.

Leopold, L. B., M. G. Wolman, and J. P. Miller, 1964. *Fluvial processes in geomorphology.* New York: W. H. Freeman and Company, 522 pp.

Miller, G. C., and M. D. Bowman, 1985. Progress report, in G. C. Miller, ed., Ecosystem management in the Colorado Division of Wildlife (unpublished report), Denver: Colorado Division of Wildlife.

Simons, D. B., 1979. Effects of stream regulation on channel morphology, in J. V. Ward and J. A. Storkford, eds., *The ecology of regulated streams,* New York: Plenum Press, pp. 95–111.

Ugland, R. C., B. J. Cochran, R. G. Kretschman, E. A. Wilson, and J. D. Bennett, 1990. *Water resources data for Colorado, Water Year 1989, Colorado River Basin.* U.S. Geological Survey, Water-Data Report CO-89-2, 402 pp.

United States Geological Survey, 1971–1989. *Water resources data for Colorado.* U.S. Geological Survey, Water-Data Reports CO-71 through CO-88.

Western Aquatics, Inc., 1985. Use attainability analysis of the upper Animas River (unpublished report). Laramie, WY: Western Aquatics Inc. for Standard Metals Corp., 94 pp.

Woodling, J., 1980. *Game fish of Colorado.* Denver: Colorado Division of Wildlife, 40 pp.

Woodling, J., 1985. *Colorado's little fish: A guide to the minnows and other lesser known fishes in the State of Colorado.* Denver: Colorado Division of Wildlife, 77 pp.

PART III

HUMAN HISTORY ALONG THE SAN JUAN SKYWAY

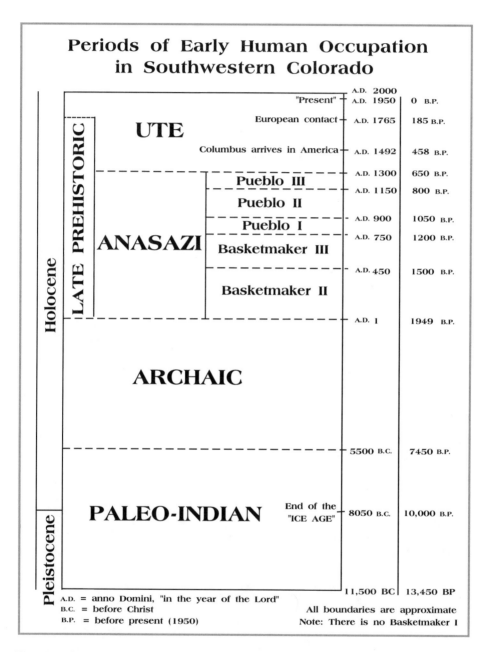

Fig. 14.1 Periods of human occupation based on artifacts.

CHAPTER 14

THE FORAGERS OF THE FOREST

PHILIP DUKE

In this chapter I will present a description of the archaeological evidence for occupation of the San Juan Skyway area by mobile hunter-gatherers (sometimes called foragers) (Fig. 14.1). Prior to the development of agriculture, hunting and gathering was the only subsistence strategy practiced in the Four Corners region. Even after the adoption of agriculture, hunting and gathering was the predominant subsistence strategy in those areas above approximately 7,000 feet (2,150 m). Hunting and gathering may have been practiced by resident forest populations, by Anasazi agriculturalists, or by both groups.

Archaeological research in the higher reaches of the San Juan National Forest, as elsewhere in the Rockies, has only relatively recently begun. Obvious reasons for this late start include the region's relative inaccessibility and harsher environmental conditions, even during the summer, compared to those of lower elevations. Another reason is the erroneous assumption that mountain sites are shallow and eroded and thus unsuitable for excavation. A final and more pernicious reason is that because archaeology in North America has been relegated to a subdiscipline of anthropology, scholars have in the past tended to organize their research along the lines of ethnographic culture areas. The original formulations of these areas were based on the assumption that the mountains were essentially impenetrable and unusable by native Americans except during the summer months or prior to their acquiring the horse. The mountains were conceived, therefore, as "refugia," used only when absolutely necessary. Consequently, in a splendid example of a self-fulfilling prophecy, archaeologists tended not to look in the mountains for prehistoric occupation, thereby "confirming" the ethnographers' predictions.

Fortunately, this perception is changing, and although work is still tentative and provisional, a much clearer picture of prehistoric occupation of the mountains is now emerging. Most important, numerous archaeologists, not only in Colorado (Benedict 1992, Black 1991) but also in other parts of the Rockies, now seem comfortable proposing indigenous cultural traditions.

CULTURE HISTORY

Culture history is normally the first research objective whenever archaeologists enter terra incognita. This phase of research attempts to organize data into preliminary classification schemes and to answer four cardinal questions: *what* (what are the artifacts? what are the sites? what were they used for?); *when* (when were they made?); *where* (where are these artifacts? where are the sites found?); and *who* (who made them? who left them behind?).

Culture histories for the Colorado Rockies are modified versions of ones borrowed from other areas, such as the Great Plains. The Paleo-Indian Period (12,000–5500 B.C.) is characterized by the exploitation of megafauna, seasonal nomadism, and the manufacture of large, finely worked projectile points. The succeeding Archaic Period (5500 B.C. to A.D. 1) is characterized by the appearance of a more generalized hunting and gathering economy and the production of distinctive dart points and is fairly well represented throughout the mountains (Fig. 14.1).

The Late Prehistoric Period (A.D. 1 to European contact) is defined archaeologically by the appearance of the bow and arrow. Study of this period in the northern Southwest is dominated by the Anasazi, whose cultural tradition is described in detail in Chapter 15. It is likely that at some point in this period the prehistoric ancestors of the Utes arrived. In the first definitive statement of Ute prehistory, Buckles (1971) was very cautious in linking prehistoric and historic cultures and did not see any strong evidence for an in situ development of Ute culture (Buckles 1988, p. 224).

Others, based on linguistic and other evidence, have suggested an immigration into western Colorado between A.D. 1200 and A.D. 1400 (Reed 1988, pp. 79–80). Estimates of how long Utes and other native American tribes have been in the area depend partially on their being recognized in the archaeological record. Unfortunately, this is a hazardous undertaking for numerous theoretical and methodological reasons. For example, some scholars believe that such artifacts as the Desert Side-notched points, Uncompahgre brownware pottery, certain rock-art styles, and even wickiup types are diagnostic of the Utes; others violently disagree. A recent symposium on Eastern Ute archaeology (Nickens 1988) has clearly demonstrated that Buckles's pioneering study of Ute archaeology provides only the initial impetus to such work and that much scholarship still needs to be done.

Within this context, some archaeologists have attempted a more specific culture-historical scheme for the mountains. For example, Black (1991) has defined the Mountain Tradition, which is characterized by seasonal movements between the foothills and tundra zones. This tradition may have continued as late as 700 years before the present (B.P.) (A.D. 1250) in some areas of the southern Colorado Rockies.

PREHISTORIC SITES IN THE SKYWAY AREA

The foregoing abbreviated discussion provides the backdrop for a more specific discussion of archaeology in the San Juan National Forest. It is important to reiterate at the beginning that, until recently, virtually all archaeological work in the San Juan Mountains has been conducted in the form of cultural resource surveys.

Paleo-Indian occupation of the San Juan National Forest and adjacent areas has recently been summarized by York (1991). A total of twelve points have been found so far, all of which belong to the Plano (late Paleo-Indian) Tradition. Of these, eight were found on the Dolores Plateau, north of the town of Dolores. York argued that these points represent the remains of a definite occupation of the area — perhaps beginning as early as 10,000 B.P. (8050 B.C.) — rather than simply containing artifacts brought into the area by later peoples. Several of these sites, in fact, have multiple components. One such, the Glade Road site, located northwest of Dolores at an altitude of 7,620 feet (3,330 m), also contains Archaic and Anasazi artifacts (King and Bradley 1985).

Archaic sites exist as isolated finds, campsites, and specialized activity areas and are far more prevalent than Paleo components. The single best source of information on the Archaic in the area comes from the excavation of two habitation sites, 5ML45 and 46, at Piedra Pass (Reed 1981, 1984). Artifacts, as well as pollen samples, indicate that a wide-spectrum subsistence economy was practiced at the sites: tansy mustard, huckleberry, wild onion, blackbrush, currants, groundberries, and goosefoot *(chenopodia)* were all exploited (Reed 1981, p. 62), and deer and elk were hunted. It is likely that the sites were occupied in late summer. Tests yielded radiocarbon dates of approximately 5900 B.C. and 1800 B.C.

A government-sponsored survey of Ridges Basin and upper Wildcat Canyon, located approximately 3 miles southwest of Durango, recovered thirty separate Archaic components (Winter et al. 1985). This was the first indication of a large Archaic presence in the area, and more likely will be found. The failure to discover Archaic components locally prior to this survey almost certainly is due to the nature of previous archaeological investigations there, most of which were conducted by amateur archaeologists interested primarily in Anasazi remains.

Late Prehistoric sites are found throughout the forest. These comprise scatters of lithic artifacts and waste material. Some sites have pottery affiliated with the Anasazi, Ute, or other ethnic groups. Recently we have found Anasazi pottery west in the vicinity of Kennebec Pass (at the headwaters of the La Plata River) at an altitude over 12,000 feet (3,670 m). It is unclear, however, whether the sherd was dropped by an Anasazi hunter or represents the remains of some type of exchange system between high-altitude hunter-gatherers and Anasazi farmers.

During the succeeding Historic Period, aboriginal groups, primarily the Utes, summered in the project area and surrounding locales. Their sites comprise objects of European origin and possibly bottle glass that was shaped into tools. Historic Ute occupation in the lower elevations is represented by hundreds of "scarred" ponderosa pine trees, the scars left by the removal of inner bark for human consumption (Martorano 1981, Martorano 1988, Swetnam 1984). Martorano (1988, p. 13) dated the majority of these trees in Colorado to between 1815 and 1875. This date is consistent with the trees' use as stress food, because during this period the Utes were being pushed from their traditional territory under the onslaught of Euro-American invasion. Structure 5 at Talus Village, a few miles north of Durango, may also be of Ute origin. This structure was tree-ring-dated to between the fifteenth and eighteenth centuries and was associated with a Desert Side-notched point (although my earlier caveat on the problems of ethnically diagnostic artifacts still applies). The remains of hogans and wickiups are also found throughout the forest, some of them built within the last thirty years. It is unclear in most cases, however, whether they were built by Utes, Navajo, or other native Americans.

Although not strictly archaeological, the Beaver Creek Massacre site, 16 miles north of Dolores, marks the location of Colorado's last Indian "battle." Here, on June 19, 1885, six Utes (three men, two women, and one child) were killed by a band of local cowboys. The site is held to be sacred by the Utes.

The precise details of the Anasazi presence in the study area are covered in Chapter 15. Worthy of mentioning in this chapter, however, is the need for future research to investigate fully the precise nature of this presence (whether it be the result of seasonal excursions into the mountains or trade with resident hunter-gatherer populations) and the temporal dynamics to the relationship between foragers and agriculturalists.

PREHISTORIC WAYS OF LIFE

Despite the emphasis on culture history, it has become more feasible over the past few years to begin to understand the forest dwellers' way of life. For example, a survey of the Elk Creek valley, southeast of Silverton, was intended to answer some elementary questions about prehistoric occupation of the high-altitude regions of the San Juan National Forest (Duke 1991, Duke and Blackshear 1992). A total of 490 acres (1,211 ha) between elevations of 9,800 and 12,800 feet (3,000 and 3,600 m) were surveyed. The nine prehistoric finds, which all consisted of isolated stone debitage or tools, are enigmatic, and their nature precludes many substantive conclusions. Their value lies in their revealing some elementary propositions about prehistoric utilization of the area and, more important, in their providing initial data that can structure future work. For instance, the different ecological zones, primarily controlled by altitude, are highly compressed because of the rapid elevation increase in the study area. Prehistoric groups, therefore, had access to a wide array of resources within a fairly confined territory.

The isolated lithic finds demonstrate that humans inhabited the Elk Creek area during the prehistoric period. Significantly, although the bulk of the material was found in the lower reaches of the valley at an altitude of approximately 10,000 feet (3,100 m) above sea level, three pieces were found at significantly higher elevations. These pieces are the remains of stone-tool manufacturing or food-processing activities. Interestingly, no projectile points were found.

Future work in the area should attempt to determine the location of prehistoric campsites. It is possible that the campsites are hidden by vegetation or soil deposition, especially in the lower areas of Elk Creek, where deposition as a result of the meandering of the creek itself can be expected and where grass and duff layers are thick. This lower part of the valley also lacks the side terraces on which campsites are often located in this type of terrain. Alternatively, the absence of campsites may reflect the absence of habitation. Elk Creek may merely have served as a communication corridor between the headwaters of the Rio Grande and the Animas River. It is significant that a local archaeologist reported two large lithic scatters on the eastern side of the Continental Divide, just across from the eastern end of Elk Creek.

The absence of major sites (of all types) along the Divide is also puzzling. It may simply reflect that too small an area was surveyed (a caution that may apply to the whole survey area). Alternatively, perhaps this section of the Continental Divide was sufficiently distant from lower elevation areas not to have attracted peoples on summer hunting and vision-quest expeditions.

CONCLUDING REMARKS

It is clear that work on the prehistoric and historic foragers of the San Juan National Forest is still in its infancy. The list of questions still to be answered is no doubt infinite, but several areas of need are immediately obvious.

First, the data base is constantly growing as the pace of government-mandated cultural resource studies quickens. However, as is so often the case, these data need to be synthesized and organized into regionally applicable culture histories. As long as the majority of work in the area is limited to surface surveys, we will be unable to develop the detailed chronologies that the excavation of both single- and multicomponent sites can offer.

Second, archaeologists still need to investigate the precise nature of human occupation of the area through time, and they can only accomplish this by developing precise paleoenvironmental sequences and models of seasonal movement based on the changing accessibility of faunal and floral resources.

Third, archaeologists need to understand the precise nature of the relationship between Anasazi groups and contemporary hunter-gatherers resident in the forest.

Finally, and perhaps most important, work on the later prehistory of the area needs to involve, at a fundamental level, the participation of contemporary native American groups, especially the Utes. Archaeology needs to demonstrate its relevance to these peoples, to their traditions, and to their history. If, in the past, these groups have been unwilling to contribute to archaeological studies, it behooves archaeologists to ask why and to encourage their participation.

REFERENCES

Benedict, J. B., 1992. Footprints in the snow: High altitude cultural ecology of the Colorado Front Range, U.S.A. *Arctic and Alpine Research*, v. 24, no. 1, pp. 1–16.

Black, K., 1991. Archaic continuity in the Colorado Rockies: The mountain tradition. *Plains Anthropologist*, v. 36, pp. 1–29.

Buckles, W. G., 1988. Discussion, in Paul R. Nickens, ed., *Archaeology of the Eastern Ute: A Symposium,* Colorado Council of Professional Archaeologists, Occasional Paper 1, pp. 218–232.

Buckles, W. G., 1971. The Uncompahgre complex: Historic Ute archaeology and prehistoric archaeology on the Uncompahgre Plateau in west-central Colorado (Ph.D. thesis). University of Colorado, Boulder, CO.

Duke, P., 1991. A Class II Archaeological Survey of Portions of the Weminuche Wilderness Area, San Juan National Forest, San Juan County, Colorado, in *The Grenadier Archaeological Project-1990 season report,* Durango, CO: San Juan National Forest.

Duke, P., and B. Blackshear, 1992. Public archaeology in the San Juan National Forest: The 1990 Grenadier Archaeological Project, *Southwestern Lore,* no. 58, pp. 15–34.

King, T. J., Jr., and S. R. Bradley, 1985. Investigations at the Glade Road site (5DL 775), a possible late paleo-Indian, archaic, Anasazi base camp. *Southwestern Lore,* v. 51, pp. 1–29.

Martorano, M. A., 1988. Culturally peeled trees and Ute Indians in Colorado, in P. R. Nickens, ed., *Archaeology of the Eastern Ute: A symposium,* Colorado Council of Professional Archaeologists, Occasional Paper 1, pp. 5–21.

Martorano, M. A., 1981. Scarred ponderosa pine trees reflecting cultural utilization of bark (M.A. thesis). Colorado State University, Fort Collins, CO, 127 pp.

Nickens, P. R., ed., 1988. *Archaeology of the eastern Ute: A symposium* Colorado Council of Professional Archaeologists, Occasional Paper 1, 232 pp.

Reed, A. D., 1988. Ute cultural chronology, in P. R. Nickens, ed., *Archaeology of the Eastern Ute: A symposium,* Colorado Council of Professional Archaeologists, Occasional Paper 1, pp. 79–101.

Reed, A. D., 1984. Archaeological investigations of two archaic campsites located along the continental divide, Mineral County, Colorado. *Southwestern Lore,* no. 50, pp. 1–34.

Reed, A. D., 1981. Archaeological investigations of two archaic campsites located along the continental divide, Mineral County, Colorado (unpublished report). Durango, CO: San Juan National Forest.

Swetnam, T. W., 1984. Peeled ponderosa pine trees: A record of inner bark utilization by Native Americans. *Journal of Ethnobiology,* v. 4, pp. 177–190.

Winter, J., W. E. Reynolds, and J. A. Ware, 1985. The cultural resources of Ridges Basin and Upper Wildcat Canyon (unpublished report). Salt Lake City, UT: U.S. Bureau of Reclamation.

York, R., 1991. Evidence for paleo-Indians on the San Juan National Forest, southwestern Colorado. *Southwestern Lore,* v. 57, pp. 5–22.

CHAPTER 15

THE ANASAZI: PREHISTORIC FARMERS

GARY MATLOCK

Two major groups of prehistoric peoples inhabited the San Juan Skyway region, the Archaic and the Anasazi. Of the two, the Anasazi are by far the better known (see Fig. 14.1, p. 192). Visitors flock from throughout the world to see the famous cliff dwellings at Mesa Verde, the silent stone cities at Chaco Canyon, and the hundreds of other prehistoric Anasazi sites in parks and monuments scattered throughout the Four Corners. Less well known, but equally important, are the thousands of Anasazi sites found on private property, Indian reservations, and lands managed by the U.S. Forest Service and Bureau of Land Management in the Four Corners area.

The Anasazi were a prehistoric farming people who lived in southwestern Colorado for more than thirteen centuries, from just before the birth of Christ until A.D. 1300. They left behind tens of thousands of large and small villages, hamlets, towers, ceremonial kivas, and other structures built of stone, adobe, and wood. Though most of these structures have fallen into low mounds of rock over the centuries, many ruins remain virtually intact in protected sandstone canyon alcoves. In southwestern Colorado today, it almost impossible to walk through a piñon forest, along a canyon rim, or across a farmer's field without encountering a scattering of broken pottery, chips of stone, and tumbled masonry walls of a prehistoric village. What is common to the residents of the Four Corners is rare and exciting to those from other parts of the country and the world.

Unlike the Archaic peoples and other mobile hunter-gatherers found in the San Juan Mountains and discussed in Chapter 14, the Anasazi were sedentary farmers. Their primary crop was corn, or Zea maize, a multicolored form of the corn we grow today. They also grew substantial quantities of squashes and pumpkins and several varieties of beans, a staple crop still grown by dryland farmers in southwestern Colorado today.

The Anasazi are classified by archaeologists as belonging to the Formative Period of human society. This period is characterized by subsistence farming, construction of permanent or semi-permanent dwellings, production of a large variety of tools and crafts such as pottery and jewelry, use of storage vessels and rooms, and the development of socially integrative structures for community rituals and ceremonials. Formative peoples also usually conducted substante trade with nearby groups.

Many of these unique Anasazi sites can be found along the Skyway or within a short drive of it. Several dozen of these sites have been excavated and are open to visitors.

A BRIEF HISTORY OF ANASAZI CULTURE

Anasazi remains in southwestern Colorado are at the northern edge of the prehistoric world of the Anasazi (Cordell 1984). At its peak, this world stretched from the lower slopes of the San Juan Mountains in Colorado throughout most of the Four Corners region and much of the Colorado Plateau (Fig. 15.1).

The Four Corners is a region of great environmental and topographic diversity, with landscapes ranging from the green, well-watered San Juan Mountains to the hot, dry, sandy Navajo desert. In between lie miles of flat mesas cut by sheer-walled sandstone canyons. These mesas are covered with dense gray-green piñon and juniper forests and expanses of great sage plains, broken here and there by the wide, tree-lined river valleys of the Colorado, the San Juan, the Rio Grande, and smaller connecting streams.

This land possesses beauty as diverse as the environments and landforms themselves. The former Anasazi realm includes the

Grand Canyon, Monument Valley, Canyonlands National Park, Canyon de Chelly, Mesa Verde, the San Juan Mountains, and numerous other places known for their outstanding scenery. Because Anasazi farmers needed a long growing season, most of the Anasazi sites along the Skyway lie at lower elevations between Durango and Dolores, south of the San Juan National Forest.

The Anasazi lived in southwestern Colorado for more than thirteen centuries. Emerging from the Archaic hunters and gatherers, they developed slowly, over many centuries, the culture we recognize today. Archaeologists have carefully tracked that development and have divided the culture into a number of different time periods (Matlock and Warren 1988). Change from one period to another was slow, imperceptible to the Anasazi themselves, and erratic from place to place.

THE BASKETMAKER PERIODS (200 B.C.–A.D. 750)

The earliest evidence for the Anasazi culture in southwestern Colorado was found near the modern town of Durango. In the mid-1930s a local amateur archaeologist, Zeke Flora, discovered two deep sandstone caves, or rock shelters, in a remote valley just north of Durango. At the back of the cave he found scores of small red, white, green, and black figures painted on the sandstone walls but observed little else that would indicate a major archaeological site. However, when he excavated a section of the North Shelter, he found, buried in a natural sandstone "vault," the most remarkable mummified human remains ever encountered in the United States. The dry cave environment had preserved intact the bodies of over half a dozen 2,000-year-old Anasazi people. Included with them, or nearby, were also well-preserved baskets, sandals, nets, cordage, beads, necklaces, and many other rare objects.

Recognizing that he had discovered a site of great importance, Flora called the University of Colorado Henderson Museum in Boulder and talked to Earl Morris, a prominent southwestern archaeologist of the time. After a preliminary assessment, Morris concluded that the site, called variously the Falls Creek Caves or Durango Rock Shelters, was from what archaeologists called the Basketmaker II Period of Anasazi culture, a period previously unknown in Colorado.

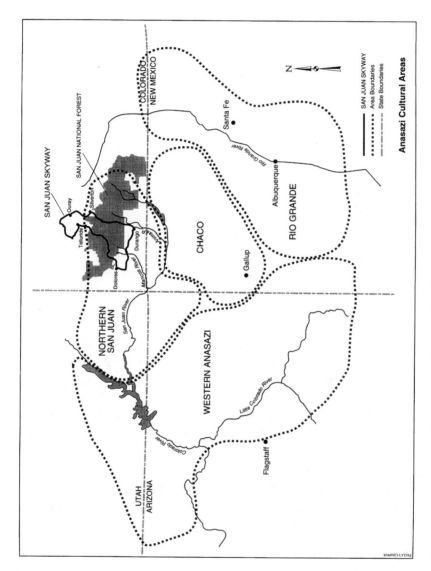

Fig. 15.1 Area occupied by Anasazi. Courtesy U.S. Forest Service.

Before Flora's discovery archaeologists working at these early Basketmaker II sites had found only small stone-slab-lined pits. Further excavation at the Falls Creek Caves by Morris led to the discovery of actual houses used by the Basketmaker people (Morris and Burgh 1954). Even more important, wooden logs used in the wood and adobe structures had also been preserved. These wooden beams yielded dates of between 200 B.C. and A.D. 200, the oldest dates known for Anasazi people (Dean 1975).

Though the wide Animas River valley, north of Durango, is littered today with shoddy trailer houses, condominiums, golf courses, and other leavings of our own society, it would have looked very different 2,000 years ago. Across the flat river valley from Durango almost to the present site of the Tamarron resort, one would have seen small garden plots of corn and squashes laid out to conform with the land and the figures of Anasazi men, women, and children working the farm plots.

Based on the discoveries at the Falls Creek Caves and later sites found in the valley, the Basketmaker Anasazi probably wore elaborate necklaces of juniper berry, shell, and ground, polished colored stone (Morris and Burgh 1954). Women carried babies on their backs in elaborately prepared cradle boards.

Basketmaker Anasazi sites are rare, and the population probably was relatively small. The people lived in small family groups and probably hunted and gathered as much food as they raised by farming. By the end of this period, the Anasazi were well established in the Four Corners, and from this base they expanded throughout a large area of the Southwest.

During the next period of Anasazi culture, the Basketmaker III Period (ca. A.D. 450–750), the Anasazi continued to live in the Animas Valley north of present-day Durango. But they had by now spread widely throughout the Four Corners and over the full range of the prehistoric Anasazi world (Nickens and Hull 1982). Basketmaker III culture varied from earlier Anasazi culture in a number of significant ways: the development of a distinctive type of subterranean or semisubterranean "pithouse" with an associated storage room or rooms; the development of ceramic storage and cooking vessels to supplement the baskets used almost exclusively during the earlier period; the addition of beans to the agricultural inventory; and other changes (Fig. 15.2).

During the Basketmaker III Period, nearly all Anasazi people lived in pithouses near their farm plots and close to available water sources. The pithouses seem to be single family units, although excavations have revealed some two- to five-unit pithouse villages that were probably occupied by extended families. Each pithouse would normally contain the generally circular subterranean main living structure, a slightly smaller attached antechamber or storage room, a central firepit (often constructed of stone or with a clay collar), and a seemingly random set of subfloor pits and storage vaults, some filled with sand on which to set hot pottery vessels. The occasional presence of outdoor firepits attests to the cooking and processing of foods out of doors. Careful excavations of these plaza areas have encountered large, bell-shaped storage pits dug into the ground surface. These pits were ordinarily lined with clay and would have been relatively insect-, rodent-, and human-proof.

All of these storage pits tell us that the Basketmaker III Anasazi must have been very successful in their farming, hunting, wild-plant gathering, and other subsistence activities and that surplus foods must have been available. The fact that these pithouses and small villages are scattered widely and in open, unprotected locations suggests that the Basketmaker III peoples must have been relatively free of hostilities from outside groups or from disagreements and rivalries within.

THE PUEBLO I PERIOD (A.D. 750–900)

The Pueblo I (PI) Period extends from about A.D. 700 or 750 to A.D. 900 or 950, depending on what part of the Anasazi world you happened to be in. During this period, the pithouse continued to be used for living, but the first above-ground structures were built. These small, contiguous rooms were made of upright wooden poles coated on both sides with a thick adobe or mud plaster, an architectural form known worldwide as "wattle and daub" (Plog 1979). The rooms tended to be arranged in a semicircle and generally faced south, capturing the sun's warmth in the plaza work

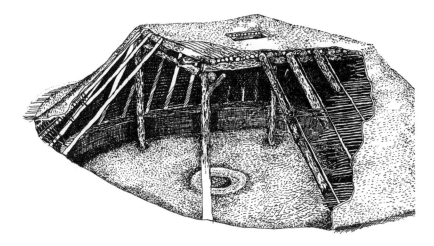

Fig. 15.2   Basketmaker pithouse. Sketch courtesy Mesa Verde National Park.

areas. The Anasazi and other peoples in the Four Corners region regularly made very effective use of solar energy.

In its most typical form, a PI village consisted of several fairly large pithouses with an arc of above-ground wattle and daub structures nearby. Occasionally some of these structures used stone masonry in portions of the walls, with upright stones providing a stabilizing foundation for the vertical post and adobe walls.

Another major characteristic of the villages of this period was their increased size and the presence of structures for ceremonial and/or community use. Over time pithouses became larger and larger, then more and more standardized in terms of their internal features, with a great deal of care being taken in their construction. These elaborate pithouses became, in time, the well-known multifunction (ceremonial and social) kivas of the Anasazi and their modern descendants, the Pueblo Indians, who continue to use them today.

As you might expect, the other crafts, tools, and material items manufactured by the Anasazi during the PI Period were also more elaborate and greater in kind and number compared to the Basketmaker III Period. Ceramic vessels with black and white painted decorations were well made. Baskets and sandals continued in use, as did many elaborate forms of jewelry in shell, turquoise, jet, clay, and other materials (Fig. 15.3).

Fig. 15.3   Anasazi artifacts from southwestern Colorado. National Park Service photo by Fred E. Mang, Jr.

Evidence of these early periods, the first 1,000 years of Anasazi culture, is hard to see from the Skyway itself, but Mesa Verde National Park and the Anasazi Heritage Center in Dolores provide excellent displays of sites from this era.

THE PUEBLO II AND PUEBLO III ANASAZI PERIODS (A.D. 900–1300)

By about A.D. 900, the Anasazi were living in masonry villages in large family or clan groups. These settlements and the highly distinctive pottery from the Pueblo II and III Periods probably represent the best known and most distinctive characteristics of Anasazi people. During both of these last periods of their history, the Anasazi produced unique and enduring contributions to world culture.

During the Pueblo II Period, the Anasazi splintered into a number of regionally distinct groups in various parts of the Four

Corners, each with its own unique masonry, pottery, and other cultural items. The Anasazi of southwestern Colorado are called the Northern San Juan or Mesa Verde Branch. Evidence of this branch can be seen along the Skyway, and therefore it is the focus of this discussion.

The masonry walls that form the homes and villages of the PII and PIII sites were made of shaped sandstone set in a simple adobe or clay mortar. The villages consist of clusters of mostly rectangular rooms that by the later part of the PII Period were often two stories in height. Within or outside these living and storage rooms were found circular masonry-walled subterranean kivas (Fig. 15.4).

Fig. 15.4 Photo of Cliff Palace at Mesa Verde National Park in southwestern Colorado. Courtesy Mesa Verde National Park.

These Anasazi manufactured hundreds of fine craft items. Foremost of these were beautifully made ceramic bowls, pitchers, specialized ritual jars, finely corrugated cooking and water-storage vessels, and unusual effigy and ritual forms. Though they are best known for their fine, creamy-white, almost perfectly smooth vessels bearing deep black geometric designs, the Anasazi in southwestern Colorado manufactured and traded for scores of different types and forms.

During the PII and PIII Periods, the population and size of Anasazi villages grew dramatically. Whereas early PII masonry villages had four or five rooms and a single kiva, by the mid-1100s large Anasazi settlements such as the Yellow Jacket site and others contained hundreds of rooms, kivas, and other structures within what by now had become substantial towns (Rohn 1989). Most of these large communities have yet to be excavated, and much remains to be learned about the Anasazi.

During the PII Period, the Anasazi of southwestern Colorado became part of or were influenced by so-called regional systems that developed out of Chaco Canyon to the south (Judge 1991). Several scores of small, specialized villages with traits of the Chaco people were constructed throughout the Four Corners. A number were built in southwestern Colorado, including the Escalante ruin and the Chimney Rock site (Reed et al. 1979, Eddy 1977). The regional sites probably served as trading centers, ritual centers, or processing centers for raw materials needed by the Chacoans. The Chacoan regional system collapsed in the late 1100s. Other, more complex features of Anasazi culture in southwestern Colorado at this time included the development of irrigation and water-control systems, extensive and intensive farming, large population centers or central towns, and communities exerting influence on surrounding smaller villages. All of these phenomena bespeak the elaborate and complex nature of Anasazi society at this time.

Despite these indications that Anasazi life was flourishing, troubles set in by the early thirteenth century, and many of the Anasazi in southwestern Colorado moved into large sandstone caves or overhangs, where they built large villages, apparently for defensive purposes. These are the cliff dwellings for which the

Anasazi are so well known. In fact, they represent only the very latest period of Anasazi culture and certainly one of its most unusual, if also most intriguing, forms.

At the end of the PIII Period, the Anasazi abandoned southwestern Colorado and other parts of the Four Corners. Most moved south to settle in or near existing villages along the Rio Grande River and its close tributaries. A few may have drifted into the villages of the Hopi in Arizona. This unusual total exodus from Colorado by a people so very successful in the past has puzzled archaeologists and visitors to the region since the Europeans first encountered the ruins in the late 1800s (Cordell 1984). Although some of the reasons have begun to emerge, a full explanation remains unclear. The most common and certainly one of the strongest theories is that environmental stress caused by a period of extreme dryness during the last part of the thirteenth century forced the abandonment. But drought alone cannot explain the migration into New Mexico.

With the collapse of the Chacoan branch in the latter part of the 1100s, a century of turmoil and instability seemed to follow for the Northern San Juan Anasazi. Some of them reoccupied the great cities at Chaco after its downfall. There may have been hostility and violence between the two branches or increased raiding and warfare between the Anasazi and nearby hunting and gathering groups. The location of villages in the cliffs would seem to suggest strongly that the Northern San Juan Anasazi sought protection against someone. There may have been too many people, too little food, and/or too little firewood to provide warmth, and Anasazi society may have been disrupted and distressed from the events leading to the collapse itself. Many archaeologists today look strongly to social and or organizational problems among the Anasazi (Cordell 1984).

In any case, there is no doubt that as the Anasazi left Colorado, they migrated into New Mexico and Arizona, where their descendants live today. They did not, as you will frequently hear, disappear mysteriously. The Pueblo Indians along the Rio Grande and the Hopi in northeastern Arizona include some of the descendants of the Anasazi. The way of life of the Anasazi, changed and altered in the last 700 years, is alive and well with them. But that is another story.

SUMMARY

Although the San Juan Skyway unquestionably offers some of the most beautiful mountain grandeur in the United States, it is well to remember that people have lived in and used the resources of these mountains, mesas, and canyons of southwestern Colorado for more than 8,000 years. The idea of pristine natural areas unused and unvisited by humans is a modern misconception. The Anasazi, the modern Ute Indians, and the Archaic people and Paleo-Indians before them have considered the wilderness areas of the San Juans home for a very long time. The lower mesas and canyons were intensively used by native American agriculturists for centuries. The farms you see today in southwestern Colorado are simply the latest example of a use that has been going on for almost 2,000 years.

VISITING ANASAZI SITES ALONG THE SKYWAY

Travelers who plan on visiting various Anasazi sites in the vicinity of the Skyway should stop by the local chamber of commerce in any town along the route or go to the U.S. Forest Service or U.S. Bureau of Land Management office in either Durango or Cortez. Below is a list of interesting and informative sites (Fig. 15.5).

Falls Creek Caves, Durango, Point of Interest 16

Anasazi Heritage Center, Dolores, Point of Interest 138

Lowry ruin and Pigg site, Pleasant View

Hovenweep National Monument

Crow Canyon Archaeological Center

Mesa Verde National Park, Point of Interest 143

Ute Mountain Tribal Park

The Colorado University Center, Cortez

Chimney Rock Archaeological Area, Chimney Rock

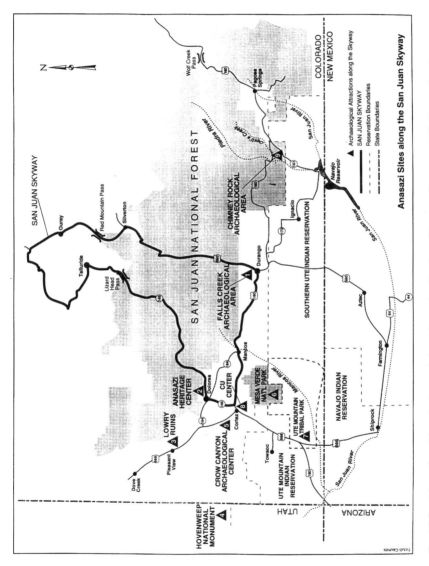

Fig. 15.5   Map of prehistoric Anasazi sites along the San Juan Skyway. Courtesy U.S. Forest Service.

REFERENCES

Cordell, L. S., 1984. *Prehistory of the Southwest.* Orlando, FL: Academic Press, Inc., 409 pp.

Dean, J., 1975. *Tree ring dates from Colorado, west Durango area.* Tucson, AZ: University of Arizona, Laboratory of Tree Ring Research, 89 pp.

Eddy, F. W., 1977. *Archaeological investigations at Chimney Rock Mesa, 1970–1972.* Boulder, CO: Colorado Archaeological Society, Memoir 1, 91 pp.

Judge, W. J., 1991. Chaco: Current views of prehistory and the regional system, in P. Crown and W. Judge, eds., *Prehistoric regional systems in the American southwest,* Sante Fe, NM: School of American Research Press, 369 pp.

Matlock, G., and S. Warren, eds., 1988. *Enemy ancestors: The Anasazi world with a guide to sites.* Flagstaff, AZ: Northland Press, 116 pp.

Morris, E. H., and R. F. Burgh, 1954. *Basket maker sites near Durango, Colorado.* Washington, D.C.: Carnegie Institution, Publication 604, 135 pp.

Nickens, P. R., and D. A. Hull, 1982. San Juan resource area, in *Archaeological resources of southwestern Colorado,* Denver: U.S. Bureau of Land Management, Cultural Resources Series 13.

Plog, F., 1979. Prehistory: Western Anasazi, in W. Sturtevant and A. Ortiz, eds., *Handbook of North American Indians, southwest,* Washington, DC: Smithsonian Institution, pp. 108–130.

Reed, A. D., J. A. Hallasi, A. S. White, and D. A. Breternitz, 1979. *The archeology and stabilization of the Dominguez and Escalante ruins.* Denver: U.S. Bureau of Land Management, Cultural Resources Series 7, 496 pp.

Rohn, A. H., 1989. Northern San Juan prehistory, in L. S. Cordell and G. J. Gunermans, eds., *Dynamics of southwest prehistory,* Washington, DC: Smithsonian Institution Press.

CHAPTER 16

THE SPANISH

RICHARD N. ELLIS

Long before Anglo-Americans visited the Southwest, the area was explored and settled by the Spanish. In 1540, almost seventy years before the founding of Jamestown or the landing of the pilgrim fathers at Plymouth, Francisco Vásques de Coronado led an exploring expedition into the Southwest that took his men from western Arizona to Kansas. More than fifty years later, in 1598, Juan de Oñate undertook the colonization of New Mexico.

New Mexico was a small and isolated frontier province at the farthest edge of the Spanish frontier, and even in the 1630s Santa Fe had a population of only some 250 Spaniards in addition to mestizos and christianized Indians. In 1680 the Pueblo Indians of New Mexico organized against the Spanish, and the Pueblo Revolt of that year successfully drove the Spanish from the province. It was not until 1693 that New Mexico was recolonized by Diego de Vargas, and three years later the population of New Mexico numbered only approximately 2,000 Spaniards and mestizos. The population of New Mexico grew in subsequent years, but it remained an isolated region whose people depended upon agriculture and stock raising for subsistence. New Mexico also was surrounded by Indian tribes, including Navajos, Utes, Apaches, and Comanches, who resisted Spanish efforts to control and to Christianize them and who were willing to fight to maintain their freedom and independence.

Though Spanish-Indian hostility was common in New Mexico, such conflict was intermittent, and many of those same Indian tribes also engaged in economic interchange with New Mexicans and with the Pueblo population of the Rio Grande Valley. Taos became a center for such trade, as Comanches, Apaches, and Utes began to make frequent commercial visits to that area, and in the latter half of the eighteenth century Taos began to host an important annual trade fair. The community of Abiquiu, in the Chama Valley, also became a center of commerce. The trade was important to both Indians and New Mexicans, and tribes such as the Utes were important suppliers of deerskins, which New Mexicans used themselves and exported to the south. "Without this trade," wrote one governor in the 1750s, the settlers "could not provide for themselves, for they have no other commerce other than that of these skins."

The Utes were an important commercial partner for New Mexico because they were generally more friendly than tribes such as the Comanches. In time their trade became significant enough that New Mexicans began to go into Ute country rather than waiting for the Utes to come to the trade fairs. It is not known when the first Spanish traders entered southwestern Colorado, for such trade was illegal and the participants were careful not to leave a written record. The trade probably began sometime about 1700, for one governor of that era proclaimed such activity by Spaniards and Indians illegal. In 1712 the governor indicated that New Mexicans were unaware of the royal order that outlawed trade on Indian land and commonly made such expeditions.

Spanish miners also explored the San Juans, although no contemporary written record of their activity exists in Spanish archival sources. Such prospecting was illegal without specific authorization, but physical evidence of mining clearly indicates that the Spanish penetrated into the San Juans in their search for precious metals.

The first recorded Spanish expedition into southwestern Colorado was led by Juan Maria de Rivera in 1765. Though the account of this trading expedition lacks detail, it is apparent that Rivera traveled into the La Plata Mountains and then proceeded westward. He journeyed down the Dolores River, turned to the San Miguel in the vicinity of present Naturita, and crossed the Uncompahgre Plateau, reaching the bottomlands of the Gunnison

Valley west of present-day Delta. He returned by ascending the Uncompahgre Valley and then crossed back over the Uncompahgre Plateau and retraced his original route. Along the way Rivera met Utes who told him he was the first Spaniard to go that way. Rivera, who returned to southwestern Colorado in the autumn of 1765, blazed the trail into Colorado and played an important role in making contact with the Utes in that country. In all likelihood other Spaniards followed Rivera's example, and in 1775 three members of his initial expedition returned to the vicinity of modern-day Delta.

The next major Spanish expedition into the region was led by Fray Francisco Atanasio Dominguez and by his subordinate, Fray Silvestre Vélez de Escalante, who kept the journal of the expedition. The Dominguez-Escalante expedition of 1776 was a major event. Spain's colonization of California and its fear of foreign encroachment in the area caused it to seek connections between the Pacific coast and other parts of the Spanish borderlands. Although Dominguez and Escalante did not accomplish the task of opening a route from New Mexico to California, they did undertake a remarkable exploring expedition. The small group included several members of Rivera's party from more than a decade before, and the fathers also had a copy of Rivera's journal, to which they referred from time to time.

The expedition left Santa Fe, ascended the Chama River, and ultimately reached the San Juan River. Traveling northwestward, they crossed the Animas River below present-day Durango and generally followed the route of the San Juan Skyway to the vicinity of present-day Mancos, whereupon they headed to the Dolores Valley. They paralleled the canyon of the Dolores, heading northwest, before turning northeast to the valley of the San Miguel River. The explorers proceeded across the flank of the Uncompahgre Plateau and entered the Uncompahgre Valley just south of present-day Montrose. The expedition continued northwest to Utah Lake, whereupon the fathers turned southward, ultimately returning to Santa Fe by way of the Hopi villages and the Pueblo of Zuni.

Although the Dominguez-Escalante expedition failed to open a road to California or to establish a frontier mission among the Utes and other Indians, their journey was of epic proportions. It indicated that the Spanish already were familiar with at least some of the area through which the expedition traveled, because the fathers already knew many of the place-names. It also is evident from comments by Dominguez, Escalante, and other Spanish officials that Colorado, at least as far as the valley of the Gunnison, was well known to traders from New Mexico.

The next recorded Spanish expedition that approached the vicinity of the San Juan Mountains was led by Juan Bautista de Anza in 1779. Anza was an experienced frontier officer when he assumed the governorship of New Mexico. He had served with distinction on the Sonoran frontier and also had led the overland expedition that founded San Francisco. By the time Anza was appointed governor of New Mexico, the province had suffered from more than seventy-five years of conflict with the Comanches. To surprise the Comanches under Cuerno Verde (Green Horn), Anza moved north from Santa Fe in August 1779. He crossed the Rio Grande to avoid detection and moved northward through Ojo Caliente and then along the west side of the San Luis Valley. Anza ultimately turned eastward and found and defeated Cuerno Verde near the mountain northwest of modern Walsenburg that bears the Comanche's name.

Though no evidence exists of official expeditions that returned to the area Anza explored, there is ample proof that private parties followed the general routes of Rivera and Dominguez and Escalante to penetrate southwestern Colorado. We know, for example, from 1805 reports by the governor of New Mexico that an individual who had served as a Ute interpreter made several trips into the Four Corners country, reaching as far northwest as the region of Utah Lake. We also know of a private expedition that left Abiquiu in 1813 and traveled to the general vicinity of Utah Lake. Upon learning of this expedition, the governor of New Mexico ordered the members of the small party to appear before a Spanish official and swear out affidavits. It appears from the testimony that the route was well known and that contacts with Indians along the route were well established, leading scholars to believe that trading parties seeking pelts and slaves penetrated this area with some frequency.

Documentary evidence of Spanish expeditions into Ute country to the north generally does not exist, but there are hints of such activity. During his expedition into the San Luis Valley and beyond, for example, Anza learned that civilians had explored to the headwaters of the Rio Grande. There also was an account of a three-month journey into Ute country in 1811, apparently stimulated by rumors from the Utes of a Spanish settlement that lay beyond their country. Because such expeditions were illegal, private parties certainly would not have left a written record, but trips of this sort must have been reasonably common because Spanish officials made repeated efforts to prevent them. In 1775, for example, the governor of New Mexico issued a proclamation prohibiting any trade in Ute territory, but the decree seems to have had little influence, as it was reissued three years later. At that time it was noted that traders had broken the law repeatedly with "rash impudence and obstinate disobedience." Several parties actually were brought to trial for conducting illegal trade in Ute country during the 1780s.

In all likelihood expeditions into Ute country increased during the last decade of the Spanish period, which was marked by the turmoil resulting from the independence movement. With the achievement of independence in 1821, Mexico abandoned the old Spanish policy of excluding foreign traders and allowed Americans into New Mexico, causing such communities as Taos and Santa Fe to become major commercial centers.

Despite the activity of Anglo-American traders, Hispanic traders continued to operate out of New Mexico, maintaining their connections with the Utes in the San Juan country and beyond. These individuals apparently were most interested in trading for Indian captives, and such activity attracted the attention of Mormon authorities following the founding of the Mormon colony in the Salt Lake Valley in 1847. In 1851 Utah authorities brought twenty Mexicans to trial for attempting to trade horses for Indian children, and in 1853 Governor Brigham Young noted that "a horde of Mexicans" had invaded Utah Territory and sent troops to the southern part of the territory to protect that area, directing them to arrest any Mexican traders. Undoubtedly most, if not all, of these traders reached the Utah area from New Mexico via the traditional trail of Rivera and the Dominguez-Escalante expedition, which took them through the San Juan country of southern Colorado.

During the Mexican period, Hispanics and Anglos opened trade between New Mexico and California, which brought increased travel through southwest Colorado. Antonio Armijo led the pioneering expedition in 1829. Armijo left Abiquiu in November with a party of thirty-one men and ascended the Chama Valley, crossed the Continental Divide, and followed Largo Canyon to the San Juan River. They continued on through southern Colorado, stopping at the Animas, La Plata, and Mancos Rivers before traveling westward to Los Angeles. Shortly afterward William Wolfskill journeyed from New Mexico to California by a more northerly route, which followed that of Dominguez and Escalante and became known as the Old Spanish Trail. Both Anglos and Hispanics used this pathway in years to come.

During the 1700s the community of Abiquiu, in the Chama Valley, was a major jumping-off point for exploring and trade expeditions to the north and to the west. Settlers in the area included both Spaniards and *genizaros* (detribalized Indians); the community of Abiquiu had its origin in a 1754 land grant to a genizaro population. Abiquiu played a major role in the expansion of the Hispanic frontier to the north and northwest. Local residents pushed their way up the Chama Valley toward present-day Colorado, and a significant number of Hispanic-surnamed pioneers in the San Juan Basin originally came from Abiquiu.

Hispanics from Abiquiu and elsewhere moved into the San Luis Valley and into the upper Chama Valley after the Treaty of Guadalupe Hidalgo in 1848. The Mexican governor had made the Tierra Amarilla land grant to Abiquiu residents in 1832, but the land initially was used for grazing. Permanent settlement apparently did not occur until after the Mexican War. By the late 1860s there were a number of small communities on the upper Chama, including Los Ojos and Tierra Amarilla, and these communities would become jumping-off points for further expansion to the north and west.

Exploration for gold in the San Juan Mountains drew Hispanics further north in the 1860s. Hispanics inhabited the two nearby towns of Del Norte and La Loma in the western part of the San Luis Valley. The area became a base for transportation across Stoney Pass to Baker's Park, the future site of Silverton. A road also was opened from Abiquiu to Pagosa Springs and then westward to bring supplies to the mining camps in the San Juans. In 1876 a wagon road was built from the Chama Valley to the San Juan River by way of Canyon Largo, which provided direct access to the San Juan mines and to the farming country in the valleys of the Animas, Los Pinos, Florida, and La Plata Rivers.

Hispanics settled in the San Juan Valley from Bloomfield and Blanco eastward to the mouth of the Piedra River. Some ranched or farmed; others found work on the Ute reservation in southern Colorado. They also found employment as construction workers on the Denver & Rio Grande Western Railroad, which crossed the reservation, reaching Durango in 1881. Many settled in communities such as La Posta in the Animas Valley and, ultimately, in Durango and the mining camps throughout the San Juan country (Fig. 16.1).

Hispanics engaged in agriculture, raised stock, and traded with their Ute neighbors. Some worked on the Southern Ute and Ute Mountain Reservations as employees of the U.S. government; others became construction workers, cowboys, and sheepherders.

Fig. 16.1   Telles Ford and Thomas Herrera with unnamed youth posing before the old Durango smelter. Courtesy Antonio Gilbert Herrera.

Fig. 16.2   The Herrera family portrait. Courtesy Antonio Gilbert Herrera.

Many labored on the railroad, in lumber camps, or in the mines and the smelters in Durango (Fig. 16.2). The lumber camp of McPhee, for example, had a significant Hispanic population. In some towns, such as Durango, they were subjected to discrimination and were forced to live in totally segregated barrios at the south end of town. During the 1920s Hispanics were targeted by the Ku Klux Klan, which was openly anti-Catholic and anti-Mexican.

Although largely ignored in textbooks, Rivera, Dominguez and Escalante, and a host of unknown New Mexicans carried out the earliest European explorations of southwestern Colorado. In the nineteenth century, Hispanos pushed northward up the Chama Valley, founding small communities along the San Juan and its tributaries, finding employment in mining, ranching, agriculture and railroading and working on the Ute reservations (Fig. 16.3). Although targets of prejudice and discrimination, Hispanics contributed to economic and population growth in the San Juan country.

Fig. 16.3 Portrait of Doloritas Valencia Sanchez. Courtesy Antonio Gilbert Herrera.

REFERENCES

Bannon, J. F., 1970. *The Spanish borderlands frontier 1513–1821.* New York: Holt, Rinehart and Winston, 308 pp.

Bolton, H. E., 1950. *Pageant in the wilderness: The story of the Escalante expedition to the Interior Basin, 1776.* Salt Lake City: Utah State Historical Society, 265 pp.

Cutter, D. C., 1977. Prelude to a pageant in the wilderness. *Western Historical Quarterly,* v. 8, pp. 5–14.

Hafen, L. R., 1954. *Old Spanish trail: Santa Fe to Los Angeles.* Glendale, CA: The Arthur H. Clark Co., 377 pp.

Sarah Platt Decker Chapter, Daughters of the American Revolution, 1942. *Pioneers of the San Juan Country,* 4 volumes. Colorado Springs, CO: Out West Printing.

Swadesh, F. L., 1974. *Los primeros pobladores: Hispanic Americans of the Ute frontier.* Notre Dame, IN: University of Notre Dame Press, 262 pp.

Twitchell, R. E., 1912. *Leading facts of New Mexico history,* volume II. Cedar Rapids, IA: The Torch Press.

Warner, T. J., ed., 1976. *The Dominguez-Escalante journal, Fray Angelico Chaves* (translation). Provo, UT: Brigham Young University Press, 203 pp.

Weber, D. J., 1982. *The Mexican Frontier, 1821–1846.* Albuquerque, NM: University of New Mexico Press, 416 pp.

Weber, D. J., 1971. *The Taos Trappers.* Norman, OK: University of Oklahoma Press, 263 pp.

Weigle, M., 1976. *Brothers of light, brothers of blood.* Albuquerque: University of New Mexico Press, 300 pp.

CHAPTER 17

THE UTES

RICHARD N. ELLIS

When the Spanish arrived in the Southwest, the people they called the Yutas, or Utes, ranged across much of present-day Colorado, northern New Mexico, and Utah. According to anthropologists, the Utes were organized into loosely defined bands, but the basic social unit was the extended family, which could most efficiently utilize the available natural resources. These small family units of perhaps ten to forty people followed a seasonal migration pattern, moving into the higher country in the spring and summer and returning to lower elevations in the autumn. They hunted deer, elk, antelope, and occasionally mountain buffalo and other animals and gathered seeds, fruits, and wild berries in the summer and fall.

Each extended family had a recognized use area. Every autumn the Utes moved southward out of the high country of southern Colorado to exploit the antelope herds in the canyon and mesa country south of the San Juan Mountains. In spring they gathered in large groups for the annual Bear Dance, which was an important ceremonial and social event, and then moved into the high mountain valleys of the San Juans and the Uncompahgre Plateau.

Because they were a nomadic people, the Utes had a relatively simple material culture, but that changed dramatically after the arrival of the Spanish. Like other Indians in the Southwest, the Utes began to acquire horses, which revolutionized their way of life. Because of their proximity to Spanish settlements in New Mexico, the Utes had relatively easy access to horses and quickly amassed large herds, which allowed them to trade the animals to other tribes. Horses greatly increased the Utes' mobility and made their life easier by enhancing their ability to utilize the available food resources. Hunters could now travel over greater distances, and the tribe could exploit the food resources of a larger area. Thus, the Utes began to consolidate into larger camps. The band replaced the family as the basic social unit, and large Ute camps were now able to travel to the Great Plains to hunt buffalo. The organization of large camps and large hunting expeditions led to the development of more powerful and influential leaders, and the movement to the Great Plains to hunt brought the Utes into contact with hostile Plains Indians, spurring the rise of war leaders.

Plains Indians such as Cheyennes, Arapahos, and Comanches often tried to keep Utes off of the buffalo grounds and raided traditional Ute areas in the mountains. The Utes learned from their Plains adversaries, adopting the tepee and utilizing buffalo hides for items of clothing. The Utes also copied Plains techniques of using quill, bone, and paint for decoration, and about 1900 they adopted the Plains Indian Sun Dance.

As Ute bands became more clearly defined, four laid claim to the San Juan Mountains in southwestern Colorado: the Muache, Capote, Weeminuche, and Tabeguache (Uncompahgre). The Muache lived in the mountains of the Front Range in southern Colorado and northern New Mexico, ranging as far north as the present site of Denver and as far south as Santa Fe. The Capotes frequented the San Luis Valley and the adjacent region of New Mexico, especially the Chama Valley area, but they and the Muache hunted as far east as the Texas panhandle. The Weeminuche were located west of the Continental Divide and north of the San Juan River and made use in particular of the La Plata and San Miguel Mountains. The Tabeguache inhabited the valleys of the Gunnison and Uncompahgre Rivers in Colorado, the northern part of the San Luis Valley, and the area of South Park. Other Ute bands inhabited northern Colorado and Utah.

As the Utes traveled through this country, they used trails that subsequently have been replaced by modern highways. They crossed passes such as Poncha and Cochetopa in the east and Dallas Divide in the west. Both Vallecito Creek and the Los Piños River provided routes to the north, and Baker's Park, which later became the site of Silverton, was a summer camp area. In the late nineteenth century the present site of Vallecito Reservoir was a favorite recreation area, and future tribal leader Buckskin Charley frequently camped there. The Utes enjoyed hot springs such as Pagosa Springs and those in the vicinity of Ouray, Ridgway, Hermosa, and Dunton. They hunted in the high San Juans, on Grand Mesa, and on the Uncompahgre Plateau and took refuge in sheltered valleys such as the Mancos during cold weather. Today much of the route of the San Juan Skyway follows traditional Ute trails.

Before 1848 and the Treaty of Guadalupe Hidalgo, which transferred present-day New Mexico, Arizona, southern Colorado, southern Utah, and southern California to the United States, the Utes generally were on good terms with the Spanish and then with the Mexicans, despite suffering from slave-raiding expeditions by the Spanish. Gradually, however, white settlement in the vicinity of Taos and up the Chama Valley encroached on land that the Utes saw as theirs. This trend would accelerate after 1848.

After the Mexican War, the United States and the Utes signed a treaty of peace and friendship in 1849 in which the Utes recognized the jurisdiction of the United States. Soon thereafter settlers from New Mexico moved north into Ute territory in the San Luis Valley, and a few years later the 1859 gold rush to Colorado brought hordes of newcomers to the area. These two events marked the beginning of a new phase in Ute history and established what would become the major theme in Ute-U.S. relations in the nineteenth century: constant pressure by the United States on the Ute land base. The first mining camps developed in areas that had not been purchased from any Indian tribes, and thus mining interests were constantly demanding that Indians, including Utes, be removed from those areas. The resulting series of treaties and agreements, negotiated over approximately twenty years, reduced the Ute land base to a thin sliver along the Colorado–New Mexico border.

In 1863, at the behest of Coloradans, the United States negotiated with the Utes for the acquisition of the San Luis Valley and other areas of Colorado. The treaty provided an indication of things to come: only the Tabeguache Utes signed the treaty, whereas the Capote Utes, to whom the San Luis Valley actually belonged, did not sign the treaty. Virtually all subsequent agreements would be marked by some kind of chicanery by the United States and its representatives.

Demands for Ute land continued, and in 1868 a Ute delegation was taken to Washington and encouraged to agree to a second cession. By the Treaty of 1868, the Utes were restricted to a rectangular reservation that lay mostly west of the Continental Divide. The Utes retained the area west of approximately Pagosa Springs and south of the present-day Moffat County line. The government promised to exclude all non-Utes except for government officials and pledged to create two agencies, one of which would be located on the Rio de Los Piños. The government wished to encourage the Utes to become farmers, but it established the Los Piños Agency on a previously unnamed creek in the Cochetopa Hills at a high elevation rather than in the more fertile Rio de Los Piños region in present-day La Plata County. Moreover, the new agency was not even within the boundaries of the reservation (Fig. 17.1).

Fig. 17.1   Ute Agency at Los Piños Creek near Cochetopa Pass. Courtesy Center of Southwest Studies.

Americans almost immediately violated the terms of the treaty by participating in a mining rush into the San Juan Mountains. Soon miners were active in the vicinity of the present-day communities of Lake City, Silverton, Ouray, Rico, Durango, and

Hesperus. The Utes protested the presence of miners; some tribal leaders attempted to persuade the miners to leave the reservation, whereas others threatened to drive them out. Colorado officials sought to solve the problem by reducing the size of the reservation, but efforts to do so in 1872 failed; the Utes insisted that the government enforce previous treaties and prevent trespass on their lands. At one point federal officials were preparing to use the army to expel non-Ute trespassers, but howls of outrage by Coloradans caused the government to cease such efforts and to seek instead a new agreement to reduce the size of the reservation.

In 1873 the United States renewed its efforts to purchase the San Juan mining country and succeeded in negotiating the Brunot Agreement, which was ratified in 1874. By this agreement, the United States acquired a block of land with a northern boundary approximately at present-day Ridgway and a southern boundary just south of present-day Durango. However, the Brunot Agreement was blatantly fraudulent; the Utes thought they were selling only the mines, but by the terms of the pact they lost an entire block of territory. The testimony of Utes and reliable Anglo observers unanimously supports the Ute position. The agreement also specifically reserved for the Utes an area between Ouray and Ridgway known as Uncompahgre Park. However, soon thereafter non-Indians moved into the area, and the Utes were never able to retain possession. During the 1870s the government also closed the Ute agencies in New Mexico and removed the Utes from the vicinity of Cimarron and from the Abiquiu and Tierra Amarilla areas of the Chama Valley, placing them all in southern Colorado.

Coloradans continued to seek further reductions of the Ute reservation, and the Meeker Massacre in 1879 gave them an excuse to accomplish that objective. Under the terms of an agreement concluded the year following the uprising, the Northern Utes, who had participated in the affair, were moved to Utah. The treaty provided that the friendly Tabeguache or Uncompahgre Utes should be moved to the junction of the Colorado and Gunnison rivers if sufficient arable land was available there. However, the government chose to ignore this provision and sent these Utes to Utah as well. These people once inhabited the area crossed by the northern part of the San Juan Skyway, and their leader, Ouray, had houses near the hot springs on the eastern side of the present-day town bearing his name and in the vicinity of Montrose, Colorado.

These events left the Weeminuche, Capote, and Muache as the only remaining Ute bands in Colorado, and they occupied a narrow strip of land that was 15 miles wide and 110 miles long on the southern boundary of Colorado. In the fifteen years following the agreement of 1880, Coloradans attempted to have the remaining three Ute bands removed from their state. Every session, the Colorado congressional delegation introduced bills to secure the expulsion of the Utes. In 1895 legislation finally passed to provide for the allotment of land to Utes on the reservation. In keeping with the general thrust of federal Indian policy, the bill provided that land would be allotted to individual adult Indians and would be held in trust for them for twenty-five years, at which time a fee simple patent would be issued. Because many Utes opposed the agreement, the government decided to make the allotments on the eastern part of the reservation and leave the western half for those who wished to live in traditional communal camps.

By 1896 land had been allotted to 371 Utes, and soon thereafter the unallotted land on the eastern part of the reservation was made available to white settlers. As a result, the eastern portion of the reservation, now known as the Southern Ute Reservation, is a checkerboard of Indian and non-Indian ownership. The Utes who opposed allotment, largely members of the Weeminuche band under the leadership of Chief Ignacio, moved to the western portion of the reservation. In time a subagency was established for them at Navajo Springs, although eventually it moved to the present location at Towaoc (Fig. 17.2). In time, the western part of the reservation was established as a separate jurisdiction and became known as the Ute Mountain Ute Reservation.

The early twentieth century was a time of transition for the Southern Utes. They had to adjust not only to reservation life but also to the shrinkage of their land base caused by the allotment and the sale of surplus land to non-Indians. Gradually they began to rely on agriculture and stock raising to replace the traditional activities of hunting and gathering. The goal of federal Indian policy was to "civilize" American Indians, to destroy traditional culture and replace it with the culture of white Americans. The

Bureau of Indian Affairs agency at Ignacio provided the focal point for these programs. Schools were located at the agency and at Fort Lewis (south of modern Hesperus, Colorado), which was transferred from the army to the Bureau of Indian Affairs in 1891.

During these years, Buckskin Charley and Severo (Figs. 17.3, 17.4) were the principal leaders of the Southern Ute Reservation. Severo died in 1913, and Buckskin Charley continued to fill that role until his own death in 1936. That same year the Southern Utes formally accepted the Indian

Fig. 17.2 Chief Ignacio with Indian police badge. Courtesy Center of Southwest Studies.

Reorganization Act and adopted a constitution that provided for a chairman and a tribal council. In subsequent years the Southern Utes developed an efficient tribal government with administrative departments to manage fish and wildlife, oil and gas, irrigation, and so forth. Today the tribe operates a modern motel and restaurant, the Southern Ute Cultural Center, and Sky Ute Downs, a modern equestrian facility. The council sponsors social programs for tribal members and maintains close ties with nearby Fort Lewis College, which has educated many Utes. Those interested in Ute culture can attend the annual Bear Dance and Sun Dance at Ignacio.

Life has been more difficult in the twentieth century for the Ute Mountain Utes because of the lack of resources on their reservation. The lack of water, in particular, has inhibited the development of agriculture and stock raising. Although Bureau of Indian Affairs officials recognized in the nineteenth century that the absence of water was a significant problem, little was done about it. The Ute Mountain Utes accepted the Indian Reorganization Act

Fig. 17.3 Buckskin Charley, standing. Courtesy Center of Southwest Studies.

Fig. 17.4 Severo and family, 1899. Courtesy Center of Southwest Studies.

and adopted a constitution in 1940. Exploration for oil and gas in the 1950s provided needed revenues, and McPhee Reservoir, completed in 1986 near the town of Dolores, will provide desperately needed water for the Ute Mountain Ute Reservation.

In the 1990s the Utes rely heavily on revenues from oil and gas, and both Southern Utes and Ute Mountain Utes have established casinos to increase their income. Today Ute leaders seek to develop economic and educational opportunitites while preserving the Ute language and traditional culture.

REFERENCES

Delaney, R. W., 1989. *The Ute Mountain Utes.* Albuquerque: University of New Mexico Press, 134 pp.

Delaney, R. W., 1974. *The Southern Ute People.* Phoenix, AZ: Indian Tribal Series, 102 pp.

Ellis, R. N., 1989. *The Ute legacy.* Ignacio, CO: Pinon Press, 12 pp.

Hughes, J. D., 1977. *American Indians in Colorado.* Boulder, CO: Pruett Publishing Co., 143 pp.

Jefferson, J., R. W. Delaney, and G. C. Thompson, 1972. *The Southern Utes: A tribal history.* Ignacio, CO: Southern Ute Tribe, 106 pp.

Linton, R., 1940. *Acculturation in seven American Indian tribes.* New York: Appleton-Century Co., 526 pp.

Marsh, C. S., 1982. *People of the Shining Mountains.* Boulder, CO: Pruett Publishing Co., 190 pp.

Pettit, J., 1990. *Utes, the mountain people.* Boulder, CO: Johnson Books, 174 pp.

Smith, P. D., 1990. *Ouray, Chief of the Utes.* Ouray, CO: Wayfinder Press, 222 pp.

Thompson, G. C., 1972. *Southern Ute lands 1848–1899.* Durango, CO: Fort Lewis College, Center of Southwest Studies, Occasional papers, 62 pp.

Wood, N., 1980. *When buffalo free the mountains.* Garden City, NY: Doubleday, 293 pp.

CHAPTER 18

THE MINERS: "THEY BUILDED BETTER THAN THEY KNEW"

DUANE A. SMITH

They intrigued the Spanish, lured the fifty-niners, and provided a home for several generations of eager prospectors and determined hard-rock miners. To all of them they were known as the San Juan Mountains. Some of Colorado's highest and most rugged peaks insured a challenge for anyone who sought to wrestle their mineral resources from the granite-ribbed depths (Fig. 18.1). For over 250 years, determined men have attempted to extract the treasure.

The Spanish came first in the eighteenth century; the Utes, who earlier had traversed these mountains for centuries, did not stop to mine. The Utes objected to the Spanish intrusion, one reason that the trespassers from the Rio Grande Valley did not linger. Certainly by the time of Juan Maria de Rivera's expedition of 1765, many of the intriguing Spanish place-names were already in common use. New Mexican miners had come, worked for a season or two, and gone home; they were trespassing on the king's resources and did not wish to give him his royal fifth of all the ore mined, as the law demanded.

There can be no doubt that the Spanish explored deeply into the San Juans. The *Ouray Times* (September 4, 1876), for example, stated that "old openings and tools" were found in Poughkeepsie Gulch, and a year later the *Engineering and Mining Journal* described an "abandoned open cut" that had been found along a silver vein on the shore of Lake Como. The Spanish came and went, leaving behind names and fascinating stories of lost mines and buried treasure that still lure people today and trap the unwary into futile searches.

In the 1820s trappers were working the San Juan streams for another natural resource — beavers. According to later reports, the well-known Kit Carson, among others, "strongly insisted" that these southern ranges were "prolific in mines of gold, silver and other precious stones." By the time of the famous 1859 Pikes Peak rush, the legends and stories of the San Juans were wafting on the wind, hard to pin down but tantalizing to ponder. The fifty-niners rushed instead to Gregory's Diggings and Payne's Bar on the eastern slopes of the Rockies, where Central City and Idaho Springs soon would be. The San Juans lay weeks of mountainous travel away, a trip that seemed unnecessary in light of the great strikes of that glorious year on the Front Range. Nevertheless, within a year Charles Baker would be in the park on the western side of the mountains that bears his name and where Silverton now sits.

Baker led a small party into the San Juans in August 1860, after which he enthusiastically promoted his discoveries. One member of the party described the mountains he had just visited as "the highest, roughest, broadest and most abrupt of all the

Fig. 18.1   This 1875 William Henry Jackson photo from the top of King Solomon Mountain shows the ruggedness of the San Juans. U.S. Geological Survey photo.

ranges." He concluded his article in the October 12, 1860, *Rocky Mountain News* with the exhilarating observation that in this "range the metalliferous development of this region, if not of the North American continent, reaches its culminating point." That was what the readers wanted to see, as plans for a rush in the spring of '61 got underway.

The rush came as anticipated, generally by way of New Mexico and up the Animas River on Baker's toll road, which passed through Animas City, another Baker-inspired creation. Unfortunately, this rush failed for several reasons: not enough placer gold, unfriendly Utes, an isolated site, and a climate and elevation not conducive to months of prospecting. By fall the rushers were gone, and the San Juans had regained their customary solitude. Not for long, however, would they remain quiet. Those rumors and legends still beckoned, and others came to try their luck. Once the Civil War ended and peace returned to a troubled United States, more rushers moved in. The fact that the San Juans remained, in the words of contemporary Colorado author Frank Fossett, "terra incognita" only enhanced the speculation of what might be found among those high peaks and deep canyons.

In 1869 prospectors worked their way up the Dolores River as far as present-day Rico; the next year, men struggled back into Baker's Park. This time they came to stay, although initially they worked only from late spring to fall, when the snows forced the closing of operations. No longer was the search simply for placer mines; lode mines were discovered and opened, and by 1874 small settlements were appearing near the gateways to the San Juans and in some of the mountain valleys. Permanent settlement took root when year-round mining became possible.

One of the most interesting of the early pioneers, John Moss, focused his attention on La Plata Canyon. Moss negotiated a treaty with the Utes for the land and brought in California capital to underwrite his mining. Parrott City, at the mouth of the canyon, served as his headquarters. For several years he and his followers prospected and mined in the area, digging not only for precious metals but also for coal. Isolation, scant profits, and Moss's own eccentric nature doomed his effort. His was the first, but not the last, of the attempts to find the mother lode in that canyon's depths.

Among the first results of the renewed interest in the San Juans was conflict with the Utes, who had been guaranteed this land by treaty. Most San Juan miners, unlike Moss, did not stop to negotiate with the Utes, simply assuming the land to be theirs by frontier right. Government was under pressure from both sides, one that had treaty rights, and another that wanted better (meaning more profitable) use made of the region. The result was the signing of the Brunot Agreement (September 1873), in which the Utes ceded 3.5 million acres, the heart of the mining country. In return, the Indians received $25,000 annually and retained the right to hunt on the ceded land as long as game lasted and peace was maintained.

Within a decade, the Utes were gone from much of Colorado's Western Slope as a result of the continuing friction between the two peoples and the killing of Nathan Meeker. Meeker, a sincere but misguided agent to the White River Utes, had served in the northwestern part of the state. The misunderstandings and conflicts that characterized confrontations between these different cultures and races elsewhere in the West were repeated in the San Juans, and in the end the Indians gave way. As was typical in the mining West, the end for the Utes came quickly and decisively.

Meanwhile, settlement and development of the San Juans went on apace. Through the gateways at Lake City and Del Norte swarmed the miners, crossing over high mountain passes, searching on mountainsides and in canyon valleys for their golden dream. Others followed the longer, more roundabout route up the Animas Valley. Some of them remained there to begin farming and ranching to serve the needs of their contemporaries in the mountains, where the growing season seemed virtually nonexistent. They founded the little settlement of Animas City (the second), south of Baker's original site; the village's population had grown to 286 by the time of the 1880 census.

In Baker's Park, the towns of Silverton, Howardsville, and Eureka took root to serve the miners who worked in the surrounding mountains. At higher elevations, Animas Forks and Mineral Point nestled among the peaks, maintaining a precarious existence while anticipating that nearby mines would produce a bonanza. The largest high-country town, Silverton, neared 1,000 inhabitants by 1880, showing the drawing power of mining. Else-where in the San Juans, other camps struggled for their share of business and some permanence. Ouray emerged as the natural ri-val of Silverton, each struggling to dominate an economic sphere of mines and small settlements. Let a rival try to take away some of a town's trade and influence and a nasty newspaper war could erupt. Lake City, too, had a string of dependent satellite camps strung out along Cinnamon and Engineer Passes — Sherman and Capitol City, for example. Across the mountains, the little camp of Columbia (soon to be renamed Telluride) clung to existence in a beautiful valley, isolated from all its neighbors.

For the miners, the 1870s were a decade of waiting — for investors to appear with needed funds, for mills and smelters to work the ores profitably, and, most of all, for the railroad to pro-vide desperately needed efficient transportation. The railroad had the potential to solve the rest of the problems. San Juan denizens had no doubts that their district contained an abundance of min-erals that would make it one of the Rocky Mountains' great min-ing regions.

In late 1879 the world looked brighter than ever before to isolated, land-locked Silverton. Denver & Rio Grande surveyors were at work in the Animas Canyon; the wonder of the age was about to challenge the San Juans. The editor of the *La Plata Min-er* (December 29) could not restrain himself: Silverton, "queen of the Silver land," was about to begin a "boom for this country that would not cease growing for a hundred years to come." Three weeks before, the same newspaper had observed, "in fact, it is im-possible to estimate the great advantage in every way the comple-tion of this road will be to our camp." The town with railroad connections had a bright future; the one without them faced con-siderable obstacles to success.

For years a railroad into these mountains had been envi-sioned, but the lack of finances and engineering problems delayed the coming of the iron horse. Surveyors had to be belayed down canyon walls to complete their work. The D&RG became em-broiled in a debate with Animas City about its future as a railroad hub. When the city fathers of the small agricultural community re-fused to meet the railroad's terms, the D&RG did what it had done before: it threatened to launch a rival community. The *La Plata Miner* reported on December 20 that railroad officials were busy buying up townsites and coal lands in anticipation of locating a new community 2 miles below Animas City. The company town would "knock the stuffing out of the present town, yet it will be a good thing for us all, and especially our San Juan neighbors."

The forecast could not have been more accurate. In September 1880 the first survey stake for the new town of Durango was driven, and within three months 2,500 people had crowded into the site along the banks of the Animas. Soon it emerged as the regional smelter center, with its San Juan and New York smelter providing the most advanced technology available. Durango also emerged as the business and banking center of the region and became, briefly, the largest town on Colorado's Western Slope.

Silverton watched and waited as the "plucky road" attempted to advance into the San Juans. One problem after another created delays. Silverton quickly realized that the railroad would be a mixed blessing. The local Greene smelter was purchased by a D&RG-backed entrepreneur, dismantled, and carted south to be erected as an economic bulwark for Durango, Silverton's new rival. The railroad reached that community in July 1881, and the tracks quickly moved beyond it toward the primary goal of the mines.

The D&RG built as far as Rockwood, 17 miles north, before winter closed in and ended construction. For one glorious season that little camp enjoyed a boom as the end-of-the-track supply point. The following spring the D&RG encountered its most difficult terrain, the "high line," immediately beyond Rockwood. A narrow shelf had to be blasted out of the granite cliffs to accommodate the rails. Overcoming that obstacle, the railroad moved on, and the first train steamed into Silverton in July 1882. As the *La Plata Miner* (July 15, 1882) observed, "So far, all that can be done by the outside world has been done, for by this medium it has been opened to us — what now remains is for us to do — to commence to make ourselves and make good our statements!" The *San Juan Herald* (July 6, 1882) was even more exhilarated: Silverton, the "Gem City of the Mountains, the most prosperous and promising camp in the entire San Juan," was the "center of the richest mineral area on the face of the earth."

Every other San Juan town and camp would have been eager to debate those statements, and each awaited only its own railroad connections to give Silverton a run for its money. The arrival of the D&RG inaugurated two decades of railroad building within the district. The D&RG built extensions from its main line over Marshall Pass to Ouray in 1887 and to Lake City in 1889, and it purchased the line that Colorado mining man and railroader David Moffat built into Creede in 1892. Nevertheless, the D&RG never had the San Juans all to itself. Three short lines were constructed out of Silverton to tap its nearby mines — the Silverton Railroad (to Red Mountain, 1888–1889), the Silverton and Northern (eventually reaching Animas Forks, 1904), and the Silverton, Gladstone, and Northerly (to Gladstone, 1899). These three routes made the community the narrow-gauge (3 feet wide, as opposed to standard gauge of 4 feet, 8.5 inches) capital of the country, but each was tied into the D&RG line at Silverton and remained dependent on that larger system.

In 1890–1891 Otto Mears, who had built two of the three smaller lines, constructed the 172-mile Rio Grande Southern Railroad, which curved from Durango to Ridgway, tapping Rico, Telluride, and mines along the route. Mears, who had first built toll roads into the district back in the 1870s, became the transportation king of the San Juans, but even he could not free himself from the D&RG (Fig. 18.2). His Rio Grande Southern tied into its rival at both Ridgway and Durango; when hard times hit in the mid-1890s, the D&RG took over control of the Rio Grande Southern, which became a feeder line.

Now that the San Juaners had the railroad connections they had always coveted, it was up to them to develop their mining potential. Quite literally, they sat atop a mineral bonanza. Gold had first attracted their attention in the early 1870s, and then silver veins were discovered. Into the 1890s silver reigned as the predominant metal. Copper, lead, and zinc were recovered as by-products, and coal was mined in the Durango area, an important reason the D&RG had been so eager to establish itself there.

The San Juans were not settled by one rush. Interdistrict rushes kept the miners moving for nearly twenty years. Prospectors ventured into what became the Telluride district in the mid-1870s

and found some prom-
ising lodes. But, as au-
thor David Lavender
pointed out, "In the
late 1870s, the upper
San Miguel district was
as tough a place to
work a mine as any in
the United States."
The lodes with the
most potential stood at
11,000 feet or more
above sea level, where
snow limited digging
to the summer months,
and ore had to be taken
by pack train over Imo-
gene Pass to Ouray to
be milled. It was a cost-
ly and time-consuming
process. Major develop-
ment awaited the arrival
of the Rio Grande
Southern. With trans-
portation connections
completed, Telluride
developed into the

Fig. 18.2 Building the road between Ouray and
Silverton — transportation was the key to open-
ing the San Juans. Photo courtesy of 1st Federal
Savings, Durango.

greatest of the San Juan mining towns, and its mines finally were giv-
en the opportunity to show that they were the region's richest.

The Red Mountain district briefly pushed Telluride from the
front page in the 1880s. It soon had its own camps, newspaper,
and rich producing mines (Fig. 18.3). The *Red Mountain Pilot*
(June 2, 1883) hailed the "pride of Red Mountain," the Yankee
Girl Mine (whose shaft house can still be seen from U.S. 550, opposite the Idarado Mine), for its "possibilities unlimited with an
ore body which grows richer at every foot of depth." Every foot of
depth also produced more natural acid, which seeped into the
mines to corrode pipes, pumps, and "everything of iron." It took

Fig. 18.3 The mines and mining camps snuggled among the mountains as the Red Mountain district illustrates. U.S. Geological Survey photo.

some experimentation and a good deal of expense before the problem was solved. Mining in the Red Mountain district was more expensive than in neighboring areas.

Rico envisioned itself as another Leadville, that most famous of all Colorado silver towns, but found itself relegated to a lesser role. So, too, did Ouray, until the Camp Bird Mine made it famous in the late 1890s. Ouray, however, capitalized on its scenery and hot springs to become the first of the San Juan tourist attractions. Even small camps such as Dunton, Summitville, Ophir, and La Plata would have moments of glory before sinking into oblivion.

The Silverton area remained a steady producer for decades, experiencing mineral excitements at Animas Forks, Mineral Point, Eureka, and Cunningham Gulch (Fig. 18.4). Those districts kept up interest until well past the turn of the century. Eureka, with its famous Sunnyside Mine, would not come into its own until an economical process to work zinc was devised. Thus, it boomed just before World War I.

Although Lake City never panned out as well as its boosters had hoped, even it had moments of feverish activity into the 1890s, when new strikes portended more ore than would actually be produced. The last great silver rush came in the early 1890s at

Fig. 18.4   Miners above Cunningham Gulch in 1875. U.S. Geological Survey photo.

Creede. "It's day all day in the day time, and there is no night in Creede," sang newspaperman-poet Cy Warman about the town. Creede attracted the national attention that had escaped earlier San Juan rushes. Just about the time the San Juans were ready to open one of their new areas, the greater discoveries at Leadville and Aspen would dominate the Colorado scene and push the San Juans out of the limelight. Also helping Creede was the railroad, which ran almost to the town's doorstep from the time the rush started.

Creede's candle flickered brightly only for a moment before it dimmed. Silver mines in the San Juans and throughout Colorado suffered a devastating setback, one from which they never recovered, with the crash of 1893 and the subsequent depression. If the San Juaners needed proof that they were dependent on a national and international silver market, now they had it. The price of silver had been declining for years as production increased and the world market stabilized. San Juan miners and western silver miners in general had demanded government purchase and price supports, but Uncle Sam responded with only half a loaf, purchasing silver with which to coin dollars. As part of the reaction to the crash, government help ended, and the price of silver collapsed to the 50-cents-an-ounce range. Colorado's great days as the top silver producer in the United States had ended.

Those had been heady years, years to be savored. Fortunately, the San Juans still had gold mines, particularly within a triangle defined by Ouray, Silverton, and Telluride. This area endured as the heart of San Juan mining, and mines such as the Tomboy, Smuggler-Union, Camp Bird, and Liberty Bell rose to take up the slack. Well into the twentieth century the San Juans would continue to be a major mining district. The last major mine, the famous Sunnyside, did not close until 1991. At long last, Silverton's economy was forced to look to something besides mining.

The crash of 1893 did more than close silver mines; it also marked the end of the widespread opportunity to venture out on one's own, select a likely outcropping of rock, file a claim, and start mining. Mining had become big business, dominated by large corporations owned by outsiders. The miners who worked the mines became little more than daily wage earners, laboring long hours in a dangerous, difficult industry. Their pay did not appear to compensate them adequately for the risks they took. As San Juan poet Alfred King, himself blinded in a mining accident, wrote:

> *Thus the battle he fights for his daily bread;*
> *Thus our gold and our silver, our iron and lead,*
> *Cost us lives, as true as our blood is red,*
> *And probably always will.*

To try to improve their bargaining position in this new industrial world, the miners joined the Western Federation of Miners, a union despised by management. The San Juans became one of the union bastions of the Rocky Mountains. Management seethed and waited for a chance to crush the WFM.

The result was predictable: labor tension increased, and finally, in 1903–1904, Telluride and another famous gold district, Cripple Creek, exploded in turmoil. When the smoke finally cleared, communities had been disrupted, people driven from the district, lives lost, and civil rights trampled into the dust. When National Guard companies marched in on behalf of the owners, lasting hatreds were generated, and the state paid a high price in money and a tarnished reputation. The union had been broken, but at what sacrifice? Neither the San Juans nor the other portions of the state where these battles had been fought would ever be the same again. The camaraderie of the old days was history. The end came, as one young lady in Creede observed, when the "people did not have the faith that Creede would come back." There were other indications that an era had come to an end. The Silverton Commercial Club promoted the San Juans in 1913 as a place for recreation and tourism, and the *Engineering and Mining Journal* reported on January 10, 1914, that the Camp Bird Mine was "virtually exhausted," that Hinsdale County "is comparatively inactive," and that, apart from the big three mines, the output from the rest of the Telluride district "is not large."

Those had been wonderful decades since the 1870s, nevertheless. The San Juans had been opened, settled, and developed. The production figures for these years give only a partial idea of the impact they had made. San Miguel County produced over $70 million in gold, silver, lead, zinc, and copper; San Juan County topped $53 million, and Ouray County, $67 million. San Juan mining operations had made pioneering advances in the use of tramways to transport ore, in industrial use of electricity, and in utilizing various new types of equipment. Mining camps had been born, had prospered and died; the survivors proudly remembered their heritage. Along with the good things there had, of course, come disappointment, failure, and tears — mining never produced just profits and success. In the end it may be said, along with the unknown poet who published these lines in the *Silverton Standard* on January 3, 1903:

> *And when the throng of eager men —*
> *Men of heroic mould and true —*
> *Wrought mines that silver might be had*
> *They builded better than they knew —*
> *These men now gone.*

REFERENCES

Crabb, P., and Dunn, S., eds, 1991. *Ridgway Colorado Centennial 1881–1991.* Ridgway, CO: The Ridgway Sun, 28 pp.

Engel, C. M., 1968. Rico, Colorado: A century of historic adventures in mining, in J. Shoemaker, ed., *San Juan–San Miguel–La Plata Region: New Mexico Geological Society Guidebook,* nineteenth Field Conference, pp. 88–93.

ADDITIONAL SOURCE

Nossaman, A., 1989. *Many more mountains,* volume 1: *Silverton's roots.* Denver: Sundance Books, 352 pp.

PART IV

POINTS OF INTEREST
AROUND THE
WESTERN SAN JUAN MOUNTAINS

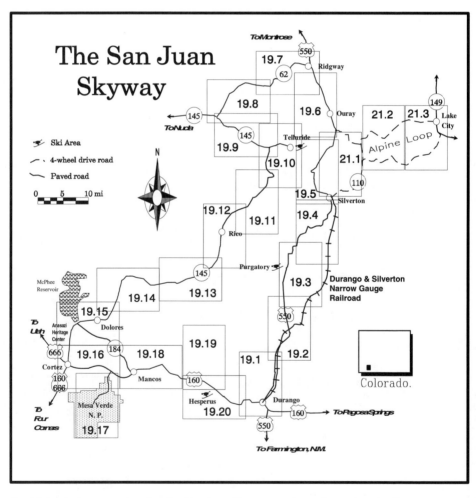

Fig. 19.1   Index map showing the San Juan Skyway route and associated reference maps.

CHAPTER 19

POINTS OF INTEREST ALONG THE SAN JUAN SKYWAY

ROB BLAIR

This road guide is meant for the visitor who wishes to delve into the geology, ecology, archaeology, and history of the San Juan Skyway region. The guide is designed to be flexible so that a traveler can enter the highway at any point and circle the loop in either direction. The points of interest are identified on topographic maps (Fig. 19.1, Maps 19.1 through 19.20, and Maps 21.1 through 21.3) by open circles, with corresponding numbers referenced in this chapter. Areas of interest are designated with black-filled circles. Many of the points of interest are referenced to the green milepost (mp) signs found along the side of the road. Each winter, unfortunately, snowplows destroy some signs, and after major road construction the new signs may not measure true miles.

The information for this road guide was obtained from numerous sources, including a number of previously published geologic road logs. These and other references are included at the end of each area of interest (dark-filled circles on maps). The flora and fauna information was provided by Preston Somers of the Biology Department at Fort Lewis College. Unless otherwise stated, all photographs were taken by the author. No guide of this sort can be exempt from errors; please bring to our attention oversights and misinformation.

1. **(Map 19.1) Durango.** Elevation: 6,512 feet (1,985 m). Population: 12,430 (circa 1990). Durango! Even the name conjures

up an image of the Old West. Although lacking cowboys on saddled horses, the town still retains much of its original flavor through its friendly people and architectural style. The Durango & Silverton Narrow Gauge Railroad, Purgatory ski area, and Mesa Verde National Park make this community one of the most popular tourist centers in the Southwest.

Basketmakers II and III occupied the region thousands of years ago. These people were followed by the Anasazi and eventually by the Mountain Utes. Spanish explorers Juan Maria de Rivera in 1765 and Escalante and Dominguez in 1776 passed just a few miles south of the future townsite as they explored the fringes of the San Juan Mountains. With the arrival of white settlers in the 1870s, the first townsite in the San Juans, called Animas City, was established; in less than a decade, it became a thriving agricultural community. However, because the town was not willing to meet the demands of the Denver & Rio Grande Railroad in 1879–1880, a new town was created 2 miles (3.2 km) south. The territorial governor, Alexander Hunt, named the new community Durango after a town in Mexico. With the establishment of the narrow-gauge railroad, Durango became a boomtown supporting local mining for coal, gold, and silver. Animas City was eventually annexed by Durango in 1947.

Before European settlers entered the valley in 1870 and began planting and cultivating trees, the site of Durango was much more open (Figs. 19.2A and 19.2B). A shrubland of big sage dominated the area, with a scattering of piñons, junipers, and ponderosa pines. All of the elms, maples, ashes, willows, Russian olives, and fruit trees seen today are exotic to the Durango area. The cottonwoods, blue spruces, white firs, box elders, quaking aspen, and chokecherries are native. The dense and diverse growth of both native and ornamental species in town today is appropriate for a well-watered river valley, but it exceeds any plant community nature would produce by itself in this semiarid environment.

The average annual precipitation in the Durango area is 18.6 inches (47.2 cm), including the average snowfall of 69 inches (175 cm). Forty-two percent of the precipitation falls from August through October.

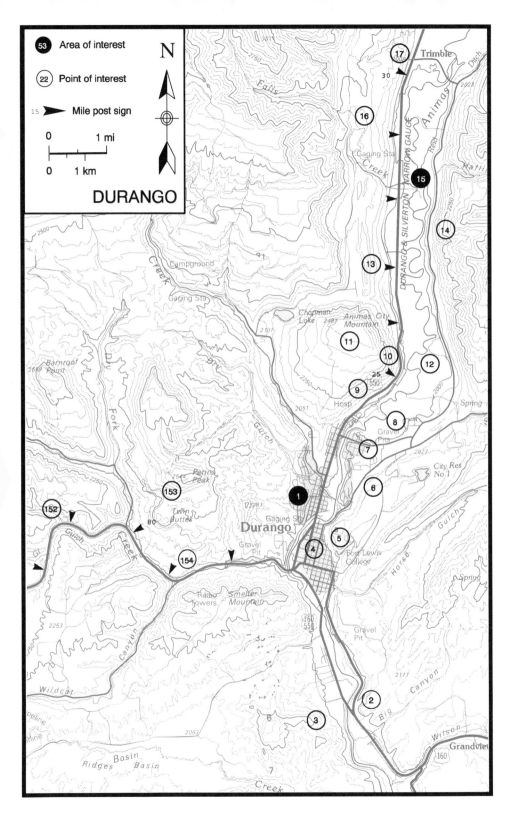

Map 19.1

Durango is built on Animas River gravels, which rest upon late Cretaceous sedimentary rocks, principally the Mancos Shale. Perins Peak (west) and Raider Ridge (east) are capped by the Point Lookout Sandstone. Animas City Mountain (north) is capped by the Dakota Sandstone and forms a conspicuous sloping surface dipping to the southwest at about 7 degrees. All formations in the Durango area dip south, toward the center of the San Juan Basin, a structural basin with a sedimentary thickness of nearly 12,000 feet (3,700 m). Just south of town the formations steepen to 35 degrees and form prominent hogbacks that represent the Hogback Monocline and mark the approximate physiographic boundary between the Southern Rocky Mountain province to the north and the Colorado Plateau province to the south (Fig. 1.1, Chapter 1). Five miles (8 km) south of town the beds become nearly horizontal. References (POI 1–9): Gillam, Moore, and Scott 1984; Lee et al. 1976, Maher 1961, Molenaar et al. 1968, Smith 1980, Vanderwilt 1934, Wengerd and Baars 1957.

2. The Pictured Cliffs Sandstone is exposed 2 miles (3.2 km) south of Durango and forms the white, resistant layer dipping steeply toward the south. It is part of the Hogback Monocline. The formation is one of the major natural gas producers in southern Colorado and northern New Mexico. The Fruitland Formation overlies this sandstone and contains economic bituminous coal deposits and associated methane gas. An open-pit coal mine lies about a mile northeast of here. Beneath the Pictured Cliffs Sandstone lies the Lewis Shale.

3. The Carbon Mountain landslide forms the hummocky debris seen beneath the siltstone and shale bluffs to the west of the highway, just above the local shooting range. The slide formed in the winter of 1932–1933, when the water-saturated Fruitland Formation collapsed and slid onto the sloping Pictured Cliffs Sandstone ledge. The maximum rate of movement was clocked at 30 feet (9 m) per day. It became such a popular tourist attraction that an enterprising young man set up a hot dog stand one weekend in early January 1933.

Fig. 19.2   A. Photo of Durango looking north taken in 1888 by J. A. Boston (contributed by Ed Boucher). B. Photo of Durango 1994.

4.   River terraces form the flat areas upon which Durango is constructed. For example, Main Street is built upon an 18,000- to 25,000-year-old Wisconsin glacial outwash terrace, and East Second Avenue is built upon a higher, 36,000- to 40,000-year-old glacial outwash terrace. The steep rise between these terraces can be seen along any east-west street in downtown Durango. These terraces merge to the north with late Wisconsin glacial end moraines.

5.   The Centennial Nature Trail begins at the end of 10th street in downtown Durango and leads to Fort Lewis College. A booklet available at the college bookstore describes the plants, geology, and history of the area and is keyed to 25 numbered stations along the trail.

6.   The Lions Club shelter provides the best views of north Durango and the Animas Valley. The shelter is built upon approximately 300,000-year-old end moraines called the Durango Moraines. The Fort Lewis College campus is built upon glacial outwash gravel of this same age. Mantling the gravel is 10 to 30 feet (3–9 m) of red loess, a windblown silt deposit thought to be derived from the vicinity of Monument Valley.

7.   Glacial end moraines form the east-west parallel ridges along 32nd Avenue. These glacial deposits are the Animas City Moraines and formed between 18,000 and 25,000 years ago. An older suite of end moraines, called the Spring Creek Moraines, are 80,000 to 150,000 years old and can be seen capping the hills just north of Florida Road before it leaves town to the northeast.

8.   The Animas River was originally called El Rio de las Animas Perdidas, Spanish for "The River of Lost Souls." River discharge generally ranges from 400 cfs (cubic feet per second) in the fall to more than 5,000 cfs in the spring (Fig. 19.3). The river overflows its banks in the lower Animas Valley when the discharge exceeds 6,500 cfs. The largest flood recorded in Durango history occurred on October 5, 1911, when approximately 25,000 cfs flowed down its channel. At that time water covered low areas of the railway tracks and the land where U.S. 550 is today.

9.   The Junction Creek Sandstone of Jurassic age forms a prominent cliff (upper white layer on middle slopes) on both sides

Fig. 19.3 View looking east of lower Animas Valley. The formations exposed are, from youngest to oldest, Picture Cliffs Sandstone (Kp), Lewis Shale (Kl), Point Lookout Sandstone (Kpl), Mancos Shale (Km), Dakota Sandstone (Kd), Morrison Formation (Jm), Junction Creek Sandstone (Jjc), Wanaka Formation (Jw), Entrada Sandstone (Je) and the Dolores Formation (TRd). Note the oxbow lakes occupying abandoned meander loops.

of the valley. This cliff is a favorite play area with the local rock climbers (Fig. 19.3).

10. (mp 25.1) The Entrada Sandstone of Jurassic age forms the lowest white layer in the valley and represents a fossilized dune field noted for its distinct cross-bedding. The cross-bedding indicates that the wind direction was variable 180 million years ago but was mostly from the west.

11. Animas City Mountain is encircled by rimrock composed of the late Cretaceous Dakota Sandstone. Landslide deposits on the south side of the mountain, beneath the rimrock, are associated with shales of the Morrison Formation. Note the ponderosa pine forest below and above the rimrock on slopes facing south. The northern slopes of Animas City Mountain are forested with Douglas fir. There are scattered stream cobbles on the summit of Animas City Mountain. How and when do you suppose they got there?

12.   Oxbow Lakes are the comma-shaped bodies in the Animas Valley formed when the Animas River cut off meander loops. The Animas here is a textbook example of a meandering river in a sandy flood plain. Cattails and red-winged blackbirds are common residents of these oxbow lakes.

13.   (mp 27) The Durango Anticline and Perins Peak Syncline form the gentle folds seen on both sides of the valley. In 1926 a group of enterprising local businessmen decided to drill an oil well just west of the highway at the crest of the Durango Anticline. They drilled and reportedly penetrated more than 600 feet (180 m) of unconsolidated sediment before abandoning the project. This indicates that the valley is a deep eroded trough in bedrock, probably U-shaped, filled with lake sediment and outwash gravel from the last retreating glacier. From this point looking east up the prominent canyon one can see drag folding associated with the east-west-trending Woodard Canyon Fault, which crosses beneath the valley and reappears to the west. Which side of the fault went up, the north block or south block?

14.   The red beds that make up the upper valley walls consist of the Triassic Dolores Formation, and the lower slopes comprise the red beds of the Permian Cutler Formation. These layers were deposited by streams in a humid continental environment.

15.   (Map 19.1) Lower Animas Valley. This glacial valley (Fig. 19.3) was made flat by lake and stream sediment. Over the last 100 years, and especially during the last decade, the valley has changed from a natural inherited setting to one reshaped by civilization. The riverbanks are mined for their gravel, and the valley floor is developed for its agricultural, residential, and recreational uses.

Ecologically, the Animas Valley represents a mosaic of communities, including riparian, piñon-juniper, mountain shrub, sagebrush, and ponderosa pine–Douglas fir forests. Slope, soil, and moisture control community type in this region. At and below the elevation of Durango, piñon-juniper woodland dominates the thinner soils, especially on south-facing slopes. North-facing slopes are cool and moist and subject to heavy snow loads, therefore favoring a mountain shrub community. Elevated river terraces with deposits of loess support sagebrush shrublands. Mixtures of two or three of the above communities are quite common on east- and west-facing slopes, burned sites, and soils of moderate depth.

Elevations above that of Durango are typically dominated on south-facing slopes by ponderosa pine forests with an understory of Gambel oak and Rocky Mountain juniper. North-facing slopes support dense groves of Douglas fir.

Along the riverbanks groves of narrowleaf cottonwood dominate, but to the south one can also find the less common, paler, and more triangular-leaved Fremont cottonwood. Common understory species include hawthorn, river birch, thinleaf alder, box elder, silverleaf buffaloberry, red-osier dogwood, and willow. Russian olive and tamarisk are escaped ornamentals that are now invading the native riparian communities in the southern valley.

The farm meadows are dominated by grasses and alfalfa irrigated from ditches fed by the Animas River. These meadows and pastures provide winter range for several hundred elk. Canadian geese may be seen in the valley year-round. This bird species is a relatively recent addition to the local fauna, and its success has been made possible by the erection of nest platforms along the river by the Colorado Division of Wildlife. These platforms protect the eggs and goslings from predation by dogs, coyotes, foxes, raccoons, and other animals.

Whether viewing the scenery from a bicycle, car, or train, visitors seem most struck by the red, white, and tan sedimentary layers inclined gently to the south. However, they often fail to appreciate that as one progresses from Durango to Baker's Bridge, one is moving back in time: the layers exposed at valley level get older to the north because of the southerly dip of the layers. For example, the rock layers 5 miles (8 km) south of Durango are about 60 million years old; those at Durango, about 90 million years old; and those at Hermosa, about 300 million years old.

One often-asked question is: Why are the rocks red? The red is a natural rust from oxidized iron finely disseminated throughout certain layers. The iron oxides and hydroxides form common minerals such as hematite and limonite. It takes very little oxidized iron to impart a reddish color.

Most glacial valleys are U-shaped from glacier erosion, but the Animas Valley floor is flat, having been filled with sediment. At the time of glacial retreat, a proglacial lake called Lake Durango filled the lower valley. Today the valley is a broad, flat floodplain filled with lake sediment and outwash gravel. Lateral moraine deposits located 1,000 feet (300 m) above the valley floor suggest that the ice was 1,500 feet (460 m) or more thick when the Animas Glacier last occupied this valley, some 18,000 years ago. References (POI 10–20): Atwood and Mather 1932, Bear 1985, Lee et al. 1976, Maher 1961, Molenaar et al. 1968, Osterwald 1989, Steven et al. 1974, Wengerd and Baars 1957.

16.   Hidden Valley lies parallel to the Animas Valley, west of the long north-south ridge. This ridge is mantled by a lateral moraine deposited by the Animas glacier 18,000 years ago. The valley probably carried the drainage from Hermosa Creek during the last glacial advance, when ice filled the Animas Valley. An Anasazi mummy called Ester was discovered in a cave in the southern part of this valley in the late 1930s and for many years was on display at Mesa Verde National Park. A residential community called Falls Creek Ranch now occupies much of the valley.

17.   (mp 28) Trimble Hot Springs is a public resort with outdoor hot tubs and swimming pool. Hot waters percolate up from several thousand feet beneath the area along faults and emerge at the surface at about 111 degrees F (44 °C). Such celebrities as Marilyn Monroe and Clark Gable have taken advantage of these medicinal hot springs.

18.   (mp 32.8, Map 19.2) The **glacial till** east of the highway forms the small hill with the house on top. The hill's exact nature is unknown but it has been called a glacial kame, a drumlin, and a remnant of a recessional moraine.

19.   The Hermosa Formation, comprising the gray layers beneath the red beds, records cyclic sedimentation during the Pennsylvanian Period. The alternating limestones, shales, and arkosic sandstones have a total thickness of more than 2,000 feet (600 m).

The formation is divided into three members: the Pinkerton Trail (the bottommost unit), the Paradox, and the Honaker Trail. The type section for the Pinkerton Trail Member is located near here. Numerous fossils, including crinoids, brachiopods, and bryzoans, have been found in these shallow marine limestones.

20.   Braided stream channels make up the Animas River north of Trimble Lane and south of Baker's Bridge. This type of channel is associated with coarse gravels, which accounts for the numerous gravel mining operations seen along the river banks.

21.   Sheepback rocks have been carved out of the granite just east of and again north of C.R. 250 (East Animas Road). These glacially rounded bedrock knobs, or sheepbacks, are sometimes known by their French name, *roche moutonnee*. They were formed by the abrasive action of rocks and debris trapped and dragged along the base of moving valley glaciers. They characteristically are asymmetric, with the steeper slope, often a blocky cliff, facing downvalley because of plucking beneath the ice.

22.   The hot springs visible just west of the highway produce prominent yellowish calcareous tufa mounds made of travertine. These and other nearby springs make up the Pinkerton Hot Springs, which are located along an east-west-trending fault zone with the north side down. The fault can be seen across the valley to the east. Active thermal springs lie only on the west side of the valley, suggesting that the hot waters may originate deep underground to the west. The waters are highly carbonated and maintain a temperature of around 98 degrees F (37 °C). Tamarisk, attracted by water and high salt content, is beginning to invade the area around the hot springs.

23.   (Map 19.2) Baker's Bridge. The first mining camp in southwestern Colorado was established on the east side of the Animas River in 1860 and 1861 by a group of about 100 people under the leadership of Charles Baker. This camp was originally called Animas City, and the log bridge built across the river was called Baker's Bridge. The miners found little placer gold, and the Indians were a constant hazard. When word of the Civil War arrived, most of the party went east. Within a year the Animas City

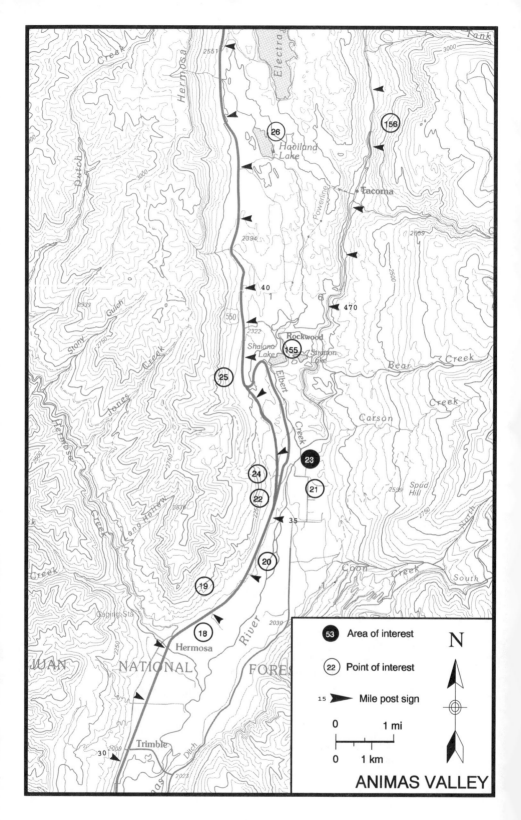

Map 19.2

settlement disappeared, but the name was resurrected about fifteen years later for a new community that stood in the north part of present-day Durango. In 1867 Baker again passed through this area and later that year was killed by Indians while exploring the Grand Canyon. Parts of the movies *Naked Spur* and *Butch Cassidy and the Sundance Kid* were filmed just north of the bridge. Remember the scene in which Butch and Sundance keep asking "Who are those guys?" and then make that incredible leap off granite cliffs into the river below?

The slopes around the Baker's Bridge area are dominated by ponderosa pine forest mixed with Rocky Mountain juniper and an understory of Gambel oak. Tall narrowleaf cottonwood can be found along the Animas River channel, with an understory of chokecherry, silverleaf buffaloberry, and willows. At Baker's Bridge, belted kingfishers feed on minnows and small trout. The American dipper nests in protected crevices in the cliffs of Precambrian granite near the river. Steller's jays, mountain and black-capped chickadees, and white-breasted nuthatches are common in the ponderosa and oaks. Mallards and other waterfowl may be seen on the Animas or on nearby Elbert Creek.

The 1.7-billion-year-old Baker's Bridge Granite surfaces here and remains exposed to the north for several miles along the Animas River. From here south the granite is buried under alluvium and Paleozoic rocks. The contact between the granite and overlying Upper Devonian Elbert Formation is an unconformity and represents a missing time gap of 1.2 to 1.3 billion years. The unconformity is clearly displayed just west of the west bridge (Fig. 19.4). This 400-plus-million-year-old erosion surface is noted for its weathered granite hillocks, which lie beneath the 70-foot-thick (21 m) McCracken Sandstone Member of the Elbert Formation. The overlying 40 feet (12 m) of the Elbert consists of shales containing scales and plates of primitive fish.

At the bridge site, glacial and fluvial erosion have stripped off the sedimentary cover to expose the Precambrian granite. Glaciation, in particular, has produced prominent rock steps visible east of the main highway and north of the bridge. Lateral moraines found high on the west and east sides of the valley indicate that the Animas glacier maintained a thickness of 2,000 feet (600

Fig. 19.4 Photo of nonconformity (line) just west of Baker's Bridge between the Baker's Bridge Granite (1.72 billion years old) and overlying McCracken Member of the Elbert Formation (400 million years old). The unconformity represents a missing time gap of 1.3 billion years.

m) or so in this part of the valley. North of Baker's Bridge, the Animas River cuts through granite to form a narrow gorge. As can be seen from the bridge, the path of this channel is largely controlled by jointing. Previously, the river split into two channels just above Baker's Bridge; it once flowed in the abandoned channel just west of the main bridge. South of the bridge, where the granite disappears below the surface, the river takes on the characteristics of a gravel-bedded channel and is braided for much of the next 5 miles (8 km). References (POI 21–24): Baars and Ellingson 1984, Lee et al. 1976, Molenaar et al. 1968, Nossaman 1989, Wengerd and Baars 1957.

24.   (mp 36) The Ouray-Leadville Limestone forms the prominent 100- to 150-foot thick (30–35 m) cliff band just west of the highway. These upper Devonian–Mississippian limestones contain numerous solution channels and small caves such as Bell's Cavern, found 2 (3.2 km) miles north of here.

25. **(mp 37.5) White fir trees** form the band of light blue-green conifers seen at the base of the Hermosa Cliffs to the west. These trees are very common in this area, extending as far north as Haviland Lake. Ponderosa pine and Douglas fir intermingle with white fir on these slopes. In the flatter areas, ponderosa pines dominate.

26. **(mp 41.8) Haviland Lake** rests upon the Irving Formation, which is considered the oldest Precambrian rock exposed in the San Juan Mountains. The rock is believed to be at least 1.8 billion years old. Compositional and structural analysis of mafic inclusions within this formation suggest that the rock is derived from basaltic rock of an ancient oceanic crust.

27. **(mp 43.9, Map 19.3) Electra Lake**, a large reservoir used to supply water to the Tacoma Hydroelectric Power Plant, lies adjacent to the Animas River. Prior to the building of the Electra Lake Dam, a smaller, natural body of water called Ignacio Lake occupied the basin. West of the lake, along Elbert Creek, is the type locality for the upper Cambrian Ignacio Formation. The northern half of the lake overlies the Electra Lake Gabbro (1.4 billion years old), and the southern and east sides overlie the Irving Formation (1.8 billion years old).

28. **(mp 45.5) The Needle Mountains** form the bold peaks east of the road (Fig. 19.5). From north to south, they are: Pigeon Peak (13,972 ft, 4,259 m), Turret Peak (13,835 ft, 4,217 m), and Eolus Peak (14,084 ft, 4,293 m). All are glacial horns surrounded by cirques, tarns, and U-shaped valleys. Glacial ice thickness in this area has been estimated to have been between 2,500 and 3,000 feet (750–900 m). These peaks and others, such as Engineer Mountain, rose above the San Juan ice field like rock islands surrounded by a sea of ice. The Needle Mountains are eroded from the Eolus Granite (1.46 billion years old). These mountains lie within the Weminuche Wilderness Area, the oldest and largest (459,804 acres, 186,082 hectares) designated wilderness in Colorado. Mountain View Crest, south of the Needle Mountains, is

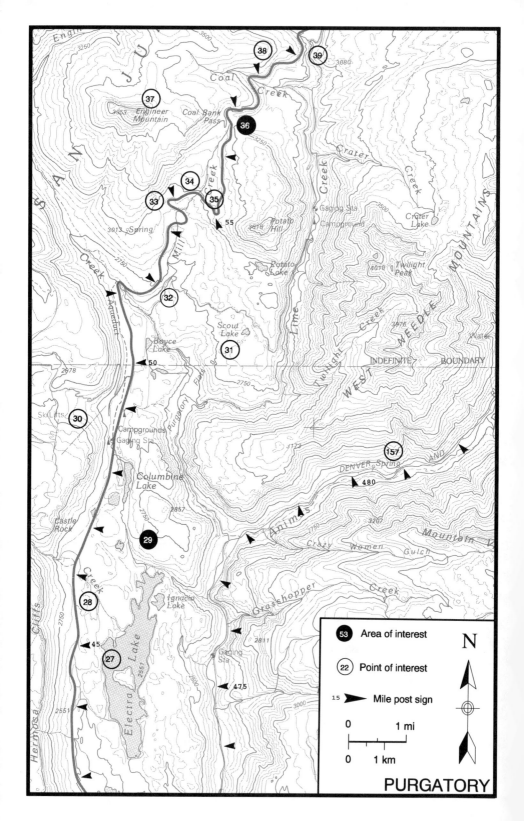

Map 19.3

Fig. 19.5   Looking east at Pigeon (left) and Turret Peaks. These are two of the better-developed glacial horns along the San Juan Skyway. They are carved from Eolus Granite (1.46 billion years old).

covered with lower Paleozoic strata that show the regional southerly dip down off the south flank of the San Juan Dome.

29.   (Map 19.3) Upper Animas Valley. This broad glacial valley was carved from Paleozoic sedimentary rocks and ancient Precambrian metamorphic basement rocks. Numerous glacial lakes lie on the west side of the valley. The two largest, Electra Lake and Haviland Lake, were enlarged with artificial dams. South of Haviland Lake, ponderosa pine forests with Gambel oak dominate, but north of Haviland Lake blue spruce becomes the dominant conifer, with Douglas fir mixed in. Ordinarily the Douglas fir would prevail over the blue spruce, but over the past decades budworms have killed many of the firs. In addition to the conifers there are numerous scattered groves of aspen, each of which typically comprises one or more clones. The stems in each clone are genetically identical and sprout up from a common root stock that forms a massive network beneath the soil of the grove. The clones are obvious in the fall, when colors change and the forest becomes a patchwork quilt, each clone a different shade of yellow, orange, or red.

U.S. Highway 550 is constructed principally upon a bench of Leadville Limestone. Occasionally the highway also passes through reddish outcrops of the overlying Molas Formation. The majestic Hermosa Cliffs, to the west, are composed of the Pinkerton Trail Member. The Twilight Peaks, northeast and east of Engineer Mountain, belong to the West Needle Mountains. They are carved from the Twilight Gneiss (1.78 billion years old). These rocks also surface at Purgatory Flats, east of the Purgatory ski area, and along Lime Creek Road. The Twilight Gneiss is strongly foliated in a northeast-southwest direction and contains numerous dikes and mafic inclusions.

References (POI 25–32): Atwood and Mather 1932, Cross and Hole 1910, Lee et al. 1976, Molenaar et al. 1968, Steven et al. 1974, Wengerd and Baars 1957.

30.　(mp 48.9) Purgatory ski area opened in 1965 with one lift and a few runs. By 1992 it had grown to nine lifts and sixty-five runs. Total snowfall averages about 20 feet per year. The original east-west stagecoach road from Rockwood to Rico passes by the base of the ski area.

30.　Wetlands occupy many of the shallow, glacially scoured basins south of Lime Creek Road. Here yellow pond lilies grow, and a beaver lodge often stands among them. What appears to be solid ground around the water is really a saturated and very springy mat of peat with a cover of sedges, mosses, and bog bean. The more solid ground is covered with willows.

32.　(mp 52) Joints in the Twilight Gneiss can be seen south across the valley. They are expressed as lines of aspen cutting through the spruce-fir forests. These aspen are growing along fractures, which collect water.

33.　(mp 53.9) An igneous intrusion is exposed on both sides of the road as a tan cliff within the Molas Formation. This trachyte porphyry sill contains fingernail-sized crystals of sanidine, a variety of potassium feldspar. The age of the intrusion is not known precisely, but it is believed to be lower Tertiary.

34. (mp 54.5) The Ignacio Formation is exposed north of the road. This upper Cambrian silty sandstone is the oldest sedimentary formation exposed in the San Juan Mountains. Its age is based upon the presence of a Cambrian brachiopod species found at this and other nearby outcrops.

35. (mp 54.7) Twilight Gneiss (1.78 billion years old) has been scoured by glacial ice and displays grooves and striations indicating the southerly flow of the Animas glacier. At this location the Twilight Gneiss is a metamorphosed extrusive igneous rock.

36. (mp 56.7, Map 19.3) Coal Bank Pass. Elevation: 10,640 feet (3,243 m). The modern highway follows an old Indian trail and stagecoach road. The first automobile road, however, originally followed the Lime Creek Road, which today skirts the pass to the east. It was abandoned as a major thoroughfare because of high maintenance costs. Prior to completion of the Durango to Silverton Railroad in 1882, the only coal for heating houses and feeding smelters in Silverton had to be mined from some local source or packed in by mule. Near Coal Creek, just north of the pass, some poor-grade coal, mostly carbonaceous shale, was extracted from the Honaker Trail Member — hence the names Coal Bank Hill and Coal Creek.

The surrounding forest is predominantly Engelmann spruce and subalpine fir, with occasional Douglas fir on drier south-facing slopes. Common juniper and scattered groves of aspen can also be found. The meadow due west of the pass is at the base of an avalanche chute and during the summer comes ablaze with wildflowers such as Indian paintbrush, bluebell, daisy, larkspur, king's crown, and blue columbine.

From the parking lot at Coal Bank Pass, a short walk can traverse a variety of geology. Three hundred feet (100 m) or so south and just west of the highway, a thinner than normal lower Paleozoic section is exposed. Here the Cambrian Ignacio Formation is a coarse conglomerate. It is exposed above the dark purple, weathered Precambrian Twilight Gneiss and is overlain by the Upper Devonian McCracken Sandstone Member of the Elbert Formation. The upper shales of the Elbert are, in turn, overlain by thin carbonate layers of the upper Devonian and Mississippian

Leadville-Ouray Limestones, and several tens of feet of red Molas Formation. Overlying the Molas is the Pennsylvanian Honaker Trail Member, which forms the cliff bands above the pass. The lower members of the Hermosa Formation are missing, which suggests that this region was a highland in early Pennsylvanian time.

The trace of the Coal Bank Fault follows the prominent gully just north of the pass. The toilets at Coal Bank Hill are built upon the upthrown block. This fault is one of a swarm of fractures trending generally east-west that have a long history of complex movement beginning in the Precambrian. The initial episodes of movement along the fault were apparently oblique-slip, with the north block dropping down and to the east. This sense of movement was determined north of and below the pass, where the fault separates the younger Uncompahgre Formation from the older Twilight Gneiss. The fault may have been reactivated during the Cambrian, when the north block went up, shedding coarse Uncompahgre sediment to the south and producing a basal conglomerate of the Ignacio (?) Formation. During or prior to the late Devonian Period, the north side again went down, according to Don Baars (1992), who cites as evidence the deeper water sediments north of the fault in the late Devonian Ouray Formation. The Leadville and lower Hermosa are missing north of the fault, suggesting that prior to and during Pennsylvanian time the north block again went up, only to drop down again some time after the Hermosa was deposited. If you are confused about this history, you are not alone. Geologists are still arguing over the details of the evidence and its interpretation.

Today the Precambrian Twilight Gneiss is exposed at the pass on the south block of the fault. The sedimentary beds of the late Pennsylvanian Honaker Trail Member make up the north block. The Twilight Gneiss on the north side of the fault is approximately 750 feet (229 m) lower than the same Twilight Gneiss exposed at the pass. References (POI 33–40): Baars 1992, Baars, Ellingson, and Spoelhof 1987, Lee et al. 1976, Molenaar et al. 1968, Nossaman 1989, Wengerd and Baars 1957.

37. Engineer Mountain is capped by a quartz trachyte porphyry laccolith that was forcibly intruded into the Cutler Formation.

Fig. 19.6 Drag folding associated with the south downdropped block of the Hermosa Formation along the Sheep Camp Fault.

Note the red beds beneath the columnar jointing of this Tertiary intrusive. The trachyte has not been dated, but it is thought to pre-date the Oligocene volcanic activity in the San Juans. Similar intrusions occur southwest of Cascade Creek on Graysill Mountain.

38.   (mp 58.4) Upturned strata of the lower Honaker Trail Member can be seen in the roadcut, west of the road (Fig. 19.6). This flexure represents drag folding associated with growth faulting during and after deposition of this part of the Hermosa Formation.

39.   (mp 59.1) Lime Creek Turnout. The Twilight Peaks to the southeast are eroded from the Twilight Gneiss (1.78 billion years old). The valley to the southeast is carved from vertically oriented quartzites and phyllites of the Uncompahgre Formation (1.69 billion years old). The rounded, polished, and scratched bedrock surfaces are the legacy of the erosive action of the Animas glacier. The Lime Creek Syncline is seen due east (Fig. 19.7). Its axis crosses the highway just north of the parking area. This doubly plunging syncline's low point (nadir) lies just east of Lime Creek. The south limb of the syncline was formed from drag along the

Fig. 19.7 Looking east toward Snowdon Peak. The lower slopes of the Hermosa Formation have been folded into a syncline.

Snowdon Fault, while the north limb was tilted from the injection of the Lime Creek Pluton, a laccolith perhaps of the same age as the intrusive cap of Engineer Mountain. The roadcut west of the parking area displays steeply inclined strata of the Honaker Trail Member on the southern limb of the syncline. Note the channel scour in the more southerly and middle sandstone layers.

40. (**mp 60.5, Map 19.4**) A **sill,** probably an arm of the Lime Creek Pluton, separates layers of the Honaker Trail Member. Only the upper contact of this sill is exposed in the highway roadcut to the south of the road. Minor hydrothermal alteration, pyrite, and fluorite mineralization can be found along the contacts.

41. (**mp 61.3**) **Springwater** emerges from a limestone solution hole 50 feet (15 m) above the road and plunges as a waterfall over an igneous sill at road level. The limestone layer is part of the Honaker Trail Member.

42. (**mp 62.5**) A **forest fire** in the summer of 1879 burned 26,000 acres (10,530 hectares) of Engelmann spruce and subalpine fir. The Lime Creek burn apparently started around Purgatory Flats

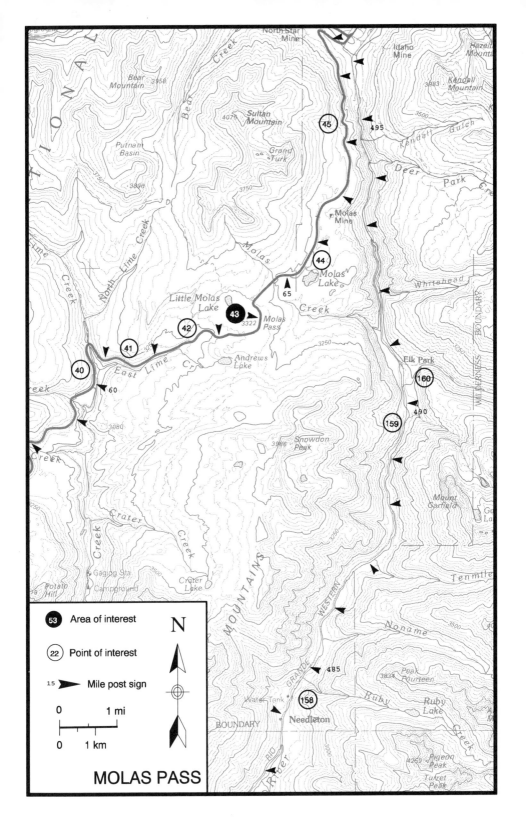

North Star Mine

Idaho Mine

Hazel Mountain

Bear Mountain 3958

Sultan Mountain 4075

Grand Turk

Kendall Mountain 3983

495

3500

Kendall Gulch

Deer Park Creek

3750

Molas Mine

Molas Creek

44

Molas Lake

Whitehead

45

65

43 3322

Molas Pass

Little Molas Lake

42

Andrews Lake

3250

Elk Park

160

41

East Lime Cr.

490

60

159

40

3080

Snowdon Peak 3986

Mount Garfield

Ga Lak

Crater Creek

Crater Creek

Tenmile

Noname 3500

Gaging Sta.

Campground

Potato Hill

Crater Lake

WESTERN

485

Peak Fourteen 3834

Ruby

Ruby Lake

Water Tank

158

Needleton

RIO GRANDE

BOUNDARY

RIO RIVER

3000

Pigeon Peak 4269

Turret Peak

53 Area of interest

22 Point of interest

15 Mile post sign

N

0   1 mi

0   1 km

MOLAS PASS

Map 19.4

along Cascade Creek in June and burned for ten days up the Lime
Creek drainage, spread over Molas Pass, and came within 2 (3.2
km) miles of Silverton. The fire was devastating because of dry conditions and intense winds from the south. Careless campers or lightning probably started the blaze; however, rumors at the time
suggested the Ute Indians may have set it as a protest against broken treaties and the continued invasion of white settlers. Replanting
of trees was initiated in 1911, but even today large areas remain
open, subalpine meadow. Early efforts to reforest the Lime Creek
burn utilized lodgepole pine, which is not native to the San Juans
and proved of limited success. These trees did best in sheltered lower elevations around Lime Creek, but the heavy snowloads and extreme drying conditions at higher elevations near the top of Molas
Pass proved too severe. Later plantings of lodgepole pine were
more successful because workers used locally adapted nursery stock.
Engelmann spruce has been used in the most recent plantings, and
it has survived well.

As recently as 18,000 years ago this area had no vegetation.
It was buried under 1,000 feet (305 m) of glacial ice.

43. (mp 64, Map 19.4) Molas Pass. Elevation: 10,910 feet
(3,325 m). This area is noted for its exposed south-sloping benches with little forest cover. The original spruce-fir forest was deci-
mated by the 1879 fire, and even today, after years of replanting
with lodgepole pine and Engelmann spruce, full reforestation is
still decades away. Islands of the old subalpine forest, however, can
still be seen north of the pass.

Molas Pass is unexpectedly wet. Karst topography abounds
in the vicinity of Molas Lake, and holes eroded in underlying limestone leave moist depressions filled with dense willow thickets,
sedge meadows, and bogs. The willows frequently resound with
the song of the white-crowned sparrow, a common summer inhab-
itant. During the growing season, the meadows are a mosaic of colorful wildflowers, such as pink and red Indian paintbrush, marsh
marigold, elephant's head, bluebell, king's crown, and yarrow.

Eighteen thousand years ago this region was buried beneath
an ice field 500 to 1,000 feet (115–330 m) thick. The ice surface
was at a level close to that of the present tree line, about 12,500
feet (3,830 m). The high peaks in the area were islands of rock

projecting above the ice surface. This ice field fed the Animas glacier, one of the longest valley glaciers documented in the Rocky Mountains of Colorado. Glacial features abound. Look for cirques, horns, and U-shaped glacial valleys (Fig. 19.8). Many outcrops display scratches and grooves carved as the ice dragged stones across the bedrock. Which direction was the ice moving locally?

The sloping benches at and above road level are of the Honaker Trail Member and consist of carbonate-clastic sequences representing cyclic sedimentation. The benches are the resistant limestones or arkosic sandstones, and the slopes are siltstones. The limestones are fossiliferous and contain phylloid algae, pelecypods, crinoids, fusulinids, gastropods, and brachiopods. Many of these 300-million-year-old fossils can be found in the local outcrops scattered about the area.

From the pass one can see structural elements of the Grenadier Horst, a Paleozoic highland. The horst is expressed as the high peaks making up the Grenadier Range to the southeast. The Molas Creek valley, seen south of Molas Lake, is the topographic expression of the Molas Graben, a local downfaulted block bounded on the north by the northeast-trending Molas–Andrews Lake

Fig. 19.8   Looking east toward the Grenadier Range from Molas Pass.

Fig. 19.9   Snowdon Peak is eroded from the Uncompahgre Formation. Note the rock glacier in the center of photo.

Fault and to the south by the Snowdon Fault, which passes just north of Snowdon Peak, seen due south (Fig. 19.9).

To the north, Grand Turk Mountain is capped by the San Juan Formation. This 30- to 35-million-year-old volcanic unit overlies a thin, prominent cliff of the Telluride Conglomerate, a late Eocene pediment-fan gravel, which rests upon a late Eocene erosion surface locally called the Telluride Peneplain. This surface is an angular unconformity and indicates the uplifting and erosion of the San Juan Dome during the Laramide Orogeny in late Cretaceous and early Tertiary time. Note the red Permian Cutler Formation dipping slightly southwest beneath the Telluride Cliff below Grand Turk. Can you pick out any faults that offset these formations? References (POI 41–45): Atwood and Mather 1932, Baars, Ellingson, and Spoelhof 1987, Blair 1985, Cross, Howe, and Emmons 1905, Lee et al. 1976, Maslyn 1977, Molenaar et al. 1968, Steven et al. 1974, Wengerd and Baars 1957.

44.   (mp 65.5) A paleokarst tower is partially exposed in an old quarry east of the road. This quarry exposes the contact between the light gray Mississippian Leadville Limestone and the overlying dark red shales of the Pennsylvanian Molas Formation. The quarry was excavated into the west side of a buried 330-million-year-old karst tower and karst breccia. The Leadville Limestone is partly re-crystallized and contains bryozoa, coral, brachiopods, and crinoids. These fossils indicate that this area was once a shallow-water carbonate platform. After the sea withdrew, the region became humid subtropical to tropical. This led to aggressive solution weathering of the exposed limestone and to the eventual development of numerous karst towers, sinkholes, and caves. Around the lake at least three buried karst towers have been located, one with a height of 65 feet (20 m). The Molas siltstones and shales are thought to represent a paleo-oxisol soil similar to the type of soils now forming in Java and North Vietnam.

45. **(mp 68.3)** A **quartz monzonite pluton** is exposed west of the road. Here a late Tertiary intrusive (26–27 million years old) is in contact with Paleozoic sedimentary rocks. The resulting contact metamorphism altered the sedimentary rocks to quartzites, hornfelses, marbles, and skarns. The altered sediments may be seen on the canyon wall east of the highway.

46. **(Map 19.5) Silverton**. Elevation: 9,318 feet (2,840 m). Population: 716 (circa 1990). Silverton lies just north of the junction of the Animas River (northeast) and Mineral Creek (northwest). The town (Fig. 19.10) was built in a meadow named Baker's Park after Capt. Charles Baker, who in 1860 and 1861 entered here with a party of miners in search of gold. The settlement grew in the 1870s and supposedly was named Silverton after a miner explained, "We may not have much gold, but we've got silver by the ton." Success of mining resulted in the birth and growth of the nearby mining towns of Howardsville, Eureka, Animas Forks, and Chattanooga. Silverton, in fact, is purported to have grown to a community of 1,500 during the heyday of mining activity. The principal supply route to Silverton from the east was completed in 1875 over Stoney Pass, and in July 1882 the Denver & Rio Grande Railroad arrived from Durango.

Many of the buildings in town were constructed out of local quartz monzonite and red sandstone and thus have held up to the

Fig. 19.10   A. Silverton looking north. Photo by W. Cross 1900. B. Silverton 1991. Photo by R. Blair.

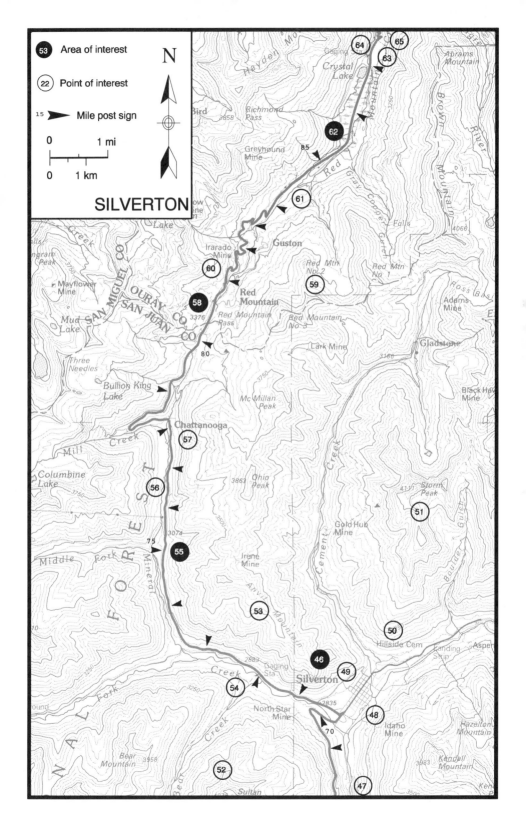

Map 19.5

elements. A display of minerals from just about every mine in the area is embedded in mortar in a monument in front of the courthouse.

Silverton lies in a mountain park. This type of sheltered valley typically supports grasses and drought-resistant shrubs on the drier ground, with sedges, rushes, and willows at wetter sites. Although they sit below timberline, mountain parks commonly lack trees. The valleys act as cold-air sinks, especially at night in spring and fall. This cooling shortens the growing season and, along with boggy soils in places, deters forest growth.

Silverton lies along the southern margin of the Silverton Caldera, the collapsed interior of an ancient volcano that last erupted about 27 million years ago. The caldera rim is outlined by the Mineral Creek and upper Animas River valleys. References (POI 46–51): Cross, Howe, and Ransome 1905, Gregory 1990, Kelley et al. 1957, Molenaar et al. 1968, Nossaman 1989, Nossaman 1993, Petersen 1988.

47. Animas Canyon is a narrow gorge cut below a broad U-shaped valley above. The narrow canyon was incised primarily by the Animas River, whereas the broad valley above resulted from the work of glacial ice. It is speculated that during the last glaciation ice filled both the canyon and valley but sheared off at the top of the canyon, leaving relatively stagnant ice in the chasm below. As a result, the canyon is not U-shaped like a typical glacial valley. The spectacular peaks rising above the upper Animas Canyon are part of the Grenadier Range, a playground for mountaineers.

48. Snow avalanche paths can be seen on Kendall Mountain to the southeast. Kendall Mountain slide (north) and Idaho Gulch slide (south) have both run periodically. In the winter of 1913–1914, Idaho Gulch produced an avalanche that covered the area where the present ballpark, chamber of commerce, and highway are located.

49. Christ of the Mines Shrine, located immediately northwest of town, is built on an old landslide (Fig. 19.11). The shrine was constructed in 1959 as a monument to the local miners. The alcove is constructed from local stone, but the twelve-ton statue is carved from the Italian Carrara marble.

50. The Hillside Cemetery is located north of town. Of the approximately 2,600 people buried here, 117 died in snow avalanches. By contrast, 143 miners died from silicosis of the lungs.

51. Storm Peak, north of Silverton, is composed of 27-million-year-old quartz latites of the Henson and Burns Formations. These units are composed of porphyritic flows, tuffs, and landslide deposits from inside the collapsed Silverton Caldera.

52. (mp 71) Sultan and Bear Mountains consist of a late Tertiary quartz monzonite intrusive stock. Both mountains are capped at about 11,000 feet (3,350 m) with remnants of the Telluride Conglomerate and overlying San Juan Formation. The remains of the North Star–Sultan Mine can be seen to the south of the road. This lead-silver mine opened in the 1880s and produced from pyrite- and galena-rich veins within the monzonite stock that trends parallel to the valley.

Fig. 19.11   Christ of the Mines Shrine.

53. Anvil Mountain is noted for the brilliant red and yellow alteration streaks caused by the oxidation of iron minerals descending toward Mineral Creek. The deep valleys to the west and northeast exist here in part because rivers and glacial ice more easily eroded the shattered rocks that encircle the Silverton Caldera rim.

54. (mp 72.3) Red beds of the Permian Cutler Formation can be seen to the west up the South Fork of Mineral Creek. Overlying the red beds is the gray volcanic San Juan Formation. The Cutler

Formation here forms the outer rim of the Silverton Caldera. In places this rim zone was faulted down in steps toward the interior of the caldera to the north.

55. (Map 19.5) Mineral Creek. Mineral Creek runs through a typical U-shaped glacial valley whose walls are now marked by numerous snow avalanche tracks (Fig. 19.12). Many of these tracks follow gullies eroded along fractures and faults associated with caldera rim faulting. The aspen occupying the avalanche chutes are able to survive because they resprout from roots after the above-ground parts of the trees are swept away by snowslides. In adjacent, undisturbed areas, Engelmann spruce have established a canopy and have existed for such a long period of time that they overshadow and eradicate the shade-intolerant aspens.

Mineral Creek is carved along ring fractures that outline the southwestern rim of the Silverton Caldera. In general, the rocks to the south and west of the road represent the walls of the Silverton Caldera. The rocks to the north and east are the 3,000-foot-thick (900 m) Henson and Burns Formations. These volcanic rocks inside the caldera rest upon a collapsed, complexly fractured caldera

Fig. 19.12   Looking south at Bear Mountain down Mineral Creek.

floor at some unknown depth. The slopes of Anvil Mountain exhibit brilliant reddish and yellowish scree derived from the highly altered volcanic rocks. After the collapse of the Silverton Caldera some 27 million years ago, sulfataric fluids percolated along fractures and escaped from around the caldera rim, in the process altering the enclosing rocks to colorful iron oxides and silicified clays. References (POI 52–57): Cross, Howe, and Ransome 1905, Cross and Larsen 1935, Kelley et al. 1957, Lee et al. 1976, Molenaar et al. 1968, Steven et al. 1974.

56. (mp 76.5) Old beaver ponds form catchment terraces in the valley floor (Fig. 19.13). Some of these have been partly overgrown with sedges. Beavers are important geomorphic and ecologic agents because their dam building levels out the valley floor, creates boggy areas, and reduces forest cover, especially aspen and willows. These modifications to the valley floor, along with nighttime cold-air drainage in the spring and fall, create valley floors with open mountain parks. When the beavers disappear, the valleys become more heavily forested.

Fig. 19.13 Beaver Pond on floor of Mineral Creek valley.

57. (mp 78) Chattanooga, an old mining settlement, was established in 1883 with 75 buildings and a population of 300. In 1884 an avalanche ripped its way from west to east across a hairpin turn and settled on Chattanooga's main street, a reminder to the residents that nature is in control. With the constant threat of avalanches and the devastating fire of 1892, the townsite was finally abandoned. To the north, Mineral Creek follows the trace of the caldera rim faults. The highly altered Henson and Burns Formations make up the valley wall east of the fault zone and the lower third of the west valley wall. The upper two-thirds of the west valley wall are the San Juan Formation, derived from ancient volcanoes located northeast of Silverton, and a sequence of rhyolite ash flows, including the Ute, Blue Mesa, and Sapinaro Mesa Tuffs. These later volcanic rocks are air-fall deposits from the caldera-forming explosions of the Ute Creek, Lost Lake, and San Juan–Uncompahgre Calderas, respectively (see Chapter 6).

58. (mp 80, Map 19.5) Red Mountain Pass. Elevation: 11,018 feet (3,371 m). Red Mountain Pass is the highest point along the San Juan Skyway. Originally called Sheridan Pass, it was the principal access route to the mines located to the north in Ironton Park. In the early 1880s silver ore wagons commonly crossed here. Business was so brisk that Otto Mears decided to extend his Silverton Railroad to Ouray. In September 1888 the first train steamed into Ironton Park, making this the highest railroad pass in the United States. The extension from Ironton Park to Ouray was never built because of the steep grades in Uncompahgre Canyon and because the price of ore collapsed in the silver panic of 1893.

Red Mountain Pass and the mountains around it are covered by alpine and subalpine vegetation. The subalpine forests comprise Engelmann spruce, subalpine fir, and scattered groves of aspen. Above timberline, at around 12,000 feet (3,660 m), the tundra community dominates, with krummholz (dwarfed subalpine fir), bunchgrass, lichens, mosses, and numerous alpine flowers, such as alpine avens, sky pilot, marsh marigold, and elephant's head.

Altered volcanic rocks make up the pass area. The Burns Formation, a hornblende latite, dominates the valley walls at road level on both sides of the pass. Off to the west, the mountaintops are capped by a series of ash-flow tuffs whose source lies to the east. The western rim of the Silverton Caldera follows the Mineral Creek drainage to the south, goes over Red Mountain Pass, and curves northeast parallel to Red Mountain Creek, north of the pass. U.S. Highway 550 essentially outlines the rim of this arcuate ring-fracture zone, where high-angle faults have dropped the east side of the fault down. Note that when traveling from Ridgway to Red Mountain Pass or from Durango to Red Mountain Pass one passes through progressively older rocks (sedimentary, metamorphic, and intrusive igneous rocks) until reaching the margins of the Silverton Caldera, where suddenly the rocks get younger (Cenozoic volcanic rocks). The older rocks are here, but they are buried hundreds to thousands of feet beneath the volcanic pile. References (POI 58–60): Cross, Howe, and Ransome 1905, Cross and Larsen 1935, Gregory 1990, Kelley et al. 1957, Lee et al. 1976, Molenaar et al. 1968, Steven et al. 1974.

59. The **Red Mountain Peaks**, east of the highway, consist of a complex system of flows, flow breccias, and pyroclastics of rhyolite and latite making up the Burns Formation. These units, in turn, have been penetrated by fingers of rhyolite and quartz latite porphyry intrusives. Most of the rocks have been highly altered by late Tertiary hydrothermal activity and have subsequently weathered to a variety of iron oxides, with shades of red, orange, and yellow-brown. Fresh exposures of the altered rock are commonly white, greenish white, or gray and represent an assortment of clay minerals mixed with primary alteration minerals such as pyrite, chlorite, alunite, and quartz. Throughout there are patches of silicified breccias derived from replacement of shattered parent rock. Landsliding is common on the slopes of these highly altered and fractured rocks, especially on the west slope of Red Mountain No. 2.

60. (**mp 81.7**) The **Idarado Mine** (Fig. 19.14) connects this valley with Telluride's Pandora Mine, 6 miles to the west, via 80 miles of anastomosing tunnels and vertical shafts. The maze of drifts and crosscuts converge on the Black Bear and Argentine veins. This entire region generated more than $30,000,000 of ore. The mine closed in 1978.

Fig. 19.14   Idarado Mine. Looking north toward Ironton Park.

61.   (mp 84.5) The **second-longest suspension bridge** in Colorado can be seen looking southeast up Corkscrew Gulch (Fig. 19.15). This bridge was designed such that it is upbowed without load. When under load, the weight removes the upbow and maintains the bridge crossing at perfect grade. The famous turntable used to get railcars into the valley was located above the bridge and to the south of Corkscrew Gulch. Ironton Park was the end of the line for the railroad, which was completed in 1888 over Red Mountain Pass.

62.   (Map 19.5) Ironton Park. Between 1888 and 1893 this region bustled with mining activity, which centered around the settlements of Red Mountain and Ironton. Between them, the two communities totaled more than 1,000 inhabitants. This glacial valley has a flat alluvial floor that supports extensive and well-developed riparian plant communities and wetlands. Willows are the dominant woody plant. The glacial ice carved the valley bottom out of the Hermosa Formation, the Molas Formation, and perhaps the Leadville Limestone. The presence of these formations is not obvious and is known principally from exploratory

Fig. 19.15   Corkscrew Gulch suspension bridge.

drilling and mining operations. Most likely this valley held a lake after the withdrawal of glaciers 18,000 to 16,000 years ago and subsequently filled with lake sediment, alluvium, and landslide debris from both sides of the valley. The lower slopes on the eastern side of the valley display the hummocky topography typically associated with landsliding.

The rocks exposed on both sides of the valley are volcanic, but the western volcanic rocks lie outside the Silverton Caldera, whereas those to the east lie within it. The oldest volcanic rocks found on both sides of the valley are part of the San Juan Formation, a well-bedded, greenish-gray to purplish conglomerate that attains thicknesses between 1,500 to 2,000 feet (450–600 m) to the north, toward Ouray. It is largely a coarse accumulation of angular andesitic boulders and cobbles held in a matrix of sandy tuffaceous material. This 30-million to 35-million-year-old debris fan accumulated upon the flanks of a stratovolcano prior to the deposition of the Crystal Lake Tuff associated with the Silverton Caldera.

The rocks on the west side of the valley belong predominantly to the San Juan Formation, with the top of Hayden Mountain capped by Blue Mesa (Lost Creek Caldera) and Ute Ridge (Ute Creek Caldera) ash-flow tuffs. The east side of the valley consists of the San Juan Formation overlain by the Burns Formation within the Silverton Caldera. The top of the San Juan Formation is a depositional contact surface that dips slightly south, but it is about 1,000 feet (300 m) lower on the east side than the west. This difference in elevation has been attributed to a combination of stepped-down block faulting and a thinning of the San Juan Formation, both toward the east. References (POI 61–63): Burbank and Luedke 1964, Cross, Howe, and Ransome 1905, Kelley et al. 1957, Molenaar et al. 1968, Steven et al. 1974.

63. (mp 87.3) Hendrick Gulch, to the east, exposes jointed cliffs of the San Juan Formation. In the summer of 1940 a large mudflow from the upper part of Hendrick Gulch ran for about twenty-four hours and spread debris across the highway 5 to 6 feet (1.5–2 m) deep.

64. (mp 87.5) The **Uncompahgre Formation** is exposed at the northern edge of Ironton Park. These Precambrian quartzites appear to form a resistant bedrock "dam," which has provided a base-level control for Red Mountain Creek in Ironton Park. This would explain why the park is so flat. Glaciers gouged out the softer rocks within the valley but not the hard quartzites at the north end. The valley was then later filled level with sediment.

65. (mp 88.1) Riverside snowslides have accounted for at least seven lives as of 1993 and an uncounted number of injuries and close calls. These slides converge from both sides of the canyon and have a well-deserved reputation as "killer avalanches." In March 1963, for example, the Reverend R. F. Miller and his two daughters were swept to their deaths while putting on tire chains. The latest victim was a highway employee, who died while clearing avalanche debris from the road in the winter of 1992. A memorial exists at milepost 87.6 (Fig. 19.16).

66. (mp 88.8, Map 19.6) A **breccia zone** is exposed in the roadcut. The breccia is composed of rounded and angular fragments of Precambrian quartzites and slates cemented by pyrite. This breccia, along with others found nearby, was possibly formed by explosive hydrothermal activity or possibly from hydrothermal solutions percolating through a fault breccia.

67. (mp 88.9) The **Dunmore Fault** trace, west of the road, follows the prominent gash and avalanche gully. The fault slices through the crest of a broad anticline in the Uncompahgre Formation and results in 2,800 feet (850 m) of vertical separation and 4,500 feet (1,370 m) of horizontal offset. The south block went east and down relative to the north block.

68. (Map 19.6) Uncompahgre Gorge. U.S. Highway 550 drops 2,000 feet (600 m) in 6 miles (10 km) as it winds along the eastern wall of the Uncompahgre Gorge from Ironton Park to Ouray. This highway follows the original toll road built by Otto Mears in the early 1880s. In the 1920s the road was redone and became the "Million Dollar Highway" because it cost $1.2 million to build.

Fig. 19.16 Memorials from Riverside snowslides.

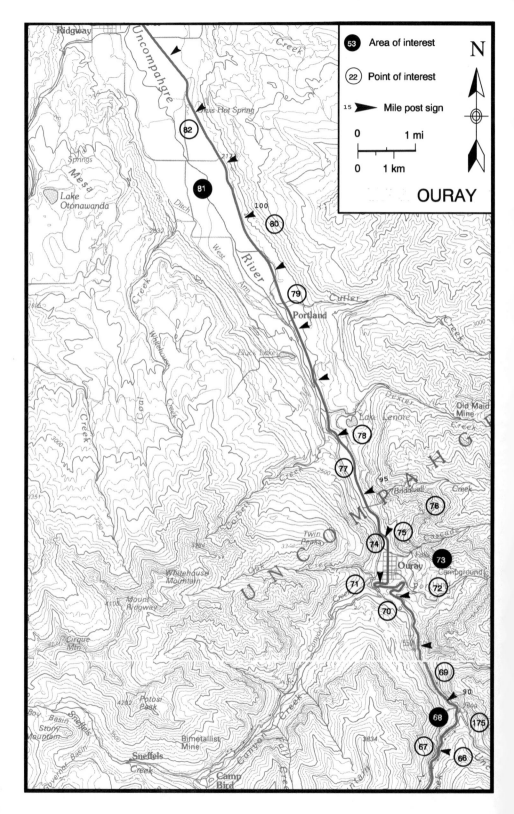

Map 19.6

The little vegetation that does cling to the steep walls of the gorge consists of aspen groves intermixed with Engelmann spruce, Douglas fir, and some subalpine fir. White fir tends to be more common in the lower, northern end of the canyon.

The gorge was carved out of Precambrian quartzites and slates of the Uncompahgre Formation by the erosive action of glaciers and streams. The quartzites and slates were metamorphosed between 1.72 billion years ago and 1.46 billion years ago and tipped up on edge so that many of the layers are now near vertical. The formation is thought to be more than 8,000 feet (2,448 m) thick.

These Precambrian rocks represent part of an uplifted, east-west-trending fault block known as the Sneffels Horst, which is bounded on the south by the Dunmore Fault and on the north by the Ouray Fault. The tectonic history of the Sneffels Horst has had a profound influence on the rock sequence in this region. Just north of Ironton Park, for example, the Paleozoic section is absent, and the San Juan Formation rests unconformably on the Uncompahgre Formation. However, when following this erosion surface north one encounters a wedge of Paleozoic rocks that thickens to approximately 800 feet (245 m) just north of Ouray. This Paleozoic section spans from the Devonian Elbert Formation through the Pennsylvanian Hermosa Formation, and these sedimentary rocks are in turn overlain by the Telluride Conglomerate and the San Juan Formation. The unconformity on top of the Precambrian rocks is tilted toward the northwest and in certain localities marks the lower boundary of late Tertiary mineralized veins and near Ouray constitutes the upper boundary of late Cretaceous mineralization. References (POI 64–69): Cross, Howe, and Ransome 1905, Gregory 1990, Harris 1990, Kelley 1957, Kelley et al. 1957, Molenaar et al. 1968.

69.   (mp 90.6) Bear Creek Falls Overlook is situated upon the Uncompahgre Formation. Bear Creek is a hanging valley, and the falls plunge 227 feet (69 m) to the Uncompahgre River below. Rock surfaces in the gorge display glacial polish, grooves, and scratches, and the mound of debris just south of the Bear Creek Bridge is probably a remnant of a lateral moraine. The glacier is believed to have been more than 3,000 feet (915 m) thick in this area and flowed another 12 miles (19 km) north to Ridgway. The west wall of the gorge exhibits a striking set of ripples in steeply dipping quartzite, which are interpreted as current ripples formed over 1.5 billion years ago (Fig. 19.17). The old tollgate was located at the bridge across Bear Creek.

70. (mp 91.5–92.1) The **Ouray Fault zone** crosses here, trending generally east-west. The uplifted fault block to the south forms the Sneffels Horst. The fault zone separates the Precambrian Uncompahgre Formation on the south from upper Paleozoic rocks on the north. The fault is expressed as an erosional scarp

Fig. 19.17 Current ripples in the Uncompahgre Formation formed about 1.5 billion years ago.

upon the more resistant quartzites of the Uncompahgre Formation. At milepost 92 there is a turnout on the west side of the road with a grand Ouray overlook from which points of interest 70 through 74 can be seen.

71. Box Canyon, 20 feet (6 m) wide and 285 feet (87 m) deep, is associated with the Ouray Fault. The initial escarpment was formed by glacial erosion of the relatively soft sediments north of the fault, which left the resistant Precambrian quartzites as a cliff on the south. Water plummeting over the cliff from Canyon Creek created plunge pools and potholes from the vigorous turbulent water charged with swirling stones. Erosion is greatest at the base of the falls; thus, a vertical channel is cut. The vertical channel is slowly migrating upstream. A view from the high trail west across Box Canyon shows a textbook angular unconformity, with the

Fig. 19.18   Angular unconformity at Box Canyon between the Uncompahgre Formation (1.5 billion years old) and the overlying Elbert Formation (400 million years old).

vertical Uncompahgre Formation capped by the nearly horizontal Elbert Formation (Fig. 19.18).

72.   The **Amphitheater** is a large bowl-shaped valley surrounded by 3,200 feet (975 m) of San Juan Formation. The San Juan Formation is composed of angular volcanic debris, which here fills a prehistoric valley 1,000 feet (300 m) deep. The amphitheater exhibits a hummocky topography, which reveals its origin as a large landslide.

73.   (Map 19.6) Ouray. Elevation: 7,760 feet (2,365 m). Population: 644 (circa 1990). Ouray occupies the floor of a glacial valley in a small mountain park at the juncture of five creeks. Within a 2-mile (3.2 km) radius, peaks rise from 3,000 feet (915 m) to 4,600 feet (1,400 m) above the valley floor. This region lives up to its nickname, "Switzerland of America."

The town, named after the Ute chief Ouray, was established in 1875 when Gus Begole and Jack Eckles came from Silverton in search of gold. They found it, and by 1876 Ouray was officially incorporated. The community thrived until the silver panic of 1893. After three years of recession, Thomas Walsh learned that much of the waste rock up Canyon Creek contained gold and silver tellurides. This discovery led to the creation of the Camp Bird Mine, which quickly became one of the world's largest gold mines.

At least five plant communities can be identified from Ouray because of the steep vertical relief. The flat valley floor harbors a riparian woodland consisting of box elder and narrowleaf cottonwood. The low, dry, south-facing valley slopes support ponderosa pine and Gambel oak, which grades upward into an Engelmann spruce–Douglas fir forest with scattered aspen groves. High above the town, at timberline, the subalpine forest gives way to alpine meadows.

Ouray is surrounded on the west, north, and east by about 4,000 feet (1,200 m) of Paleozoic and Mesozoic sedimentary rocks dipping gently to the north and northwest. To the south the dominant rocks are the Precambrian quartzites and slates of the Uncompahgre Formation that lie south of the Ouray Fault. The first 1,500 feet (450 m) of ledgy gray and buff strata above the valley floor to the west and northeast are the sandstone and limestone layers of the Pennsylvanian Hermosa Formation. Above these layers are the red beds of the Permian Cutler Formation and the Triassic Dolores Formation. An angular unconformity separates these two formations and suggests that several episodes of uplift occurred along the Ouray and other local faults around 245 million years ago. All of these formations are blanketed by a thick sequence of volcanic rocks, mostly of the lower Tertiary San Juan Formation. References (POI 70–76): Cross, Howe, and Irving 1907, Gregory 1990, Kelley 1957, Kelley et al. 1957, Luedke and Burbank 1962, Molenaar et al. 1968.

74. Hot springs emerge from faults buried beneath the valley floor alluvium. Some of the hot water is used to heat local buildings in the winter and to supply the waters for the public thermal pools (Fig. 19.19).

75. (mp 94) A **dike** can be seen to the west slicing across and vertically through the Hermosa beds at road level.

Fig. 19.19   Public hot springs at Ouray.

76.   The **Blowout** is a broad, yellowish-stained gully above the valley northeast of Ouray. This altered zone was a feeder pipe to a pancake-shaped laccolithic intrusion injected during the late Cretaceous or early Tertiary. The Ouray Pluton, as it is called, flowed like molasses between the Mancos Shale and Dakota Sandstone. This laccolith of granodiorite porphyry is associated with precious and base metal mineralization and has been discolored from subsequent hydrothermal activity.

77.   (**mp 94.8**) A **monoclinal fold** in the Cutler Formation is visible on both sides of the valley.

78.   (**mp 95.8**) **Bachelor Mine** Road, to the right, also provides access to Lake Lenore. This mine occupies the south side of Dexter Creek and was an important producer of high-grade silver-lead ores during the late 1880s and 1890s, producing more than $3,000,000. To the west side of the valley one can occasionally get glimpses of the old railroad grade brought in from Montrose during the mining boom days.

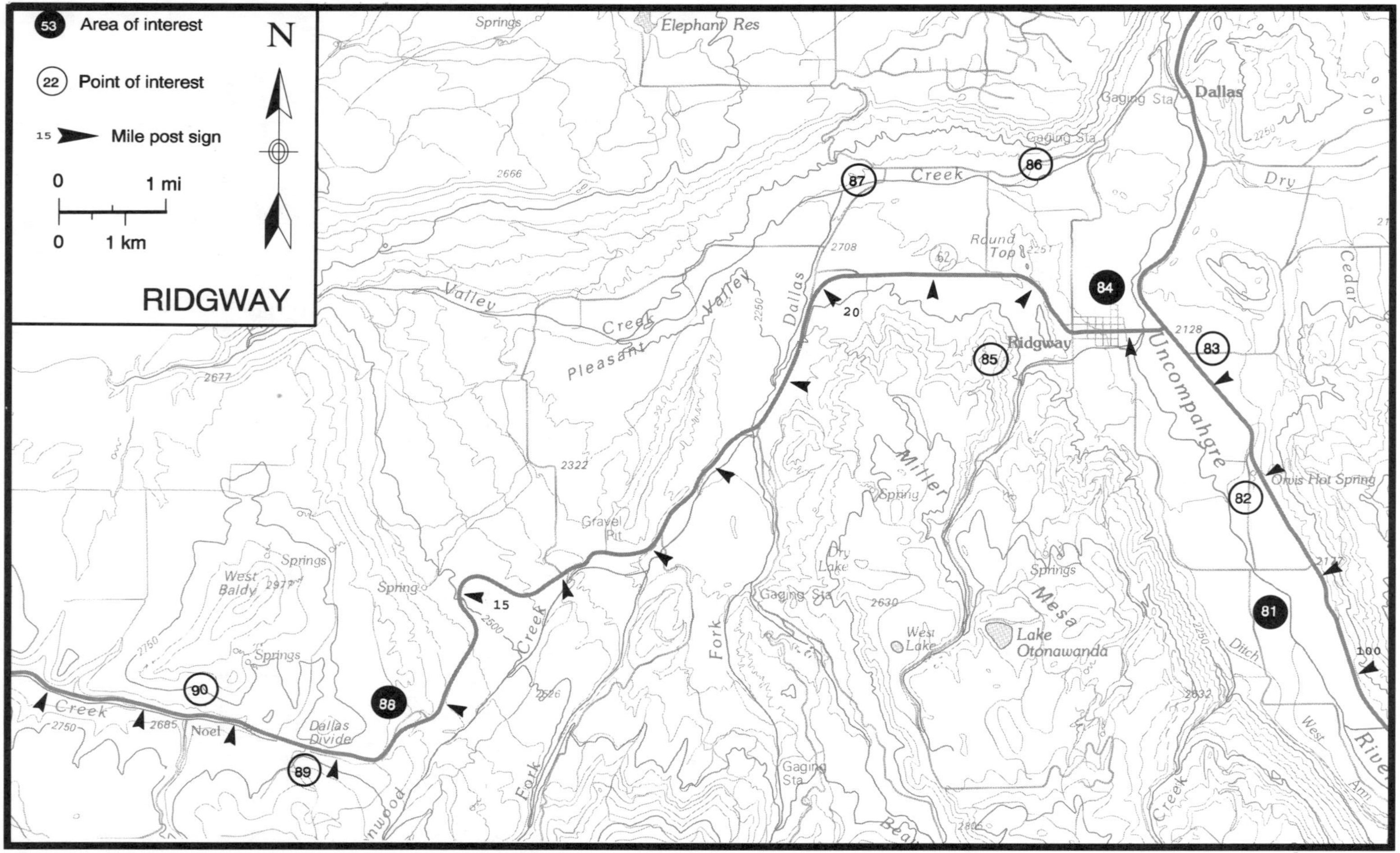

Area of interest
Point of interest
Mile post sign
0
1 mi
0
1 km
N
RIDGWAY
Springs
Elephant Res
Dallas
Gaging Sta
Creek
Dry
Cedar
Round Top
Ridgway
Dallas
Valley
Creek
Pleasant
Valley
Uncompahgre
Orvis Hot Spring
Miller
Spring
Gravel Pit
Dry Lake
Gaging Sta
West Lake
Lake Otonawanda
Mesa
Springs
Ditch
West
River
Fork
Creek
West Baldy
Springs
Spring
Dallas Divide
Noel
Creek

Map 197

79. (mp 98.4) Cutler Creek, to the east, offers an exceptionally good exposure of the Cutler Formation (red beds). The formation was first measured and examined in detail here, and thus the name was selected from this type section.

80. (mp 100.2) Entrada Sandstone is exposed as a white cliff high up on the valley walls. It is overlain by the Morrison Formation. Both are of Jurassic age.

81. (Maps 19.6 and 19.7) Uncompahgre Valley. This is the northern gateway into the heart of the San Juan Mountains. Chief Ouray and the Mountain Utes occupied this valley until the late 1870s. Intense mining activity and the growth of white population centers drove the native Americans from their residences and hunting grounds. This valley is an important winter range for mule deer and elk, but today they, too, feel the pressure of encroaching civilization.

Vegetation cover in the valley is a mixture of natural species and agricultural crops. Stream banks are revealed through the presence of box elder, narrowleaf cottonwood, and the occasional blue spruce. Near Ouray the lower slopes on the west side of the valley are dominated by Douglas fir, and farther down the valley piñon-juniper and mountain shrub communities become more prominent. The upper valley slopes support white fir, Douglas fir, piñon pine, and the occasional Rocky Mountain juniper and ponderosa pine.

This valley is almost a mirror image of the lower Animas Valley north of Durango. The valley from Ouray to Ridgway was buried beneath 1,000 feet (330 m) or more of glacial ice some 18,000 years ago. Originally the valley was probably U-shaped, but subsequently it was filled with alluvium and lake sediments to produce the flat-floored valley we see today.

Between Ouray and Ridgway the Uncompahgre Valley is bounded on both sides by cliffs composed of Paleozoic and Mesozoic strata dipping to the north and northwest. Near Ouray the Pennsylvanian Hermosa Formation forms the valley walls and is overlain by 2,150 feet (655 m) of Permian red beds of the Cutler Formation. The boundary between the Hermosa and Cutler is marked by the uppermost occurrence of limestone in the Hermosa and is not based on color, making it difficult to detect. The north-ward-dipping beds of the Cutler Formation are, in turn, truncated by the flatter-lying Triassic Dolores Formation. The resulting an-gular unconformity marks a time of tectonic instability and ero-sion. The northern part of the valley is bounded by strata from the Jurassic Entrada Sandstone and Morrison Formation followed by the Cretaceous Dakota Sandstone and Mancos Shale. References (POI 77–82): Cross, Howe, and Irving 1907, Kelley et al. 1957, Molenaar et al. 1968.

82. **(mp 102.2) Orvis Hot Springs** have been a popular rest stop ever since they were discovered by the Indians. The first com-mercial operation began in 1917, when Louis and Irma Orvis built a public pool called the "Orvis Plunge." The land was sold in 1933, and the springs were not developed for public use until 1987 under the ownership of Jeff and Andrea Kerbel. Swimsuits are optional. The natural waters seep out of the ground at temper-atures ranging from 115 to 125 degrees F (46–52 °C). The pool temperatures range from 100 to 105 degress 5F (38–40.5 °C). These springs are associated with nearby tufa mounds of travertine and are most likely connected with either a buried fault or fracture system. However, no such structures have been mapped.

83. **Cimarron Ridge** forms the eastern skyline and is jagged from pinnacles carved from the Tertiary volcanic conglomerate San Juan Formation, which here rests upon the upper Cretaceous, coal-bearing Fruitland and Kirtland Formations. The square-topped peak is Courthouse Mountain.

84. **(Map 19.7) Ridgway**. Elevation: 6,983 feet (2,128 m). Population: 423 circa 1990. The Tabeguache Utes lived, hunted, and traveled through the Ridgway region for several centuries be-fore the first white settlers entered. One of the Utes' favorite stops was the "sacred" Orvis Hot Springs, 2 miles south of Ridgway. With the exploration for gold and silver in the nearby mountains in the 1870s, the town of Dallas, 2 miles north of Ridgway, became a thriving community. However, when the Denver & Rio Grande Southern Railroad made plans to expanding the Montrose-Ouray rail line to the west, Dave Wood, an enterprising Dallas man in the

Fig. 19.20   View west of Ridgway at the "Ridgway Tillite" (R), Telluride Conglomerate (T), San Juan Tuff (SJ) and Mancos Shale (Km).

freight business, refused to sell his land. Wood wanted to enter the rail business, but on his own terms. Otto Mears acquired land at the site of Ridgway on behalf of the railroad and established the Rio Grande Southern link over the Dallas Divide to Telluride. Ridgway was incorporated in 1891 and quickly became the hub of all meaningful enterprise. Dallas, by contrast, evaporated the same way Animas City, north of Durango, did.

In 1951 the railroad succumbed to competition from trucking and closed its lines. Shortly thereafter, in 1956, the Bureau of Reclamation laid out its plans for the Ridgway Dam and Reservoir, which would place the town under 100 feet of water. Times looked grim. The dam, fortunately, was relocated 5 miles north and was dedicated in 1990. Three movies have been filmed around Ridgway: *Tribute to a Bad Man* (James Cagney), *How the West Was Won* (James Stewart), and *True Grit* (John Wayne, Katharine Hepburn).

Ridgway's soil, derived from Mancos Shale, is saline and so fine-grained that it does not absorb water readily. Consequently it is inhospitable to many plant species. In addition, the area's steep slopes are subject to erosion; therefore, many bare patches exist. The shale weathers to a distinct yellowish gray. Because of their greater moisture concentration, north-facing slopes favor mountain shrub communities with piñon pine, Rocky Mountain juniper, and, occasionally, Gambel oak. Big sage is common on south-facing slopes.

Ridgway is built upon alluvium deposited by the Uncompahgre River. The low-lying hills east, north, and northwest are end moraines deposited by the last advance of the Uncompahgre glacier 18,000 to 16,000 years ago. These riverine and glacial deposits rest directly upon the Mancos Shale.

The Ridgway Fault runs east-west, just south of Log Hill Mesa. This fault represents the southern edge of the Uncompahgre Uplift and has a displacement of about 1,500 feet (459 m) with the adjacent block to the south. One of the strongest earthquakes recorded in Colorado had an epicenter about 10 miles (16 km) east of Ridgway, just north of Owl Creek Pass. It occurred on October 11, 1960, with a magnitude of 5.5 on the Richter scale. References (POI 83–87): Atwood 1915, Atwood and Mather 1932, Crabb and Dunn 1991, Cross, Howe, and Irving 1907, Lee et al. 1976, Steward et al. 1968, Tweto et al. 1976.

85.   The **"Ridgway Tillite,"** a conglomerate of disputed origin, is exposed beneath the San Juan Tuff and Telluride Conglomerate but above the Mancos Shale in the east-facing slopes near the top of Miller Mesa (Fig. 19.20), due west of Ridgway. Atwood (1915) described this conglomerate as a glacial moraine deposit, which would suggest an origin in glacial conditions during Eocene time some 45 to 55 million years ago. The most recent geologic information, however, suggests that mild Mediterranean-like climates existed during this time. Closer examination of this deposit by geologists in the 1950s and 1960s indicated that this conglomerate is most likely an old mudflow, not a glacial till, and may be more closely associated in age and origin with the Paleocene Animas Formation exposed south of Durango.

86. The **Ridgway Fault** lies just south of Log Hill Mesa and trends east-west. Mancos Shale on the south downblock is juxtaposed with the Morrison Formation to the north.

87. Earthship home, built by movie actor and environmentalist Dennis Weaver, was completed in 1989 (Fig. 19.21). Constructed of 300,000 recycled aluminum cans, 2,000 auto tires, wood, and adobe, it stands along the trace of the Ridgway Fault.

Fig. 19.21   Earthship home, outside of Ridgway.

88.   (mp 13.1, Map 19.8) Dallas Divide. Elevation: 8,970 feet (2,734 m). This stretch of highway was opened up in 1882 as another of Otto Mears's toll roads. Initially it was not much more than a rutted trail, but it served as the main supply route to Telluride, with its booming mining industry. In the early 1900s, the first "horseless carriage" made it over the divide in just fifteen hours. In 1890 the Rio Grande Southern Railroad was completed over the pass and continued operations until 1951.

The open meadows and shrublands of the pass area present a mosaic of Gambel oak clones, grasslands, and silver sage in moist swales. Groves of quaking aspen are common, and lines of willows can be seen following the natural drainages. In July the hillsides will be yellow with the flowers of mule's ears, contrasting with blue splotches of lupine. Scarlet gilia adds a dash of red in midsummer. West of Dallas Divide along Leopard Canyon, ponderosa pine,

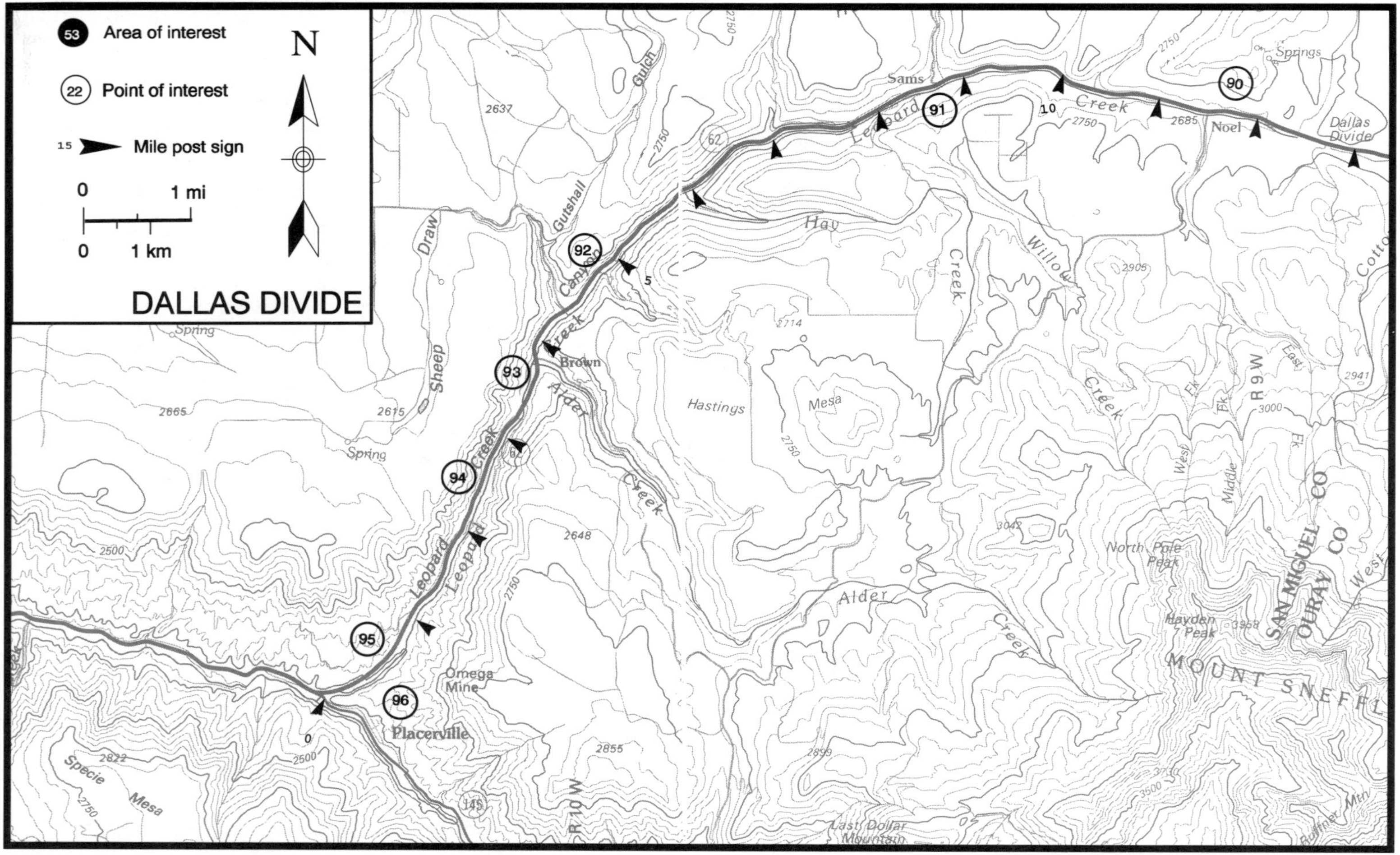

Area of interest
Point of interest
Mile post sign
0 1 mi
0 1 km
N
DALLAS DIVIDE
Dallas Divide
Noel
Sams
Leopard Creek
Hay
Willow Creek
Creek
Gutshall
Gulch
Canyon Creek
Brown
Alder Creek
Sheep Draw
Spring
Hastings
Mesa
Omega Mine
Placerville
Specie Mesa
North Pole Peak
Hayden Peak
MOUNT SNEFFL
SAN MIGUEL CO
OURAY CO
R 9 W
R 10 W
Last Dollar Mountain
Springs
90
91
92
93
94
95
96

Map 19.8

Gambel oak, and quaking aspen are found on south-facing slopes. North-facing slopes are dominated by aspen and mixed conifers.

The east side of Dallas Divide is mostly Mancos Shale. The road on the west side of the divide cuts through the local Mesozoic and upper Paleozoic section. References (POI 88–95): Gregory 1990, Steward et al. 1968, Tweto et al. 1976.

89. (mp 13.1) Mount Sneffels (14,150 ft, 4,314 m) is the triangular peak forming the centerpiece of the skyline to the south of Dallas Divide (Fig. 19.22). The peak itself is eroded from an early Miocene (?) intrusive. The intrusive rock is slightly more resistant to weathering than the weaker volcanic rocks; thus, Mount Sneffels towers over the neighboring peaks. The whole mountain crest is part of an uplifted fault block called the Sneffels Horst. The summits of the other mountains consist mostly of Oligocene ash-flow tuffs erupted from the Silverton and Lake City Calderas. These units, in turn, lie upon about 2,000 feet (615 m) of the San Juan Formation. A Tertiary sill (mp 13–14.6) is intruded into the Mancos Shale and exposed in the north roadcut. Note the contact metamorphism with the Mancos Shale where exposed.

Fig. 19.22   View south of Mount Sneffels from Dallas Divide.

90.   (mp 11–11.4) Dakota Sandstone is exposed to the north and contains lenses of carbonaceous shale.

91.   (mp 8.3, Map 19.8) The **abandoned narrow-gauge railbed** can be found south of the highway along the fence line. Roadcuts (mp 7–10) consist of Jurassic Morrison Formation.

92.   (mp 5.4) The **Alder Creek Graben** lies between two north-south-trending faults. At the easternmost fault (mp 5.4) the east block is upthrown, exposing the Jurassic Entrada Sandstone and underlying Triassic Dolores Formation (red beds). The western fault (mp 3.5) also exposes Entrada. The graben section at road level between the faults is the Morrison Formation.

93.   (mp 3.4) The **Entrada Sandstone** is exposed at road level. Along Leopard Creek one can find narrowleaf cottonwoods, willows, chokecherry, hawthorn, and Woods rose.

94.   (mp 3.2–1.0) The **Dolores Formation** of Triassic age is exposed at road level as red beds.

95.   (mp 1.0–0.0) The **Cutler Formation** (also red beds) of Permian age is exposed at road level.

96.   (mp 84) Placerville lies just east of the junction of Colorado Highways 145 and 62. A look west down the canyon will reveal bedrock strath terraces in the Cutler Formation, mostly on the north side of the river. The trend of the north wall of the canyon for the next 3 (4.8 km) miles west of here may be partly influenced by the Black King Fault, a normal fault with the north side about 500 feet (152 m) below the south. Across the river, south of Placerville, are the Placerville Hot Springs. The sulfurous springwater flows out from a fault in the Cutler Formation and maintains a temperature of about 94 degrees F (34.4 °C).

97.   (mp 82.5, Map 19.9) A **drill hole** was completed to a depth of 6,244 feet (1,903 m) in 1960 by Kerr McGee just above and north of the road. The well, called Placerville Unit No. 1, was drilled through a faulted west-plunging anticline. This dry hole bottomed out in Precambrian rocks. The main surprise was the discovery of an erosion surface that removed most of the lower Paleozoic section. The drill went directly from Pennsylvanian Molas Formation into Cambrian sands and dolomites of the Ignacio Formation.

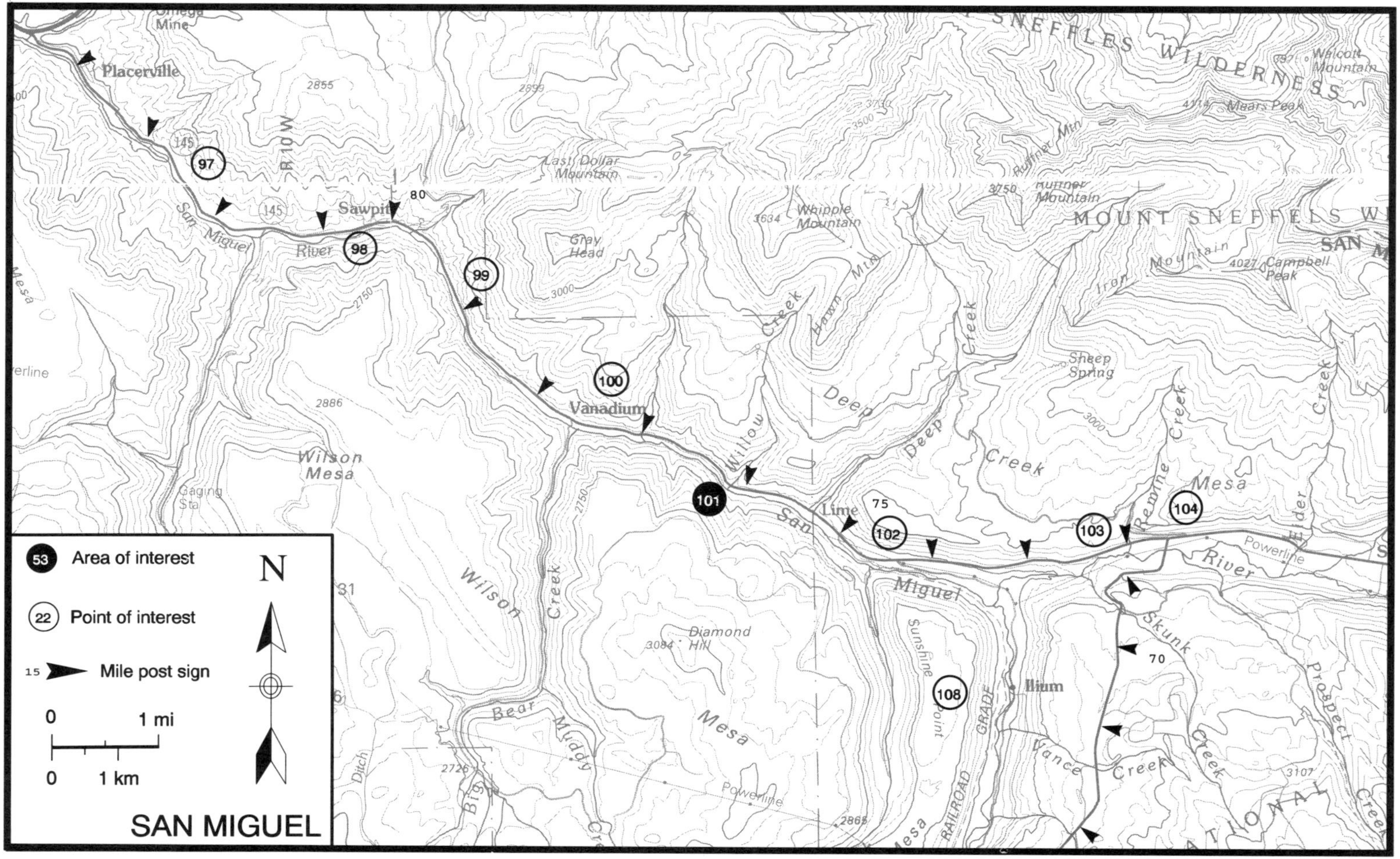
SAN MIGUEL
Area of interest
Point of interest
Mile post sign
N
0 1 mi
0 1 km
Placerville
Sawpit
Vanadium
Lime
Ilium
San Miguel River
Wilson Mesa
Wilson Creek
Diamond Hill
Sunshine Point
Gray Head
Last Dollar Mountain
Whipple Mountain
Ruffner Mountain
Iron Mountain
Campbell Peak
Mears Peak
Sheep Spring
Deep Creek
Willow Creek
Skunk Creek
Prospect Creek
Vance Creek
Muddy Creek
Bear Creek
RAILROAD GRADE
MOUNT SNEFFELS WILDERNESS
Powerline

Map 19.9

98. (mp 80.6) **Plant fossils** were discovered in the Dolores Formation just south of the river in 1952 by G. Edward Lewis and Roland W. Brown of the U.S. Geological Survey. They uncovered the palmlike leaves of *Sanmiguelia lewisi*, the oldest flowering plants, about 220 million years old, found in the Western Hemisphere.

99. (mp 78.9) A **pebble conglomerate** marks the base of the brick-red Triassic Dolores Formation. The Permian Cutler Formation disappears beneath the road (mp 78.6) toward the east.

100. (mp 77.5) The **first uranium ore** recovered in the United States was processed around 1920 at the mill at the old townsite of Vanadium, located north of the road. The access road to Silver Pick Basin, up Bear Creek, lies to the south. Marie Curie reportedly used some of this ore for her pioneering experiments with radioactivity. Uranium and vanadium were mined from the Entrada Sandstone exposed up Big Bear Creek.

An olivine basalt dike (gray) can be seen on both sides of the highway (mp 77.1 and 77.4) and has been traced for more than 3 miles (4.8 km). The dike is expressed as a slot when enclosed by more resistant bedrock or as a free-standing wall when surrounded by more easily erodible rock.

The riverbanks are lined with narrowleaf cottonwoods, river birch, willows, Woods rose, and scattered blue spruce.

101. (Map 19.9) **San Miguel Canyon.** The San Miguel River winds its way northwest through a canyon 1,200 to 1,500 feet (365–457 m) deep and joins the Dolores River just west of Uravan, Colorado. The lower portion of the canyon is dominated by piñon pine and Rocky Mountain juniper on south-facing slopes and Douglas fir mixed with Gambel oak and mountain mahogany on north-facing slopes. As the upper end of the canyon opens up, south-facing slopes support ponderosa pine on the lower reaches and aspen on the upper reaches. North-facing hillsides are dominated by aspen, blue spruce, and Douglas fir.

The canyon cuts through a sequence of Paleozoic and Mesozoic sedimentary rocks dipping gently to the south. The older sedimentary layers are found near Placerville. References (POI 96–103): Cross and Purington 1899, Steward et al. 1968.

102. (mp 74–74.4) The **Mesozoic section** is visible to the north. The Dakota Sandstone can be seen at the top overlying the Morrison Formation, Junction Creek Sandstone, Wanakah Formation, Entrada Sandstone, and Dolores Formation at road level.

103. (mp 73.1–72.4) Mudflow deposits are exposed in the roadcut. Here, weathered Mancos Shale is slipping down the trough of a faulted syncline. Landslides and mudflows in this area during wet years have caused headaches for highway maintenance crews. For example, in April 1987 a mudflow not only blocked the highway but also threatened to undermine the foundation of the Telluride airport runway, located above the road on Deep Creek Mesa.

South of the road one can see exposures of breached end moraines derived from the Main Fork glacier, which flowed west from Telluride. These Wisconsin-aged deposits have a thickness of about 500 feet (152 m) and consist of both stratified and unstratified till. When the glacier was at its maximum about 18,000 years ago, it supplied copious quantities of gravel to the San Miguel River. Evidence of pre-Wisconsin glaciation occurs as terrace gravel deposits found scattered along the canyon 100 feet (30 m) or so above the present river level.

104. (mp 71.5) Society Turn, the intersection of Colorado 145 and the road to Telluride, is so called because around the turn of the century Telluride's elite folks frequented this corner on Sunday afternoon picnics so as to see and be seen. The gravel-filled hills in the valley floor west of Society Turn are breached end moraines and acted as a natural dam during the retreat of glaciers some 18,000 to 16,000 years ago.

105. (0.5–1.5 miles east of Society Turn, Map 19.10) Wetlands occupy a large portion of the valley floor here. Stunted blue spruce and shrubbery have much of the appearance of muskeg habitats found in the Arctic. The willows, rushes, sedges, and grasses enhance this resemblance, but the parallel between the stunted blue spruce and the black spruce of the northern wetlands is most striking. The close proximity of this unusual natural area to the rapidly developing town raises disturbing questions about the wetlands' future.

106. (Map 19.10) Telluride. Elevation: 8,745 feet (2,665 m). Population: 1,309 (circa 1990). Telluride occupies the floor of the narrow, glaciated Main Fork Valley of the San Miguel River. The steep valley walls rise more than 4,500 feet (1,370 m) to the surrounding summits. Two miles east of Telluride the valley terminates in a glacial cirque with a headwall 2,400 feet (732 m) high (Fig. 19.23). The Main Fork Valley is U-shaped and filled with more than 500 feet (152 m) of lake sediment and alluvium.

Exploration for gold and silver began in 1875, and the Smuggler Mine opened that same year. After the railroad and electricity entered Telluride in 1890, the Telluride Mining District boomed. In the fall of 1896 about 400 stamp mills and nearly 2,000 men were active in milling and mining ore. Some estimate that more than 275 miles (440 km) of tunnels have been bored into the surrounding canyon walls. With so much reliance on mining, it was no wonder that the labor strikes of 1903–1904 were devastating to the local economy.

As a new frontier town, Telluride was an easy mark. On the morning of June 24, 1889, the McCarty Gang, which included Butch Cassidy (George LeRoy Parker), robbed the San Miguel Valley Bank of more than $30,000 and headed south into Utah.

Paleozoic and Mesozoic strata make up the north and south valley walls and dip gently toward the west. The reddish-brown Cutler Formation of Permian age forms the basal band of rocks seen at valley level. Overlying layers include, in order, the brick-red Dolores Formation of Triassic age, the Jurassic Entrada Sandstone, the Wanakah Formation, and the Morrison Formation, capped by the cliff-forming Cretaceous Dakota Sandstone. The Cretaceous Mancos Shale forms the dark gray slopes above the Dakota Cliff to the west. The airport runway is built upon the Mancos Shale. As many

Fig. 19.23 Looking east from Telluride at Ingram Falls.

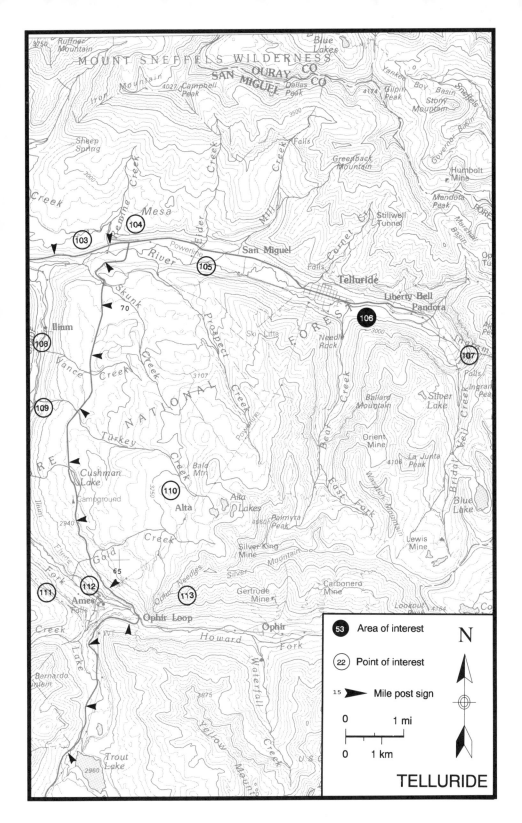

Map 19.10

homeowners can probably attest, the Mancos Shale is associated with landsliding, mudflows, and swelling soils.

Because these formations dip to the west and because an east-dipping Tertiary erosion surface truncates the layers, the formations wedge out toward the east. In fact, at the head of the Main Fork Valley, only the Cutler and Dolores Formations remain below the erosion surface. This surface has been called the Telluride Peneplain and marks a time in the late Eocene when the whole region was tectonically stable. Overlying this surface is the 250-foot-thick (76 m) Telluride Conglomerate, which forms a prominent cliff chock full of pebbles and cobbles of many lithologies. Late Tertiary volcanic tuffs are draped over the conglomerate like a blanket. The lowest and thickest (~2,000 ft, 610 m) of these volcanic formations is the San Juan Formation, followed by several rhyolite ash-flow units from the Lake City and Creede Calderas.

Fracturing and subsequent mineralization during the late Tertiary formed rich veins containing gold and silver. Much of the silver is tied up in minerals that also contain arsenic, antimony, and sulfur, such as stephanite (Ag_5SbS_4). Most of the early mined gold occurred as visible free gold. References (POI 104–109): Burbank and Luedke 1966, Cross, Spencer, and Purington 1899, Gregory 1990, Steward et al. 1968.

107. Glacial topography dominates the landscape. The head of South Fork Valley is a glacial cirque surrounded by hanging valleys and waterfalls that drain from higher cirques. Note the spectacular Ingram Falls, found north of the headwall, and Bridal Veil Falls, which has a free fall of 350 feet (107 m) south of the headwall.

108. (mp 68–69) Sunshine Mesa, seen across South Fork Valley to the west, is capped by rimrock composed of the Dakota Sandstone. The Morrison Formation forms the slopes below the rim rock.

109. South Fork Valley is a glacial valley. Much of the highway north of Ophir rests upon lateral moraine ridges superposed upon landslide. Between Telluride and Trout Lake the vegetation consists of a complex mosaic of Douglas fir, blue spruce, aspen groves, and subalpine meadows.

110. (mp 65.5–68) **Turkey Creek Mesa**, to the east of the highway, is mapped by the U.S. Geological Survey as a huge complex landslide covering an area of about 10 square miles (30 km^2). The ghost town of Alta and the Alta Lakes sit upon this landslide, which is "floating" upon the Mancos Shale. Huge blocks of Telluride Conglomerate and San Juan Formation ride piggyback upon this sliding mass.

111. (mp 65–66) A **granodiorite sill** (look across the valley) makes up most of this bold northeast-facing cliff. This 800-foot (244 m) sill connects with the quartz monzonite intrusive making up Mount Wilson, visible to the southwest. Above the sill are slopes composed of Mancos Shale.

112. The **Ames Power Plant** was conceived and financed by L. L. Nunn, who, with the help of George Westinghouse, completed its construction in 1891. This hydroelectric generating plant was the first to use alternating current as a method for distributing electricity, an idea generated by Nikola Tesla. The Ames plant supplied the Gold King Mine at Alta with the power it needed and did so at an enormous savings. The electricity was later fed to Telluride to make it one of the first all-electric cities in the U.S. The existing plant was built in 1906.

113. (mp 64–66) **Ophir Needles** form the jagged ridges and spires just above the Ophir post office and are eroded from a fine-grained, igneous rock, forming a stock. A keen eye can pick out the lower stratified, light-colored Telluride Conglomerate, split and wedged apart by the intrusive stock (Fig. 19.24). Below the Telluride are the darker beds of baked Mancos Shale.

114. (Map 19.11) **Sunshine Mountain** and **San Bernardo Mountain** are eroded from the Telluride Conglomerate, which rests upon the Mancos Shale.

115. (mp 61.1) **Trout Lake** is dammed by a glacial moraine superposed upon landslide debris. The view across the lake looks up the Lake Fork Valley toward Pilot Knob, Golden Horn, Vermillion Peak, and San Miguel Peak. All of these peaks are carved from rhyolite ash-flow tuffs overlying the San Juan Formation. The basin is a huge glacial cirque.

Fig. 19.24 Ophir Needles. The Telluride Conglomerate has been split apart by an igneous rock intrusive.

116. (mp 59.5, Map 19.11) Lizard Head Pass. Elevation: 10,250 feet (3,124 m). This pass provides the only viable southern access to Telluride. The Rio Grande Southern Railroad completed its track over the pass in 1890–1891, which became known as the "Galloping Goose" line. The Galloping Goose was a gasoline-powered locomotive with one passenger car attached.

The highway passes through a large subalpine meadow and shrubland consisting of willows and shrubby cinquefoil. The forest surrounding the meadow is composed of Engelmann spruce and subalpine fir. In the subalpine meadow, the pocket gopher is responsible for the winding solid dirt ridges, 3 to 4 inches (7–10 cm) in diameter, draped across sections of the marshy ground. These are most prevalent in the spring, after the snowpack has melted. The aspens, shrublands, and clear-cuts harbor the long-tailed vole, a tiny mouselike mammal. The long-tailed vole will also inhabit fescue meadows, but only if the closely related montane vole is not present. The red-backed vole appears to be largely restricted to the dense, old forest habitats surrounding the meadows. The chorus

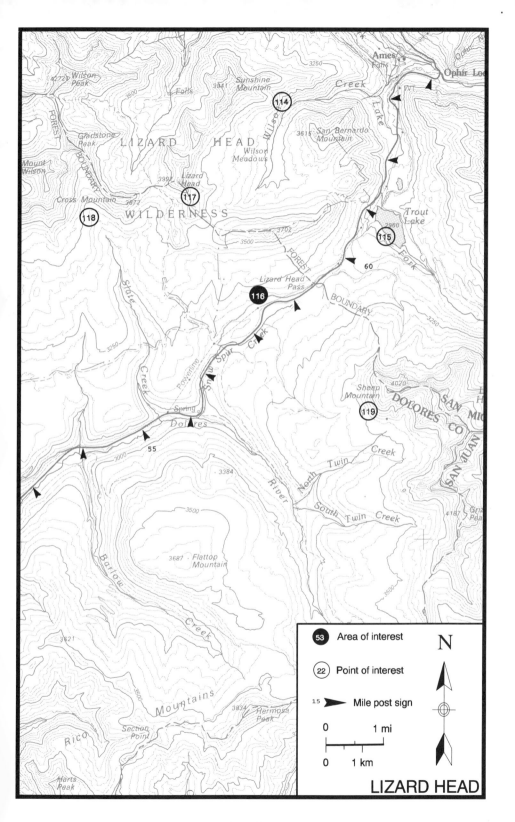

Map 19.11

frog is found near its upper elevation limit on the slopes of Wilson Peak at 11,800 feet (3,600 m).

During each of the last glacial epochs, ice covered this divide and filled the surrounding valleys. Glacial moraine deposits can be seen just south of Trout Lake and form the hummocky topography viewed there. From Trout Lake to the southern edge of the subalpine meadows (mp 57) the road is built upon upper Cretaceous Mancos Shale. South of the meadows the road is confined to the Dolores River Canyon and passes down through the Mesozoic section consisting of the Dakota Sandstone, the Morrison Formation, the Wanakah Formation, and the Dolores Formation. These formations all dip generally 5 to 10 degrees to the north off the northern flank of the Rico Dome. References (POI 110–119): Bromfield and Conroy 1963, Cross, Spencer, and Purington 1899, Gregory 1990, Steward et al. 1968.

117. (**mp 57.5**) **Lizard Head** (13,113 ft, 3,997 m) is the conspicuous spire located north of the highway (Fig. 19.25). Albert Ellingwood and Barton Hoag first climbed it in 1920. The ascent is considered to be the hardest of any 13,000-foot peak in Colorado. In fact, an early climbing guide for the mountains of Colorado described the approach to the base of the spire and then recommended that climbers take a photograph and return home. When early miners first saw the peak, it had a bulge of rock at the top on the east side, giving it the appearance of a reptile's head. This section collapsed as a rockfall in the early part of the century. The upper 500 feet (152 m) of the spire is composed of a late Tertiary ash-flow tuff resting upon the San Juan Formation and the Telluride Conglomerate.

118. **Cross Mountain,** south of Lizard Head peak, is named after Whitman Cross, the pioneer geologist who did most of the early work in the San Juan Mountains. It is capped by the remains of an eroded sill. Gladstone, the next peak west, is carved from granodiorite and associated igneous intrusives from the Wilson Peak stock. Left of Gladstone is Mount Wilson (14,246 ft, 4,342 m), which is capped by ash-flow tuff, although its northern flanks are granodiorite.

Fig. 19.25   Lizard Head is carved from Tertiary volcanic rocks.

119. Sheep Mountain (13,188 ft, 4,020 m), east of Lizard
Head Pass, is capped by more than 700 feet (213 m) of ash-flow
tuff and 600 feet (183 m) of Telluride Conglomerate. These two
formations account for the steep sides of the mountain. The break
in slope represents the approximate contact of the Telluride Conglomerate and the underlying Mancos Shale. Note at timberline
the band of krummholz between the high alpine meadow and the
spruce-fir forest below.

120. (mp 48.2, Map 19.12) A **sulfuric acid plant** was located
east of the Dolores River prior to 1964. Now only the leaching
ponds remain. Stack emissions created a pollution halo surrounding the plant and killing the vegetation. Since 1964 the area has
only partly recovered. One can see landslide debris on both sides
of the road. For example, a large landslide from the east has nar-
rowed the canyon between mileposts 48.5 and 49.3. With so
much loose debris available, floods along tributaries were able to
build massive debris fans, such as the Aztec Gulch Fan just south
and west of the road.

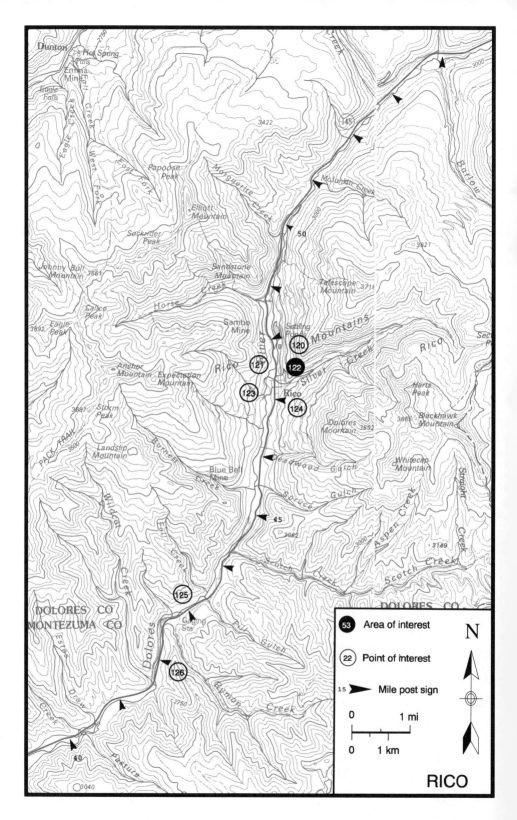

Map 19.12

121. (mp 47.5) Precambrian Uncompahgre Formation (quartzite) is exposed just south of the Dolores River bridge above and east of the highway.

122. (Map 19.12) Rico. Elevation: 8,827 feet (2,690 m). Population: 92 (circa 1990). Rico sits upon the banks of the Dolores River, which cuts through the heart of the Rico Mountains. In 1833 William Walton, a trapper from Taos, New Mexico, passed through the Dolores Valley and reported encountering many bands of Indians and even the remains of Spanish smelters. The Rico district, however, was not occupied permanently until 1860, when Gus Begole prospected and located galena ore. Mining only became a reality in 1869 with the discovery of the Pioneer lode by Sheldon Shafer and Joe Fearheller.

Early access to Rico was difficult and long. During the summer the shortest access from the east was via the Pinkerton Trail, which came from the Animas Valley over the divide and down Scotch Creek (mp 44.3). The town of Rico was incorporated in 1879. In 1891 the railroad was completed from the south and allowed the community to grow to a population of several thousand people. The silver panic in 1893 occurred after President Grover Cleveland signed the McKinley Silver Purchase Act. This panic killed the immediate future of Rico mining and caused a major drop in population in a matter of months. By 1900 the population was listed as 811. Since then several revivals of mining activity have occurred. Most recently, a sulfuric acid plant was constructed north of town with a designed capacity of 150 tons per day. The plant was partially dismantled in 1964.

Douglas fir and blue spruce dominate the canyon walls. Lining the river banks of the Dolores River are narrowleaf cottonwood, blue spruce, elderberry, and thinleaf alder.

The townsite of Rico occupies essentially the center point of the Rico Dome. The east-west axis of the dome crosses at the north edge of town. From almost any commanding position, the Paleozoic sedimentary strata can be seen dipping away from town in all directions. Exceptions to this exist when the strata are faulted or come in direct contact with igneous intrusives.

The two dominant formations of the valley walls and the core of the dome are the Pennsylvanian Hermosa Formation (1,200 ft, 366 m) and the Permian red beds of the Cutler Formation (2,100 ft, 640 m). Both are laced with numerous Tertiary igneous dikes and sills.

The center of the dome has been shattered by numerous faults, most trending east-west and northwest-southeast. These faults produced pathways for mineralized fluids, which reacted with some of the limestones in the Hermosa Formation and replaced them with pockets of silver, lead, zinc, and pyritic ore. The intense fracturing also contributed to the instability of the surrounding outcrops, because within a 2-mile (3.2 km) radius of the town center more than 70 percent of the bedrock is associated with either landslide or talus. References (POI 120–124): Engel 1968, Pratt 1968, Pratt, McKnight, and DeHon 1969, Steward et al. 1968.

123. A **monzonite stock** makes up the west valley wall (mostly tree-covered). It pierced through the Hermosa Formation and probably contributed to the uplift of the dome. The most widespread igneous rock, however, is the hornblende latite porphyry, which produces the numerous sills and dikes seen in this region.

124. **Newman Hill**, located southeast of town, generated the most successful silver production in the Rico district, especially from the Enterprise Mine.

125. (**mp 44.3**) An **igneous sill** can be seen forming the steep slopes on both sides of the river. The Scotch Creek road joins the highway on the east side.

126. (**mp 43, Map 19.13**) The **Hermosa Formation** is exposed along the road from here to Rico. Early maps by the U.S. Geological Survey showed the uppermost Hermosa as the Rico Formation. However, geologists now find the supposed contact of the Rico with the Hermosa difficult, if not impossible, to define. As a result, many workers have abandoned the Rico and have lumped it in with the Honaker Trail Member of the Hermosa Formation.

127. (**mp 39–42**) The **Cutler Formation** is exposed at road level. The Permian-aged Cutler is about 1,600 feet (488 m) thick

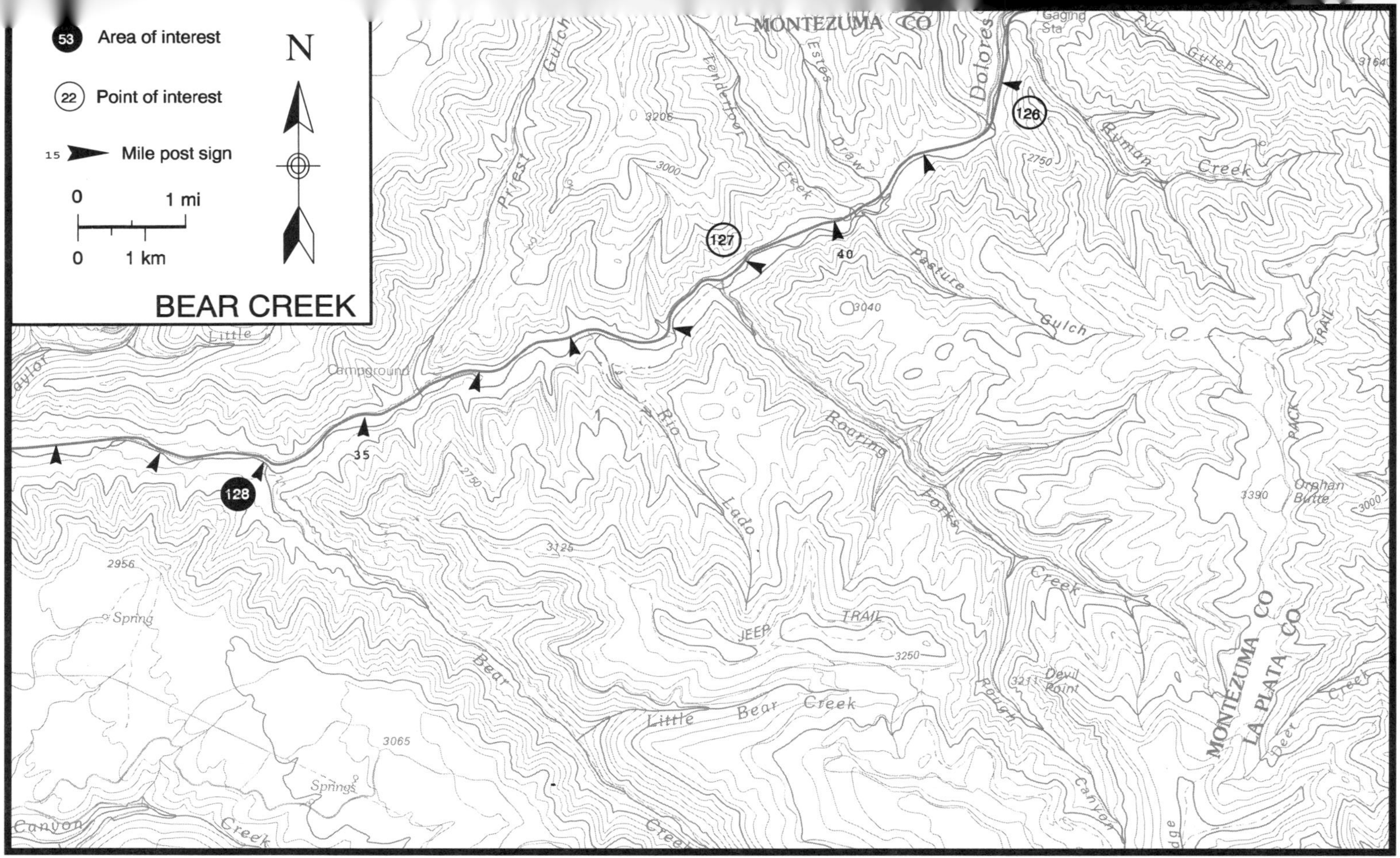

Map 19.13

BEAR CREEK

53 Area of interest

22 Point of interest

15 Mile post sign

0   1 mi
0   1 km

N

in this area and consists of pink to maroon arkosic sandstone with lenses of conglomerate. The large clast size indicates the Cutler's close proximity to its source area from the north, where the Uncompahgre Plateau is today. These rocks represent braided stream deposits that accumulated upon a giant alluvial fan sloping toward the south and southwest.

128. (Map 19.13) Upper Dolores River Canyon. This colorful canyon provides the easiest access from the south to Rico and Telluride and was heavily traveled by early trappers and miners. The Dolores River flows west-southwest in this canyon, with a gradient of about 53 feet per mile (10 m/km). At the western end, the river is 1,200 feet (366 m) below the top of the canyon, 2,400 feet (731 m) below it to the east.

The valley floor is lush with meadows and riparian woodland. Narrowleaf cottonwood dominates the floodplain, but other important trees found here include box elder, blue spruce, and even species from the canyon walls, such as ponderosa pine and Gambel oak. Riparian shrubs make up the understory plants in the woodland, including willows of various species, silverleaf buffaloberry, hawthorn, chokecherry, and Woods rose. Golden rabbitbrush is common in drier disturbed sites, especially along the road. The meadows are typically artificially maintained by irrigation, mowing, cutting of woody species, and grazing. Often the herbaceous species that dominate these meadows are exotics that invade because of the disturbance of agricultural practices. Prominent examples are thistles, dandelions, orchard grass, alfalfa, and yellow sweet clover.

Upper Paleozoic and Mesozoic strata make up the canyon walls. These sedimentary formations dip 1 to 2 degrees toward the west and southwest; thus, the oldest layers encountered along the road are to the east toward Rico and youngest to the west toward Dolores. Little structure is encountered; however, note the fault exposed in a northwest outcrop at milepost 33.9, opposite the Bear Creek trailhead. References (POI 125–135): Cross, Howe, and Ransome 1905, Steward et al. 1968.

129. (mp 28–29, Map 19.14) The Dolores Formation is exposed in the roadcuts. These Triassic sandstones and siltstones are

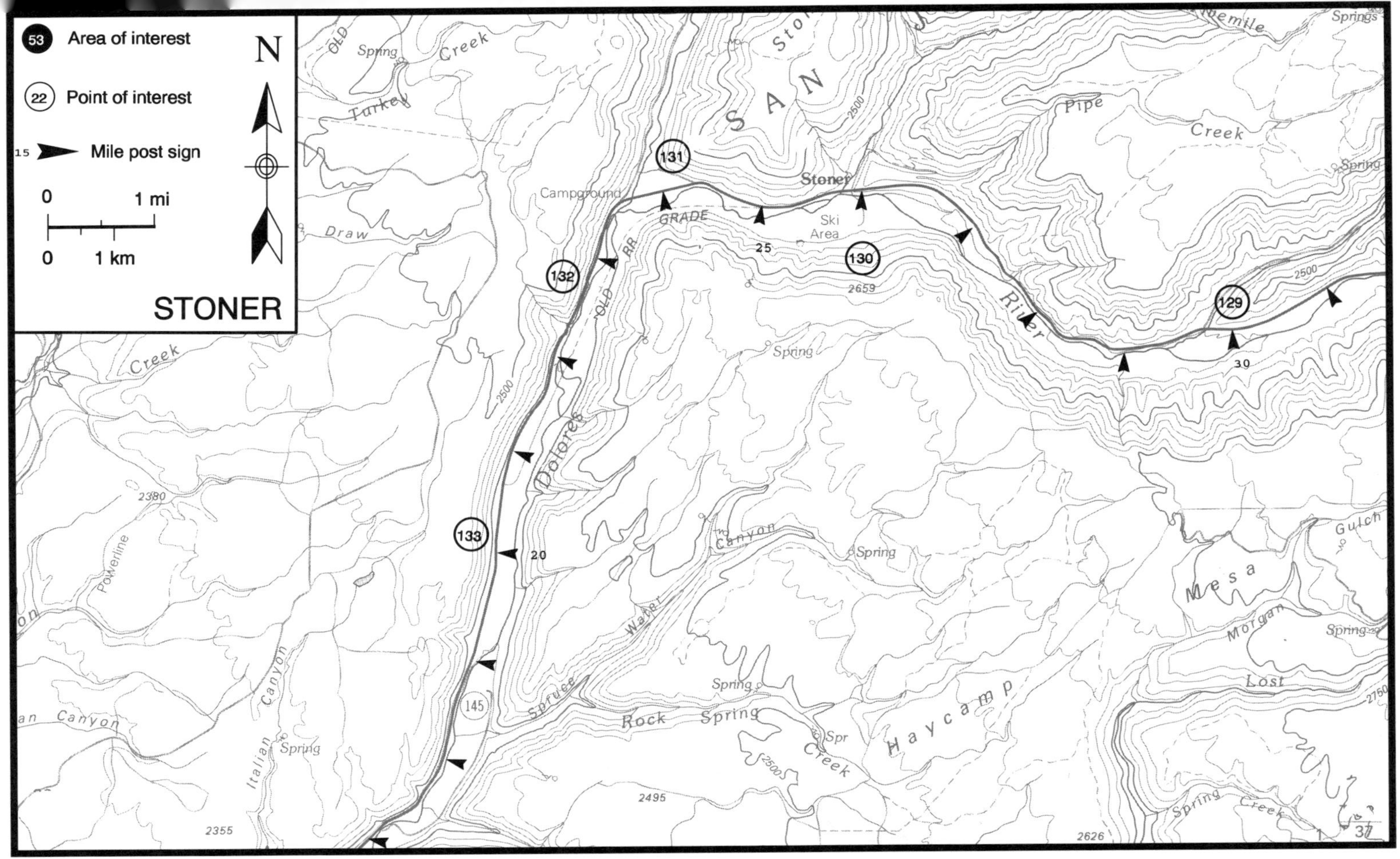

53 Area of interest
22 Point of interest
15 Mile post sign
0 1 mi
0 1 km
N
STONER
Stoner
Campground
Ski
Area
GRADE
OLD RR
Dolores
River
SAN
Pipe
Creek
Turkey
Creek
Draw
Spring
Canyon
Water
Spruce
Rock Spring
Spr
Creek
Haycamp
Mesa
Morgan
Lost
Gulch
Italian Canyon
Powerline
131
132
133
130
129
145
25
20
30
2500
2659
2380
2495
2355
2626
2750

Map 19.14

known for their bright red colors, caused by the oxidation of iron. The formation is about 840 feet (256 m) thick in this area and represents floodplain deposition in the lower layers and lake and cross-bedded river channel deposits in the upper layers.

The contrast between south-facing versus north-facing slopes is quite distinct here. Cliffs of bedrock are more exposed on the south-facing slopes, where the greater annual sunshine creates drier conditions and more frequent freeze-thaw cycles. Thus, these slopes tend to support an open forest of ponderosa pine, with scattered Rocky Mountain juniper and piñon pine and an understory of Gambel oak. In contrast, the north-facing slopes receive more moisture and thus are more favorable for aspen and Douglas fir.

130. (**mp 25.5**) The **Stoner ski area**, once called Sky-Hi Ski Hill, was abandoned in the early 1980s. The ski runs are still obvious, but now aspens are beginning to reclaim them. Eventually the three ski slopes will be completely covered again by aspen forest. Aspen has an advantage in the early invasion of such north-sloping areas because it is tolerant to mechanical damage; its young shoots spring back up after being weighted down by snow or bent downhill by snow creep. Also, aspen can sprout back from its rootstock after fires. In areas adjacent to the ski slope, the hillsides are covered by a mosaic of Douglas fir and aspen stands. The areas that aspen dominate are probably the sites of forest fires that occurred 100 or more years ago. The Douglas fir stands represent little islands of unburned vegetation.

131. (**mp 24–26**) The **Entrada Sandstone** is pinkish in color and forms a smooth slickrock ledge 100 feet (30 m) thick above the road (Fig. 19.26). It is early Jurassic in age and is noted for its distinct cross-beds, suggesting an ancient sand-dune environment.

132. (**mp 22.7**) The **Wanakah Formation**, of Jurassic age, is about 60 feet (18 m) thick and consists of siltstones and sandstones associated with a coastal tidal-flat environment. These layers are weakly cemented and tend to form debris-covered slopes rather than bold cliffs.

133. (**mp 17.2–22.5**) The **Junction Creek Sandstone** forms the bold 300-foot (91-m) cliff seen along the road. Its color is

Fig. 19.26   The Entrada Sandstone is exposed above the highway in Dolores Canyon.

light red to tan, and it is distinctly cross-bedded, indicating a sand-dune depositional environment.

134.   (mp 15, Map 19.15) The **Salt Wash Member** of the Morrison Formation is exposed along the road. This unit is dominantly composed of braided stream deposits.

135.   (mp 12) The **Brushy Basin Member** of the Morrison Formation rises from here to the base of the rimrock, making up the Dakota Sandstone. The Brushy Basin Member consists of fine silts associated with lake beds mixed with river sediments. These lake beds frequently weather to form green, purple, and orange sandy slopes.

136.   (Map 19.15) Dolores. Elevation: 6,936 feet (2,113 m). Population: 866 (circa 1990). The town of Dolores is named after the river, which in turn was named by eighteenth-century Spanish explorers. Supposedly, one of the exploring parties lost two members of its group while attempting to cross the raging channel.

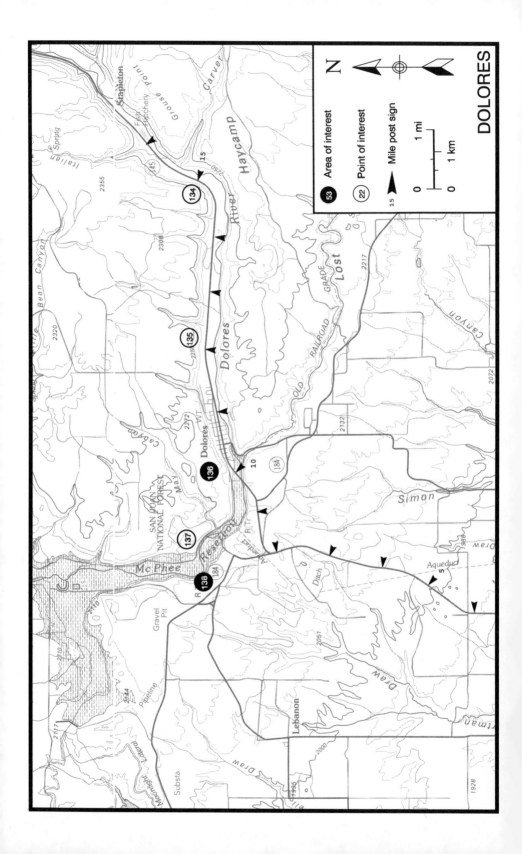

Thereafter, the stream was referred to as El Rio de Nuestra Senora de las Dolores, or the "River of Our Lady of Sorrows." In 1891 the townsite became the western junction for northern destinations on the Rio Grande Southern. Nine years later, in July 1900, Dolores was officially incorporated. The railroad was abandoned in 1951, but the town still remains the gateway to the western San Juan Mountains.

The river flows west through town and into the McPhee Reservoir. About 2 (3.2 km) miles west of Dolores the water, having traveled southwest from the San Miguel Mountains for 50 miles (80 km), goes through a 135-degree turn back to the north. This radical change in flow direction has caused many geologists to ponder the early history of the stream. Charles Hunt of the U.S. Geological Survey and other geologists have speculated that the river may once have continued south and joined the San Juan River as a tributary. Imbricated stream cobbles with San Juan Mountain lithologies have been found in a gravel pit on Haycamp Mesa, southeast of Dolores. These gravels indicate that a south-flowing ancestral river once existed here. What caused the stream to change course and when is still a mystery. Some combination of uplift and stream capture is likely, and it may have occurred within the last 5 million years.

The stratified canyon walls are composed of Mesozoic sedimentary rocks. The slopes surrounding the town comprise the late Jurassic Morrison Formation, which is best exposed north and east of the town. This formation is divided into an upper and lower unit, the Brushy Basin Member and Salt Wash Member, respectively. The prominent cliff capping the north canyon wall is Dakota Sandstone. This late Cretaceous formation is the uppermost rimrock for nearly the full length of Dolores Canyon. References (POI 136–137): Haynes, Vogel, and Wyant 1972, Hunt 1956, Steward et al. 1968.

137. The **McPhee Dam and Reservoir** was completed in May 1986 by the Bureau of Reclamation as part of the Dolores Project. This 4,470-acre (1,810 ha) impoundment provides irrigation water to Montezuma Valley, the Great Sage Plain, and a small portion of the Ute Mountain Ute Indian Reservation. Municipal and industrial water is also supplied to the towns of Cortez, Towaoc, and

Dove Creek. Fishing and boating are popular activities on this reservoir, which fills from spring snowmelt in April, May, and June. The greatest draw from the reservoir occurs from April through October. A minimal amount of water is released through the dam to maintain a live stream and sport fishery downriver.

138.   (Map 19.15) Anasazi Heritage Center. This museum is located 3 miles (4.8 km) west of Dolores. To get there, turn north from Colorado 145 to Colorado 184 at milepost 8 and drive about 1 mile north-northwest. The center was built by the Bureau of Reclamation as part of the McPhee Dam and Reservoir project. Permanent exhibits include a hands-on discovery area, an Anasazi-style pithouse, and a nature trail.

The Anasazi moved into this region about 1,500 years ago. After farming the red soils for about 800 years, they mysteriously left. In 1776 the Dominguez-Escalante expedition arrived at the Dolores River and came upon the ancient ruins of a small Indian village (Fig. 19.27). Escalante made note of them in his journal. The center is believed to stand upon the site of the ruins Escalante observed, making it the first archeological site recorded in Colorado.

Fig. 19.27   The remains of an Anasazi Indian structure at the Anasazi Heritage Center.

The hilltops are covered by a piñon-juniper woodland that grades into a mountain shrub community on the north-facing slopes. The nature trail passes through a plant association that mixes species from both the piñon-juniper woodland and the mountain shrub community. Representatives of the mountain shrub community include squaw-apple, fendlerbush, mountain mahogany, Utah serviceberry, Gambel oak, and occasionally three-leaf sumac.

The observation tower at the top of the trail offers a good view of the Great Sage Plain to the west. Much of this plain has been converted to agriculture, specifically for the dryland cultivation of pinto beans and winter wheat.

Along the trail to the ruins one can see many of the birds and mammals common to this area. Rufous-sided towhees and scrub jays are year-round residents, and noisy flocks of piñon jays occasionally appear, especially when the large, edible piñon seeds mature in the fall. Blue-gray gnatcatchers and black-headed grosbeaks nest here in the summer. Chipmunks and cottontail rabbits frequent the woodlands and shrublands, and black-tailed jackrabbits and Gunnison's prairie dogs may be seen in the open areas below the museum. References (POI 138): Bureau of Land Management pamphlets 1988, Haynes, Vogel, and Wyant 1972.

139. (mp 3, Map 19.16) The **Great Sage Plain**, visible to the west and northwest, is mostly an eroded surface upon the Dakota Sandstone. Some of the scattered hills, however, are remnants of Mancos Shale. Most of the surface is mantled with a reddish-brown loess, which in places is more than 10 feet thick. The loess, an airborne silt derived from the Southwest, is believed to have slowly accumulated over hundreds of thousands of years. This area north and west of Cortez is now green and agricultural, but a hundred or more years ago it was a mosaic of sagebrush shrubland and piñon-juniper woodland. Today alfalfa hay production and apple orchards provide an economic base for many of the local farmers.

140. (Map 19.16) Cortez. Elevation: 6,201 feet (1,890 m). Population: 7,284 (circa 1990). This town lies in the Montezuma Valley in the shadow of the Sleeping Ute Mountain to the west and Mesa Verde to the southeast. The town took its name from Hernando Cortez, the sixteenth-century conqueror of Mexico, and the val-

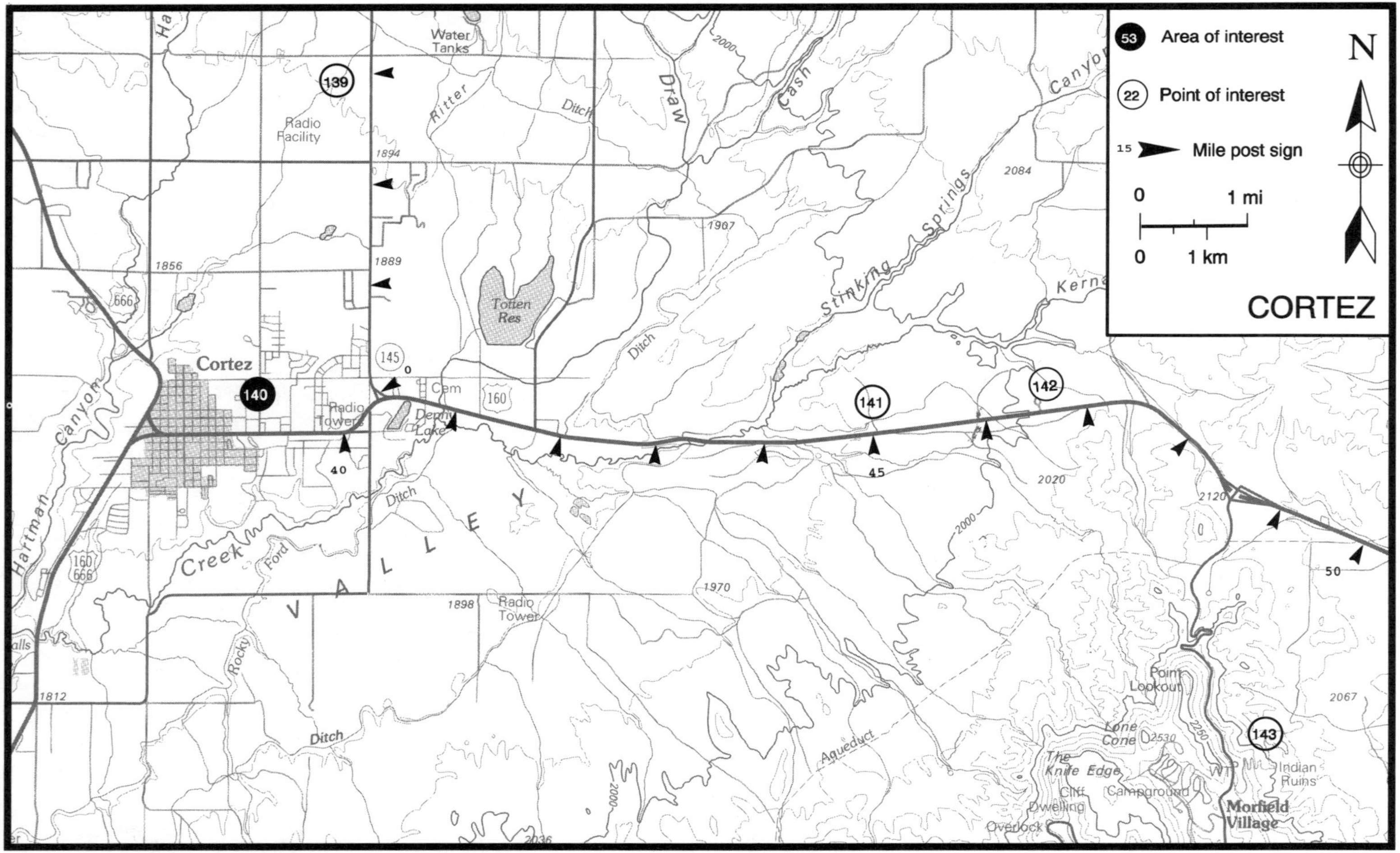

CORTEZ

N

Area of interest
53

Point of interest
22

Mile post sign
15

0   1 mi
0   1 km

Kernal

Canyon

Sitkawa Springs

Cedar
Draw
2084
2000
1907
Ditch
Totten Res

Water Tanks
1894
1889
Ritter
Ditch
160

139
Radio Facility

Cortez
140
1856
999
Ha
Hartman Canyon
160
666
1812

142
2020

141
45

2120
2020
2000

50

2067

143
Mt. Indian Ruins
Mesa Verde

Morfield Village

Point Lookout
2250
Lone Cone
2530
The Knife Edge
CH4 Campground
Overlook
Dwelling

Aqueduct

1970
2000
2036

Radio Tower
1898

Cem
Depot
Creek
145
Radio Tower
40
Ditch

V A L L E Y

Creek
Ford

Rocky
Ditch

Map 1016

ley was named after Montezuma, the Aztec warrior vanquished by Cortez. The community began in 1885, when a group of settlers living south of the present town conceived of a scheme to bring water from the Dolores River into the Montezuma Valley. With the establishment of the Montezuma Valley Water Supply Co., M. J. Mack laid out plans for a new townsite, and in 1886 the city of Cortez officially replaced the existing Mitchell Springs settlement.

Cortez has been called the archaeological center of the United States because more than half a dozen major archeological sites, including Mesa Verde and Hovenweep, lie within a 20-mile (32-km) radius of town.

The city and roads in the Montezuma Valley are built upon the eroded surface of the Mancos Shale. A good exposure can be seen to the southeast, where the shale slopes sweep up to the rim-rock (Point Lookout Sandstone) of Mesa Verde. The Mancos Shale has been eroded in places down to the underlying Dakota Sandstone, which serves as the platform for the Great Sage Plain, the vast, relatively flat surface to the west and northwest. To the southwest is the Sleeping Ute Mountain, a series of laccolithic intrusives that formed about 84 million years ago. References (POI 139–142): Haynes, Vogel, and Wyant 1972, Molenaar and Werts 1968, Smith and Bochard 1957.

141. (mp 45) A **cold desert shrubland** exists on both sides of the highway on soils developed from the underlying Mancos Shale. The Mancos Shale is rich in salts such as sodium sulfate and sodium bicarbonate. These salts are water soluble and leave a white coating on the surface after evaporation. Big sage thrives on the higher, better-drained sites, and golden rabbitbrush is common along the roadside. The lower areas often contain salt-tolerant shrubs that have a competitive advantage in the saline and alkaline conditions created by the Mancos Shale. Four halophytic species are common here: the large greasewood, the four-wing saltbush, the smaller shadscale, and the very small sea blight.

142. (mp 46.4) The **Sleeping Ute Rest Area** represents a fairly typical piñon-juniper woodland. South of the road this woodland grades into a mountain shrub community on the steep, north-facing slopes of Mancos Shale. The mountain shrub community consists principally of Gambel oak, fendlerbush, and mountain mahogany. From this vantage point one can see the north-facing slope of Mesa Verde. Above the cliffs of Point Lookout Sandstone there are patches of Douglas fir; these are at the high point of the park at an elevation of approximately 8,000 feet.

143. (Map 19.17) Mesa Verde National Park. Take a thick sandstone slab, elevate it to 8,000 feet, and tip it to the south. Carve in canyons with hollows, add a healthy sprinkling of trees and shrubs, and you have Mesa Verde, meaning "green tableland" in Spanish.

Human habitation of the Mesa Verde area probably began around the time of Christ. The first residents were the Basketmakers, a group of seminomadic hunters. There is no direct evidence that these people ever lived within the national park boundaries, but they may have lived in the lowlands surrounding the park. The modified Basketmakers (Basketmakers III), who lived between A.D. 550 and 750, did inhabit the mesa tops; they left evidence of their pottery, bows, arrows, and, of course, baskets. They lived in pithouses with low walls and flat thatched roofs.

Between A.D. 750 and 1100, the Pueblo Indian culture evolved. The Pueblo I and Pueblo II people also inhabited the mesa tops but developed a more complex architecture than the Basketmakers. Their homes (pithouses) differed from their ceremonial meeting rooms (kivas). They used cotton and designed water projects to retain moisture. The "golden age" of the Anasazi was during the Pueblo III Period (A.D. 1100–1300). During this time many of the people built and lived in mud-brick and stone apartment houses in the hollows of cliffs (Fig. 19.28). The move from mesa-top living to cliff dwellings apparently came quickly around A.D. 1200. Tree rings date a severe drought between A.D. 1276 and 1299. The environmental pressures associated with this drought, along with other factors, forced the Indians to seek refuge somewhere south. Many anthropologists believe the Pueblo Indians of today are descendants of the Anasazi.

In August 1776 the Franciscan Friars Dominguez and Escalante traveled north of the mesa and perhaps gave the region the name Mesa Verde, but more than likely the name was already in use

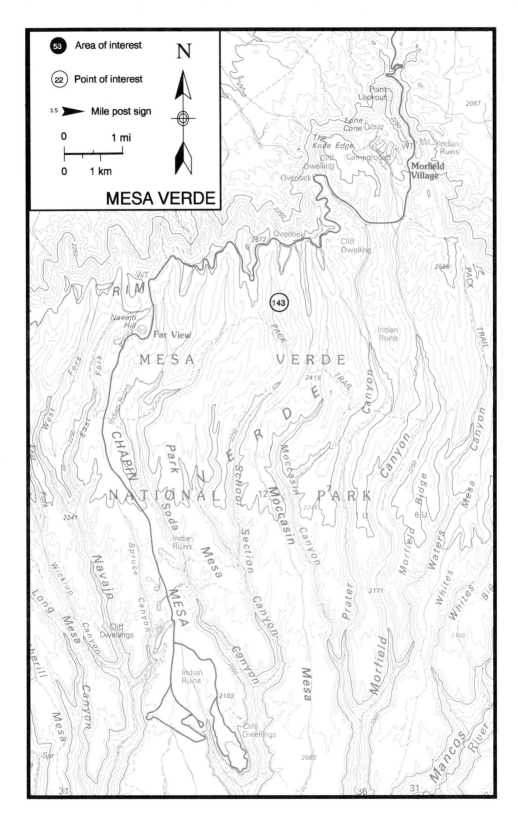

Map 19.17

Fig. 19.28   Ruins at Cliff Palace before renovation (compare with Figure 15.4). Courtesy Center of Southwest Studies, Fort Lewis College.

by then. The first English-speaking explorers to penetrate the mesas were connected with the 1859 expedition of Captain J. N. Macomb. The expedition geologist, J. S. Newberry, climbed to the crest near Point Lookout and surveyed the area but apparently did not explore the canyons or discover any cliff dwellings. In 1874 a small party of explorers led by John Moss and William H. Jackson, photographer for the U.S. Geological and Geographical Society, made the first recorded discovery of cliff houses. Jackson was following up on stories from Moss, a gold miner and ex-soldier, who claimed to have seen cliff houses built in caves. In December 1888 local cowboys Richard Wetherill and Charlie Mason discovered the Cliff Palace and Spruce Tree House ruins while searching for stray cattle. Wetherill and his brothers soon became the local experts and guides to the region. In 1906, after years of persistent lobbying by Virginia McClurg and Lucy Peabody, Congress passed and President Theodore Roosevelt signed a bill creating Mesa Verde National Park, the first national park in the United States dedicated to preserving the culture of native Americans. It has since been recognized by the United Nations as a World Heritage Site.

Topography and elevation control the distribution of the different plant communities found within the national park. At higher elevations, near the park's north end, Douglas fir grow on the cool, moist, north-facing slopes and in canyons near intermittent streams and springs. Annual precipitation is greater at the north end than at the south end for two reasons. First, higher altitudes are usually associated with greater precipitation; second, the northern end lies closer to the Ute and La Plata Mountains, which produce a greater buildup of clouds and moisture. Ponderosa pine are scattered on the higher south-facing slopes and in a few meadow areas, where the soils are drier. In some of the moist valleys, small aspen groves thrive. Gambel oak and serviceberry are abundant across the upper mesa.

The dominant plant community below 7,800 feet (2,377 m) is the piñon-juniper forest, which blankets the south-sloping mesa tops in the southern portion of the park. In general, neither the Utah juniper nor the piñon pine exceeds 30 feet (9 m) in height, but these trees were adequate for the building materials and firewood used by the Anasazi. Under ideal conditions the piñon pine produces a crop of nuts every two years. These seeds are a very important food source for many birds and mammals. The piñon-juniper forest can be dense with dead wood and an undergrowth of mutton grass, making it ripe for forest fires. Lightning-caused blazes are a constant concern in the park region. A burned area in this community usually requires 200 to 300 years to proceed through the succession of communities leading up to a mature piñon-juniper woodland.

The canyons make their own environment. The cliffs support only lichens and occasional shrubs anchored in cracks. The valley floors tend to be dry, despite what one might expect, and are dominated by big sage mixed with cheatgrass, other herbaceous plants, and cactus.

The mesa tops are like islands surrounded by desert lowlands and thus provide a home for a variety of animals that frequent cooler, moister habitats. Rocky Mountain mule deer are common, as are coyotes. Bighorn sheep, cougar, black bear, and elk have been seen within the park, but with the exception of the sheep these may be transients.

Masters of the air over Mesa Verde include turkey vultures, red-tailed hawks, golden eagles, and the great horned owl. Perhaps the noisiest bird in the park is the steller's jay, whose squawking takes attention away from the various species of chickadees, titmouses, nuthatches, towhees, and warblers that also inhabit the region.

Physiographically, Mesa Verde is a 200-square-mile (500 km^2) plateau tipped toward the south with a gradient about 115 feet per mile (22 m/km). The north end of the plateau sits just above 8,000 feet (2,438 m), while the lower end, 13 miles (21 km) to the south, is at 6,500 feet (1,981 m). The plateau has been incised by more than a dozen parallel drainages trending south and southeast, toward the Mancos River.

The medium to dark gray Mancos Shale makes up the lower two-thirds of the north-facing steep slopes of the Mesa Verde area. The slopes on these late Cretaceous rocks form numerous steep gullies with little to no vegetative cover. The road that climbs up to the mesa top from the park entrance passes across these steep shale slopes, which each spring rearrange themselves through landsliding and creep to form a new geometry. The old entrance road to the west of Point Lookout was abandoned in favor of the present road in 1957 because of the constant landsliding. Unfortunately, the new road is not much better. Engineers have tried a variety of strategies to stabilize the road and prevent landslides. This may be the true million-dollar highway, because it is one of the most expensive sections of road to maintain in the Southwest.

The Mesa Verde Group overlies the shale. It was originally described and named by W. H. Holmes, who in 1877 divided the group into three formations: the lowermost layer, or Point Lookout Sandstone; the middle, Menefee Formation; and the topmost unit, the Cliff House Sandstone. These three formations are sandwiched between two thick shale units, the Mancos and Lewis Shale, to the south. Together they represent one of the best records of a shoreline that retreated and advanced some 90 million years ago.

The shale units represent an offshore marine environment in which only the finest silt settled out. The silt was eroded off a highland located to the west. To the east lay a large continental interior seaway. Through time the sea slowly withdrew eastward, and the shoreline crept toward the northeast, bringing with it a sandy beach (Point Lookout Sandstone), followed by a swamp deposit with meandering streams (Menefee Formation). The plant material from the swamp eventually turned into coal and can be seen along the national park road in places. The sea later invaded the area again, bringing back the beach (Cliff House Sandstone) and eventually flooding the land and depositing fine silts (Lewis Shale). During the Tertiary the region was tilted to the south from the uplift of the San Juan and La Plata Domes, located to the northeast. This tilting established streams that flowed south and eventually cut the canyons now seen at Mesa Verde. During the past 5 million years, streams to the west and north removed the sedimentary cover to create the Montezuma Valley and the north-facing mesa front. This mesa escarpment continues to this day to slowly retreat southward. All of the south-trending stream valleys on the mesa were subsequently beheaded by the retreating mesa front (Fig. 19.29). This phenomenon can be seen at the Montezuma Valley overlook, which is built upon the old floor of a beheaded stream valley.

Fig. 19.29   The old entrance road into Mesa Verde National Park as it passes beneath Point Lookout and a beheaded drainage to the right of the cliff. Courtesy Center of Southwest Studies, Fort Lewis College.

Typically, if one follows such a valley southward, it will suddenly end in a cliff marking the beginning of an open canyon. It was in these canyons, carved in the Cliff House Sandstone, that the Indians constructed their cliff dwellings. Most of the alcoves are situated beneath surface drainages that plunge over cliffs. Runoff from storms funnels into these drainages and flows along the stream bed, plunging over the cliff as a waterfall. Much of the water seeps into the sandstone to flow within the formation and drip out at the base of the cliffs. This leakage creates a damp environment, which accelerates weathering and erosion below the cliff. This process forms horizontal hollows that can grow into large caves or alcoves. During extended wet climatic intervals some of these alcoves contained continuously flowing springs, which, along with roof protection from rain, snow, and wind, made for an ideal living environment. References (POI 143): Gregory 1990, Griffitts 1990, Haynes, Vogel, and Wyant 1972, Molenaar and Werts 1968, Smith and Bochard 1957, Wenger 1980.

144. (Map 19.18) Mancos Valley. Elevation: 7,030 feet (2,142 m). Population (Mancos): 842 (circa 1990). This valley, with its lazy river, lies in the heart of farming and cattle country in southwestern Colorado (Fig. 19.30). Hundreds of years before white settlement, the Anasazi hunted and farmed in the valley. The name Mancos comes from early Spanish explorers who ventured through the valley in the mid-eighteenth century. *Mancos* is Spanish for *crippled* and apparently refers to the condition of one of the explorers after crossing the local river. By 1874 homesteaders occupied the valley, and with the completion of the railroad in 1891 this region became a center for both the mining and cattle industries.

The valley's altitude and climate are best suited for a piñon-juniper woodland. This plant community can be seen in abundance between meadows and open range. The broad alluvial floor of the Mancos Valley harbors wet meadows, irrigated fields, and extensive mature riparian woodlands consisting of narrowleaf cottonwoods, silverleaf buffaloberry, willows, and tamarisk. This latter shrub is exotic and was introduced from the Middle East. It is salt-tolerant, but because of its dependence on water it grows only along watercourses and springs. It now dominates the banks of

Fig. 19.30   The La Plata Mountains and the Mancos Valley.

many southwestern rivers. In 1913 the San Juan National Forest supervisor received forty-five head of elk from Jackson Hole, Wyoming, and these were turned loose in the nearby forest. It is believed that most of the elk in the San Juan Basin descended from this herd.

Underlying the valley is the Mancos Shale, an open-water marine deposit of silt and clay laid down in a calm, warm, late Cretaceous sea. A fingerprint of this ancient sea can be seen along gullies and evaporated ponds as a white salt deposit. These sodium bicarbonates and sodium sulfates give the soils their alkaline character. The 2,000-foot-thick (610-m) layer of shale was first described in detail, just south of the valley, by Whitman Cross in 1899. The upper shale has several fossiliferous horizons containing remains of a variety of cephalopods, brachiopods, and pelecypods. The Mancos Shale is a valley-forming unit because it erodes easily. Nearly every large town in western Colorado is built upon it, including Cortez, Durango, and Grand Junction. References (POI 144–149, 151–154): Molenaar and Werts 1968, *Mancos Times* 1991, Smith and Bochard 1957.

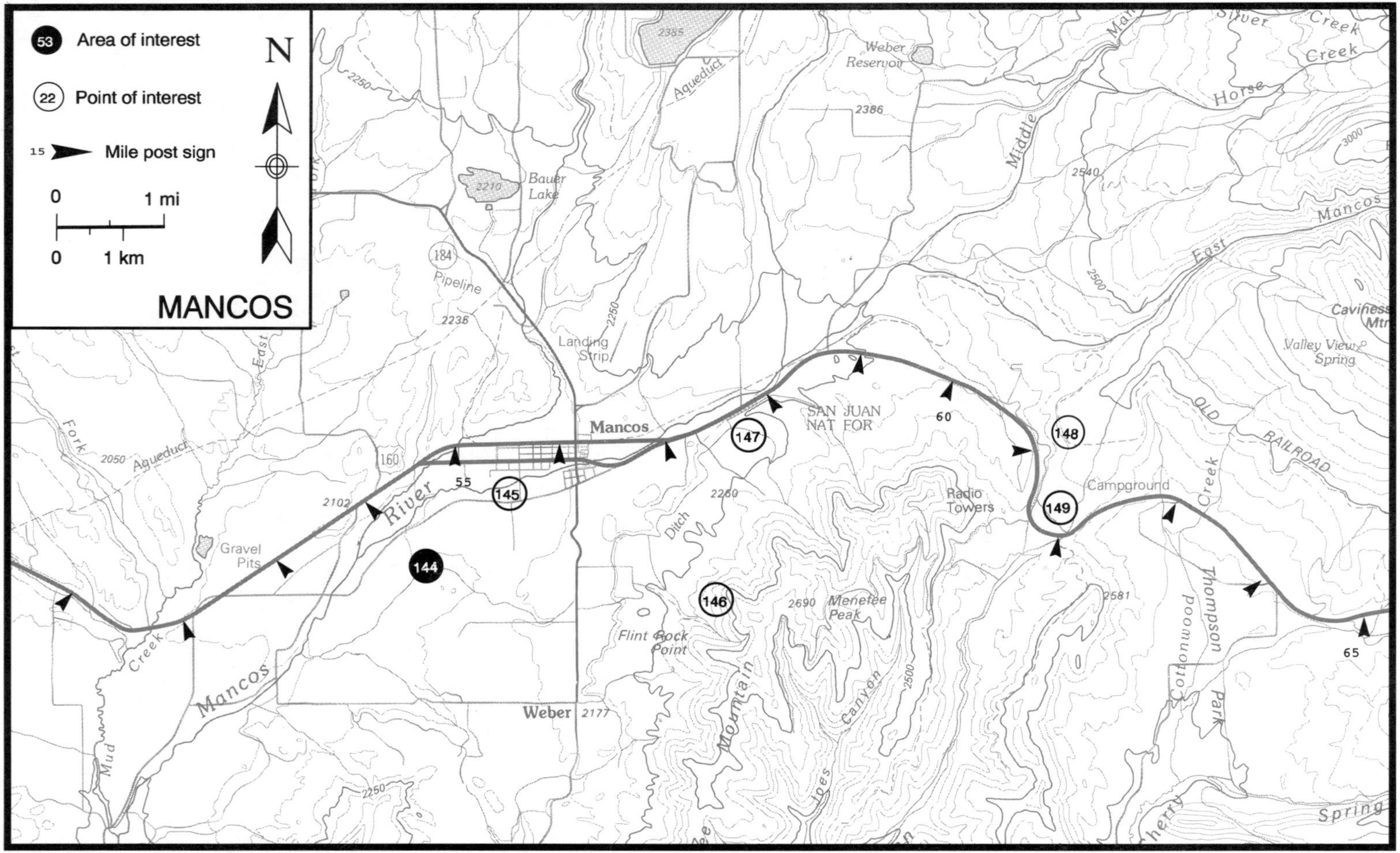

Area of interest
Point of interest
Mile post sign
N
0
1 mi
0
1 km
MANCOS
Mancos
Bauer Lake
Weber Reservoir
Aqueduct
Pipeline
Landing Strip
Gravel Pits
River
Mancos
Creek
Mud
Fork
Ditch
Flint Rock Point
Mountain
Menefee Peak
Canyon
Joes
SAN JUAN NAT FOR
Radio Towers
Campground
OLD RAILROAD
Creek
Thompson Park
Cottonwood
Cherry
Spring
East
Middle
Horse
Creek
Valley View Spring
Weber
55
60
65
144
145
146
147
148
149
160
184

Map 19.18

145. A **timber processing plant** (Western Excelsior Corporation) produces wood shavings from local aspen trees. The wood shavings are used as packing material, erosion-control sheets, holiday-basket filler, archery targets, and garden mulch. Prior to 1989 the plant was called the Ohio Blue Tip Match Factory.

146. The **Mesa Verde Group** makes up the sandstone bluffs seen to the south above the steep gray slopes of the Mancos Shale. These bluffs comprise a series of three formations that all dip south into the San Juan Basin. The lowermost formation is the Point Lookout Sandstone, followed by the Menefee Formation, which consists of alternating lenticular beds of yellowish-brown cross-bedded sandstone, grayish brown shale, and coal seams. The uppermost unit, the Cliff House Sandstone, is not visible because it has eroded back from the northern edge of the escarpment.

147. (**mp 56.7**) A **wetland** and small pond occupy an abandoned gravel quarry just south of the road. The open water is surrounded by pond lilies, cattails, and dark green bull rushes. Surrounding the wetland are narrowleaf cottonwood, box elder, silverleaf buffaloberry, and several species of willows. Waterfowl that breed here in the spring and summer include mallard ducks, cinnamon teal, and American coot. In spring flocks of red-winged blackbirds arrive to establish their individual territories within the cattail zone by singing and displaying their red shoulder patches. Later the females arrive, and each selects a nest site within a male's territory. Other birds seen inhabiting this wetland include the locally rare great-tailed grackle, violet-green swallow, tree swallow, rough-winged swallow, and common flicker. Beavers and muskrats inhabit this community, along with the chorus frog, leopard frog, Woodhouse's toad, and tiger salamander.

148. The **hogback** (view to north) is an east-west trending prominent ridge with columnar jointing exposed along a south-facing escarpment. This ridge is the eroded arm of a laccolith of quartz diorite that pushed its way horizontally through the Mancos Shale. This laccolith is part of the intrusive complex that makes up the La Plata Mountains. Hesperus Peak (13,232 ft, 4,038 m), the highest peak seen to the north, was carved from baked Mancos Shale and older Mesozoic sedimentary rocks.

149. **(mp 62) Mancos Hill** is a drainage divide that provides a good view of the La Plata Mountains to the north and Thompson Park to the east. The hill is composed of Mancos Shale, which dips gently to the south. In spring the wet shale wreaks havoc with the road base, resulting in displacement and actual landsliding of the highway in places. A shrubland of Gambel oak surrounds the divide, with occasional ponderosa pine trees and meadows interspersed. A Gambel oak just south of the divide crest was measured with a diameter of 29 inches (74 cm) at breast height in 1991, making it the second-largest in Colorado (Fig. 19.31). The largest Gambel oak known in Colorado stands north of Durango. The few ponderosa pine present appear to be growing on a substrate of stream gravel. The gravel, made up of rocks from the La Plata Mountains and a distinct valley to the south, suggests that the East Mancos River, which now flows west off the La Plata Mountains, may have once flowed south across this divide and into East Canyon. Apparently, a tributary from the Middle Mancos River lengthened itself eastward and eventually captured the East Mancos River, forcing it to flow west. It is not known when this happened.

Fig. 19.31   The second-largest Gambel oak in the state of Colorado.

150. (Map 19.19) La Plata Mountains. This circular mountain range, 9 miles (14 km) in diameter, encompasses some twenty-two major peaks and numerous other minor summits. The La Plata River and glaciers have carved out a deep valley that bisects the heart of the range. From satellite images, a radial drainage pattern can be traced, radiating away from the range center like the spokes of a bicycle wheel.

Spanish explorers passed by and into the La Plata Mountains in the mid- and late eighteenth century and possibly found ore there, but serious prospecting and discovery only began in 1878 with the opening of the Comstock Mine. Between 1878 and 1900, additional mines became operational, but their production was comparatively small. However, between 1900 and 1937 several productive deposits were discovered, and nearly $6 million worth of ore was processed, mostly from the Mayday and the Idaho Mines. Gold was the principal objective, but more than 2 million ounces of silver, lead, and copper have been recovered.

The La Plata Mountains are the erosional relics of a structural dome uplifted from the forceful injection of magma 65 to 67 million years ago into a thick sedimentary sequence of upper Paleozoic and Mesozoic rocks. The injected igneous bodies produced more than half a dozen stocks and multiple sills, dikes, and pipes. Some of the stocks could be called laccoliths because of their near mushroomlike geometry.

The sedimentary strata, which ring the flanks of the La Plata range, generally dip down and away from the dome's crest, located in the vicinity of Diorite Peak. However, variations in formation dip do occur in close proximity to local intrusions and faults.

The igneous rocks can be classified into two broad groups, an older, porphyritic intrusive and a younger, nonporphyritic intrusive. The quartz diorite porphyry is the most abundant rock type and constitutes most stocks, sills, and dikes. The younger nonporphyritic intrusives form singular stocks and associated dikes with compositions of syenite, monzonite, and diorite.

The district is best known for its veins and replacement deposits of gold-bearing and silver-bearing telluride ores, which account for the greatest production. An incredible variety of deposit types have been identified within the district. These include gold-bearing

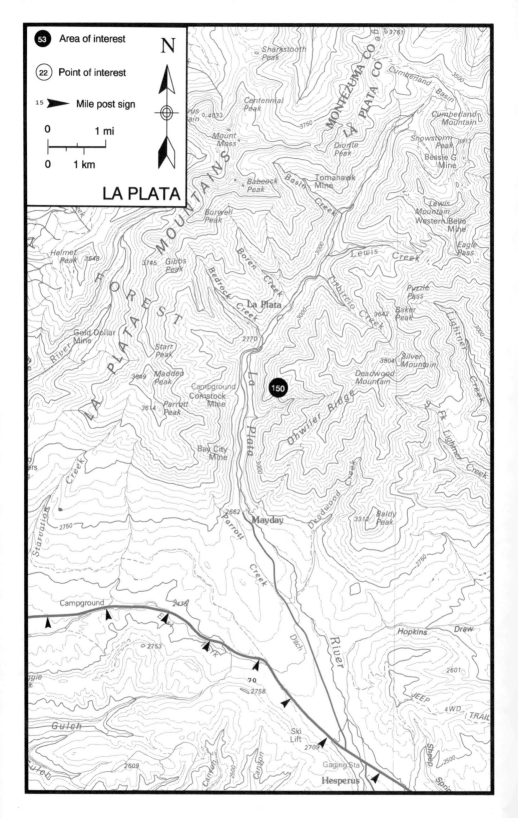

Map 19.19

contact ore, disseminated platinum-bearing chalcopyrite, veins of ruby silver, and veins of mixed base-metal sulfides containing silver or native gold. Gold-bearing placers also have been mined but generally have been nonproductive.

The relationships among these different deposit types have been confusing, but it seems certain that they were formed through a wide range of temperatures and, to a lesser degree, pressures. Some of the ore bodies are zoned. Several lines of evidence suggest that all the deposits (excluding placers) were formed during one general period of hydrothermal activity that followed closely on the heels of the last igneous event associated with the nonporphyritic rocks.

The La Plata Mountains have been glaciated, but they did not support glaciers as large or extensive as those found in the San Juan Mountains. Remnants of an end moraine, found near the town of Mayday, grade into a glacial outwash terrace to the south called Gold Bar. References (POI 150): Cross, Spencer, and Purington 1899, Eckel et al. 1968, Molenaar and Werts 1968.

151. (mp 73.8, Map 19.20) Hesperus Hill separates the La Plata River drainage from the Animas River drainage. The hill is underlain by the Cliff House Sandstone. The view east shows the boundary between two major physiographic provinces, the Southern Rocky Mountains to the north and the Colorado Plateau to the south. The boundary is marked by the parallel hogback ridges seen near the southern edge of Durango. These hogbacks represent a sudden steepening of the sedimentary section into the San Juan Basin over a fold called the Hogback Monocline. To the north the section slowly rises up toward the San Juan Mountains, where the sedimentary cover has been stripped off by erosion. Northeast of here, the northeast-southwest-trending fold axes of the Durango Anticline and Perins Peak Syncline can just be made out, broad, open folds plunging gently to the southwest. Their axes are nearly parallel to the northeast-southwest-trending Hogback Monocline; thus, they are probably related to this structure.

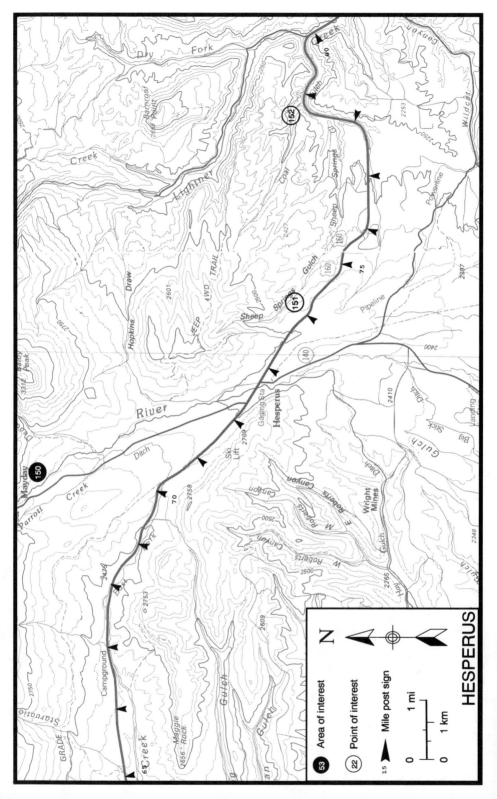

HESPERUS

N

53 Area of interest

22 Point of interest

15 ► Mile post sign

0   1 mi
0   1 km

152. (mp 78.7) Abandoned coal mines can be identified to the north from the decayed mine workings. This area supported the Peerless, Victory, and OK Mines. The coal was mined from the Menefee Formation and was used to fire local home furnaces and steam engines. These coal mines are located virtually on the axis of the Perins Peak Syncline.

153. Perins was the site of a turn-of-the-century coal town. This community thrived on coal mined from the Menefee Formation, which in this area is preserved along the trough of the Perins Peak Syncline. Perins Peak and the prominent Twin Buttes are capped by the Point Lookout Sandstone.

154. (mp 81) Landslide debris is exposed above the riverbank just north of the road. Angular blocks of Point Lookout Sandstone can be seen "floating" in and on top of a matrix of chaotic weathered Mancos Shale.

REFERENCES

Atwood, W. W., 1915. *Eocene glacial deposits in southwestern Colorado.* U.S. Geological Survey, Professional Paper 95, pp. 13–26.

Atwood, W. W., and K. F. Mather, 1932. *Physiography and Quaternary geology of the San Juan Mountains, Colorado.* U.S. Geological Survey, Professional Paper 166, 176 pp.

Baars, D. L., 1992. *The American Alps: The San Juan Mountains of southwest Colorado.* Albuquerque: University of New Mexico Press, 194 pp.

Baars, D. L., and J. A. Ellingson, 1984. Geology of the western San Juan Mountains, in D. C. Brew, ed, *Field Trip Guidebook,* Geological Society of America, Rocky Mountain Section, 37th Annual Meeting, pp. 1–45.

Baars, D. L., J. A. Ellingson, and R. W. Spoelhof, 1987. Grenadier fault block, Coalbank to Molas Passes, southwest Colorado, in S. S. Bues, ed., *Geological Society of America Centennial Field Guide,* Geological Society of America, Rocky Mountain Section, pp. 343–348.

Bear, Leith Lende, 1985. *Trimble Hot Springs: A historical tale.* Durango, CO: Trimble Hot Springs, Inc., 39 pp.

Blair, Jr., R. W., 1985. *Road Log — Day one Molas Pass to Durango.* Friends of the Pleistocene, 21 pp.

Bromfield, C. S., and A. R. Conroy, 1963. *Preliminary geologic map of the Mount Wilson quadrangle San Miguel County, Colorado.* U.S. Geological Survey Map MF-273.

Burbank, W. S., and Robert G. Luedke, 1964. *Geology of the Ironton quadrangle, Colorado.* U.S. Geological Survey, Geologic Quadrangle Map GQ-291.

Crabb, P., and S. Dunn, eds, 1991. *Ridgway Colorado Centennial 1881– 1991.* Ridgway, CO: The Ridgway Sun, 28 pp.

Cross, C. W., and A. D. Hole, 1910. *Geologic atlas of the United States, Engineer Mountain quadrangle, Colorado.* U.S. Geological Survey, Folio 171, 14 pp.

Cross, C. W., E. Howe, J. D. Irving, and W. H. Emmons, 1905. *Geologic atlas of the United States, Needle Mountain quadrangle, Colorado.* U.S. Geological Survey, Folio 131, 14 pp.

Cross, C. W., E. Howe, and J. D. Irving, 1907. *Geologic atlas of the United States, Ouray quadrangle, Colorado.* U.S. Geological Survey, Folio 153, 20 pp.

Cross, C. W., E. Howe, and F. Ransome, 1905. *Geologic atlas of the United States, Silverton quadrangle, Colorado.* U.S. Geological Survey, Folio 120, 40 pp.

Cross, C. W., and E. S. Larsen, 1935. *A brief review of the geology of the San Juan region of southwestern Colorado.* U.S. Geological Survey Bulletin 843, 138 pp.

Cross, C. W., A. C. Spencer, and C. W. Purington, 1899. *Geologic atlas of the United States, La Plata quadrangle, Colorado.* U. S. Geological Survey, Folio 60, 14 pp.

Eckel, E. B., J. Williams, and F. Galbraith, 1968, Geology and ore deposits of the La Plata District, Colorado, in J. W. Shomaker, ed., *Guidebook of San Juan, San Miguel, La Plata Region, New Mexico and Colorado, nineteenth field conference,* Albuquerque: New Mexico Geological Society, pp. 41–62.

Engel, C. M., 1968. Rico, Colorado: A century of historic adventures in mining, in in J. W. Shomaker, ed., *Guidebook of San Juan, San Miguel, La Plata Region, New Mexico and Colorado, nineteenth field conference,* Albuquerque: New Mexico Geological Society, pp. 88–93.

Gillam, M. L., D. Moore, and G. R. Scott, 1984. Quaternary deposits and soils in the Durango area, southwestern Colorado: in D. C. Brew, ed., *1984 Field Trip Guidebook,* Geological Society of America, Rocky Mountain Section, 37th Annual Meeting, 209 pp.

Gregory, L., 1990. *Colorado scenic guide, southern region.* Boulder, CO: Johnson Books, 208 pp.

Griffitts, Mary O., 1990. *Guide to the geology of Mesa Verde National Park.* Mesa Verde Museum Association, Inc., 88 pp.

Harris, C. W., 1990. Polyphase suprastructure deformation in metasedimentary rocks of the Uncompahgre Group: Remnant of an early Proterozoic fold belt in southwest Colorado. *Geological Society of America Bulletin*, v. 102, pp. 664–678.

Haynes, D., J. Vogel, and D. Wyant, 1972. *Geology, structure, and uranium deposits of the Cortez Quadrangle, Colorado and Utah*. U.S. Geological Survey, Miscellaneous Investigation Series Map I–629.

Hunt, C. B., 1956. *Cenozoic geology of the Colorado Plateau*. U.S. Geological Survey Professional Paper 279, 99 pp.

Kelley, V. C., 1957. Geology of Ouray and environs, in F. F. Kottlowski and B. Baldwin, eds., *Guidebook of southwestern San Juan Mountains, Colorado, eighth field conference*. Albuquerque: New Mexico Geological Society, pp. 203–207.

Kelley, V. C., J. R. Hillebrand, R. G. Luedke, and W. S. Burbank, 1957. Silverton to Ouray, Ridgway, and return to Silverton, in F. F. Kottlowski and B. Baldwin, eds., *Guidebook of southwestern San Juan Mountains, Colorado, eighth field conference*. Albuquerque: New Mexico Geological Society, pp. 53–71.

Lee, K., R. C. Epis, D. L. Baars, D. H. Knepper, and R. M. Summer, 1976. Road log: Paleozoic tectonics and sedimentation and Tertiary volcanism of the western San Juan Mountains, Colorado, in R. C. Epis and R. J. Weimer, eds., *Studies in Colorado field geology*, Colorado School of Mines, Professional Contributions 8, pp. 139–158.

Luedke, R. G., and W. S. Burbank, 1962. *Geology of the Ouray quadrangle, Colorado*. U.S. Geological Survey, Geologic Quadrangle Map GQ-152.

Maher, L. J., 1961. Pollen analysis and post-glacial vegetation history in the Animas Valley (Ph.D. thesis). University of Minnesota, Minneapolis, MN.

Mancos Times-Tribune, 1991. Tourism edition. Mancos, CO: Times Publishing Co., 12 pp.

Maslyn, R. M., 1977. Fossil tower karst near Molas Lake, Colorado. *The Mountain Geologist*, v. 14, no. 1, pp. 17–25.

Molenaar, C. M., and L. L. Werts, 1968. Road log from Farmington, New Mexico to Cortez, Colorado, via Four Corners Power Plant, La Plata Canyon, La Plata Mining area and Mancos, in J. W. Shomaker, ed., *Guidebook of San Juan, San Miguel, La Plata region, New Mexico and Colorado, nineteenth field conference*. Albuquerque: New Mexico Geological Society, pp. 11–23.

Molenaar, C. M., J. W. Shomaker, L. L. Werts, and J. A. Campbell, 1968. Road log from Ouray, Colorado to Farmington, New Mexico via Silverton, Eureka, Durango, and Aztec, in J. W. Shomaker, ed., *Guidebook of San Juan, San Miguel, La Plata region, New Mexico and Colorado, nineteenth field conference*. Albuquerque: New Mexico Geological Society, pp. 104–129.

Nossaman, A., 1993. *Many more mountains*, volume 2: *Ruts into Silverton*. Denver: Sundance Books, 352 pp.

Nossaman, A., 1989. *Many more mountains*, volume 1: *Silverton's roots*. Denver: Sundance Books, 352 pp.

Osterwald, D. B., 1990. *Cinders and smoke*. Lakewood: Western Guideways, Ltd., 152 pp.

Peterson, F. C., 1989. *The story of Hillside Cemetery — burials 1873–1988, San Juan County, Colorado*. Oklahoma City: F. C. Peterson, 718 pp.

Pratt, W. P., 1968. Summary of the geology of the Rico region, Colorado, in J. W. Shomaker, ed., *Guidebook of San Juan, San Miguel, La Plata Region, New Mexico and Colorado, nineteenth field conference,* Albuquerque: New Mexico Geological Society, pp. 83–87.

Pratt, W. P., E. T. McKnight, and R. A. DeHon, 1969. *Geologic map of the Rico quadrangle, Dolores and Montezuma Counties, Colorado*. U.S. Geological Survey, Geologic Quadrangle Map GQ-797.

Smith, D., 1980. *Rocky Mountain boom town: A history of Durango*. Albuquerque: University of New Mexico Press, 215 pp.

Smith, K. T., and J. R. Bochard, 1957. Durango to Cortez, in F. F. Kottlowski and B. Baldwin, eds. *Guidebook of southwestern San Juan Mountains, Colorado, eighth field conference*. Albuquerque: New Mexico Geological Society, pp. 91–94.

Steven, T. A., and P. W. Lipman, 1974. *Map of the Durango quadrangle, southwestern Colorado*. U.S. Geological Survey, Miscellaneous Investigations Series Map I-764.

Steward, J. H., E. T. McKnight, A. L. Bush, L. R. Litsey, C. T. Sumsion, and C. M. Molenaar, 1968. Road log from Cortez, Colorado to Ouray, Colorado via Dolores, Rico, Lizard Head Pass, Telluride, Placerville, Dallas Divide and Ridgway, in J. W. Shomaker, ed., *Guidebook of San Juan, San Miguel, La Plata region New Mexico and Colorado, nineteenth field conference*. Albuquerque: New Mexico Geological Society, pp. 63–82.

Tweto, O., T. A. Steven, W. J. Hail, Jr., and R. H. Moench, 1976. *Preliminary geologic map of Montrose 1°x2° quadrangle, southwestern Colorado, 1:250,000*. U.S. Geological Survey, Miscellaneous Field Investigations Map MF-761.

Vanderwilt, J. W., 1934. A recent rockslide near Durango in La Plata County, Colorado. *Journal of Geology*, v. 42, no. 2, pp. 163–173.

Wenger, G. R., 1980. *The story of Mesa Verde National Park*. Mesa Verde Museum Association, Inc., 79 pp.

Wengerd, S. A., and D. L. Baars, 1957. Durango to Silverton, in F. F. Kottlowski and B. Baldwin, eds., *Guidebook of southwestern San Juan Mountains, Colorado eighth field conference*. Albuquerque: New Mexico Geological Society, pp. 39–52.

CHAPTER 20

POINTS OF INTEREST ALONG THE DURANGO-TO-SILVERTON NARROW-GAUGE RAILROAD

ROB BLAIR

The mournful whistle of the narrow-gauge train echoes between the canyon walls as much today as it did in 1882, when service began between Durango and Silverton. The train ride is only 46 miles, but it takes more than three hours to complete. From Durango to Rockwood follow the log given for the highway (Points of Interest 7 through 25).

The rail bed rises from 6,500 feet (2,000 m) at Durango to just over 9,300 feet (2,850 m) at Silverton. Because the line follows the Animas River, it is mostly confined to a riparian environment. Thus, narrowleaf cottonwood, box elder, and willows dominate. As the train moves north past Rockwood one encounters the spruce-fir forest encroaching upon the narrow floodplain. Only glimpses of the subalpine and tundra regions can be viewed between the cliffs and trees.

For the most part, the rail bed rests directly upon Quaternary alluvium, but these river sediments, in turn, rest upon old Phanerozoic and Precambrian rocks. The incessant eroding action by the Animas River, along with multiple episodes of glaciation, has carved the Animas Valley and the gorge. For the most complete guide to the train ride and history of the railroad, refer to the excellent book *Cinders and Smoke* (1990) by Doris Osterwald.

155. (mp 468.5, Map 19.2) A **nonconformity** is exposed on the north side of the tracks and forms the contact between the pinkish Baker's Bridge Granite and overlying Ignacio Formation. The contact is noted for the weathered granite lying beneath a coarse basal conglomerate, thus revealing the nature of this buried Cambrian erosion surface. The Baker's Bridge Granite is exposed from here to just past milepost 470 (Fig. 20.1).

Fig. 20.1   The train makes its way toward Silverton along the "High Line" cut from the Baker's Bridge Granite at milepost 469.6.

156. (mp 473.5) The **Irving Formation**, a metamorphic rock, is exposed in the canyon walls. This hornblende gneiss is believed to be over 1.8 billion years old and includes pods of black amphibolite, which may represent ancient sea-floor basalt.

157. (mp 480.7, Map 19.3) The **Irving–Twilight Gneiss** contact shows up to the west in the railroad cut. The Twilight Gneiss is more granitic in its composition and therefore is more resistant to erosion than the Irving Formation.

158. **(mp 484.5, Map 19.4)** The **Grenadier Range** is visible to the northeast. These mountains are carved into quartzites and phyllites from the Uncompahgre Formation. Spectacular peaks such as Mount Garfield are glacial horns.

159. **(mp 489.5)** A **fault** separates the Twilight Gneiss from the Uncompahgre Formation. This latter formation is part of a large fault block, which because of its resistance forms a highland trending northwest-southeast. The Uncompahgre quartzites and phyllites are nearly vertical in this area and exhibit folding. Erosion has occurred along the fault trace on the slopes of Mount Garfield to the east to form a V-cut valley. Landslides now partly fill the valley.

160. **(mp 490.5)** At **Elk Park,** the Colorado Trail (coming from Durango) crosses the track and continues toward the east up Elk Creek and onward to Denver. The slopes to the east are part of a large moraine deposited from a glacier emerging from the Elk Creek Drainage.

REFERENCES

Osterwald, D. B., 1990. *Cinders and Smoke.* Lakewood, CO: Western Guideways, Ltd., 152 pp.

CHAPTER 21

POINTS OF INTEREST
ALONG THE ALPINE LOOP

BARBARA BYRON

[L]ofty mountains are most worthy of deep study. For every-
where you turn, they present to every sense a multitude of objects
to excite and delight the mind. They offer problems to our in-
tellect; they amaze our souls. They remind us of the infinite va-
riety of creation, and offer an unequaled field for the
observation of the processes of nature.
— Josias Simler, *De alpibus commentarius* (1574)

The Alpine Loop provides easy access into the lofty San Juan
Mountains and offers the inquisitive eye an "unequaled field for
the observation of the processes of nature." There are no milepost
signs along the Alpine Loop; therefore, points of interest are located by odometer readings beginning in Silverton. The traveler is
guided north up the Animas River toward Animas Forks and over
Cinnamon Pass to Lake City. Odometer readings begin again at
0.0 at Lake City, where the route turns up Henson Creek, over
Engineer Pass, and on toward Ouray.

The Alpine Loop follows the original wagon route pio-
neered in the late 1870s to meet the needs of the burgeoning new
San Juan mining area. Much of the 65 miles (105 km) of dirt and
gravel roads between Silverton, Lake City, and Ouray is accessible
by passenger car, but four-wheel drive capability is required for
travel over Cinnamon (12,598 ft, 3,840 m) and Engineer (12,800

ft, 3,901 m) Passes. Snowfall at high altitude can close the road anytime after late September and keep it closed until the end of June, when snowplows from San Juan and Hinsdale Counties vie to clear their way to the county line first.

The Loop passes by numerous abandoned mines and mining camps, relics of a bygone era when prospectors came seeking their fortunes. Climbing to altitudes in excess of any reached along the Skyway, the route presents a "multitude of objects to excite and delight the mind": alpine meadows with a luxuriant profusion of brightly colored flowers, caldera structures related to mid-Tertiary volcanism, and spectacular mountain landscapes sculpted by Pleistocene glaciers.

Rising beyond the limit of tree growth, the Alpine Loop passes through the forest-tundra transition zone, marked by increasingly stunted and wind-deformed trees called *krummholz* (a German word meaning "crooked wood"). Streamlined islands of dwarfed cushion trees dot the landscape. Also curious are flag trees, whose crowns have become one-sided because gales have killed the branches on the windward side. The alpine tundra is a windswept, treeless area characterized by intense solar radiation, cold temperatures, strong winds, and extended periods of snow cover.

Flora and fauna of the alpine life zone are specially adapted to survive the rigorous climatic conditions of their harsh environment. Alpine plants tend to be small, low-growing perennials able to withstand a frost-free growing season that averages less than forty days. The first leaves and stems to appear after snowmelt are characteristically tinged reddish-blue by the pigment anthocyanin. Anthocyanin, accumulating in the cell sap of the epidermal cells, absorbs ultraviolet radiation and protects the inner mesodermal cells from its damaging effects. The dark pigment is also capable of converting incident light rays into heat energy.

"Watermelon snow" can be seen throughout the summer. The reddish-pink patches on late-lying snowbanks indicate high concentrations of pigmented resting spores of the flagellated, unicellular snow alga *Chlamydomonas*. A freshly scraped surface even smells like watermelon.

A variety of survival strategies are employed by high altitude fauna. White-tailed ptarmigan, permanent residents of the alpine tundra, are experts in camouflage. In winter their pure white plumage blends imperceptibly with the snow. In summer their feathers become a mottle of brown, gray, and black, making them nearly indistinguishable from their rocky surroundings. The yellow-bellied marmot lives in rocky outcrops and copes with severe environmental conditions by avoiding them through hibernation. Active above ground only four months of the year, it feeds heavily, building critical fat reserves. Its loud, shrill warning calls can be heard across the windy tundra, giving rise to the nickname "whistle pig."

The pika, like the marmot, is found almost exclusively in rocky habitats. However, this diminutive member of the rabbit family does not hibernate. Its small ears, feet, and tail reduce heat loss through the extremities. Summer is haying season, and these little critters are frequently seen with their mouths stuffed full of grasses and wildflowers as they gather vegetation for their winter stores.

The geology of the Alpine Loop consists of middle Proterozoic intrusive and metamorphic rocks unconformably overlain first by early Oligocene volcanic rocks of intermediate composition erupted from stratovolcanoes and later by late Oligocene to early Miocene silicic ash-flow tuffs and associated lavas and sediments. The San Juan and Uncompahgre Calderas collapsed simultaneously in response to the voluminous eruption of the Sapinero Mesa Tuff (28 to 29 million years old). Collapse of the Silverton Caldera (27 million years old), nested within the San Juan Caldera, soon followed. Joint resurgent doming of these calderas resulted in numerous distentional fractures known as the Eureka Graben, a downdropped keystone fault zone trending northeast across the crest of the elliptical resurgent dome. At 23.1 million years ago the Lake City Caldera, nested within the older Uncompahgre Caldera, collapsed during eruption of the Sunshine Peak Tuff.

Mineralization in the Lake City area is closely associated with intrusive activity in the waning stages of the caldera cycle. Even though mineralization in the Silverton area did not occur until 5 to 15 million years after the caldera collapsed, deposition of base (lead, copper, zinc) and precious (gold and silver) metals was localized by structures associated with subsidence and resurgence of the San Juan, Uncompahgre, and Silverton Calderas.

Caldera structures also influenced the route of the Alpine Loop. Leaving Silverton, the road follows the ring fault zone along the eastern margin of the Silverton Caldera as reflected by the arcuate drainage of the Animas River. The route then circumvents the Lake City Caldera along the Lake Fork of the Gunnison and Henson Creek, streams superimposed on the moat of the caldera.

The following odometer readings begin with 0.0 at the north end of Silverton, where Colorado Highway 110 breaks northeast from Greene Street.

161. (mi 2.2, Map 21.1) The **aerial tramline** was first constructed in the late 1880s to bring ore to the Silver Lake Mill. The existing tramline was constructed in the early 1930s to convey ore, miners, and equipment between mines located up Arrastra Gulch (to the southeast) and the Mayflower Mill, located just north of the road. Several tram towers lie twisted at the bottom of Arrastra Gulch, victims of powerful avalanches. The Mayflower Mill was restored in 1960 to process ore from the Sunnyside Mine, the largest underground gold mining operation in Colorado. August 1991 saw the closure of the Sunnyside, more than a century old, and the commencement of reclamation activity. During the summer of 1992 the mill tailings were blanketed with topsoil and planted with young aspen trees.

162. (mi 7.9) Lake Emma collapsed into the Sunnyside Mine on June 4, 1978, filling nearly 5 miles of tunnels with more than a million tons of mud. Had the disaster not fortuitously occurred on a Sunday, 125 men would have been killed as the mud swept through the Spur vein, 70 feet beneath the bottom of Lake Emma.

163. (mi 11.3) Animas Forks, established in 1877, is situated near timberline at two prominent branches of the Animas River. The town prospered during the late 1870s and 1880s and boasted a population approaching 1,500. It even enjoyed the luxury of a telephone line brought in over Cinnamon Pass from Lake City. The architectural style of the dwellings at Animas Forks is in sharp contrast to the crude log construction used in most mining camps. Many of the buildings still standing today are built with dressed and finished lumber and have shingled roofs, gables, and bay windows.

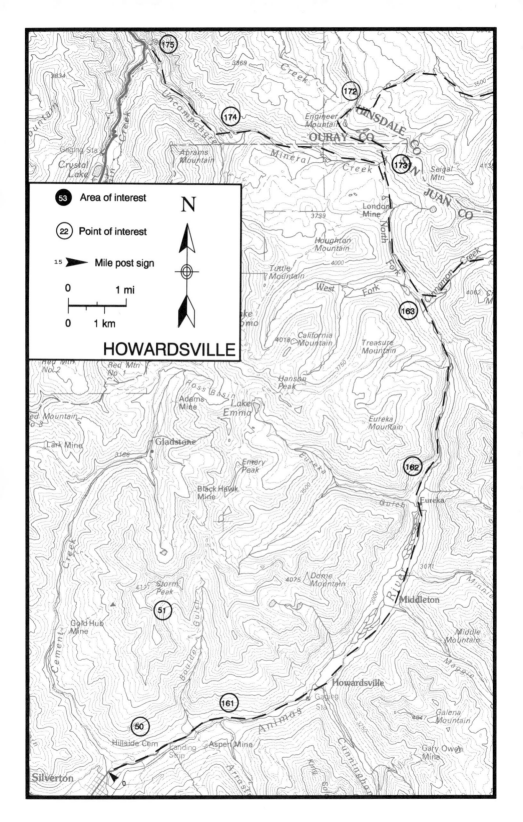

Map 21.1

164. (mi 13.8, Map 21.2) Cinnamon Pass (12,598 ft, 3,840 m) affords fine views of fault relationships within the Eureka Graben system. Cinnamon Mountain (13,328 ft, 4,062 m), to the southwest, is the most downdropped block in the core of the graben. To the north the Cinnamon fault, a major bounding fault of the Eureka Graben, cuts the lower southeast shoulder of Wood Mountain (13,660 ft, 4,164 m). The dark rugged cliffs of younger pyroxene andesite on the southeast are downdropped against the older, rust-colored, iron-stained Burns Formation on the northwest.

Three-tenths of a mile (0.5 km) down the east side of the pass, the road crosses a conspicuous quartz vein that follows the Rainbow Fault, another of the several northeast-trending faults comprising the Eureka Graben system. The vein can be followed both southward up to the ridge and northeastward, where it parallels the road for 0.3 mile (0.5 km) before cutting uphill toward Edith Mountain. Here again, the younger, post-collapse pyroxene andesite is juxtaposed against older Burns lavas and Eureka tuffs.

165. (mi 16.0) American Basin drains the headwaters of the Lake Fork of the Gunnison River and features classic examples of many glacial erosional landforms. The basin itself is a cirque (an amphitheaterlike depression) at the head of a U-shaped glacial valley. The clear blue waters of Sloan Lake are typical of a glacial tarn, formed when glaciers removed loose debris and left a smooth bedrock surface as the lake bottom. The sawtooth ridge on either side of an unnamed peak (13,806 ft, 4,208 m) is an arête formed by headward erosion of cirque glaciers on opposite sides of the ridge. Pyramid-shaped glacial horns are formed by headward erosion of cirque glaciers on all sides of the summit. Three excellent examples, Uncompahgre Peak (14,309 ft, 4,361 m), Wetterhorn Peak (14,015 ft, 4,272 m), and Matterhorn Peak (13,590 ft, 4,142 m), can be seen to the north from just east of Engineer Pass. A rock glacier heads in the cirque and is easily recognized from the road by the steep face of its lobate front. Striations on bedrock along the creek trend N10°E and reflect the direction of glacial movement. Not surprisingly, the axis of the glacially carved U-shaped valley also trends N10°E.

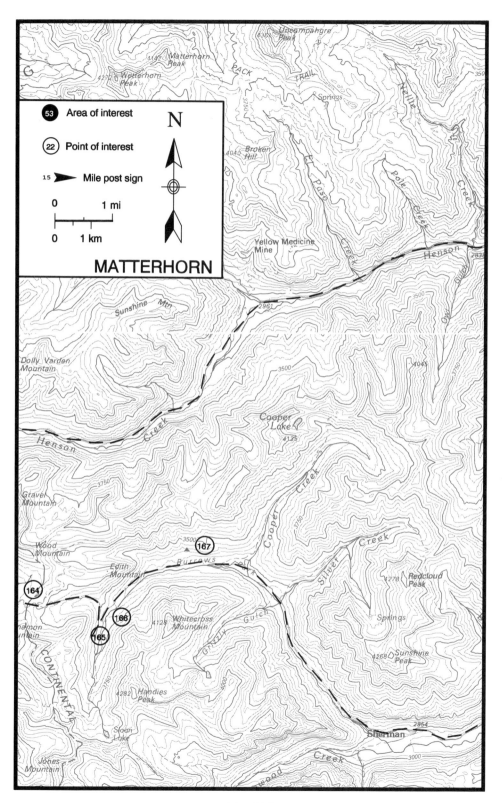

Map 21.2

166. (mi 16.2) Precambrian granite forms a structurally high ridge at road level and separates the San Juan and Uncompahgre Calderas. Ahead is Whitecross Mountain (13,542 ft, 4,128 m), composed of the same Precambrian granite of Cataract Canyon (1.45 billion years old) that lies in the roadbed. The mountain is bounded on the north and south by faults of the Eureka Graben system and on the east by the ring fault of the Lake City Caldera. It gets its name from two quartz veins that form a "white cross" on the summit's northeast ridge.

167. (mi 17.7) The **Lake City Caldera** (22.5 million years old) and its steeply inward-dipping ring fault can be seen from Burrows Park. The western arc of the ring fault is exposed to the northwest along a steep gully where bright reds and yellows mark a zone of intense hydrothermal alteration. A quartz vein cuts a rhyolite porphyry ring dike and separates coherent Precambrian granite in the caldera wall on the west from intracaldera breccias and ash flows on the east. A hike up this gully is strongly recommended. Sunshine Peak (14,001 ft, 4,268 m) and Redcloud Peak (14,034 ft, 4,278 m), both within the Lake City Caldera, dominate the view to the east. The ash-flow tuffs on Sunshine Peak represent more than 1.5 kilometers of caldera fill.

168. (mi 31.2, Map 21.3) The **Red Mountain intrusive complex,** located along the eastern ring fault of the Lake City Caldera, is visible up Red Mountain Creek. Potassium feldspars of the porphyritic quartz latite lava dome have been hydrothermally altered by the action of sulfur-bearing fluids to alunite, a potassium aluminum sulfate. Alunite is considered a potential aluminum resource.

169. (mi 33.9) Slumgullion earthflow dammed the Lake Fork of the Gunnison River and impounded 2-mile-long (3.2-km) Lake San Cristobal (Fig 21.1). Seven hundred years ago supersaturated clays (altered volcanic rocks) slipped off Mesa Seco from the head scarp at 11,400 feet (3,475 m) and traveled 4.5 miles (7.2 km) downslope before coming to rest across the Lake Fork at an elevation of 8,800 feet (2,682 m). Continued movement of the debris flow is reflected in the "drunken aspens" growing on the still-active lobe.

The following roadlog begins with 0.0 at the bridge over Henson Creek on Colorado Highway 149 in Lake City.

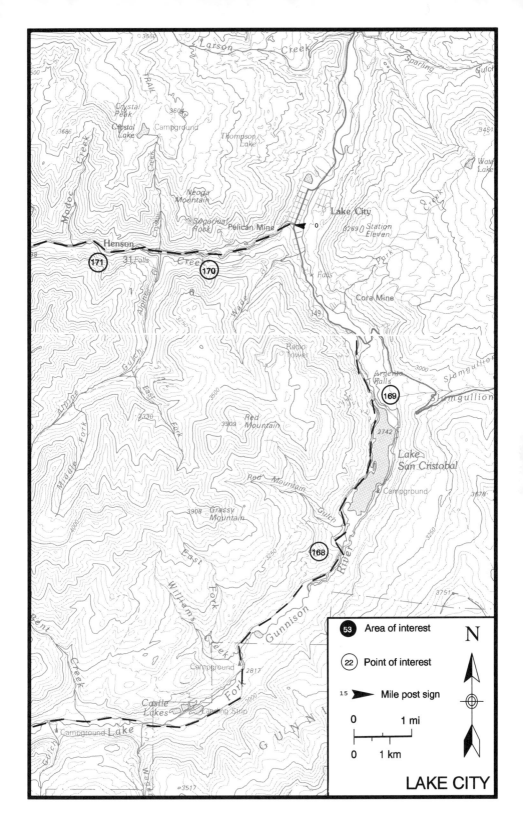

Map 21.3

Fig. 21.1   Photo looking east at the Slumgullion mudflow. Photo by W. Cross, 1905. Courtesy U.S. Geological Survey.

170.   (mi 2.0) Caldera-collapse megabreccia is exposed along Henson Creek. Large, jumbled blocks of San Juan Formation (conglomeratic mudflows) and densely welded Eureka Member of the Sapinero Mesa Tuff are embedded in less densely welded, propylitically altered Eureka. These clasts are interpreted to be blocks of the caldera rim that slumped from the oversteepened wall of the Uncompahgre Caldera both during and after collapse.

171.   (mi 3.7) Ute-Ulay Mine was the leading producer of lead and silver in the Lake City district. The buildings are on private property, so please respect the owner's "shotgun-enforced" no-trespassing request. The mine had its own smelter, processing mill, and gravity-driven rail tramway. A cement dam built in 1925 provided water for a hydroelectric generating plant, and its breached remnants can still be seen spanning Henson Creek. Nearly half of the miners at the Ute-Ulay went on strike in 1899 in armed protest of the requirement that all single miners board at the company boarding house. The state militia intervened at the request of the Lake City sheriff, and a week later work resumed at the mine. It is not known where the single miners slept thereafter.

172.   (mi 17.9, Map 21.1) Engineer Pass (12,800 ft, 3,901 m) presents a unique opportunity to "bag a thirteener" with very little effort. A short walk uphill to the south leads to Engineer Mountain (13,218 ft, 4,029 m), a 23-million-year-old dacite porphyry intrusion. Thumb-sized reddish-brown euhedral phenocrysts of sanidine can be found on the summit.

The western skyline is punctuated by flat-topped Potosi Peak (13,786 ft, 4,202 m) and the sharp summit of Mount Sneffels (14,150 ft, 4,313 m). Potosi consists of a sequence of welded ash-flow tuffs recording the outflow stratigraphy of several western San Juan calderas. The Sneffels stock, northwest of the Silverton Caldera, is similar both in age and composition to the Sultan Mountain monzonite stock, emplaced 26 to 27 million years ago along the southwest structural margin of both the Silverton and San Juan Calderas.

173.   (mi 20.1) Elephant Heads are growing in a typical alpine wetland community situated on a flat surface covered by shallow standing water. The distinctive magenta flowers, complete with ears and trunk, do indeed resemble an elephant's head. A lush growth of Rocky Mountain sedge dominates this community but shares its habitat with queen's crown, marsh marigold, and alpine bistort.

174.   (mi 24.2) Three genera of rock lichen reside on a flat knob of the San Juan Formation at a pulloff in the aspens west of the road. Here one can see an excellent exposure of a laharic breccia with angular greenish volcanic clasts in a reddish-purple muddy matrix. The chartreuse map lichen, *Rhizocarpon geographicum,* is very slow growing and can live for several thousand years. The jewel lichen, *Caloplacia elegans,* is a rusty red-orange color, and *Parmelia,* the leafy foliose boulder lichen, is pale gray-green with a black underside. The view to the south is up Poughkeepsie Gulch and the headwaters of the Uncompahgre River.

175.   (mi 26.8) The Precambrian and a 1.5-million-year unconformity can be seen from the pulloff at a hairpin curve 0.2 miles (0.3 km) from the highway. Westward, on the opposite river bank, is a convoluted, flexural fold in the quartzite beds of the Uncompahgre Formation. To the northeast an angular unconformity is exposed where the Tertiary San Juan Formation lies upon the Precambrian Uncompahgre Formation. This unconformity reflects a gap in the geologic record where 1.5 billion years' worth of rock are missing.

REFERENCES

Arno, S. F., and R. P. Hammerly, 1984. *Timberline: Mountain and arctic forest frontiers.* Seattle: The Mountaineers, 304 pp.

Bird, A. G., 1986. *Silverton gold: The story of Silverton's largest gold mine.* A. G. Bird, 152 pp.

Burbank, W. S., and Robert G. Luedke, 1964. *Geology of the Ironton quadrangle, Colorado.* U.S. Geological Survey, Geologic Quadrangle Map GQ-291.

Casadevall, T. J., and H. Ohmoto, 1977. Sunnyside mine, Eureka mining district, San Juan County, Colorado: Geochemistry of gold and base metal ore deposition in avolcanic environment. *Economic Geology,* v. 72, pp. 1285–1320.

Duft, J. F., and R. K. Moseley, 1989. *Alpine wildflowers of the Rocky Mountains.* Missoula, MT: Mountain Press Publishing Company, 196 pp.

Fandrich, J. W., 1968. *The Slumgullion earthflow.* Lake City, CO: J. W. Fandrich, 22 pp.

Hon, K., and P. W. Lipman, 1989. Western San Juan caldera complex, in Charles E. Chapin and Jiri Zidek, eds., *Field excursions to volcanic terranes in the western United States,* volume 1, *Southern Rocky Mountain region,* New Mexico Bureau of Mines & Mineral Resources, Memoir 46, pp. 350–380.

Lipman, P. W., 1976. *Geologic map of the Lake City caldera area, western San Juan Mountains, southwestern Colorado.* U. S. Geological Survey, Miscellaneous Investigations Map I-962.

Luedke, R. G., and W. S. Burbank, 1987. *Geologic map of the Handies Peak quadrangle, San Juan, Hinsdale and Ouray Counties, Colorado.* U.S. Geological Survey, Geologic Quadrangle Map GQ-1595.

Mutel, C. F., and J. C. Emerick, 1984. *From grass-land to glacier, the natural history of Colorado.* Boulder, CO: Johnson Publishing Company, 238 pp.

Panze, A. J., M. G. Cruson, and T. A. Watkins, 1983. Gold-silver deposits of the San Juan Mountains, Colorado, in *Proceeding of the 86th National Western Mining Conference, 1983 Mining Yearbook,* Colorado Mining Association, pp. 64–73.

Price, L. W., 1981. *Mountains and man.* Berkeley, CA: University of California Press, 506 pp.

Wolle, M. S., 1949. *Stampede to timberline: The ghost towns and mining camps of Colorado.* Denver: Sage Books, 544 pp.

Wright, C., and C. Wright, 1964. *Tiny Hinsdale of the Silvery San Juan.* Denver: Big Mountain Press, 196 pp.

Zwinger, A. H., and B. E. Willard, 1972. *Land above the trees: A guide to American alpine tundra.* New York: Harper & Row, Publishers, 489 pp.

GLOSSARY

This glossary includes some of the more commonly used terms in the text. It is not a complete listing of all technical terms. For more in-depth definitions please consult technical dictionaries or general texts in geology, biology, and archaeology.

ablation: processes by which snow and ice are lost from a glacier (wastage).

adsorption: adhesion of gas molecules or gas molecules in solution to a solid surface by weak molecular bonding.

algal mounds: small hill-shaped limestone structures formed by the remains of calcium-carbonate-producing algae.

alluvial: associated with or formed by running water (e.g., streams or rivers).

alpine: associated with high mountains (e.g., the Alps of Europe); more specifically, associated with areas above timberline.

andesite: a dark-colored, fine-grained rock of volcanic origin containing sodic plagioclase feldspar and one or more of the mafic minerals (e.g., biotite, hornblende, pyroxene).

angular unconformity: an erosion surface in which younger sediments rest upon tilted or folded older rocks.

annual: a plant that completes its entire life cycle and dies within a single year.

anticline: a fold, sides down and center up, wherein the core contains older rocks.

arboreal/arborescent: associated with, or living in, or having the form of a tree.

Archean: the earlier part of Precambrian time (see Stratigraphic Chart, p. 2).

arête: a sharp-edged ridge or spur, commonly found above the snowline in rugged mountains, formed by glacial action in the heads of valleys and the backward growth of adjoining cirques.

asexual reproduction: reproduction that does not involve sex (i.e., there is only one parent, and the offspring are genetically identical to the parent).

association: a group of plant species that tend to occur together in places having similar environmental conditions.

asthenosphere: the layer of the earth below the lithosphere; the soft, probably partially molten layer where magmas are generated.

basalt: a fine-grained, dark, mafic igneous rock composed largely of plagioclase feldspar and pyroxene.

basement: the oldest rocks in a given area, a complex of igneous and metamorphic rocks that underlies all of the sedimentary formations.

basin: 1. a depressed area with no surface outlet; 2. the drainage area of a stream; or 3. a low area in the earth's crust where sediments have accumulated.

batholith: a large igneous body formed from the cooling of magmatic rock at depth with extensive surface exposure.

biota: all of the various forms of plants, animals, and microorganisms that live in an area.

breccia: rock formed by angular broken fragments of older rocks held together by a mineral cement or a fine-grained matrix.

caldera: a large, basin-shaped, generally circular volcanic depression commonly formed by collapse of the magma chamber beneath a volcano after venting.

carbonaceous: rich in carbon or organic matter; perhaps containing coal.

carbonate: 1. a mineral containing the anionic structure of CO_3^{-2} (e.g., calcite and aragonite $CaCO_3$); 2. a sediment formed of the carbonates of calcium, magnesium, and/or iron, e.g. limestone and dolomite.

carnotite: a strongly radioactive, canary-yellow to greenish-yellow secondary mineral; an ore for uranium and vanadium.

cirque: a steep-walled semicircular hollow, high in a mountain valley, formed by erosive glacial action.

clastic: formed from mineral particles (clasts) that were mechanically transported.

co-evolution: adaptation or other forms of evolution that takes place in two closely associated species in response to the effects of one on the other.

Colorado lineament: a hypothesized belt of Precambrian faults or zones of weakness in the basement about 100 miles wide, extending northeastward from the Grand Canyon to the Rocky Mountain front near the Colorado-Wyoming border.

columnar jointing: the breaking of an igneous rock into parallel, prismatic columns by cracks produced by thermal contraction upon cooling.

community (biotic community): an assemblage of organisms of many different species that all live and interact with one another within a particular area.

cordillera: an extensive series of mountain ranges.

creep: 1. the slow, imperceptible downslope movement of rock and soil caused by gravity; 2. slow deformation of solid rock resulting from constant stress over a long period of time.

cuesta: a landform consisting of a ridge with one steep side and one gently sloping surface (often less than 5 degrees dip).

debris flow: a moving mass of rock fragments, soil, and mud, more than half of the particles being larger than sand size. Rates vary from less than 1 meter per year to more than 150 kilometers per hour.

desiccation: the process of drying out.

dike: a roughly tabular body of igneous rock that cuts across the structure of adjacent rocks or cuts massive rocks.

diorite: a plutonic rock with composition intermediate between granite and gabbro; the intrusive equivalent of andesite.

ecosystem: a biotic community and the physical environment within which it lives.

endogenetic: a term describing processes that originate within the earth.

ephemeral pond: a pond that has water in early summer or after rain but that dries out during periods without rain.

exogenic: originating at or near the surface of the earth.

extrusive: igneous rock that has been erupted onto the earth's surface (e.g., lava flows and volcanic ash).

fault: a fracture along which there has been displacement.

fauna: a list of the species of animals living in an area.

fellfield: a slope covered with large boulders and little or no vegetation.

felsic: an adjective, derived from *feldspar* and *silica*, applied to an igneous rock having abundant light-colored minerals; also applied to those minerals (quartz, feldspar, feldspathoids, muscovite).

flora: a list of the species of plants living in an area (the adjective is "floristic").

foliation: a planar set of minerals or banding of mineral concentrations found in a metamorphic rock, or any planar arrangement of textural or structural features in a rock.

footwall: the rock beneath an inclined fault.

gabbro: a black, coarse-grained, intrusive igneous rock composed of calcic feldspars and pyroxene. The intrusive equivalent of basalt.

geomorphology: the study of the nature and origin of surface landforms.

gneiss: a foliated metamorphic rock that commonly displays bands of light, granular minerals and bands of dark, flaky, or elongate minerals.

graben: an elongate downdropped crustal block bounded by faults on its long sides.

granite: a coarse-grained, intrusive igneous rock composed of quartz, orthoclase feldspar, sodic plagioclase feldspar, and micas.

granodiorite: a group of coarse-grained plutonic rocks intermediate in composition between quartz diorite and quartz monzonite.

gravity anomaly: the difference between the observed value of gravity at a point and the theoretically calculated value. Excess observed gravity gives a positive reading.

habitat: a place where an organism lives (i.e., where it finds all that it requires for life).

halophyte: a plant that can tolerate high concentrations of salt in the soil.

hanging valley: a tributary glacial or stream valley whose mouth is high above the floor of the main valley.

hanging wall: the overlying rock above an inclined fault.

herbaceous plant: an herb (i.e., a plant having no wood tissue).

herpetofaunal center: a region having high diversity (i.e., many different species) of reptiles and amphibians.

hogback: a ridge formed by the slower erosion of hard strata and having two steep, equally inclined slopes.

horn: a high pyramidal peak with steep sides formed at the intersection of several cirques.

horst: an elongate, upthrown crustal block bounded by faults on its long sides.

hydrothermal: of or pertaining to hot water or the action of hot water.

igneous: 1. solidified from molten rock or magma; 2. the processes related to the formation of igneous rocks (from the Latin word ignis, meaning fire).

intermediate igneopus rock: describing a rock that is transitional between basic and silicic (or between mafic and felsic), with a silica content of 54 to 65 percent.

intrusion: 1. the emplacement of magma into preexisting rock; 2. the rock so formed.

intrusive rock: igneous rock formed by emplacement into existing rock.

joint: a large and relatively planar fracture in a rock across which there is no relative displacement of the two sides.

laccolith: a roughly mushroom-shaped igneous intrusion that has domed the overlying rocks.

leeward: on the side of an object away from the oncoming wind; protected from the wind.

lithify: 1. to change to stone; 2. to consolidate a loose sediment into a solid rock.

lithosphere: the outer, rigid shell of the earth above the asthenosphere containing the crust, continents, and plates.

mafic: describing an igneous rock made up mainly of dark, iron- (*ferric*) and *ma*gnesium-rich minerals, or the minerals themselves (e.g. basalt, hornblende).

magma: molten rock material generated within the earth from which igneous rocks are derived (adj.: magmatic).

marine: of, belonging to, or caused by the sea.

mass wasting: a general term for the downslope movement of soil and rock material due to gravity.

metamorphic rock: a rock whose original mineralogy, texture, or composition has been changed by pressure, temperature, or gain or loss of chemical components.

metamorphism: mineral, chemical, and structural changes to solid rocks caused by pressure and heat at depth.

metasomatism: the process of practically simultaneous capillary solution and deposition by which a new mineral may grow in the body of an old mineral, usually with little disturbance of the textural or structural features.

microclimate: climatic conditions (e.g., temperature and moisture availability) within a very small area, perhaps as small as a square meter; compare with "regional climate," which affects very large areas and is the kind of climate measured by the National Weather Service.

microorganisms: very small organisms such as bacteria, fungi, and algae; usually visible only with a microscope.

monocline: a stair-stepped fold that connects two relatively horizontal parts of the same stratum at different elevations.

moraine: a deposit of glacial till left at the margin of an ice sheet.

nunatak: an isolated knob of bedrock that projects prominently above the surface of a glacier and is surrounded by glacial ice.

nurse plant: a larger plant that creates a more favorable environment (e.g., shade) for a smaller plant of the same or a different species.

oolite: a rock, usually limestone, made up of many small rounded bodies resembling fish eggs and formed of calcium carbonate in concentric layers around a nucleus such as a sand grain.

orogeny: the processes of mountain building by which large areas are folded, faulted, metamorphosed, and subjected to plutonism.

perennial: a plant that can live longer than a single year.

Phanerozoic: the part of geologic time (570 million years to present) represented by rocks in which the evidence of life is abundant; Cambrian and later time.

phenocryst: a large crystal surrounded by a finer matrix in an igneous rock.

photosynthesis: the chemical process by which green plants convert solar energy into food energy.

phyllite: a metamorphosed rock, intermediate in grade between slate and mica schist.

plate tectonics: a theory of global geology in which the lithosphere is divided into a number of rigid plates that move horizontally and interact with each other at their boundaries.

playa: the flat floor of a closed basin in an arid region.

pluton: an igneous intrusion formed at depth in the crust (e.g., dike, laccolith, batholith).

plutonic: pertaining to igneous activity at depth.

porphyry: an igneous rock that contains two distinct crystal sizes. The larger crystals are often called *phenocrysts.*

Proterozoic: the more recent of the two great divisions of Precambrian time (see Stratigraphic Chart, p. 2).

pyroclastic rock: a rock composed of airfall fragments derived from an explosive volcanic eruption.

pyroclastic texture: the unsorted, angular texture of the fragments in a pyroclastic rock.

quartz monzonite: a granitic rock in which quartz makes up 10 to 50 percent of the felsic components but in which alkali feldspar content is lower and plagioclase content is higher than in granite.

quartzite: 1. a very hard, clean, white metamorphic rock formed from a clean, quartz sandstone; 2. a clean, quartz sandstone so well cemented that it resembles (1).

rhyolite: the fine-grained volcanic equivalent of granite, light brown to gray, typically porphyritic.

ring fault: a steep-sided fault pattern that is cylindrical in outline and commonly associated with caldera subsidence.

salt anticline: an anticlinal structure formed by the squeezing-up of salt in a plastic state, rupturing and deforming the overlying rocks.

schist: a metamorphic rock characterized by the strong foliation of a dominant platy or prismatic mineral assemblage (e.g. mica schist).

sedimentary rock: a rock formed by the accumulation and cementation of mineral grains transported by wind, water, or ice or chemically precipitated at the site of deposition.

sexual reproduction: process by which two parents contribute genetic material to produce offspring that are genetically different from either parent.

silicic: rich in silica; usually applies to quartz and feldspar.

sill: a horizontal tabular intrusion that parallels the planar structure of the surrounding rock.

skarn: limestones and dolomites that have been altered into lime-bearing silicates by the introduction of large amounts of silicon, aluminum, iron, and magnesium.

slate: the metamorphic equivalent of shale; compact, fine-grained, hard, and splits into slabs and thin plates along cleavage planes.

solifluction: a process in which soil that is saturated with water slowly creeps or flows downhill.

species: a group of organisms that all share similar physical characteristics and are capable of interbreeding.

spreading center: a zone of tectonic plate divergence, commonly found at ocean ridges, where partially molten mantle upwells and new lithosphere is created.

stock: an exposed intrusion (pluton) covering less than 100 square kilometers.

strataform: refers to a mineral deposit confined to a specific stratigraphic unit.

stratovolcano: a volcano consisting of alternating layers of lava and pyroclastic rock, with abundant dikes and sills.

stratum: a layer of sedimentary rock, separable from layers above and below; a bed (plural: strata).

structural: pertaining to rock deformation or features that result from it.

subalpine: just below the alpine zone (i.e., just below timberline).

subduction: the process of one lithospheric plate descending beneath another.

sublimation: a physical process in which a solid is transformed into a gas without passing through the liquid state (e.g., ice turning into water vapor without melting first).

substrate: the kind of rock out of which a soil has developed or on which a plant is growing.

symbiosis: a very close ecological relationship between two different species of plants, animals, and/or microorganisms.

talus: a deposit of large, angular fragments of physically weathered bedrock at the base of a cliff or steep slope.

tectonics: the study of movements and deformation of the crust on a large scale.

tectonism: a general term for all movement of the crust by tectonic processes, including the formation of ocean basins, continents, plateaus, and mountain ranges.

till: an unconsolidated sediment containing all sizes of fragments from clay to boulders deposited by glacial action, usually poorly sorted.

timberline: the highest elevation at which trees or forests grow.

transform fault: a strike-slip boundary along which the displacement suddenly stops or changes form or along which plates slide past each other.

tuff: a rock composed of pyroclastic debris and fine ash. If particles are melted slightly together from their own heat, it is a "welded tuff."

unconformity: a buried erosion surface that separates two different ages of rocks.

upwarp: the uplift of a broad region without extensive faulting.

uraninite: a strongly radioactive metallic mineral, the chief ore of uranium.

vegetation zone: a range of elevation in the mountains in which one finds a similar set of plant species and similar climatic conditions.

volcaniclastic: pertaining to a rock containing fragments of volcanic material.

volcanism: the processes by which magma and associated gases rise through the crust and are vented onto the earth's surface and into the atmosphere.

windward: on the side of an object facing toward the oncoming wind, without any protection from the wind.

CONTRIBUTORS

GEOLOGY

Rob Blair is a professor of geology at Fort Lewis College in Durango, Colorado. He holds a Ph.D. from the Colorado School of Mines and specializes in geomorphology and quaternary research. He is the author of twenty-four publications. His interests in geology and mountaineering have taken him to more than two dozen countries.

Douglas Brew has taught at Fort Lewis College in Durango, Colorado since 1980, having also taught at Prescott College and the University of Minnesota. He is a graduate of Dartmouth College and has a Ph.D. from Cornell University, where he specialized in stratigraphy and paleontology. He has written many papers on invertebrate paleontology, his main area of research, while also enjoying the many outdoor opportunities afforded by life in southwestern Colorado.

Terence L. Britt is a senior geological advisor for Meridian Oil in Denver. He was Meridian's exploration manager in Farmington from 1987 to 1991, when coal-bed methane development was at its zenith. In addition, Britt has worked in uranium, coal, and non-metallic exploration for the Anaconda Company. He has published several papers on oil and gas exploration and holds a B.S. in geology from the University of Notre Dame and an M.S. in geology from the University of Arizona.

Barbara Byron has a B.A. in biology from the College of Saint Teresa in Winona, Minnesota, and a B.S. in geology from Fort Lewis College. She has worked with the U.S. Geological Survey on the Kilauea Volcano in Hawaii, in the basin-and-range province of Nevada, and in the San Juan Mountains of Colorado. She is an avid mountaineer.

John (Jack) A. Campbell is a professor of geology at Fort Lewis College, where he teaches on a variety of subjects, including groundwater geology, depositional systems, natural resources, and the environment. He earned his Ph.D. from the University of Colorado. He has been involved in oil and gas exploration, taught geology at Colorado State University, worked for the U.S. Geological Survey as a research geologist, and served on the Colorado Oil and Gas Conservation Commission.

Tom Ann Casey has worked mainly as a consultant geologist with Emerald Gas in Durango, Colorado since 1990 in the development and characterization of coal gas reservoirs. She has worked on a variety of projects, including Gulf Coast and Alaskan geology with Sun Oil Company, exploration for helium in the San Juan Basin, and well-site geology in the western states. She has also been involved with technical writing and organizational and resource management projects for the Southern Ute and Jicarilla Indian tribes. She holds a B.A. from Colorado College and an M.S. in geology from Stanford University.

Jack A. Ellingson is a professor of geology at Fort Lewis College in Durango. He received his Ph.D. from Washington State University, with emphasis on the Cenozoic volcanism in the White Pass area near Mount Rainier, Washington. Mineralogy and the petrology of volcanic rocks are his major geological interests.

Scott Fetchenhier has a B.S. in geology from Fort Lewis College and worked in the San Juan mines as a geologist and laborer for several years. He now mines a different kind of gold in Silverton, having been in the retail gift business for the past fourteen years.

James M. Hornbeck is a senior staff geologist with Meridian Oil in Farmington, New Mexico. He holds an M.S. in geology from the State University of New York, Oneonta, and has spent the last seventeen years working on a variety of oil and gas projects in the Four Corners area. His experience includes development of tight-gas sandstone reservoirs and coal-bed methane in the San Juan Basin, exploration for oil in the Paradox Basin, application of new technologies (such as horizontal drilling) to enhance recovery from fractured reservoirs, and a recent regional study of the Four Corners Platform.

Richard Keen is a member of the American Meteorological Society. He has a Ph.D. in climatology and has conducted weather research for the National Center for Atmospheric Research, the U.S. Army, and the University of Colorado. He is the author of several popular books on weather and meteorology.

BIOLOGY

Lisa Floyd-Hanna was born in Surabaja, Indonesia and studied botany in Hawaii. She earned her B.S. and M.S. degrees from the University of Hawaii in cell biology and botany and a Ph.D. from the University of Colorado. She is currently studying characteristics of threatened plant populations in the Southwest as well as twentieth-century changes in forests and shrublands of Mesa Verde National Park and the San Juan National Forest.

David W. Jamieson received his bachelor's and master's degrees in botany from Humboldt State University and was awarded a Ph.D. in botany/bryology from the University of British Columbia. For seventeen years Jamieson has been a member of the Biology Department at Fort Lewis College, where he pursues interests in vascular plant and bryophyte floristics in southwestern Colorado. He is particularly interested in problems of Arctic and alpine floristics.

William Romme was born in Denver, Colorado and grew up in Albuquerque, New Mexico. He received his B.A. from the University of New Mexico and his Ph.D. in plant ecology from the University of Wyoming. He is now a professor of biology at Fort Lewis College in Durango, where his primary professional interests are in fire ecology, landscape ecology, and undergraduate science education. He is researching prehistoric fire history, twentieth-century changes in the forests and shrublands of Mesa Verde National Park and the San Juan National Forest, and the ecological effects of the Yellowstone fires of 1988.

Preston Somers earned a B.S. degree from Wake Forest University in North Carolina and a master's and Ph.D. at the University of Colorado, Boulder. He is a professor of biology at Fort Lewis College. Hiking, camping, and photography are favorite activities that complement his interest in ecology.

Albert W. Spencer is professor emeritus in biology at Fort Lewis College. He earned his Ph.D. from Colorado State University in 1965. He has been a member of the biology faculty at Fort Lewis College since that time. His principal interest has been the study of vertebrate populations.

ANTHROPOLOGY AND HUMAN HISTORY

Philip Duke is a professor of anthropology at Fort Lewis College. He has conducted archaeological research in southwestern Colorado since 1980. In 1990 he began a long-term research project on the archaeology and human history of the San Juan mountains northwest of Pagosa Springs, Colorado.

Richard N. Ellis of Durango, Colorado specializes in the history of the Southwest and has written numerous books and articles. He works closely with the Southern Ute tribe and has done many studies for the U.S. Justice Department on behalf of southwestern tribes.

Gary Matlock, a native of southwestern Colorado, recently retired after almost 34 years as an archaeologist for the U.S. Forest Service, the National Park Service, and the Bureau of Land Management. He is the author of more than forty technical and project reports and has published a variety of monographs and articles on the archaeology of the southwestern United States. He co-authored *The State of Colorado Archaeology* and *Enemy Ancestors* with Philip Duke. Currently he is a visiting professor at Fort Lewis College and is a partner in a private archaeological consulting firm in Durango.

Duane A. Smith has been a professor of history and Southwest studies at Fort Lewis College since 1964. He earned his Ph.D. from the University of Colorado. His areas of research and writing include Colorado mining, urban history, the history of baseball, and western history. He has published numerous books and articles and is fondly known as Durango's local historian, always available to tell a good story or to remind citizens of the colorful past.

INDEX